MONTGOMERY MCFATE
JANICE H. LAURENCE
(*Editors*)

Social Science Goes to War

*The Human Terrain System
in Iraq and Afghanistan*

HURST & COMPANY, LONDON

First published in the United Kingdom in 2015 by
C. Hurst & Co. (Publishers) Ltd.,
41 Great Russell Street, London, WC1B 3PL
© Montgomery McFate, Janice H. Laurence and the Contributors, 2015
All rights reserved.
Printed in India

A Cataloguing-in-Publication data record for this book is
available from the British Library.

978-1-84904-421-9 *paperback*

This book is printed using paper from registered sustainable
and managed sources.

www.hurstpublishers.com

CONTENTS

CONTENTS

FOREWORD

General (Ret) David H. Petraeus

General (Ret) David H. Petraeus is Chairman of the KKR Global Institute. Prior to joining KKR, General Petraeus served over thirty-seven years in the U.S. military, including command of coalition forces in Iraq, command of US Central Command, and command of coalition forces in Afghanistan. Following his service in the military, General Petraeus served as the Director of the Central Intelligence Agency. General Petraeus graduated with distinction from the US Military Academy and subsequently earned MPA and Ph.D. degrees in international relations from Princeton University's Woodrow Wilson School of Public and International Affairs. General Petraeus has received numerous US military, State Department, NATO, and United Nations medals and awards, and he has been decorated by thirteen foreign countries. He also serves as a Visiting Professor of Public Policy at CUNY's Macaulay Honors College, as a Senior Fellow at Harvard University's Belfer Center, and as Judge Widney Professor at the University of Southern California. General Petraeus is a member of the advisory board of Team Rubicon and a number of other veterans' organizations.

* * *

Counterinsurgency operations are sometimes described as "armed social work." This description is meant to convey that counterinsurgency campaigns require more than *just* the tasks associated with offensive and defensive operations—that counterinsurgency campaigns have to include a host of so-called "stability operations" tasks as well.

The term "armed social work" thus highlights that, in addition to lethal force to combat the enemy, a counterinsurgency campaign has to include a variety of activities beyond those of vital conventional military operations that seek to *clear* areas of insurgents and then to *hold* them. The additional tasks range from assisting with the development of military and police forces and the re-establishment of critical governmental institutions, to helping restore basic services, rebuild damaged infrastructure, and restore (or build) various components of the rule of law. Additionally, and very importantly, all of these endeavors have to be undertaken in a manner that reflects a granular understanding of the local cultures, religions, customs, laws, and social organizing principles and structures if the overall effort is to succeed in the long run. Indeed, outside approaches should not be imposed on a foreign society; rather, sustainable change has to emerge from the efforts of the nation itself in line with the unique conditions of the local area. As T.E. Lawrence famously cautioned in his *Twenty Seven Articles* in 1917, "Do not try to do too much with your own hands. Better [they] do it tolerably than that you do it perfectly. It is their war, and you are to help them, not to win it for them."

Carrying out "armed social work" in a foreign country thus necessitates considerable knowledge of that country and its culture, traditions, laws, and practices. Indeed, such knowledge can be decisive in a counterinsurgency. Unfortunately, this critical lesson has been forgotten from time-to-time, and it has cost intervention forces dearly in certain cases. As I noted while still in uniform, for example, American military elements were not nearly as well prepared as we should have been at the beginning of the wars in Iraq and Afghanistan for the situations that we faced. In fact, at the outset of both those campaigns we lacked the detailed, granular understanding of the countries we were invading. Our forces were, moreover, primarily organized, trained and equipped for major combat operations rather than for a mix of those operations *plus* the myriad additional tasks essential to the conduct of a counterinsurgency campaign. Beyond that, as I also noted while in uniform, it took us years just to get the *inputs* right in both Afghanistan and Iraq—that is, to get the "big ideas" (the strategy) right, to communicate the big ideas effectively throughout our forces, to establish the organizational elements and architecture needed to properly implement the big ideas together with our coalition and host nation partners, and to deploy the military and civilian resources required to conduct the resulting comprehensive civil-military campaign.[1]

Among the many areas in which U.S. military forces sought to improve their capabilities in Iraq and Afghanistan was that of knowledge of the local cultures, traditions, religions, languages, and social organizing principles and structures. We learned quickly in each case that sociocultural knowledge was essential if we were to understand the specific contexts in which we were operating. And over time, the U.S. military pursued a number of initiatives to promote such understanding, including: emphasis on the importance of such knowledge in the Army and Marine Corps Counterinsurgency Field Manual published in late 2006; the creation of new institutions such as the Army Training and Doctrine Command Cultural Center of Excellence at Fort Huachuca, Arizona; revamping pre-deployment training to include instruction on the local population and its customs and practices; and creating Female Engagement Teams (FETs) to establish links with a population segment—women—that often had the most to lose from the violence in their communities.

The focus of this book is another important action that we pursued—the Human Terrain System (HTS) initiative. The objective of the HTS program was to provide our Soldiers and Marines in Iraq and Afghanistan with knowledge about the local communities in which they were operating based on social science concepts and extensive research rather than on anecdote, rumor, conjecture, or opinion. HTS was a result of the recognition that, if the US government was going to deploy military and civilian personnel to conduct operations among a foreign population, it needed to provide those personnel with mission-critical knowledge about the culture, political system, economy, religious beliefs, and other features of those countries and populations.

The HTS initiative was pursued in recognition of one of the biggest of the "big ideas" that guided the Surges in Iraq and Afghanistan, recognition that, "The decisive terrain [in a counterinsurgency campaign] is the human terrain." The HTS initiative sought to help our leaders and our units understand the human terrain.

Ultimately, and despite organizational challenges and the pressure of meeting ever-evolving requirements, the HTS initiative contributed significantly to the conduct of our missions in Iraq and Afghanistan. To be sure, as with any endeavor, the contribution of each Human Terrain Team varied with the experience, expertise, and skills of the individuals in it. In general, though, the good teams provided increasingly invaluable support at the brigade combat team level as the program gathered momentum.

The contributions of the HTS program were typically four-fold:

First, Human Terrain Team (HTT) members acquired important knowledge of the local area in which the unit they supported was operating. This was, after all, their mission, and the knowledge understandably was gained from a variety of sources—the unit's members, Iraqi Security Force leaders in the area, local leaders and citizens, study of the available books, articles, and other works on the features of the population in the area, and so on.

Second, HTT members helped our unit commanders and staffs establish relationships, prepare for meetings with local leaders, understand the roles of relevant actors, and so forth.

Third, HTT members typically participated in planning sessions and rehearsals for potential operations, and they often were able to contribute to answering the key question we repeatedly posed: "Will this policy, initiative, or operation take more bad guys off the street than it creates by its implementation?"

Fourth, HTS teams were generally deployed on timelines that ensured that they would stay in an area beyond the departure of one unit and well beyond the arrival of the replacement unit, thereby bridging the gap and providing a source of continuity in knowledge, relationships, and situational awareness.

Commanders in theater agreed widely that the teams assisted them in understanding their operational environment, and in a number of cases this improved knowledge and communication reduced friction and even conflict between the military and local civilians.

To be sure, some in the academic anthropologist community saw HTS as a tool to oppress Iraqi and Afghan populations or to perform other equally reprehensible tasks. Sadly, these viewpoints, in contrast to the generally positive reviews by our commanders (and me), show the divide between the military and academic communities on this issue.

Thus, just as the Surge promoted engagement between US forces and local Iraqi populations, this book hopefully will promote engagement between the military and "the academy." Both communities have much to learn from each other.

This book was written by individuals with direct experience in program implementation on the ground; hence, it offers a unique perspective on the Human Terrain System. By giving voice to the social scientists who embedded with the Army and Marine Corps for months (and in a few cases, years) at a time, this volume explains how the Human

Terrain Teams worked hand-in-hand with military units and describes their contributions, their experiences, and their challenges. This book does much to address common misconceptions and criticisms, to explain the context in which the program was executed, and to shed light on how teams conducted their work in theater.

Conversations are now underway in the Pentagon and elsewhere on the future of post-9/11 wartime innovations such as HTS. Given budgetary pressures and anticipated missions, policy makers are understandably examining what should be done with HTS and a number of other military programs established to assist during the large, extended counterinsurgency campaigns in Iraq and Afghanistan. Although the current strategic guidance may suggest that US forces will no longer be used to support conduct of large scale stability operations, understanding the population will nevertheless remain critical in the conduct of any campaign. Indeed, an emphasis on a small foot print approach may actually increase the military's need for sociocultural knowledge.

I would submit, in fact, that regardless of the type of operations conducted in the future, we must not forget the lessons learned in Iraq and Afghanistan—many learned the hard way and at considerable cost. Among the most important lessons of our post-9/11 campaigns has been that the key terrain in irregular warfare is the human terrain. Clearly, the enemy has to be defeated in order to protect the human terrain; nonetheless, the prize is the population, without whose support no host nation can endure. As I have explained, the HTS program contributed substantially in helping us understand the dynamics of the areas in which we were operating. And, though the program was not without shortcomings at times, the general contribution that the HTS program made was substantial and important. This book helps make that point.

1

INTRODUCTION

UNVEILING THE HUMAN TERRAIN SYSTEM

Montgomery McFate and *Janice H. Laurence*

History is replete with examples of how militaries have benefited from understanding the culture and society of their adversaries. Thus, Chinese military strategist Sun Tzu admonished his readers, "If you know the enemy and know yourself, you need not fear the result of a hundred battles."[1] Effective strategy depends on understanding the adversary. How is it possible to deter one's enemy without knowledge of what they hold dear? How is it possible to achieve victory unless one understands the adversary's concept of defeat?

Equally, military organizations require knowledge of their allies in order to work effectively in coalitions. As the league of twelve kings discovered in 853 BC when they opposed Assyrian emperor Shalmaneser III, it is not so easy to work together when "each spoke a different dialect, prayed to a different god, ate different food, and adhered to a different set of rules and social norms."[2] Past *is* prologue: International Security Assistance Forces (ISAF) in Afghanistan encountered similar difficulties three thousand years later. So, how can allies work together unless they respect each other's martial traditions? How can allies cooperate without trust based on knowledge?

1

Surely military organizations require socio-cultural knowledge of both their adversaries and their allies, but must also understand the local population in the area where they are conducting operations. This type of knowledge is especially critical in irregular warfare, such as counterinsurgency and stability operations, where the local population are not just bystanders but the center of gravity. In the words of Lieutenant General Peter Chiarelli, the then Commanding General of Multi-National Corps—Iraq: "I asked my Brigade Commanders what was the number one thing they would like to have had more of, and they all said cultural knowledge."[3] Indeed, how can you engage with key leaders, develop infrastructure, distinguish friend from foe, or provide emergency relief if you know nothing about the environment and the people living in it?

This book tells the story of how the US military obtained an increased understanding of the local population in Iraq and Afghanistan through the actual lived experience of social scientists who served on Human Terrain Teams.

ORIGINS OF THE HUMAN TERRAIN SYSTEM

While it may seem like common sense to provide military forces with basic knowledge about the human dimension of the battlespace, military units deploying to Iraq and Afghanistan before 2006 knew little about the political system, economic life, or culture of the countries in which they would be fighting a war. According to General Stanley McChrystal, who commanded Coalition forces in Afghanistan in 2009–10: "Most of us, me included, had a very superficial understanding of the situation and history, and we had a frighteningly simplistic view of recent history, the last 50 years."[4] Given that in a counterinsurgency the population is the "center of gravity," this ignorance impeded the military's ability to build support for the host nation government, and decrease support for the insurgency.

Innovation from Failure

Although the historical record shows that some innovations result from peacetime planning, wargaming, and education,[5] military innovation may also result from wartime failure.[6] As military historian Theo Farrell has noted, military organizations often cease relying on standardly accepted technology, organization, and approaches "when they are at war and appear to be losing."[7] Prospective defeat often functions as a trigger of change.

For many of us working inside the Beltway at the beginning of the wars in Iraq and Afghanistan, monitoring the progress of the war through news reports, emails sent by friends downrange, and Pentagon briefings was like watching a train wreck in slow motion. Policy decisions, such as de-Baathification, were made without apparent consideration of their effect on Iraqi society or the country's security environment. What were the potential consequences of creating a large group of unemployed, dishonored, highly trained, well-armed men who had been swept from power and now must face the prospect of domination by their traditional ethno-sectarian rivals? In addition, similarly unfounded assumptions apparently guided the planning process. The DOD (Department of Defense) and US Central Command (CENTCOM), for example, believed that the Iraqi military and police, minus their Baathist leaders, would remain intact to reestablish order after the end of conventional operations.[8] As the former National Security Adviser Condoleezza Rice said, "The concept was that we would defeat the army, but the institutions would hold, everything from ministries to police forces."[9] This planning assumption demonstrated a significant misapprehension about Iraq: namely that it was a technocratic bureaucracy rather than a dysfunctional totalitarian state.

The swift, precise use of military force to topple the regime of Saddam Hussein was perhaps intended as a showcase for the revolution in military affairs focused on speed, agility, and precision propounded by Secretary of Defense Donald Rumsfeld. Echoing Rumsfeld, President Bush noted in May 2001: "I'm committed to building a future force that is defined less by size and more by mobility and swiftness, one that is easier to deploy and sustain, one that relies more heavily on stealth, precision weaponry and information technologies."[10] Indeed, warfighting based on speed, agility, and precision instead of mass had become the dominant paradigm throughout the military establishment. Leading up to the war in Iraq, the training that brigades received at the National Training Center and Joint Readiness Training Center focused on large-scale maneuver warfare, augmented by the sexiest technology taxpayer dollars could purchase. At the war colleges, military academies, and staff colleges, only a handful of classes included any assigned readings on such unpopular and outmoded forms of warfare as counterinsurgency. Moreover, the military intelligence collection and analysis process had been designed and built to identify and neutralize lethal targets.[11]

Thus, in 2004, the burgeoning insurgency in Iraq took political leaders by surprise. For all of 2003, and most of the first half of 2004, senior US officials referred to those who perpetrated attacks on Coalition forces as "terrorists" and "dead-enders," estimated their numbers at 5,000 or less, and claimed that they were "outside elements" and "former regime loyalists" (FRLs) with limited popular support.[12] The simmering Sunni–Shia tensions were ignored, as were the ethno-sectarian divisions in the north.[13] At a June 2003 press conference, Secretary of Defense Donald Rumsfeld stated, "I guess the reason I don't use the phrase 'guerrilla war' is because there isn't one."[14]

The simmering insurgency also found military commanders unprepared. When General David Petraeus took command of Multi-National Force—Iraq (MNF–I) in February 2007, conditions in Iraq had deteriorated significantly. Coalition forces were taking casualties daily from improvised explosive devices (IEDs), mortars, rocket-propelled grenades (RPGs), and small arms fire. In addition, ethno-sectarian cleansing was taking place in some neighborhoods with "up to 150 corpses being found daily in Baghdad."[15] In the words of General Petraeus, "The insurgencies in Iraq and Afghanistan were not, in truth, the wars for which we were best prepared in 2001; however, they are the wars we are fighting and they clearly are the kind of wars we must master."[16] The alternative to total failure was taking proactive steps to reduce the level of violence in Iraq; to improve the ability of the Iraqi government to govern the country; to fix the economy; and to reduce support (active and passive) for the proliferating insurgent groups such as the Mahdi Army, the Mujahideen Shura Council, and al-Qaeda in Iraq.

The deployed military swiftly recognized that understanding the "human terrain," like having Humvees and body armor, was critical to accomplishing the mission. Official requirements were swiftly generated from the field and sent up the chain to the Pentagon. The result was an experimental program called the Human Terrain System (HTS) that embedded teams of mixed military and civilian members with all echelons of US, Coalition, and ISAF forces in Iraq and Afghanistan. The mission of these teams was to conduct social science research and analysis, and to advise military commanders about the local population. HTS, which began in 2006 as a "good idea" on PowerPoint slides, exploded to a $150 million dollar program in three years. By conducting research on the spot in a war zone and advising military commanders and their staffs, HTS was designed to remedy the military's lack of understanding regarding the people of Afghanistan and Iraq. It was the largest single investment ever made by the DOD in applied social science, and it also exemplified institutional innovation within the military, triggered by the prospect of failure.

Origin of the Term "Human Terrain"

Before describing how the program was built, it might be worthwhile to say something about the name. To those unaccustomed to working with the military, the term "human terrain" sounds at best impersonal and at worst nefarious. To our knowledge, the phrase was first used by Geoffrey Fairburn, a scholar of revolutionary warfare, in an article for an American anti-Communist magazine that was appended to a US House of Representatives Un-American Activities Committee Report in 1968.[17] The term made a comeback in the mid-1990s, when the UN undertook security, peacekeeping, and humanitarian missions in Somalia following its civil war, catalyzing a new focus on complex operations in urban areas. US Army Lieutenant Colonel Ralph Peters used the term in his 2000 article "The Human Terrain of Urban Operations," arguing that the human terrain would be just as important as the physical terrain in future urban warfare scenarios.[18]

The term "human terrain" swiftly expanded beyond the confines of urban operations, and was informally adopted by the US military to refer to the population as a component of the battlespace in all sorts of operations. The earliest general use of the term can be attributed to Major General William G. Boykin, writing in *Special Warfare* in 2001: "United States Army special-operations forces, or ARSOF, more than any other segment of the military population, recognize the importance of the human terrain in military operations."[19] However, the true credit for the term "human terrain system" should rightly go to Colonel Joseph Celeski, a former commander of the Combined Joint Special Operations Task Force in Afghanistan. Characterizing the population in a given area of operations as a complex system, Celeski argued that the military needs to conduct a "cultural assessment" prior to entering the area of operations, to understand the local society. "This type of data provides a start point for the links and nodes sought for in the target analysis of human terrain systems."[20]

In choosing the term "human terrain," HTS program management was considering how best to communicate to military land forces the fundamental idea of the program: that the local population should be considered as a critical element of the operational environment in the same way as weather, geographical terrain, or time are evaluated. In order to be adopted and used by the military, social science concepts must be translated into terminology familiar to a military audience. As a Navy captain noted, the term "human terrain" is "the type of lexicon that has to be used to effectively communicate. If you start with semiotics and exogenous language or endogenous marriage patterns or the synchronism of ethnography I won't say no one will listen, but I'll certainly bet my next paycheck your military audience will relegate your lecture to their already overflowing trashcans."[21] The term "human terrain" helped to make a conceptual link between the well-being of the local civilian population and the warfighting function of military units. "Human terrain," rather than being a means to dehumanize civilian populations (as some anthropological critics of HTS have asserted), was actually a metaphor that used the military's pre-existing conceptual frameworks to convey the idea that the battlespace was not a blank, uninhabited domain but was actually somebody's home.

From the Ground Up

Understanding the human terrain had become critical for the military's mission in Iraq and Afghanistan, and throughout the DOD, efforts were being made to find solutions to ameliorate the socio-cultural knowledge deficit. HTS was just one of a number of such initiatives. All of these new programs faced a similar struggle within old and entrenched bureaucracies of the DOD, where most programs and organizations are heritage entities, where rice bowls are jealously protected, and where defense dollars are programmed years out in budgets. "Changing the DOD is like turning a battleship in a sea of mud," as a rear admiral once cautioned us. Change, when it does occur, often comes from outside (such as the Goldwater–Nichols DOD Reorganization Act of 1986) or during wartime as a result of the pressure to adapt to enemy tactics and technology or new operational environments. Indeed, the wars in Iraq and Afghanistan drove a great deal of innovation, as the US military adapted to conditions on the ground, recognized shortfalls, and plugged gaps. These innovations included technology (such as the

Office of Naval Research's development of QuikClot for use in treating battlefield wounds), equipment (such as up-armored High Mobility Multipurpose Wheeled Vehicles or HMMWVs), and organizations (such as the Joint Improvised Explosive Device Defeat Organization or JIEDDO, and the Asymmetric Warfare Group).

Like these other organizations, HTS was built from scratch. Unlike them, it was intended to be a wartime experiment, referred to inside the DOD as a "proof of concept." Most people who have never worked for the US government assume that starting a new program must be similar to starting a new business. This, however, is not the case. In the government, particularly the military, one must work within the extant bureaucratic system, using commonly accepted and understood concepts and language. Moreover, to grasp the challenge of undertaking a "proof of concept" fully, one must understand that the Army as a bureaucratic system does not facilitate the process of *de novo* creation. The Army is functionally organized according to the Army Universal Task List (AUTL), which lists tasks, missions, and operations performed at corps level and below. Each warfighting function performed on battlefield task is thoroughly detailed in the AUTL: movement and maneuver, intelligence, fires, sustainment, command and control, and protection.[22] Only very rarely do new tasks appear in the AUTL, and the process for adding anything new involves multiple layers of approval.[23] Needless to say, conducting social science research does not appear in the AUTL.

The AUTL provides a standardized "catalog of tasks" from which Army units build their mission-essential task list (METL). "A *mission-essential task* is a collective task a unit must be able to perform successfully to accomplish its mission."[24] These mission-essential tasks represent what Army units actually do during operations, and are therefore also what the Army trains to do. Most METLs are standardized by the Department of the Army to ensure that units have similar capabilities and are interoperable; all infantry brigade combat teams, for example, train and report on the same METL. Subordinate units use the METL of their parent unit.[25] If a unit does not have a METL (such as units which are not in an Army Force Generation pool), then commanders should "consider a unit's table of organization and equipment or table of distribution and allowances mission, plans or orders, higher command's guidance, and doctrinal principles"[26] in order to develop their METL. In other words, if a unit lacks a METL, they should refer back to other relevant documents such as a table of organization and equipment, which prescribes the number and type of personnel, their grade or rank, the composition of the command and staff, equipment, and mission. But what if you're a new unit and you have no METL? What if you have no table of organization and equipment? How can you build a METL? What if none of your basic functions appear in the AUTL?

This was the situation which HTS faced in 2006. HTS had no mission statement, it did not exist in doctrine, its tasks did not appear in the AUTL, it had no table of organization and equipment, and it had no METL. HTS was nothing more than a good idea on PowerPoint. HTS had emerged out of a predecessor project sponsored by the Joint Chiefs of Staff (JCS) J3 and JIEDDO called the Cultural Preparation of the Environment (CPE). The CPE was basically a socio-cultural database, which was intended to assist military units with situational knowledge of their operating environment. Many of us who worked on the CPE were skeptical that a technological solution would work for brigades in combat, especially given the paucity of accurate, empirical data on local populations and the limited time any brigade staff had to spend learning how to use a new piece of equipment. We were afraid that without a team of social scientists who could conduct research on the ground and advise the brigade commander and his staff, the CPE would become simply another piece of useless equipment sitting in the tactical operations center (TOC). Meanwhile, the head of the US Army Training and Doctrine Command (TRADOC) intelligence unit, Maxie McFarland, who had long been an advocate of improving cultural education for military officers, was determined to address this pressing issue. A subordinate organization, the Foreign Military Studies Office in Fort Leavenworth, volunteered to assume the task of building some sort of social science research program around the CPE. Colonel Steve Fondacaro (USA, Ret), who had just retired after thirty years in Army Special Operations, became the Program Manager in 2006.

At that point in 2006, HTS had no funding, no staff, no table of organization and equipment and no METL. What it did have was an Operational Needs Statement (ONS) from the US Army 10th Mountain Division. An ONS is a service component document that articulates the "urgent need for a nonstandard and or unprogrammed capability to correct a deficiency or improve a capability that enhances mission accomplishment."[27] Subsequently, a DOD-level requirements document, called a Joint Urgent Operational Needs Statement (JUONS), was signed by I Corps in Iraq and 82nd Airborne Division in Afghanistan, and then consolidated by CENTCOM. To our knowledge, this was the first time an ONS or a JUONS was issued for a human capability, rather than a piece of technology.

These joint requirements documents brought HTS into being as an official organization, and established its mission. The Iraq JUONS, though unclassified, was never intended for external distribution. Therefore, it offers a rare insight into what the US military believed were the most significant issues it was facing regarding the Iraqi population in 2005–6. Noting that "human terrain knowledge deficiencies" existed at all command echelons, the Iraq JUONS observed that "detailed knowledge of host populations is critical in areas where US forces are being increased to conduct counterinsurgency and stability operations in Iraq. US forces continue to operate in Iraq without real-time knowledge of the drivers of the behavior within the host population. This greatly limits Commanders' situational awareness and creates greater risks for forces." The Iraq JUONS established the objectives of the HTS experiment: to "improve operational decisions and chances for mission success" through "increased understanding of Iraqi citizens' physical and economic security needs at local/district resolution"; "increased understanding of local ideological, religious, and tribal allegiances"; and "avoidance of unintended second order effects resulting from a lack of understanding of the local human terrain." The goal for HTS, as stated in the Iraq JUONS, was to help "decrease both coalition force and local national casualties" and "avoid needless loss of life that has occurred due to lack of a systematic process and systems to enable transfer of human terrain knowledge during unit Relief in Place/Transition of Authority (RIP/TOA)."

HTS Mission Statement

The JUONs established the mission of HTS, which is to "enable culturally astute decision-making, enhance operational effectiveness, and preserve and share socio-cultural institutional knowledge."[28] Before describing the program start-up process, it might be worthwhile to discuss the mission in more detail. Culturally astute decision-making, as we often explained in briefings to the military and the general public, means that the actions chosen by the military also take into consideration the affected local populace. Many actions taken by the US military appear quite reasonable to Americans, but mystify the intended beneficiaries. For example, from an American point of view, rehabilitating a cement factory in the Diyala province of Iraq would seem like a reasonable way to alleviate the local unemployment problem, boost the economy, and keep young men off the streets. However, from an Iraqi perspective, factory labor was degrading and there was no market for cement. The priority of local Iraqis was reconstruction of the aquifers damaged by US forces so that the orchards would produce citrus fruit again. If working the land was considered a noble occupation and people were desperate for fresh oranges, why spend $17 million dollars on a project nobody wants? Yet, until the Human Terrain Team (HTT) began asking local community members what they wanted, the military had not taken the Iraqi point of view into account and had made decisions that were not as culturally astute as they might have been. As a number of chapters in this volume demonstrate, based on their research, HTTs were frequently able to help the military broaden their conceptual aperture and think about the situation from a local point of view.

Enhancing operational effectiveness, as we explained the concept in program briefs, meant helping the military execute their operations more successfully with less expenditure of effort. The objective of counterinsurgency, for example, is the increase in support (active and passive) for the host nation government and the decrease in support (active and passive) for the insurgency, operating with the assumption that the host nation government has some legitimacy in the eyes of the people. In such a fight, the likelihood of success is often inversely proportional to the amount of force used. In 1986, General John Galvin, then Commander-in-Chief of the US Southern Command, observed that the military must not only "subdue an armed adversary while attempting to provide security to the civilian population, it must also avoid furthering the insurgents' cause. If, for example, the military's actions in killing fifty guerrillas cause 200 previously uncommitted citizens to join the insurgent cause, the use of force will have been counterproductive."[29]

In military circles this formula is called "insurgent math."[30] Given this equation, the implicit goal of HTS was to help the military reduce its need for the use of lethal force. For example, in 2007–8 the Taliban were firing rockets at Forward Operating Base Salerno from a village outside the gate. The HTS team members went to the village and talked to the elders, who indicated that they "wished to be good neighbors" and that they would make the Taliban unwelcome if the Coalition would show an occasional presence in the village. In addition, the villagers indicated that they wanted a volleyball net. In the words of the Brigade S3, "we don't ask them about their needs—paratroopers just don't think that way. But we gave them what they wanted—a volleyball net—and they gave us information on their security situation. The HTT, through a completely non-lethal effort, achieved the desired effect, which was to stop the attacks on the Forward Operating Base (FOB). We couldn't have done it if we had cordoned and searched every house in the village."[31]

The third aspect of HTS's mission was to "preserve and share sociocultural institutional knowledge." In both Afghanistan and Iraq, the Army employed unit rotation, in which an entire unit (brigade, division, corps) deploys to a theater, remains about twelve months, rotates home, and is replaced with another unit. One of the drawbacks of the unit rotation policy is that knowledge about the area of operations is often lost during the shuffle and not adequately transmitted to the follow-on unit. Expeditionary warfare requires a mechanism to capture and transmit tactical cultural information during unit rotation, yet no such system had been developed when HTS began. Even as late as 2009, units would turn over shoeboxes of information (scraps of paper, PowerPoint files, and photographs) to their replacements. This continuity problem was not new to Iraq or Afghanistan. As one Marine Corps battalion commander noted about Bosnia, "it was the seventh rotation, but nothing was handed down in terms of institutional knowledge. We had no idea where the shops and schools were, who was who. It took us weeks just to gather the most basic information and we lost a major opportunity because of the RIP/TOA [relieve in place/transfer of authority] f*ck up."[32] To preserve and share sociocultural knowledge during unit rotations, HTS did not attach teams to brigades (which would have just perpetuated the problem) but instead geographically located the teams (e.g. a particular forward operating base) so that the team would become experts in a given area. Unfortunately, as a number of the chapters in this volume note, this organizational structure itself was not always effective at preserving and sharing socio-cultural knowledge.

The Learning Curve

The JUONS provided the basis of the mission statement for HTS, but it did not provide any funding, a table of organization and equipment or a METL. Not only was HTS a start-up program, it was doing something that had never been done before: sending mixed military civilian teams (including both retired and active duty military personnel) into a war zone to conduct social science research in direct support of military units.[33] Before the first team deployed, every element of the program design was based on an informed estimate of what was feasible and what might work downrange. We had to take a guess about how large the teams should be and about what skills they might need. Should the teams include a non-commissioned officer or someone with knowledge management background, or maybe an extra social scientist? We had to guess about what equipment they might want and whether we should send them downrange with tape recorders for transcription, or just pens and paper? The most critical questions that related directly to the mission of HTS were also unanswered. What kind of research would the brigades want? What kind of research would it be possible or feasible for the teams to conduct during a war? Where in the military decision-making cycle would this research add value? What was the best place on the staff for teams to provide this input? What were the collective team tasks that would hold true regardless of echelon or location? What were the individual tasks of the different positions involved that would hold true regardless of team size, team composition, echelon, or location? In 2006 and for most of 2007, HTS had a staff of seven people to answer all these questions and run the organization.[34]

Structure of HTS

The HTTs were the centerpiece of HTS's mission. As the program grew and developed, we determined that a fully-staffed HTT should have five to nine members, depending on where they were going and the type of unit they were supporting. In addition to one or two social scientists (who typically were civilians), HTTs included a research manager and cultural analysts to aid in the collection, analysis, and dissemination of data. Another key role was that of the team leader (typically a military reservist or retiree) who was expected to facilitate the relationship between the HTT and unit to which it was formally attached. Unfortunately, as a number of chapters in this volume note, not all of the teams were adequately staffed and not all of them performed as well as we had hoped, often as a result of personality issues and interpersonal dynamics.

A critical question in late 2006 when we were standing up the program was the level of military staff to which these teams should go. Where would they do the most good and have the greatest impact? Subject matter experts, when they are utilized at all by the military, tend to be embedded within military staffs at the highest level. When General Petraeus was commander of Multi-National Force—Iraq (MNF–I) in 2007, he had a PhD economist, a PhD historian, and a PhD political scientist on his staff. Presumably, the theory was that the insight provided by these highly-educated individuals would help the commander make better informed decisions, and these pearls of wisdom would trickle down to division commanders, brigade commanders, battalion commanders, company commanders, and then eventually to platoon and squad commanders. However, in practice, those young officers at the end of the chain of command often had to make do with very little information or guidance about the history, politics, or economy of the area of operations beyond what they could glean for themselves.[35]

In deciding at what echelon to put the teams, we asked ourselves two questions. What is the lowest echelon at which a military unit makes strategic decisions that affect the overall conduct of the war? What is the highest echelon at which a military unit makes tactical decisions that affect how the war is fought? The sweet spot is the brigade, and that is where the first twenty-six teams out the door went, filling requirements in both the Iraq and Afghanistan theaters. Brigade commanders have tremendous influence over the course and conduct of any given war. Yet, when one looks at the staff composition of a US Army brigade combat team (BCT) or US Marine Corps regimental combat team (RCT), the commander is lucky if he has any staff members with Master's degrees. And so, despite pressure from a few generals who pounded their fists on the table demanding an HTT at division or corps level, only after this requirement for teams at the brigade level was filled did we send teams to higher echelons. The teams working at division or corps level, called Human Terrain Analysis Teams (HTAT), conducted research just like HTTs but had the additional mandate of collating information collected by HTTs to create a fuller picture of the operational environment. Teams were designated by country in the order they deployed: thus, for example, AF1 was the first team to deploy to Afghanistan and IZ16 was the sixteenth team to deploy to Iraq.

To support those teams, HTS also built two Research Reachback Centers (RRCs) focused on Iraq and Afghanistan and staffed with analysts who conducted secondary source research on demand. Just to give readers an idea of the scope and volume of the RRCs' research, during 2008 the RRCs responded to nearly 600 requests for research, of which a third were "short notice reports" with an eight to seventy-two-hour deadline, and some of which exceeded 100 pages. Some examples of reports included the history of poppy eradication programs in Kandahar and Helmand; an analysis of the correlation of the unemployment rates and insurgent attack rates throughout Iraq by province; and the structure of influence in a Pashtun village.

In addition, HTS designed and built a training program to train the teams; a personnel system to manage the teams; an operations center to deal with immediate team requirements and movement; a database and analysis system called MAP-HT for teams to use (later taken over by CENTCOM); a contracted Social Science Research and Analysis (SSRA) capability to conduct primarily quantitative research in areas where the teams could not travel; a theater coordination element (TCE) to provide oversight and management of personnel in theater; a doctrine section to develop best practices and de-conflict HTS activities with current Army doctrine; and so on.

The HTT—with support from the RRC and SSRA—was expected to engage in "action research," meaning systematic, practical, research that could be applied to real-world problems as presented by the exigencies of the context or situation. The research conducted by the HTTs was not research for its own sake, but either directly tasked by the unit or implicit in the unit's lines of operation. Thus, for example, a brigade commander might ask very specific questions. What is the preferred means of resolving disputes concerning water rights in Helmand province? How does the segmentary lineage system of the Kurds differ from that of the Arabs? The research question might show up in a commander's critical information requirements (CIR) or priority information requirements (PIR) that was circulated within the staff. Alternatively, research topics might be implicit in the brigade's mission, such as a unit working to establish neighborhood councils in Sadr

City. In that case, the team would evaluate the socio-cultural knowledge required against the unit's current state of knowledge to identify the knowledge gap. Often research questions were implicit in various lines of operation. What was the pre-existing system for local political representation under Saddam Hussein? What are the responsibilities for management and administration at the local political level in Iraq? What are the processes for appointing or electing representatives? It may seem somewhat obvious that in order to establish a neighborhood council in a foreign country one might need this sort of information. However, as many HTTs discovered, units often did not know what they needed to know. It was the HTT's job, therefore, to indicate very gently that considering such issues might be advisable in order to achieve the mission.

Depending on the research question, a research design generally would be developed including testable hypotheses, assumptions, research methods, analysis methods, and some preliminary idea about the form of the ideal final product (such as a paper, a briefing, or a chart). The research would then be conducted in the field with secondary source supplementation, often conducted by the RRC or SSRA. During the identification of the research topic, while the research was being conducted, and after completion of the final product, the HTT would participate in the brigade's operational planning cycle. In other words, social scientists and other HTT members often had a seat at the table when courses of action were compared and plans were made. Commanders and their staffs could in theory then make decisions with reference to the local situation and develop courses of action that emphasize the use of non-lethal tactics (such as negotiation, infrastructure development, and provision of medical and veterinary care) in order to achieve desired effects (such as increased support for the host nation government, and decreased support for insurgent groups, such as the Taliban). In this way, HTS represents the first attempt (to our knowledge) to incorporate the insights of social science into the military's *operational* capability.

Complexities

During the first four years of the program, HTS can be accurately described as a live experiment to determine what worked and what did not work. This particular experiment was complicated for a number of reasons. First among them is that the teams had to support and be integrated with Army Brigade Combat Teams and Marine Corps Regimental Combat Teams *in combat*. Nobody can tell a brigade commander how to run his organization, especially when bullets are flying. Therefore, as the chapters in this volume illustrate, each HTT had to be flexible enough to adapt to the brigade's organizational culture and its staff structure.

Second, each operational environment is different in terms of level of permissiveness, attitudes towards US forces, physical terrain, population demographics, and so on. Therefore, each HTT had to accommodate its research questions and research process to the environment in which it was working.

Third, the unique environment of each area of operations meant that each BCT and RCT had to tailor its mission and lines of operation to its operational environment. Brigades whose area of operations included Sadr city in Baghdad often conducted a staggering number of "key leader engagements" with sheikhs, religious leaders, and local politicians.[36] Brigades in Khost Province in Afghanistan, on the other hand, faced both an active threat from the Taliban and a bewildering array of governance issues and property disputes.

Fourth, each HTT was unique and had to determine its own strengths and weaknesses in order to determine its own capabilities. A team with a PhD social psychologist accustomed to qualitative research methods and content analysis would most likely be unable to conduct a large-scale survey, regardless of the brigade's priorities. On the other hand, a PhD political scientist with a statistical background and an interest in voting behavior might have trouble with conducting a series of individual interviews on the topic of local female medical issues.

Because the war varied across areas of operations, brigades varied in terms of organizational culture and lines of operation, and HTTs varied in terms of their composition and skills, having a one-size-fits-all HTT would not have worked.

Program Development Team Lessons Learned

In 2006, when we started HTS, we did not fully understand the complexity of integrating mixed military/civilian teams into US military units in combat in order to conduct social science. Moreover, none of the critical questions facing HTS (such as team composition, team location, or even team equipment) could be accurately addressed in advance, but could only be answered on the basis of empirical data about what the teams were doing in theater. The intent was to draw conclusions based on real-life observations rather than assumptions. Too many chimerical concepts drafted up under fluorescent light in the Pentagon are imposed on the warfighter downrange, without any attempt to understand the pressures and problems of deployed units. Understanding what types of social science research worked in theater, understanding where the HTT should sit on the brigade staff, understanding what types of equipment and supplies were needed was all part of the experiment. Only once we had that information—based on the aggregate, not just the subjective opinions of individuals—could we validate the concept and grow the program.

Given that HTS was essentially an experiment in how to conduct social science in support of the military in combat, having what the military refers to as a "lessons learned" process was critical to discovering what worked and what did not work downrange. HTS created a Program Development Team (PDT) in 2006 to gather, analyze, and respond to feedback from the field about best practices—from both team members and from brigade staff.[37] Many of the recommendations that the PDT made were implemented, such as in-theater team management, changes to the training curriculum, and reorganization of team structure. For example, the PDT realized in 2007 after seeing AF1 in the field that brigades would split up the teams to support subordinate units during missions in the field. This was not something we anticipated, but was something that we learned from the experiment in real-time. Accordingly, HTS management immediately began planning a nine-person team to accommodate how brigades were actually utilizing the teams. Some recommendations, such as improving the quality of personnel, could not be implemented because HTS had no control over the omnibus contact under which team members were hired by the prime contractor (see below). Other recommendations, such as providing vehicles for teams, could not be implemented for financial and force protection reasons.[38]

One of the critical issues for the PDT was about research methods. What type of research questions were the brigades asking? What questions were they not asking that they should be asking? Given all that, what research was it feasible for teams to actually conduct? What research methods, given the time and operational constraints, were most effective? Over the course of two years we discovered that the non-permissive nature of most areas of operation prohibited the standard ethnographic method of research: participant observation. More commonly, HTTs conducted semi-structured interviews with individuals, which would often turn into group interviews as local people interjected their thoughts and opinions. Most of these interviews took place in relatively safe places, such as markets, doorsteps, government information centers, and so on. Sometimes, HTTs conducted interviews while soldiers conducted patrols in highly dangerous environments. In these cases, six minutes was the absolute maximum length of time the interview could run because seven minutes is how long it takes a sniper to move position and set up for another shot. The PDT discovered over the course of two years that HTTs typically researched similar topics, regardless of brigade or location. Typical research topics included tribal networks, legitimate traditional authority figures, emergent political groups, local conflict resolution mechanisms, and political ideologies.[39] Economic indicators were another common topic. For example, one HTT was able to use the presence in markets of perishable goods, such as fruit and vegetables, as an indicator of population security. Cabbage is grown in the south of Iraq and distributed in Baghdad via north-running truck routes; when al-Qaeda was active in south Baghdad, there was little or no cabbage in the market and the prices were very high.[40] Needless to say, most brigades had never before considered the cost of vegetables as a security indicator.

Organizational Process Team Lessons Learned

HTS has been criticized by former team members, bloggers, journalists, and others for having a training program that did not prepare them to perform their jobs in theater, for sending teams downrange with too much useless equipment (or alternatively, not enough), for lacking a team performance strategy, and so on. Much of this inefficiency was the by-product of an inductive approach to concept implementation, of seeing what worked in context and adapting HTS to fit the reality of the circumstances downrange. Thus, over the first few years of its existence HTS grew organically, and alterations were constantly made to the training program and organizational structure on the basis of recommendations from team members, the PDT, higher headquarters, and other sources. By 2008, the HTS experiment had been running in theater for over a year and we had enough information about what worked and what was needed to restructure the program from the ground up.

The means to accomplish this daunting task was a multi-year, in-house, working group called the Organizational Process Team (OPT). We formed the OPT in 2008 under the supervision of the Director of Training,[41] and conducted dozens of working groups, interviews, and data calls with hundreds of current and former team members. With revision of training as the goal, we went all the way back to genesis: the HTS Vision Statement, which articulated what we wanted the program as a whole to provide to the military, which was drawn primarily from the JUONS. On the basis of the Vision Statement, we developed the Mission Statement, which established the overall mission of the program: "to enable culturally astute decision-making, enhance operational effectiveness, and preserve and share socio-cultural institutional knowledge across the Department of Defense." On the basis of the Mission Statement, we began the process of developing Collective Tasks, which included team tasks, RRC (Research Reachback Center) tasks, and SSRA (Social Science Research and Analysis) tasks. As we developed the Collective Tasks, we needed to understand (1) what types of social science research were needed by the military across two theaters of war and across multiple echelons; (2) what the purpose of this research was (situational awareness, mitigation, course of action analysis, etc.); (3) how and where this research fitted in with the military decision-making process; (4) the actual research process used by multiple teams over multiple years in multiple theaters with multiple social science backgrounds, so as to distill it to something that could function as a template for future research; (5) what types of products teams commonly produced, so as to develop a standardized list of product types and a naming convention so that we had the ability to manage our own knowledge production process; (6) what the individual tasks performed by different members of the team were and how they grouped according to skill set so that we could produce accurate job descriptions, and so on. On the basis of the Collective Tasks, the OPT developed the Individual Tasks. On the basis of the Individual Tasks, we developed the Terminal Learning Objectives and Enabling Learning Objectives. On the basis of the TLOs and ELOs, we produced a curriculum design and an implementation plan.[42]

So, what did we discover at the end of a two-year process of overhauling HTS from top to bottom, pertaining specifically to social science? First, we discovered what commanders want to know, drawing our conclusions from an empirical study of the research that deployed teams had conducted over the course of three years in Iraq and Afghanistan, and the various requests for research they had sent back to the RRC from the field for supplemental secondary source research. What commanders want to know is remarkably consistent between theaters and over time: it includes social structure; the political system (both formal and informal); the economic system (both formal and informal); and interests/grievances (particularly pertaining to security, intra- and extra-group conflict, and administration of justice). As we noted, "Interestingly, 'culture' in the broad anthropological sense ... has less salience than might have been anticipated. Despite the frequent use of the term in doctrine and by policy-makers in Washington, DC, 'culture' appears to be less relevant than social structure, political and economic systems, and the grievances of the population in the context of the conflicts in Iraq and Afghanistan."[43]

Second, we identified the ways in which HTTs actually support military decision-making, discussed below. Third, we identified that the research methods most commonly used by HTTs were semi-structured and unstructured interviews, and that the methods used were not highly dependent on the permissiveness of the security environment, suggesting that the choice of methods is a result of team preference, or social scientist comfort, or other team-specific factors. Other common research methods included: direct observation, visual ethnography, "key leader engagement,"[44] participant observation, multi-party interviews, surveys, and mixed method approaches. Fourth, we discovered that the analysis most commonly used by HTTs was textual analysis of notes and transcripts, followed by structural analysis (such as flow-charts, social network analysis, and diagramming). Other analytical methods included cultural domain analysis, quantitative analysis, and "inference analysis," which was what we called the ad hoc analysis performed by team members leaning on a HMMWV when the unit commander asks, "What do you think is going on in this village?" In sum, the type and utility of the research method employed depended on the questions asked by the military and by the conditions in which the research would be undertaken.

Team Tribulations

Throughout the course of this applied social science experiment, we also learned a great deal about teams. At its height in 2009, HTS had forty-two teams deployed with every brigade, division, and corps in Iraq and Afghanistan. Over the course of the first four years about 700 people deployed in teams, serving a minimum of nine months in theater, and with a few people serving over two years. During this period not all individuals performed optimally, and not all teams performed optimally. Understanding the reasons for both success and failure begins with the recognition that the larger organization both enables and constrains the job performance of teams and individuals. Some of the problems experienced by teams downrange resulted from structural factors inherent in the organization as a whole.

First among these organizational factors was the policy of staggered replacements, where the team stayed in place at its assigned geographical location and individual members of the team rotated in and out when their tour finished. (The alternative model would have been formation of the team as a whole, and rotation in and out of theater as a whole.)[45] Unfortunately, staggered rotation was the only option open to HTS, which had a programmatic requirement from the JUONS to "enable transfer of human terrain knowledge during unit Relief in Place/Transition of Authority (RIP/TOA)." The loss of knowledge during the RIP/TOA process hindered the ability of US forces to conduct stability operations and counterinsurgency.[46] Brigades in Iraq and Afghanistan spent about a year in theater, and when they redeployed back to the US they took their knowledge and connection with them. HTS was designed (and required) to address this loss of socio-cultural knowledge by remaining in place. The benefits to the military were considerable, and we often heard comments such as this from an S3 in Iraq: "They were invaluable on the RIP, and answered the questions that young company commanders had about who was who."[47] The downside was that staggered rotation caused disruption and aggravation to members of HTTs, who were forced constantly to readjust to the personalities, intellectual capabilities, and work habits of new team members. Staggered rotation in some cases also caused bonded, high-functioning teams to fall apart. Additionally, staggered rotation was difficult for the units themselves, when well-integrated team members were replaced in stride by new personnel who had to be brought up to speed on events in the battlespace.

The second structural factor that inhibited effective team and individual performance was HTS's lack of control over contracting and hiring. Because HTS was an experimental program, it had no government billets of its own. Initially all of the civilian staff and team members were contractors. Because HTS was located within TRADOC this command's omnibus contract was the vehicle used for hiring personnel. Because the omnibus contract lacked performance standards, HTS had no means to hold the contractor accountable. Furthermore, federal contracting regulations prohibit the government from telling contractors who to hire. HTS could not choose who it wanted to hire but had to accept whoever the contractor chose. In a situation such as this, contractors have no incentive to be selective in hiring since they make their money on the basis of bodies, regardless of quality. The contractor sometimes hired individuals for HTS without an interview or even a cursory background check, such as one candidate who had a felony warrant for vehicular manslaughter. Other individuals lacked job qualifications or were clearly unable to carry 50 pounds of body armor due to age and level of physical fitness. Having personnel on teams with questionable qualifications was a disservice both to other team members and to the military as a whole.

An additional, related problem was that HTS technically had no authority to fire individuals for non-performance. If an individual appeared unsuitable during training, HTS had to rely on the contractor to fire them. (Individuals cannot be terminated for non-performance by the government unless their job requirements have been identified through a job analysis. Conducting a job analysis *de novo* generally takes over a year to complete, including research, analysis, or production of the report. HTS only received authorization from its higher headquarters to put out the contract for bid in 2008. The job analysis was finally completed in 2009, and could then be implemented in 2010.) In addition, US government regulations prohibited a *civilian* team leader from disciplining or firing a *uniformed military* subordinate, resulting in either a bifurcation of team authority or total breakdown in discipline. Moreover, once individuals deployed downrange, the team leader had no authority to fire any team members, civilian or military. According to both the Army Judge Advocate General and the Inspector General, the only recourse a team leader had to deal with a non-performing team member was to ask the brigade commanding officer to pull the individual's country clearance. Needless to say, the program's inability to fire non-performing team members was detrimental to both deployed teams and to the military units that were forced to become involved in HTT internal issues.

The third structural factor affecting team and individual performance was the inability to train and deploy teams with the brigade and regimental combat teams they would actually be working with downrange. This proved frustrating for both military units supported by HTTs and for team members themselves. In the words of one brigade S3 in Iraq in 2009, "We had high hopes after NTC [National Training Center], but these were not necessarily met because the social scientist we had there was not the same as what we had here—not that we were disappointed with what we got, we just were expecting someone qualitative and instead here was a quantitative SS (Social Scientist)."[48] Unfortunately, the Army force generation model of train/ready, available, reset is based on a thirty-six-month timeline for active duty components,[49] while the HTS deployment length was nine months not including training (based in part on US Army Reserve requirements). As a result of this mismatch in force generation models, teams could not train or deploy with the units they would eventually serve, but had to integrate quickly into the battle rhythm of units they had never met before.

These organizational factors—staggered rotation, lack of control over hiring or firing, and inability to deploy teams with the actual brigades they would support downrange—contributed to the stress and aggravation of individuals who served on teams and influenced whether teams and individuals could perform optimally. It is also worth noting the inherent difficulty of building small units with flat (and at times undefined) leadership structures that will undertake ambiguous and dangerous missions. Without stretching the comparison too far, special operations commands generally pay close attention to personality and interpersonal relations within teams. Teams are thus crafted to work optimally together. HTS did none of that: teams were simply assembled, at times only a few weeks or even days before deploying. The intense pressures from the DOD to deploy teams rapidly combined with the poor human resources support provided by the prime contractor made effective team-building quite difficult.

VALUE OF SOCIAL SCIENCE

Perhaps the biggest unanswered question facing those of us who created HTS was whether social science has any value to the military at all. On the one hand, some observers have concluded that the US military presence in Iraq was little more than democratization forced at the barrel of an M-16; that concern for the well-being of the Iraqi people was merely a pretense to justify neo-colonialism; and that US policies were insensitive and boorish at best. At the tactical level, the imposition of political authority backed by coercive force bred ethnocentric attitudes towards the local population. After observing American forces in Iraq, British Brigadier General Nigel Aylwin Foster wrote that "at times their cultural insensitivity, almost certainly inadvertent, arguably amounted to institutional racism."[50]

On the other hand, military operations can be conducted in accordance with local norms, with some regard for viewpoint and values of the local inhabitants, and in harmony with local institutions. According to COL Isaiah Wilson III, who served as an official Army historian of the Iraq campaign:

> Learning about the patronage-based (associative—kin, clan, and tribal) politics peculiar to Northern Iraq, and each of its four separate but interconnected provinces (also known as "governorates") was ESSENTIAL to getting an initial set of governance institutions reestablished and back up and running throughout the North—institutions and institutional processes that maintained a small modicum of local public trust and legitimacy. This better understanding of the local politics—the day-to-day politics of Northern Iraqi public affairs, or administration—proved critical (necessary and sufficient, in the short term) for establishing (restoring) initial essential services (production, storage, distribution), local economies (creation of jobs and employment opportunities), governance (legislative, executive, and judicial authorities), and civil society (community associations; recreation activities; etc.). Eventually, our expanding knowledge of local tribal ways and relationships were incorporated into our strategies and plans for the rebuilding of the Iraqi Ministerial system—we found that appreciating the traditional roles that some tribes and clans had once enjoyed under the old regime of Saddam Hussein (and before it) was beneficial in helping us in our support of local selected and elected Iraqi leadership to effectively determine the fair and just and effective distribution of political "spoils" (assignments and responsibilities; political power).[51]

Does understanding (and implementation of policy in harmony with) social structure, norms, institutions, communication patterns, power structure, and belief systems of the various groups in a given society make any difference to military outcomes? The short answer is that there are no formal measures of effectiveness to prove the proposition that cultural knowledge or sensitivity makes any difference to military outcomes. In many cases, culture is not even considered as a relevant variable. In three different studies on "nation building," for example, RAND identifies the six top priorities as security, humanitarian relief, governance, economic stabilization, democratization, and development.[52] While some discussion is scattered throughout these texts, culture is mostly considered to be a tactical concern.[53]

The proposition that cultural knowledge is beneficial cannot be realistically evaluated using the objective, quantitative measure by which the US military prefers to judge outcomes. It is inherently subjective and anecdotal. In Iraq's Al Anbar Province between January and August 2005, for example, the 3rd Battalion, 4th Marines conducted seven offensive operations to disrupt insurgent cells, detained more than 400 suspected insurgents, uncovered the largest cache of weapons and explosives found by the 2nd Marine Division in Iraq, and lost no Marines in combat. In part, the Marines owed their success to their knowledge of the local society. According to Lt Col. Andrew Kennedy, the commanding officer of 3rd Battalion, 4th Marines, Regimental Combat Team-8, "Basically the operation worked because we knew who the tribal power brokers were and we took advantage of the situation. We knew how they were organized, so instead of making a terrible *faux pas*, we parlayed it into a relationship with the Azawi sheikh, and that translated to relations with the sub-sheikhs, and this feeling of goodwill extended throughout the area of influence."[54]

Although there may be no empirical evidence to support the proposition that cultural knowledge makes any difference to military outcomes, the real question is one of policy. How should the government of the US behave in relations with other people and nations of the world? As Clyde Kluckholn, an anthropologist who worked for the Office of Strategic Services, noted in 1949: "Ignorance of the way of life in other countries breeds an indifference and callousness among nations, a misinterpretation and misunderstanding which becomes ever more threatening as the world shrinks."[55] Do Americans really want a national security policy based on ignorance? If the answer to this question is "no," then the policy should be informed by socio-cultural knowledge and the means of policy implementation should match the policy.

At the tactical level, socio-cultural knowledge can also provide benefits to the operational military. As mentioned earlier in this chapter, during the OPT process of programmatic restructure we needed to evaluate exactly how HTTs were conducting research to "enable culturally astute decision-making, enhance operational effectiveness, and preserve and share socio-cultural institutional knowledge."[56] Based on interviews, focus groups, and analysis of four years' worth of data, we were able to identify the specific ways in which HTTs were supporting military decision-making: by providing socio-cultural situational awareness; providing input to course of action (COA) development; recommending mitigation strategies; providing effects analysis; supporting the operations process; and providing unit specific socio-cultural training. In offering this support to the military, HTS's goal was to enable the military to make decisions based on knowledge about the local community that made sense from a local point of view. In the words of one deputy commanding officer in Afghanistan: "the HTT helps us to make decisions that aren't culturally stupid."[57]

The first way to avoid "cultural stupidity" is to understand the local society. Providing "socio-cultural situational awareness" entails giving the supported unit an understanding of the population, which is not something that most brigade intelligence elements are trained or required to do. In the words of one battalion commander in Iraq: "It's what you don't see that's most critical. I can use UAVs to see the security situation—but economics and governance are difficult to see with the sensors that the Army has provided to me to see bad people doing bad things. The HTT gives me the ability to see with confidence what's going on among the civilian population…we're well intentioned amateurs in the governance and economic development, and the HTT allows us to see those arenas much better."[58]

In general, socio-cultural situational awareness may include information about the population's wants, needs, and expectations; or specific issues affecting the population such as access to resources, political cleavages, etc.[59] For example, in 2007 a US brigade in Baghdad was attempting to facilitate a rapprochement with the Office of Martyr Sadr (OMS) in order to create peaceful preconditions for democratic governance. The brigade, however, had a limited understanding of who to engage within the Sadr leadership. In accordance with the commander's guidance, the HTT and the brigade staff developed a framework that included four separate lines of engagement for the brigade to pursue: the district advisory council (DAC), the tribal sheikhs, the imams, and the OMS leadership. The HTT developed a Sadr City leadership chart to help the commander visualize the power structure within the society and identify legitimate local leaders with whom he could engage. The brigade commander then briefed General Petraeus,

Lieutenant General Odierno, and Major General Hammond on the chart (and provided copies to each of them), which eventually led to a major division operation focused on improving governance. (General Petraeus kept this chart on his office wall during his command of Multi-National Force—Iraq.) This type of situational awareness of the Shia leadership of Iraq proved critical for developing local political representation. In the words of the brigade commander, "The HTT empowered us to engage, and this is critical because Sadr City is going to be a political solution and not a military solution. ... We've surged all over Baghdad, but we isolated Sadr City. It could have been a powder keg, but we opened discussions and prevented that. These discussions and engagements had positive repercussions back to Najaf. The HTT empowered us to be much more effective with engagements, and the third-order effect was a strategic impact on the whole region."[60] In other words, as the brigade executive officer explained, "The HTT helped shape the national strategy for negotiating with OMS."[61]

Another common means of supporting a unit's decision-making process is "input to course of action development," in which an HTT conducts research specifically to assist a commander to make a decision between various courses of action. Supporting COA development includes both the COA analysis and COA comparison steps of the military decision-making process (MDMP). During COA analysis, teams are responsible for ensuring that non-lethal COAs are represented during working groups and mission planning. In COA comparison, teams actively engage with all staff sections from the perspective of the population to minimize risk and establish a positive future posture for unit operations. In one 2008 case, the brigade commander asked IZ10 for their input on which tribal leaders of the Sunni awakening (*sawah*) should be the focus of the brigade's engagement effort. During the *sawah*, many former insurgents rejected al-Qaeda and sought out alliances with Coalition forces. Many of these Sunni sheikhs and their followers joined the Sons of Iraq (essentially a group of local militias organized to provide security to their communities and paid for initially by the Coalition). On the HTT's recommendation, the brigade commander met with one particular tribal leader, who had formerly been one of the most powerful insurgent figures in Iraq, with 3,000 fighters allegedly under his control. Various brigade staff members were displeased with this, arguing that for the commander to meet with this former insurgent leader would be "engagement fratricide." The commander was determined to continue with the planned engagement and told the staff to "sit down and shut up"—the meeting would take place as planned.[62] Shortly before the meeting, the tribal leader's family turned in the largest cache the brigade had ever uncovered, requiring a five-ton truck to pick it all up. Included were a variety of weapons and explosives, including anti-aircraft guns, all serviceable. The decision to engage turned enemies into allies.

HTTs may also contribute to brigade decision-making by performing effects analysis. Effects analysis, as an aspect of COA analysis, provides an estimation of how the population will behave if particular events occur. Effects analysis can be based on events (e.g. if X happens, then Y is likely to happen) or on actions (e.g. if the unit does X action, then Y is likely to happen). Second- and third-order effects analysis provide an estimation of a series of cascading events. For example: if a lethal operation is conducted, the first-order effect may be neutralization of the target, the second-order effect may be destabilization of the tribe, and the third-order effect may be the empowerment of new tribal leadership hostile to the Coalition.

Effects analysis was a common means by which HTTs influenced a unit's decision-making process. For example, a *sawah* leader invited members of IZ6 to see some nearby "Persian ruins," which were a *tel* or mound immediately adjacent to the patrol base on the north side. The next day, the team members discovered that the unit was planning to expand the patrol base and pave over this archeological site. The HTT immediately called brigade headquarters, informing them that if they expanded the patrol base, they would destroy Tel Arbiyah Qabir, the Fourth Big Mound, and violate the rules for operation for Coalition forces in Iraq which prohibited building on archeological sites. Arrangements were then made with the Cultural Heritage Officer at the Embassy to bring the head of the Iraqi State Board of Antiquities and Heritage (SBAH) to the site for an inspection. Subsequently, working in conjunction with the Army archeological team and faculty from Penn State, the HTT got a comprehensive list of all known sites in Iraq by latitude and longitude, archived it with the RRC, and created an ArcGIS (Global Information System mapping software) map for the brigade combat team with all the sites in their area.[63] This action definitely preserved one Iraqi archeological site, and possibly many more.

HTTs also assisted in the military decision-making by training the units they supported, on topics such as agriculture, religion, local politics, and by recommending mitigation strategies for courses of action that a supported unit has already selected (such as one team's recommendation that if a mosque had to be searched for weapons, this should not be done during prayer time on Friday, which had been the brigade's original plan). HTTs also participated in the "operations process," meaning that instead of conducting research and writing reports they were engaged in activities that directly supported the unit's lines of operations. In 2005–6, for example, many Sunnis were displaced from a part of Baghdad called Hariya because of sectarian violence. When these internally displaced Iraqis began to return home they discovered that their houses had been ransacked and that the local mosque was being used by the Iraqi Security Forces as a barracks. Although winter was coming, the Government of Iraq did not want to give any support to "squatters," leaving a large population homeless and destitute. The social scientists of IZ2 reached out to the UN High Commissioner for Refugees and used his personal network to arrange a meeting in Jordan with a number of NGOs. According to the brigade S9, "three thousand non-food item kits (worth about $1 million) would have never got there if [the social scientist] had not pried that open. Now UNHCR is delivering items all over. Everything from tarps, house repair kits, non-food kits (mattresses, cooking pots, stoves, blankets, tarps). To see 3,000 of those laid out—it was fantastic."[64]

CONTROVERSY

The US military, struggling to understand the complexities of politics, culture, and economics in Iraq and Afghanistan, innovated in many domains. New doctrine was developed in the form of Field Manual 3–24, *Counterinsurgency*, new regulations such as DOD Directive 3000.05 (which established the DOD's responsibilities in stability operations) were issued, new training was introduced such as that at the National Training Center focused on stability operations at the local level. HTS was one of many innovations that the US military introduced during the early years in Iraq and Afghanistan, as it attempted to better understand the socio-cultural dynamics.

Academic Reactions

Despite the new attention paid by the military to culture, it took a few years for the academic community to recognize the shift. The earliest attempt by the academic community to come to terms with the military's new interest in culture was a workshop organized by the Watson

Institute at Brown University, in collaboration with the Pell Center for International Studies at Salve Regina University, in December 2004. The workshop, "Prepared for Peace? The Use and Abuse of 'Culture' in Military Simulations, Training, and Education," brought together social scientists and military personnel to draw lessons relevant to training, education, and the use of simulations in operational environments. A second workshop, titled "The Production of Cultural Knowledge in the United States Military," took place in 2006 at Brown University with a focus on the production, consumption, and circulation of "cultural knowledge." Despite the organizers' attempts to create a cordial environment, many of the academics and the military attendees felt that they were the victims of hostility and misunderstanding from the other side, which served as a reminder of the wide gulf between the military and the academy.

The open-minded discourse established by the Watson Institute gave way to a different sort of discussion once the anthropology community discovered the Pat Roberts Intelligence Scholars Program (PRISP). Funded by Congress, PRISP helps to build the academic backgrounds and skills of candidates for the CIA's Directorate of Intelligence. While most people might think having qualified analysts at the CIA would be a good idea, in 2005 anthropologists David Price and Hugh Gusterson expressed concern about whether students who accept funding would be subject to "debt bondage"; whether the "increased reliance on pre-selected intelligence analysts" will "dangerously narrow the range of intelligence views at the CIA and elsewhere"; whether PRISP scholars will be "covertly compiling dossiers" on faculty members and whether "PRISP's secretive presence on campuses" would "chill open academic classroom discussions on controversial topics?"[65]

PRISP, however, was just the beginning. The military's interest in cultural knowledge came to the full attention of the anthropology community after Seymour M. Hersh published "The Gray Zone" in the May 2004 edition of *The New Yorker*. According to an allegation from an unnamed academic source, anthropologist Raphael Patai's 1973 book *The Arab Mind* was "the bible of the neocons on Arab behavior." Allegedly, US interrogators relied on Patai's depiction of Arab sexual anxieties to develop torture techniques for Iraqi prisoners in the hope that these prisoners would become informants to prevent the release of humiliating photographs.[66] The alleged "misuse" of anthropology at Abu Ghraib prison raised the hackles of many anthropologists. At the

American Anthropological Association's 2006 meeting, a resolution was passed condemning the war in Iraq and the use of "anthropological knowledge as an element of physical and psychological torture." In November 2006, *Inside Higher Education* ran an article on "Torture and Social Scientists," which quoted one anthropologist condemning "scum with PhDs who stand beside torturers."[67] In response to PRISP, the alleged "misuse" of anthropology at Abu Ghraib prison, and the appearance of Central Intelligence Agency job ads on the American Anthropological Association (AAA) website, in 2006 the AAA formed an Ad Hoc Commission on the Engagement of Anthropology with the US Security and Intelligence Communities (CEAUSSIC). Composed of academic anthropologists and anthropologists working within the national security community, the commission's task was to advise the Executive Board and the AAA on the following: the roles of anthropologists within intelligence and national security entities; the state of AAA's existing ethical guidelines on the involvement of anthropologists in national security; and the key ethical, methodological, and practical challenges faced by the discipline in engagement in intelligence/national security. According to Alan Goodman, the president of the AAA, "The decision to establish a commission represents a commitment by the AAA to facilitate an informed, educational conversation about the complex terrain linking anthropology to national security policy in the US."[68] Members of the AAA seemed to have a different view of the commission's role: "to blow wide open" the debate on "justified means to protect national security."[69]

Meanwhile, just as the CEAUSSIC project was getting underway, in 2007 HTS was excoriated by the AAA on the grounds that it was "an unacceptable use of anthropological expertise."[70] When the AAA issued their statement, it hardly came as a surprise to the HTS staff. That their condemnation was based on media reports rather than original research seemed somewhat ironic, given that anthropologists pride themselves on empirical research. Like the AAA, the Society for Applied Anthropology also passed a motion expressing "grave concerns about the potential harmful use of social science knowledge and skills in the HTS Project."[71] Shortly thereafter, the Network of Concerned Anthropologists (NCA) asked anthropologists to sign a pledge affirming that they would "not engage in research and other activities that contribute to counter-insurgency operations in Iraq or in related theaters in the "war on terror." Furthermore, we believe that anthropologists should refrain from directly assisting the US military in combat..."[72]

The AAA's 2007 CEAUSSIC report raised a number of unanswered questions about the role of social scientists working directly for the US military. Thus, the AAA determined that another two-year period was necessary to focus exclusively on HTS, releasing a final report in 2009. The central argument of the report is as follows:

> in its considerations of training and research methods, of data collection and storage, and of the relationship of HTTs to intelligence, a variety of fundamental problems arise when anthropological research priorities are determined by military missions, are not subject to external review, and where data collection occurs in the context of war, as integrated into counterinsurgency goals, or in a potentially coercive environment... And this sets the goals of the HTS program and the activities of HTTs apart from any legitimate professional exercise of anthropology.[73]

Carolyn Fluehr-Lobban, a contributor to this volume, served on both of the AAA CEAUSSIC commissions on engagement and was involved with the drafting and discussion of the previous two codes of ethics of the AAA in 1998 and 2007–9. After the second report was completed, she recalled:

> I was left with a lingering and uncomfortable feeling that HTS had not been objectively assessed by the official anthropological community charged with this historic responsibility. The initial commission in 2007—just prior to the election of the anti-war candidate Barack Obama—was politically charged and the HTS program in which anthropologists were allegedly involved was a target for possible self-righteous anti-war action. Although little was known of the actual operation of the Human Terrain Teams on the ground, condemnation was swift and complete.... Since neither of the two commissions on which I served ever met as a whole with HTS personnel—despite promises to do so and an effort on my part to convene such a meeting at the US Institute of Peace was jettisoned—I felt deprived of the knowledge needed to make an assessment of the Human Terrain System from the standpoint of professional anthropology and its code of ethics.... As a cultural anthropologist working in the challenging cultural environment of Sudan I am keenly aware of the role of perception vs. reality and of the danger of mislabeling a person. As the controversy over HTS unfolded, I observed that our professional community was in fact labeling "good" and "bad" anthropologists, and that the latter were those few anthropologists who worked professionally with the military or openly with the intelligence apparatus.[74]

While addressing the 2009 CEAUSSIC commission findings is beyond the scope of the present volume, a few words should be said about dangerous fieldwork. The report notes that "HTTs collect sensitive socio-cultural data in a high-risk environment and while working for one combatant in ongoing conflicts... the program places researchers and their counterparts in the field in harm's way."[75] Since its inception in 2006, HTS has deployed approximately 700 people downrange, of which three have been killed and others wounded. Two of the individuals killed (Paula Loyd and Nicole Suveges) both had prior military service and understood the risks. Michael Bhatia, who was killed by an IED in Afghanistan, had made seven prior trips in country and knew just how dangerous it was. Indeed, the violence associated with the current insurgencies ongoing in Afghanistan and Iraq does place team members in harm's way. In the words of one HTT member who was wounded in Iraq:

> The danger inherent to HTS members conducting research in a combat zone is obvious. Yet team members continue doing their jobs with the full knowledge of the danger. I will not speak for anyone but myself as to motivations. But, after surviving being shot by a sniper while conducting interviews as a member of a HTT I have a fairly solid frame of reference on the risks verses the rewards. As to the risk to our researchers, they are no greater than those undertaken by any infantry man in today's Army. To those that are worried about researchers being targeted, it is always a possibility, but it is one that CA, PRT, and police and military training team members live with on a daily basis. Some risk adverse individuals would prefer to remove them from harm's way and abandon their mission. To do so betrays both their courage and the hopes of the people they stand to help.[76]

How should the risks to researchers be mitigated? According to the 2009 CEAUSSIC report, "conducting field work in a tension-ridden conflict zone... raises questions about the feasibility of such work."[77] The report also observes that the deaths of three HTS members are... "a stark reminder that battle zones are first and foremost battle zones and not research spaces."[78] Presumably, according to the CEAUSSIC report, the best way to mitigate risk to researchers is to ensure that academics only work in safe, secure "research spaces." While "safe" research locations might keep scholars from harm, this would also limit their ability to conduct timely, applied research. In the words of one HTS social scientist:

> Keeping an "academic" in an academic setting makes it sound as if academics should stay in their ivory towers. No research can be completed that way whether in the US or in a combat zone. Imagine developing a research study about heroin addiction and hesitating to seek out people who are addicts to

interview? Our research space is out in the field with the Afghans. This is a war zone and there is a different set of daily activities. With that comes potential death and injury. We are people who are dedicated to making a difference in a combat zone not only by hopefully saving lives but also by advocating for the populace non-kinetically. (And, I might add, what is AAA doing to support our troops and country?)[79]

The reality of being in a combat zone is that people may be killed or injured in the line of duty. Social science field research in a war zone is feasible, but it is also dangerous. Everyone who worked on an HTT was aware of the potential danger associated with the research. During the in-briefs to new recruits, for example, we always invited them to consider several questions. On balance, does helping the military and the local people of Iraq and Afghanistan by conducting social science research outweigh the risks of being injured or killed? Is this mission something worth dying for? Those individuals who could not answer these questions affirmatively to their own satisfaction were asked to leave with no hard feelings. Not everyone believes that social science is worth dying for, although many of the people serving on HTTs believed exactly that, as many of the chapters in this volume indicate.

Military Reactions

Despite the spate of articles in military journals, the impressive number of conferences and workshops, the production of new doctrine, and the organizational attempts such as HTS to rectify the cultural knowledge gap within the military, there were still pockets of resistance within the military to "all this fuzzy stuff," in the words of one Army infantry officer.[80] The importance of culture was not universally accepted within the military, with many believing that it was a "touchy-feely waste of time."[81]

What was the source of this resistance? As a matter of organizational culture, the case could be made that the US military generally prefers the more definitive, less "squishy" approaches of hard sciences and engineering. Additionally, the military has a strong preference for traditional warfighting instead of population-centric counterinsurgency, which often involves equal measures of lethal operations and "touchy-feely" activities such as drinking tea with sheikhs, handing out soccer balls to kids, de-worming sheep, and so on.

The 2010 debate between Gian Gentile and John Nagl captures the widely divergent perspectives within the military establishment regarding the utility of force in counterinsurgency and the effect of counter-insurgency operations on the core functions of the US Army. Nagl held the view that "protecting the population was the key to success in any counterinsurgency campaign,"[82] and that "war is *not* essentially 'about death and destruction' but is fundamentally an instrument of policy designed to achieve political aims."[83] Gentile argued, to the contrary, that the Army's focus on counterinsurgency was too non-lethal and eroded core military competencies.

> The COIN straitjacket has produced within some circles in the Army and the greater defense establishment a rather curious way of thinking about firepower. It has come to be viewed as something dirty, bad, and to be avoided. This negative treatment … has replaced what should be the core principle of combined arms competencies. As a result, the Army's warfighting skills have atrophied….War essentially is about death and destruction, its hard hand. Unfortunately, the dogma of counterinsurgency has seduced folks inside and outside the American defense establishment into thinking that instead of war and the application of military force being used as a last resort and with restraint, it should be used at the start and that it can change "entire societies" for the better.[84]

Some of the criticism within military circles about HTS reflected the parameters of the Nagl–Gentile debate. For example, General Charles Dunlap in a *New York Times* editorial entitled "We Still Need Big Guns" took the position that "the lesson of Iraq is that old-fashioned force works." In his view Field Manual 3–24, *Counterinsurgency*, focuses too much on the "squishy" stuff and leads to the false conclusion that "victory over insurgents is achievable by anything other than traditional military force." In an indirect reference to HTS, Dunlap notes: "Unfortunately, starry-eyed enthusiasts have misread the manual to say that defeating an insurgency is all about winning hearts and minds with teams of anthropologists, propagandists and civil-affairs officers armed with democracy-in-a-box kits and volleyball nets. They dismiss as passé killing or capturing insurgents."[85]

Many military personnel in Iraq and Afghanistan certainly agreed with General Dunlap that "draining the swamp"—killing every enemy or potential enemy in an area of operations with little regard for civilian casualties or local norms for the use of force—was the best approach to defeating an insurgency. As some of the chapters in this volume note, HTTs supporting units whose commanders held this traditional, kinetic mindset faced a difficult struggle convincing them that non-lethal alternatives, such as jobs programs, rebuilding mosques, or even providing volleyball nets, might actually achieve national security objectives more quickly and more thoroughly than bullets.

Despite these pockets of resistance, most of the US Army and Marine Corps units were willing to experiment with new approaches, including application of the principles of population-centric counterinsurgency as laid out in FM 3–24 and using new "enablers" such as HTTs and provincial reconstruction teams (PRTs) to achieve their mission. As some of the chapters in this volume indicate, the teams sometimes had to overcome a certain amount of military prejudice against academics. Often, overcoming the military's preconceptions required proof that the HTTs were ready to eat the same food, endure the same conditions, and accept the same risks. In the words of the G2 for II Marine Expeditionary Force (Forward) in Iraq, "I expected a bunch of liberal anthropologists, and who wouldn't work well with us [Marines]. What I got were people who were anxious to help us understand the battlespace. They roundly exceeded my expectations. In this case, they were always ready to get dirty and go out there."[86]

But by far the most important element in the HTT process of integrating into a brigade was convincing them that social science research had some value. From a military perspective, is it worthwhile to fill space in a Mine Resistant Ambush Protected (MRAP) vehicle with HTT personnel when you could have an extra gunner instead? What is the benefit in having a whole platoon providing security for an HTT while they ask villagers questions about pine nuts, water rights or wild pigs? And in one case that we observed, is it worthwhile to provide air support while an HTT conducts semi-structured interviews on women's health issues in rural Iraq? Apparently, it is worthwhile. Here is the benefit from the military perspective, in the words of the Second Infantry/8 Battalion commander in Iraq: "In the run-up to the provincial elections, I wanted to know which shaykh could or would impact the locals to get out the vote (without influencing who to vote for). I wanted to know who were the players politically and how much influence they had. The HTT was able to confirm my hypothesis of the relationship between the local government and the informal leadership made up of the tribal leaders and were able to do an assessment of 2nd and 3rd order effects of the influence of tribal leaders on elections."[87] As a result of this contribution, the battalion commander ordered his company commander to take the social scientist (Leslie Adrienne Payne, a contributor to this volume) on missions, protect her, and ensure that she had the time she needed to interview subjects. The battalion commander told the company commander that "Ms Payne" would direct the mission.

Most of the military units (but certainly not all) that worked with HTTs expressed support for the program. When supported units expressed their dissatisfaction with the teams, the execution rather than the concept was generally the issue. In other words, when problems occurred, it was not because something was wrong with the concept of embedding mixed military and civilian teams in military units to conduct social science research; rather, it was because individual team performance issues hindered the team's ability to complete their mission to the satisfaction of their uniformed customers. In some cases personality dynamics of teams impeded overall performance. For example, on one team a strong-willed social scientist saw his role as directing the work of other members of the team, which naturally caused conflict. In some cases, individual behavioral issues affected team performance. For example on another team, the analyst was having a love affair with a Special Forces officer on an adjacent base. On yet another team, the social scientist believed it was his mission to bring Christianity to the Iraqis. Obviously, in the latter two cases, neither of the individuals in question was suitable for work on an HTT, and both were removed from theater.

Feedback from commanders in the field about the program filtered up the chain of command through both formal and informal channels. In a war, the warfighter's opinions and requirements outweigh almost every other consideration, and in the case of HTS those voices were overwhelmingly positive. It is important to consider that as an experimental program HTS could have been dismantled at any point. But the word from units in combat, in Iraq and Afghanistan, was that HTTs—for the most part—helped the military accomplish the mission. While much of the feedback we received was informal, we were quite surprised to discover that the Army's formal input to the Quadrennial Defense Review in 2009, based on input from brigade commanders, was strong support for HTTs. The actual quote from the document was: "Human Terrain Teams = good! Everybody wants one."[88] The result of feedback from warfighters in theater was a decision at the Army level, and the DOD level, to continue funding HTS year after year in increasing amounts.

The funding that flowed to HTS inevitably caused some dissension among organizations that held a scarcity view of DOD resources. HTS appeared as a threat to many entrenched, well-established organizations who viewed the program as intruding on their territory and resources. One expression of this particular view was Major Ben Connable's article in *Military Review*, "All our Eggs in a Broken Basket." Connable's article made a number of points: that HTS duplicates existing functions of Civil Affairs; that uniformed military personnel can do research just as well as social scientists; that academics should retreat to the Ivory Tower; and that HTS is a self-created business niche foisted on the military.

Underlying his criticism, however, is really a concern about rice bowls and funding. Connable argues that the existence of HTS has "come... at the expense of precisely those long-term programs that will develop this mandated, comprehensive level of [socio-cultural] expertise."[89] Later he asserts that "HTS has sapped the attention or financing from nearly every cultural program in the military..." and bemoans the fact that "the Army and Marine cultural training centers remain staffed primarily with contractors and subsist on fluctuating budgets."[90] Connable was certainly not alone in his view that HTS threatened the "rice bowls" of other entrenched "culture shops." However, it is worth noting that HTS competed for resources in the same arena, and under the same strict rules, as any other element in DOD. The HTS budget was annually revalidated through deployed Army and Marine unit feedback on whether or not the program was worth the cost. It is also worth noting that in DOD terms the budget for HTS is small compared to most of the enablers provided to operating forces in Afghanistan and Iraq. To put it simply: the entire yearly program budget for HTS amounts to less than a DOD accounting error.[91] Of course, the real issue is not how big a program budget is, but whether what is produced with that budget offers something of value relative to the cost. With the budget HTS was authorized, the project has deployed teams to Iraq and Afghanistan, supporting every Army and Marine brigade, division and corps; built a Research Reachback Center to support deployed teams; did the initial development of the MAP HT Toolkit in conjunction with Army Civil Affairs under CENTCOM leadership; initiated a direct support social science research and analysis capability in Iraq and Afghanistan; and provided training support to unit pre-deployment training at home stations, the Combat Training Centers, and to the Counterinsurgency (COIN) Academies.

For those of us working for HTS, the concern about rice bowls seemed somewhat misplaced given the exceptional challenges posed by the larger war effort. The goal, from our perspective, was to meet the socio-cultural knowledge requirement of the men and women in harm's way, not to ensure the bureaucratic continuation of our little program. Military requirements should drive the bureaucracy; anything else is the tail wagging the dog.

PURPOSE OF THE BOOK

As this Introduction indicates, in the first few years of the program's existence HTS garnered considerable attention from the press, the public, the academy and the military. HTS and the surrounding controversy absorbed a lot of "air time." For many anthropologists working in other arenas of the defense establishment, the focus on HTS seemed to negate or minimize their own contributions to national security. As the editors of *Practicing Military Anthropology* note, "the ethics and disciplinary dangers of the HTS seemed to be dominating much of the conversation and thinking about military anthropology. Yet, we knew that whatever the involvement of anthropologists with the HTS, it did not characterize the work and activities of the majority of military anthropologists."[92]

Although the authors of *Practicing Military Anthropology* are no doubt correct that HTS dominated much of the conversation, much of that conversation involved polemic statements about the ethics of the program. For example, Roberto J. Gonzalez in *American Counterinsurgency: Human Science and the Human Terrain* argues that "HTS hearkens back to ...the age of Euro-American empire" and is a "subversion of social science" which will allow the military to "target suspected enemies for abduction or assassination."[93]

Other academics used HTS as a bête noire to reposition the discipline of anthropology and expound their own political agenda. For example, the editors of *Anthropology and Global Counterinsurgency* aim to reformulate political anthropology to bring "ethnographic techniques and insights into discussions of war, peace, and American power."[94] In *Weaponizing Anthropology: Social Science in Service of the Militarized State*, David H. Price goes even further, advocating that the AAA should take a more direct political position on HTS, and stop using ethics as a cover for political objections to the war.[95]

With some notable exceptions, very little has been reported about the actual work done by teams in theater.[96] Whether pro or con, most of the writing about HTS has suffered from a dearth of appropriate source material.[97] Noting that the debate about HTS within the anthropological domain has mainly been about principles rather than practice, George Lucas noted that "we need case studies" and that "there is very little in the way of concrete specifics available to discuss."[98] Not surprisingly, lacking accurate and reliable source material, much of the writing about HTS by academics betrayed a distinct lack of knowledge about the program and about the military in general. For example, the primary editor of *Anthropology and Global Counterinsurgency* gets the name of HTS wrong, referring to it as the "Human Terrain Systems project,"[99] an error that could have been corrected by simply looking at HTS's website.

Good, reliable source material written by people with actual knowledge of HTS has been hard to come by. Why has so little been published by individuals who served on teams downrange? For the most part, individuals who served on teams in theater were fully engaged in conducting applied social science research for the military units they supported. With the exception of social scientist Marcus Griffin who blogged about his experiences in Iraq while he was downrange for the benefit of his students at his home university, most HTS personnel waited until they returned home to write anything for publication. Recently, a few social scientists have capitalized on their work with HTS, using it as a baseline for publishing academic journal articles. For example, social scientist Adam Silverman published "Preliminary Results from Voices of the Mada'in: A Tribal History and Study of One of Baghdad's Six Rural Districts," in *Cambridge Review of International Affairs* in 2010; and Katherine Blue Carroll published "Tribal Law and Reconciliation in the New Iraq" in the *Middle East Journal* in 2011.[100] A few HTS personnel used the research they had conducted in the field as the basis of their dissertations.[101] One social scientist wrote an article about his experiences in Afghanistan for *Geo Magazine*, the German equivalent of *National Geographic*.[102] Another HTS social scientist, AnnaMaria Cardinalli, recently wrote a book about her experiences in Afghanistan, *Crossing the Wire: One Woman's Journey into the Hidden Dangers of the Afghan War*.[103] By far the most common outlet for publications by HTS personnel has been military journals,[104] including a complete issue of the *Military Intelligence Professional Bulletin* in 2011 written entirely by HTS personnel.

As this quick literature review demonstrates, this book fills a gap: namely, the actual lived experience of social scientists who served on

HTTs in Iraq and Afghanistan. This edited volume goes beyond the anecdotes, snippets, and blogs to provide a comprehensive, objective, and detailed view of HTS. It addresses themes of enduring importance for US national security, such as the role of US forces in "nation building," challenges of inter-agency coordination and innovation during wartime, and the larger strategic issues of the need for socio-cultural knowledge in American foreign policy. This book provides an overview of the program, including the political and military context; the genesis and origin of the program; the ethical and epistemological issues; and some examples of significant research by teams and their effect on the military decision-making process. But most importantly, this books aims to capture some of the diverse lived experiences of HTS members during the wars in Iraq and Afghanistan and the overall context in which this took place. In the long run, it is the experiences of military and civilian personnel on the ground in theater that will provide the bedrock for future analysis, evaluation, and judgment of the program.

STRUCTURE OF THE BOOK

This volume has a relatively simple structure. This first chapter establishes the context for the growth and development of HTS, specifically how the US military's focus on fighting "the big war" left them unprepared for the missions they would face in the Middle East and Central Asia. Montgomery McFate then describes in Chapter 2 how HTS attempted to meet an urgent military need to narrow the socio-cultural knowledge gap that became apparent following the US involvement in Vietnam. She explores in detail the uncomfortable alliance between the military and academic communities.

The next grouping (Chapters 3–5) explores the research process involved in conducting social science in a war zone, including the adaptation of research methods from "pure" to "applied" to suit the context of military operations. These chapters also discuss the complexities of conducting research in a war zone, including ethical issues, time constraints, limited access to population, equipment malfunction, and rocket attacks.

In Chapter 3, Ted Callahan, an anthropologist specializing in Afghanistan, paints a vivid picture of what it was like to "do anthropology" in Afghanistan while under attack. He shows how military and civilian security could be enhanced through a better understanding of local economic practices. In Chapter 4, Katherine Blue Carroll, a political scientist specializing in the Middle East, transports us to Iraq, providing case studies describing what she brought to the fight in dealing with the aftermath of a soldier shooting a Qur'an, securing local elections, and mapping the political power grid. In Chapter 5, Jennifer Clark describes her experiences embedded with the Marines in Iraq's Anbar Province. Despite being an anomaly, if not an outcast, as a civilian, a social scientist, and a woman, Clark's takeaways include that by shedding the prima donna academic façade, adapting to a hostile environment, and employing ethnographic and interpersonal skills with the Marines and the local tribesmen, tolerance and understanding were enhanced.

Chapters 6–8 concern integration of teams with military units. Because of the security environment in Iraq and Afghanistan, teams could not roam around the battlespace on their own, but were embedded within supported military units and were dependent on them for housing, food, security, and transportation. In order to influence the military's decisions and actions, HTTs had to integrate with their military unit—no small task with a brigade in combat who often questioned the value of social science, had a kinetic mindset, and had a gender bias.

In Chapter 6, based upon her HTT experiences in both Iraq and Afghanistan, Kathleen Reedy, an anthropologist specializing in the Middle East, reflects on key aspects of integrating social science into the military decision-making process. Learning how to talk to both military members *and* the local people and thus serve as effective mediators and moderators proved critical. Credible HTTs were able to take, at best, vague orders, collect relevant qualitative data, and produce actionable advice under limited timelines.

In Chapter 7, James Dorough-Lewis gives a compelling vantage point on HTS's contribution as a force multiplier to US counterinsurgency and stability efforts in Iraq. Prior to serving as a civilian social scientist on an HTT, Dorough-Lewis served in uniform in Iraq as an Army human intelligence collector and Arabic linguist. He provides first-hand experience regarding the distinction between intelligence (à la military) and social science (à la HTS).

In Chapter 8, Leslie Payne, who has degrees in security studies and political science, reinforces and adds another element to the discussion of the integration challenges which HTTs encountered. While in

Helmand Province, Afghanistan, Payne recounts politics, conflicts, and clashes not just between military and HTT or military and local population but also between the HTT and British civilians, our Coalition partners.

Ethics runs as an undercurrent in many of the chapters, but is the explicit focus of the next section. In Chapter 9, anthropologist Carolyn Fluehr-Lobban and moral philosopher George Lucas bring the contentious debate regarding HTS to the surface. Although this chapter may not quell the controversy for some adamant detractors, it does provide a firmer basis from which to judge rather than "pre-judge" the program. Fluehr-Lobban and Lucas bolster the preceding chapters with interviews and opinions from HTS social scientists (none of whom are contributing authors to this volume) regarding their experiences and activities in connection with HTS. It is fitting and intentional that this chapter comes after those that describe actual HTT experience; for the ethical criticisms levied with the launching of HTS were devoid of actual data and details regarding just what the social scientists who deployed to Iraq and Afghanistan did there, and how they did it.

In Chapter 10, anthropologist Brian Brereton describes how he grappled with ethical concerns before joining HTS and deploying to the Afghan provinces of Logar and Wardak where his contributions centered on softening the hostile or aggressive nature of the military's interaction with the local residents. His experiences in conducting benign interviews in Afghanistan counter the unfounded fears that social scientists would be used to engage in lethal targeting.

The final chapter by Janice H. Laurence highlights the themes and integrates the lessons from HTS and discusses its future. All in all, it reviews HTS and why it was developed; what HTT social scientists did; what was learned; how it was used; and to what effect. In addition to noting HTS's strengths, the chapter addresses some of the key weaknesses, including training, team development, and administrative concerns.

Each of these chapters offers a unique, personal portrayal of the experience of conducting social science research within a small team in a war zone. The chapter authors are scholars and practitioners from an eclectic array of social science disciplines, including anthropology, political science, psychology, history, and security studies. Furthermore, a few of the authors could be considered "soldier–scholars," having both military and social science expertise. With the exception of Fluehr-Lobban and Lucas, all the chapter authors have direct experience of HTS, having served with HTS in Iraq and Afghanistan. Together, their applied work represents a symphony of perspectives that promises to stimulate future social science theory and practice. It is hoped that the sum of the chapters will contribute to the understanding of why and how social science is a vital part of the military's toolkit.

CONCLUSION

Bringing social science—and actual *social scientists*—to the wars in Iraq and Afghanistan was bold and challenging. After all, soldiers and social scientists are not customary colleagues but rather are "strange bedfellows." The military embraces the lethal warrior ethos, whereas humanistic values and concerns are core for the social sciences. In addition, toughness and decisiveness are not characteristics for which social scientists are known; they more often employ qualitative approaches to deal with "squishier," human nature subjects that defy deterministic, exact answers.

Despite the obvious cultural differences, the relationship between the military and social science can be mutually beneficial. For example, military requirements have shaped the broad discipline of psychology and have led to the formal discipline of military psychology that unites its numerous sub-disciplines in support of relevant military needs. "Military psychology contributes to recruiting, training, socializing, assigning, employing, deploying, motivating, rewarding, maintaining, managing, integrating, retaining, transitioning, supporting, counseling, and healing military members."[105] Although military psychology has met with criticism from those in "purer" sub-disciplinary lines, "giving psychology away"[106] to the military has led to advances in the science and practice of psychology across its numerous specialties.

Could such a symbiotic relationship develop between the military and other social science disciplines? HTS, and more broadly the engagement of social science with national security, remains a subject of deep concern for many academic social scientists. The development and implementation of HTS also highlighted the barriers to effective partnerships between the social sciences and the military. Despite these differences segments of the behavioral and social sciences have embraced the profession of arms and the military has become more comfortable with the methods and inherent limitations of the "human" sciences, we believe that such a military anthropology is not only possible but inevitable.

2

MIND THE GAP

BRIDGING THE MILITARY/ACADEMIC DIVIDE

Montgomery McFate

In 2008, I spent a number of months in Iraq and Afghanistan flying in Blackhawks, sleeping on cots, and occasionally being shelled by mortars along with the other members of Human Terrain System's (HTS) Program Development Team. The purpose of these trips was to develop a better understanding of what research the Human Terrain Teams (HTTs) were actually doing in the field, and whether the units they were supporting were satisfied. HTS was a new program, with the mission of providing socio-cultural research and advising to the military, and we needed to learn everything we could about what actually worked downrange. Sometimes the Army and Marine Corps units we visited provided frank criticism about the program or the personnel on the teams. One annoyed brigade commander in Afghanistan emphatically told me that the HTT team leader was "quite obviously insane" and needed to be removed immediately from the forward operating base (FOB). During moments such as this, I often wondered why I was wasting my time and energy on a project that was so ambitious, dangerous, and quixotic. A few weeks after arriving in Iraq, I met with the brigade commander of the 172nd Infantry Brigade. "Look, I want to tell you something," he said. "Close the door and sit down." I took out my computer, and prepared myself for some negative feedback. Then the colonel started talking, and what he said was a surprise: "This team is providing a tool that provides understanding that prevents us from killing people. Absolutely they've helped—it's a component of the mission. This fight has always been a fight of wills and personalities: if the enemy goes kinetic, that's a mindless game and you just need to shoot quicker. With an insurgency, that is just 2% of the problem. The real problem is in the fabric of the society—genocide, positioning for power, the tribes, the sectarian issues—the bottom line is that all that is in play. The HTT is the tool that's made to address the other 98%."[1] Hearing an Army colonel whose entire professional career had been dedicated to the management of violence talk about *preventing* violence through a better understanding of the "social fabric" made me feel that our original hunch was correct: social science research conducted on the ground in support of the military during a war was not only valuable to the mission, it had the potential to reduce the level of violence.

This chapter aims to answer some important contextual questions about HTS that will set the stage for the chapters that follow. First, what were the conditions inside the Department of Defense (DOD) and the military services that made HTS necessary? The socio-cultural knowledge gap that HTS sought to fill was nothing new, but had existed for many years before the wars in Iraq and Afghanistan began. Second, why was integration between military personnel and academics so difficult? HTS sought to integrate civilian academics into small teams that would then be embedded with military units. From a training and team management perspective, this process often proved challenging, in part because the worldview, work habits, ethics, and epistemological frameworks of academics differed greatly from that of the military. Third, why was there so much controversy? HTS embedded social scientists with the military, and for some academics this support to military operations amounted to an ethical violation. Answering these questions requires some understanding of the differences between the academic and military communities.

ACADEMIC/MILITARY DIVIDE

As I write this, the US has been at war for more than a decade, which is the longest sustained conflict in US history. In both Iraq and

Afghanistan, the US military found itself fighting unfamiliar adversaries with different norms of combat, whose weapon of choice in the form of the improvised explosive device (IED) was often as indiscriminate as it was deadly. In addition to its traditional warfighting function, the US military assumed a variety of "nation building" tasks that required them to work in conjunction with foreign civilian populations, whose culture, language, and social organization were markedly different from their own. These conditions led to an epiphany of sorts in the military: that "culture" was not just a conceptual framework for high-level strategic analysis but that it was also a "force multiplier" at the operational level, where this type of knowledge facilitated tribal engagement, improved economic development plans, and even led to the identification of high-value targets. "Knowledge of the cultural 'terrain,'" as then Lieutenant General David Petraeus noted, "can be as important as, and sometimes even more important than, knowledge of the geographic terrain.... Understanding of such cultural aspects is essential if one is to help the people build stable political, social, and economic institutions. Indeed, this is as much a matter of common sense as operational necessity."[2]

Perhaps at no time in history had the US military been so amenable to the insights and knowledge that social scientists could provide. As Major General Robert Scales observed, this was "the social scientists' war."[3] Yet not since the Vietnam War had social scientists done so much soul-searching about the relationship of their profession to the national security enterprise. In the end, many social scientists chose to eschew participation with the military altogether. As one anthropologist who worked with the State Department noted, "if the DOD offered $1 million in grants to professional anthropologists tomorrow, they would be hard pressed to find takers."[4]

Many military personnel struggled to understand why social scientists were so hesitant to offer their assistance to the war effort, and questioned the patriotism of the academic community. Many social scientists felt that the ethical integrity of the discipline was being threatened, and questioned the motives of the military.

On both sides, misunderstanding, preconceptions, and prejudice influenced how these communities viewed each other. While a gap exists between the US military and civil society in general, it is not nearly as deep as the trench that separates the military and academic communities in particular.[5] Both institutions are insular, and somewhat segregated from the rest of American civil society. But the academy has also intentionally and systematically separated itself from the military, and to a lesser degree the military has segregated itself from academia. This gap in institutional connectivity is compounded by the differences in organizational culture within the academy and the military.

Cultural Gap

Military institutions, like all large institutions, develop their own unique organizational cultures. Such organizational cultures are partially the result of the norms, values, and beliefs that the aggregate of individuals comprising those institutions carry with them. Military personnel tend to vote Republican, rate themselves as more patriotic than other Americans, are more likely to be married, are better educated on average than most American civilians, are generally more conservative,[6] are mostly from the middle and upper class, and tend to come from the Southern states.[7] Naturally, the military as a whole tends to reflect the cultural norms and values associated with the demographic groups it contains.

Unique among other social institutions, however, military institutions proactively indoctrinate individuals joining the military with (possibly) new and (possibly) different sets of norms, values, and beliefs than those individuals may have had prior to joining, including self-sacrifice, honor, integrity, and so forth. Military institutions are also unique in that they frequently engage in internal direct social change programs, discouraging the use of tobacco and alcohol, encouraging religious practice in the form of prayer breakfasts, fostering racial integration, promoting patriotic displays, creating new identities such as "warrior," and more recently providing training to military personnel on interacting with gay colleagues. Moreover, military institutions have the capability to ensure through direct forms of social control (such as directives, policies, and orders) that military members comply with these organizational change initiatives.

Thus, when discussing military organizational culture (distinct from the so-called American "way of war") we are really referring to two different but linked factors: the culture of the predominant demographic groups making up the organization and the culture of the organization itself. The distinction between these two factors can lead to interesting anomalies: the US military has a lower percentage of

Christians than the US population demographically,[8] yet the organizational culture tends towards Christianity of the evangelical sort.[9]

Academia, like the military, tends to reflect the cultural norms, values, and beliefs of the demographic of which it is comprised. Given the heterogeneity of the academy, it is difficult to draw broad generalizations about academic culture but some observations can be made. Like the military, academics tend to be better educated than the general population. However, academics in general tend to be liberal in their political orientation, unlike the military. One study found that Democrats outnumber Republicans at elite universities by at least six to one, and by higher ratios in the humanities and social sciences.[10] A 2007 study found that 44 percent of college faculties could be classified as liberals, with just 9 percent classified as conservative. Among social scientists, the proportion was 58 percent liberals, and 4.9 percent conservative.[11]

Academia, of course, also has its own organizational culture, which varies according to institution (e.g. Princeton's culture is different from that of the University of Texas) and discipline (e.g. the culture of an economics department is different than that of an anthropology department). Unlike the military, academic culture is inculcated gradually, often absorbed through canonical texts, encouraged through gentle persuasion of the faculty, imbibed while learning how to analyze texts from a Marxist and feminist perspective, and so on. Unlike the military, acculturation to academia tends to be a softer process, involving quiet forms of social control and indirect incentives. Although most military recruits have memorized the "warrior ethos," new students in a PhD program do not recite an equivalent "scholarly ethos" or get it tattooed on their forearms.

What are the cultural differences between academics and military personnel? While the size and heterogeneity of both the US military and US academy make it difficult to generalize, some broad cultural differences seem to hold true. First, the military tends to be highly collective in its work process orientation. Whereas all members of the military regardless of rank or branch of service will have had experience working on a team toward a common goal, few academics are accustomed to team work. Academia is, in many regards, a highly individualistic profession. Scholars conduct research on their own, write their books alone, and are rewarded for individual accomplishment rather than group achievement.[12]

Second, the preferred styles of communication of the military and the academy differ. When academics communicate to others in a professional setting (such as a lecture), they tend to use specialized terminology, emphasize the complexity of ideas and concepts, diverge on tangents to illustrate concepts, and footnote everything. The military also uses specialized terminology, which is often reduced to acronyms on PowerPoint slides. PowerPoint forces the organizer to process information in the form of bullets and outlines, and as a result tends to compress thought and increase linearity.[13] PowerPoint is dangerous, according to Major General H. R. McMaster, "because it can create the illusion of understanding and the illusion of control," and "some problems in the world are not bullet-izable."[14]

Third, the knowledge they take for granted is dissimilar. Most graduate students in the social sciences have read Foucault, Durkheim, and Said.[15] The ideas in these works (such as discourse, hegemony, solidarity, and neo-colonialism) provide the baseline conceptual frameworks through which these academics perceive the world. Similarly, most mid-grade to senior military officers have read Clausewitz, Keegan, and Sun Tzu.[16] The ideas in these works (such as center of gravity, fog of war, courage in battle) provide the baseline conceptual frameworks through which military professionals perceive the world.

Fourth, academics and military personnel have different approaches to epistemology, or the nature and scope of knowledge. "Traditionally, scholars see the world in the form of a series of interesting puzzles that require their personal attention. Importantly, in the academy, puzzles are not given to professors to solve; one seeks them out on one's own and attempts to structure a research agenda to solve (or at least address) them. Military practitioners, on the other hand, see the world in terms of problems to be solved and the military instrument of national power as merely one tool in a bag to be employed only when and where necessary."[17] Problems, unlike puzzles, require a solution. In an operational military environment, the problem must be answered quickly and sometimes literally under the gun. The "slow thinking" of academia often gives way to heuristics and rules of thumb in a military environment. As soldiers commonly say, "perfect is the enemy of good enough."

A fifth and related issue is the function of knowledge for academics versus the military. The US military's constitutionally derived mandate is the execution of foreign policy, and this imperative promotes a very utilitarian view of knowledge. For the military in a deployed environment, knowledge is often only as valuable as it can be applied to planning, decision-making, and policy execution. Academics, on the other hand, whose mission is research and education, generally value knowledge for its own sake, not just its utility. Conversely, many of them reject applied knowledge as something impure and tainted by the exigencies of external funding and client interests.[18]

Sixth, the military and the academy are both communities centered on sacred values, but their sacred values are very different. Social psychologist Philip Tetlock defined sacred values as "those values that a moral community treats as possessing transcendental significance that precludes comparisons, trade-offs, or indeed any mingling with secular values."[19] Sacred values form an impermeable psychological boundary, beyond which one is thinking the proverbial unthinkable. When sacred values are challenged, individuals will seek to protect themselves "from moral contamination by the impure thoughts and deeds implied in the taboo proposals." Ordinary values differ from sacred values. For example, challenging the official US Army values (loyalty, duty, respect, selfless service, honor, integrity, and personal courage)[20] would certainly annoy many soldiers, but in specialized military units (such as the Army Rangers) violation of the sacred value "leave no man behind" would provoke a visceral response of moral outrage.[21] Academics have an equally powerful but different set of "sacred values." At a 2011 meeting of social psychologists, Dr Jonathan Haidt asked the Democrats in the audience to raise their hands. Liberals made up more than 80 percent of the 1,000 psychologists, while conservatives were only 0.3 percent.[22] Haidt's point, which resulted in a blogosphere furor, was that this "statistically impossible lack of diversity" was evidence of the "moral force field" in social psychology organized around sacred values. The sacred values of social psychologists, according to Haidt, fall along the axis of anti-racism and anti-sexism; scientific inquiry and explanations that posit gender or race as a variable are taboo. As Haidt argues, "If a group circles around sacred values, they will evolve into a tribal–moral community.... They'll embrace science whenever it supports their sacred values, but they'll ditch it or distort it as soon as it threatens a sacred value."[23] We will return to the discussion of sacred values later in this chapter.

Connectivity Gap

In addition to a cultural gap between the military and academia, these communities lack connectedness.[24] In 2009, nearly 40 percent of professors of international relations and political science reported that they had "no impact" on foreign policy or even the public discourse about it.[25] Some of this lack of impact of scholarship on foreign policy results from a lack of institutional connection between the communities. With some notable exceptions, very few scholars have worked in the US government in any capacity. Even fewer have served in or worked with the military.[26]

The academic/military relationship was never completely cozy, but the gap was not always as wide as it is today. During the Second World War, for example, many social scientists worked for the War Department or served in the uniformed military. Those social scientists took their government experience and contacts back into academia, "where they established new styles of research and encouraged a major new emphasis on theory as the basis of scientific advancement."[27] By 1967, seven successive presidents of the American Sociological Association had wartime experience in government.[28]

So what happened? Richard Lambert argues that academics eschewed government involvement as a result of "the overlong Korean and Vietnam wars, and reaction against what was perceived as the misuse of social science in those wars; our military policy in Central America; and, more generally, the growing use of clandestine operations to achieve foreign policy ends."[29] Many social scientists came to see themselves not as formulators but as critics of American foreign policy.[30] Some academics turned that criticism inward, seeing the forces of colonialism, paternalism, and racism at play in their own disciplines. As Noam Chomsky wrote in *Objectivity and Liberal Scholarship* in 1969, "When we strip away the terminology of the behavioral sciences, we see revealed ... the mentality of the colonial civil servant, persuaded of the benevolence of the mother country and the correctness of its vision of world order, and convinced that he understands the true interests of the backward peoples whose welfare he is to administer."[31]

Given the politics of the academy and the difficulties in working with academics, DOD began to look elsewhere for expertise on policy issues. Federally Funded Research and Development Corporations (FFRDCs), rather than the academy, became the preferred means of contracting research.[32] Within the universities, military-sponsored research became "a specialized function of an enclaved, limited subset of organizations and individuals."[33] Additionally, the number of

ROTC programs on American university campuses declined, reducing the connection between the military and the academy even further.[34]

The Academic "Cult of Irrelevance"

Over the past sixty years, the academic/military gap has become a deep moat. Today, as previously noted almost 40 percent of political scientists—whose work should be the most policy relevant of all disciplines—say they have no policy relevance at all. According to Joe Nye, "The fault for this growing gap lies not with the government but with the academics."[35] This raises an important question: what pressures exist within the academic system that might foster such a "cult of irrelevance?"[36] Stephen M. Walt, who teaches on the faculty of the John F. Kennedy School at Harvard University, refers to these system pressures of the academy as "professionalization." In his view, professionalization of the academy has the unintentional effect of reducing the policy relevance of academic research.

How does this process work? The primary professional goal of graduate students is to complete their dissertation and receive their doctorate. Young scholars are encouraged to pick dissertation topics that will neither challenge well-established paradigms nor answer pressing policy issues, but make an incremental contribution to their discipline. "Doctoral students are cued early on that their program of study is more about the discipline than the world ... search committees give far more weight to a dissertation's theoretical question than policy significance, and readily ignore, if not look down upon, policy-oriented publications outside of the scholarly peer-reviewed domain."[37]

Newly minted PhDs are generally encouraged towards academic jobs. Few consider accepting positions in government, particularly the military or intelligence sector, since in many fields this type of employment has a taint that cannot be washed off. When young scholars find a faculty position, their goal is to obtain the holy grail of tenure. (Much the same as in the military, where after being commissioned, the professional goal shifts to command at different echelons.) Despite the lip-service paid to teaching quality and "academic service" in the form of serving voluntarily on committees, what really counts in tenure decisions are publications in peer-reviewed journals. (Similarly, promotion decisions in the military are based on officer evaluation reports or OERs, with little attention paid to whether or not an officer may have authored a best-seller in his spare time.) Although peer review has been criticized for suppressing dissent,[38] reproducing the dominant paradigm,[39] and being vulnerable to the prejudices and whims of referee gatekeepers,[40] it is the only sure path to tenure. Because tenure decisions are made on the basis of publications in peer-reviewed journals and university presses, rather than popular presses, "most scholars of global affairs do not try to write books or articles that would be directly relevant to policy problems or accessible to a wider public audience."[41] It is hard to be policy-relevant if very few people actually read your publications.[42]

To get published in a peer-reviewed journal one must communicate in the language of one's peers. Professionalization "encourages scholars to employ specialized jargon and arcane methodological techniques, because these devices reinforce the idea that members of the discipline are privy to specialized knowledge that non-members lack."[43] However, it is very difficult to be policy-relevant if one's writing is incomprehensible to anyone but fellow scholars.

Peer-reviewed publications tend to eschew grand theories, sweeping statements, controversial opinions, mixed methods, and interdisciplinary perspectives in favor of narrow studies on a single issue with limited conclusions. Thus, as Stephen M. Walt notes, "professionalization also discourages academic scholars from addressing controversial topics or challenging well-established taboos. Focusing one's efforts on narrow and uncontroversial topics that are of interest only to one's fellow academicians is by far the safer route to the Holy Grail of lifetime employment."[44] It is hard to be policy-relevant without a little bit of controversy.[45]

Given the pressure to "publish or perish" in the academy, rarely if ever do faculty members use their sabbatical time to work in government or industry. Time off is usually spent in research and writing. (For the same reasons, military personnel rarely have the opportunity to get a PhD, unless they can do it in two years during the course of a regularly scheduled professional military education (PME) stint.) Because academia rewards the faculty on the basis of publications, "the academic disciplines that are most concerned with global affairs (political science/international relations, history, economics, sociology, anthropology/area studies, etc.) are largely governed by university-based scholars who have little if any experience in the policy world."[46] It is hard to be policy-relevant if you know almost nothing about the realities of policy or policy-making.

By the time they achieve tenure, established professors have little inclination and few incentives to do policy-relevant research. Their reputations have often been cemented not because of their contributions to government, but because of their criticisms of government. The incentives of the system ensure that newly minted graduate students follow the same policy-irrelevant path. The social sciences, including anthropology, are not immune from the pressures of professionalization. As one graduate of London University observed, "The main thing I got from my degree was a sense of guilt for being an anthropologist and a feeling that you couldn't comment positively on anything in the world as an anthropologist; all you can do is 'deconstruct' things."[47]

The "Cult of Major Combat Operations"

As a result of system pressures, collective political views, and organizational culture, the academy has tended towards a "cult of irrelevance" that has limited its connectivity and usefulness to the national security establishment. On the military side, there is an equally formidable cult: the "cult of major combat operations." The "cult of major combat operations," arguably a significant element of the American way of war, has focused military attention on firepower, technology, and peer enemies to the exclusion of small wars and irregular enemies.

An analysis of the system pressures (such as defense budgets, Congressional constituencies, and the military–industrial complex) that produce and maintain the "cult of major combat operations" is beyond the scope of this chapter. More important here is how the "cult of major combat operations" left the US unprepared for the counterinsurgencies it would face in Iraq and Afghanistan.

One might think the US military would organize, train, and equip for the type of wars it fights most frequently. Over the past forty years, US military forces have been engaged in operations other than war in Lebanon, Panama, Somalia, Haiti, Bosnia, Kosovo, and so on. Given this record, "small wars" can hardly be considered an anomaly in US military history; they are arguably the norm.[48] As former Secretary of Defense Robert Gates noted, "the first Gulf War stands alone in over two generations of constant military engagement as a more or less traditional conventional conflict from beginning to end."[49]

Despite the fact that the US military has been consistently engaged in a variety of operations other than war since its inception, the dominant concept of warfighting in the US has always been conventional war. The experiences of the First and Second World Wars loom heavily in American military thinking about war, while counterinsurgencies, peacekeeping operations, and other "small wars" are generally of only marginal interest.[50] For example, although the US was engaged militarily in a variety of small operations during the Cold War, time and attention were primarily devoted to planning for tank warfare in the Fulda Gap against a peer adversary.

As Lieutenant General David Barno has pointed out, the prevailing attitude among US forces has been that "'real Soldiers' rode to battle in armored vehicles."[51] This conventional view of war was reflected in the Vietnam era concept of "active defense" and the post-Vietnam concept of "AirLand Battle." In the 1990s, the conventional war discourse shifted again following the Gulf War to the concept of a "revolution in military affairs" (RMA),[52] characterized by "extremely precise, stand-off strikes; dramatically improved command, control, and intelligence; information warfare; and nonlethality."[53] For a revolution, the RMA was not particularly revolutionary, and changed very little inside the military.[54] In time, other "big war" concepts followed RMA, such as rapid decisive operations, effects-based operations, full-spectrum dominance, and network-centric warfare.

Immediately preceding the war in Iraq, the buzzword inside the Pentagon was "transformation." Transformation was discussed at conferences and workshops, officers at staff colleges wrote papers about it, and an Office of Force Transformation was established. Transformation involved a number of different components, including increasing the speed of maneuver of military units, increasing the precision of weapons systems, increasing the interoperability of units, and improving the networking of systems. As Secretary of Defense Rumsfeld noted, the goal of transformation was to make US forces "faster, more agile, more balanced, more interoperable."[55] The common view was that the synergy of these changes would dramatically improve US military capability. In the words of Paul Wolfowitz, "US forces must leverage information technology and innovative network-centric concepts of operations to develop increasingly capable joint forces."[56]

Before the wars in Iraq and Afghanistan began, "culture" was not a concept that held much interest for the US defense community. If you took a random sample in the Pentagon food court before the Iraq war, most people would probably have answered the question "does culture matter?" in the negative. The notion that the local population might be a significant factor in military operations ran counter to much of the thinking in the conventional military. In the words of US Army Colonel William Darley, "the entire thrust of interest by the military in culture as a dimension of the battlefield is the unfortunate but prevailing assertion that culture is merely a kind of human-terrain obstacle that one must negotiate like any other factor impeding successful operations, similar to dealing with adverse weather or topography."[57] Indeed, the 2001 version of the Department of Defense Dictionary defined culture as "a feature of the terrain that has been constructed by man. Included are such items as roads, buildings, and canals; boundary lines; and, in a broad sense, all names and legends on a map."[58]

Science and Technology Portfolio

Military force structure, training programs, budgeting, professional military education, and even the DOD's science and technology (S&T) investment portfolio reflected the predominant institutional focus on fighting major combat operations using sophisticated technology and firepower. Supporting social science research that might be of use in counterinsurgency and stability operations was not a significant part of the DOD scientific investment portfolio prior to the wars in Iraq and Afghanistan. Of the *total* federal social science research budget of $1.2 billion (which includes basic and applied research) from 2002 through 2004, the DOD spent only 1 percent.[59] The DOD spent less money on social sciences than all other agencies except the Smithsonian, which obviously had a much smaller budget. Not surprisingly, the majority of the defense science budget was allocated to the development of technology, weapons, equipment, and materiel, rather than social science; the DOD's investment in behavioral, cognitive, and social science represented only a very small proportion of its overall S&T portfolio. In 2004, for example, the total spending on behavioral, cognitive, neural, and social science represented 3.1 percent of the defense S&T budget.[60]

In line with the military's "cult of major combat operations," S&T funding in the DOD has been overwhelmingly dedicated to advanced technology rather than basic research.[61] Within the DOD, there is considerable institutional resistance to funding qualitative social science since it is often not considered adequately "scientific." When the wars began in Iraq and Afghanistan, none of the service labs or research offices supported a robust social science program, and neither did the Defense Advanced Research Projects Agency (DARPA).[62] For example, the Army Research Laboratory's mission has historically been to "focus on technology areas critical to strategic dominance across the entire spectrum of operations."[63] Almost none of the Army Research Laboratory's (ARL's) research areas addressed the social science requirements needed for future stability operations.[64] Similarly, the Office of Naval Research, who sponsored remarkable ethnographic research during the Second World War on Japan, Germany, and Pacific territories, had no equivalent program to meet the needs of the US government sixty years later in Iraq and Afghanistan. Ironically, the most robust US government social science research program is sponsored by an agency—the National Science Foundation—that has no responsibility for execution and formulation of foreign policy, and therefore has limited incentive to provide research beneficial to operational military requirements. The DOD noted this fact in its 2000 Report to the Senate Appropriations Committee: "While the National Science Foundation (NSF) and the National Institutes of Health support behavioral, cognitive and social science research, their research products only occasionally are useful for military needs."[65]

Lack of Coordination

Because federal agencies generally fund research in order to meet their specific agency needs and frequently do not share information with other agencies about the particular type of social science they are sponsoring, there is no easy way to find out exactly who's doing what in the world of government science and technology. Without coordination, this research is often duplicative in preparing for and conducting military operations. In 2005, I conducted a number of interviews for the National Science and Technology Council's *Combating Terrorism Report* in order to determine what types of social science were actually being used in counterterrorism, and what types of information were most needed by practitioners directly involved with the so-called global war on terrorism (GWOT). During an interview, a National Security Council (NSC) staff member observed: "We need to produce a catalogue of who does what, including seeking out agencies, organizations and units including the military, State, FSI, DIA, and even the Mormon Church. We need to know what they provide, how best to access their services." According to this NSC member, had social science research been coordinated and accessible, operations in Iraq might have been conducted differently. "Nobody could tell the three star commander of V Corps what the people in Baghdad cared about. Nobody could tell him what the psyche of the Iraqis was like."[66] Part of the problem was that the members of the V Corps staff had no idea where to find this information inside the federal government, or even whether it existed.[67] Without coordination, valuable information is lost in the fog of bureaucracy.[68]

Lack of Foreign Area Officers

When the wars in Iraq and Afghanistan began, the defense S&T establishment was focused on developing technology rather than basic social science research. Moreover, the research that was being conducted or funded was not coordinated across agencies, and was not being distributed to end-users such as warfighters in theater. The military, if it wanted socio-cultural knowledge downrange, had to rely primarily on in-house expertise. For the past few hundred years of American history, however, technical competence and leadership skills were considered the most important qualification for military commanders. The curriculum at the service academies reflected the institutional emphasis on engineering and mathematics. Knowledge of foreign societies was considered to be a marginal, somewhat quirky interest that was almost entirely irrelevant for major combat operations. To put it bluntly, there was not much in-house socio-cultural expertise.

The reservoir of regional expertise among military officers was concentrated in the Foreign Area Officers (FAO). Each branch of the armed services has an FAO program. Officers selected as FAOs obtain a graduate degree (generally a Master's) with a regional focus, undergo in-country training, and develop proficiency in a foreign language in addition to continuing to master their regular military occupational specialty (MOS). While FAOs bring a rare set of skills to the US knowledge arsenal (language skills matched with local and regional knowledge), there are not enough of them to meet the military's socio-cultural knowledge needs. In 2004, there were about 1,000 FAOs in the Army. Of those, 145 specialized in the Middle East, while the largest number focused on Europe.[69] Most commonly, FAOs serve as Attachés or Security Assistance Officers at US embassies or on joint staffs. As

Brigadier General Michael A. Vane and Lieutenant Colonel Daniel Fagundes observed, "FAOs are all too often seen as "cocktail circuit riders" out of touch with the real Army."[70]

Intelligence System

In addition to the minimal S&T investment in social science, the lack of coordination of the research that was conducted, and the paucity of foreign area officers, the US intelligence system was neither structured nor tasked to provide socio-cultural information. In line with the "cult of major combat operations" at the outset of the wars in Iraq and Afghanistan, military intelligence was focused on collecting and analyzing information to identify targets for kinetic resolution. In other words, the focus of military intelligence was lethal targeting of the adversary. Indeed, the primary purpose of intelligence, according to Joint Publication 2–0, *Joint Intelligence*, is to provide "the commander with a threat assessment based on an analysis of the full range of adversary capabilities and a prediction of the adversary's likely intention."[71] Time and resources were dedicated to identification of bad actors—the "red" layer of the human terrain. Very few resources were dedicated to identification and understanding of indigenous civilians— the "green" layer of the human terrain. As one former US Army military intelligence officer noted, "When I was in MI school, we used to put a giant black X over the cities, since there was just no possibility that we would ever be conducting operations there. Too many damn people! Nobody in the Army even thought about the possibility."[72]

A PERFECT STORM

The academic "cult of irrelevance" and the military "cult of major combat operations" might have remained an interesting but irrelevant feature of American life if nothing had happened on September 11, 2001. Al-Qaeda's terrorist attacks on US soil compelled a response, and US forces subsequently deployed to Afghanistan to hunt Osama bin Laden and bring down the Taliban regime that had sheltered and assisted him. Two years later US forces invaded Iraq, ostensibly to prevent Saddam Hussein's government from further developing weapons of mass destruction and aiding al-Qaeda. The coup that Bush administration officials had hoped for in Iraq—removing Saddam Hussein from power but leaving the rest of the Iraqi bureaucracy intact—became significantly more difficult following de-Baathification and the disbanding of the Iraqi Army. After major combat operations in Iraq ended, uncontrolled looting began, the Iraqi bureaucracy fell apart, Iraqi civilians did not greet Coalition forces as liberators but as invaders, and former members of the recently outlawed Baath party began an insurgency against occupying forces. "The insurgencies in Iraq and Afghanistan," as Lieutenant General David Petraeus put it, "were not, in truth, the wars for which we were best prepared in 2001..."[73]

New Center of Gravity

The "cult of major combat operations" did not prepare the military well to fight a counterinsurgency in a foreign country. "Political power is the central issue in insurgencies and counterinsurgencies," according to US Army Field Manual 3–24, *Counterinsurgency*; "each side aims to get the people to accept its governance or authority as legitimate."[74] Because insurgency and counterinsurgency involve a struggle for political power and a competition for legitimacy in the eyes of the population, the use of lethal force by itself is an inadequate tool. In a counterinsurgency, according to classical military theory, the military should employ proportional force and use non-lethal operations (e.g. civic development, infrastructure repair, electoral reform, and so on) to increase support for the host nation government and reduce support for the insurgency. David Galula, for example, notes that successful counterinsurgency is 20 percent military action and 80 percent political. Every soldier must become a "propagandist, a social worker, a civil engineer, a schoolteacher, a nurse, a boy scout."[75] Unlike major combat operations, where the preferences and perspectives of civilians are often of little consequence, counterinsurgency takes place within the society as a whole.[76] Far from being irrelevant in a counterinsurgency, the civilian population is the center of gravity and kinship is the new order of battle.

When US forces support a host nation government in a counterinsurgency, they are drawn into a political struggle in a foreign country whose language they may not speak and whose people they may not understand. How can a soldier be effective at dispute resolution in Basra, micro-finance in Jalalabad, or constitutional reform in Baghdad with no understanding of the local society?

New Tasks

When the United States invaded Iraq in March of 2003, notwithstanding the failure to declare martial law at the cessation of hostilities, the US military de facto assumed the functions and responsibilities of the toppled Iraqi government. During the Second World War, this type of operation was known as "military governance," and is now known as civil–military operations.[77] The elements within the US military that were in any way trained and equipped to assume these functions—US Army and Marine Corps Civil Affairs—were under-staffed and under-resourced. As US Army Civil Affairs officer Chris Holshek has noted, in 2005 the whole civil affairs force totaled

> less than 6,000 in the Army and Marines. This is astounding: including PSYOP [Psychological Operations] (a total of about 10,000 with CA), less than one half of one percent of the entire US military force structure is dedicated to soft-power applications to winning the peace and leveraging the "end state" in stability operations—and the budgeted share is half again as proportionate.[78]

Because they work so closely among the local people, Civil Affairs were literally the front-line troops in Iraq and Afghanistan: although Civil Affairs specialists make up only about 5 percent of the Army's Reserve forces, they accounted for 23 percent of the combined fatalities among reservists in Iraq and Afghanistan.[79]

Given their small numbers, Civil Affairs personnel could not by themselves conduct the complex set of civil military operations required in a counterinsurgency. Few non-governmental organizations were willing to accept the security risks of operating in Iraq or Afghanistan, and the Department of State was neither organized nor equipped to reconstruct a government. As a result, as General Petraeus once said, "everyone does nation building."[80] US military personnel of all ranks and military occupational specialties—the so-called general purpose force—became responsible for such short-term tasks such as providing security to a local population, restoring essential services, and addressing immediate humanitarian needs. The whole US military became responsible for such long-term tasks as building indigenous capacity for essential services, encouraging a viable market economy, developing the rule of law, promoting democratic institutions, and assisting in the creation of a robust civil society. As one Marine officer noted regarding Al Anbar province in 2007: "The majority of money and logistics are focused at the national level in Baghdad, but it's been difficult to establish a system where the government in Baghdad pushes those resources down to the Provinces... and then for the provinces to push that down to the cities. I know that sounds like it should be a simple system to implement, but it didn't exist under Saddam Hussein and *we have had to create it from scratch.*"[81]

Unlike major combat operations, stability and reconstruction operations must be conducted among, and with the support of, an indigenous civilian population. How can the US military train a police force in Helmand, establish a local banking system in Diwaniya, or create provisional councils in Anbar without working in conjunction with local civilians? Understanding the environment is critical in stability operations. As General Anthony Zinni once observed, "On one hand, you have to shoot and kill somebody; on the other hand, you have to feed somebody. On the other hand, you have to build an economy, restructure the infrastructure, and build the political system. And there's some poor lieutenant colonel, colonel, brigadier general down there, stuck in some province with all that saddled onto him, with non-governmental organizations and political wannabes running around, with factions and a culture he doesn't understand."[82]

Socio-cultural Knowledge Shortfall

In both Iraq and Afghanistan, the US military found itself combating insurgencies while simultaneously trying to reconstruct a government. To do this, military personnel needed knowledge about the societies they were supposed to reconstruct.[83] Yet arguably neither the US military nor policy-makers inside the Beltway had the requisite level of knowledge about either Iraq or Afghanistan to support this type of population-centric warfare. According to General Stanley McChrystal, who commanded coalition forces in Afghanistan in 2009–10: "Most of us, me included, had a very superficial understanding of the situation and history, and we had a frighteningly simplistic view of recent history, the last 50 years."[84] This gap existed from top to bottom. For example, in 2004 the Defense Science Board, a group of scientific experts who advise the DOD, released a report entitled *Transition to and from Hostilities.*[85] In the report, the Geographic Combatant Commands were asked to assess their knowledge of societal, cultural, tribal structure, economic, infrastructure, and evolving threats, and to identify the number of in-house specialists in its respective area of responsibility (AOR). Pacific Command (PACOM) rated itself as "generally inadequate," while European Command (EUCOM) and Central Command (CENTCOM) rated themselves as "inadequate."[86] At the lowest level, soldiers on the ground struggled because of a lack of knowledge. For example, a platoon leader in the 101st Airborne Division wrote to the author seeking assistance: "I'm very confused about the tribal relations in this AO [Area of Operations] and how they interact. You would think that we would have this down by now, but the MI [Military Intelligence] community isn't getting the info down to the user."[87]

Moreover, neither the US military nor the policy community had a clear idea of what they needed to know to support stability operations and counterinsurgency.[88] Following the operations in Haiti and Somalia, the US military identified the lack of socio-cultural knowledge as one of the key causes of operational failure. According to JP 3–06, *Joint Urban Operations*, for example, "during UNOSOM II, US leaders failed to take certain factors of Somali culture into consideration, contributing to the operation's failure."[89] Although the shortfall had become apparent, only limited attempts were made to identify precisely what information was required to support non-traditional military operations. In 1996, for example, a CIA analyst named Jeffrey B. White wrote an insightful paper called *Some Thoughts on Irregular Warfare*, in which he noted that "Cultural geography also needs to be understood in the micro sense. The geography of small areas becomes important in a tribal context. Who are the tribesmen? Where are they? What do they do? How do they live? What are their towns and houses like? These are important questions as US operations are planned and then executed."[90] Despite the lessons of Haiti and Somalia, and despite the prescient observations of a few US government personnel, only very broad socio-cultural knowledge requirements found their way into doctrine.[91]

In sum, the US military was relatively well prepared to fight a major land war against a peer competitor enemy in 2001. The war one prepares for, however, is not always the war one is called upon to fight. The conflicts in Iraq and Afghanistan involved forms of warfare (counterinsurgency, counterterrorism, and stability operations) which the US military was not equipped, manned, or trained to fight. In addition, these forms of warfare involved new tasks (agricultural development, conflict mediation, "key leader engagements", and so on) which in turn required different types of knowledge from what the intelligence system was geared to provide. The imperatives of transformation—faster, more precise, networked, and interoperable—became less relevant than understanding the social and political environment of Iraq and Afghanistan. As Major General Robert Scales noted, "Reflective senior officers returning from Iraq and Afghanistan have concluded that great advantage can be achieved by out-thinking rather than out-equipping the enemy. They are telling us that wars are won as much by creating alliances, leveraging non-military advantages, reading intentions, building trust, converting opinions, and managing perceptions—all tasks that demand an exceptional ability to understand people, their culture, and their motivation."[92] Yet, because the "cult of major combat operations" emphasized engineering and mathematics at the expense of other branches of knowledge, in-house experts who understood something about non-Western societies were few and far between. The S&T social science portfolio was minimal, the intelligence system was not geared towards producing this knowledge, and the research that was produced that might have been relevant to the warfighter was not coordinated. Lacking socio-cultural knowledge about Iraq and Afghanistan, the US military certainly needed the help that the academy could provide. The "cult of irrelevance" in academia, however, meant that few US scholars were able or interested in offering practical assistance. This combination proved to be a perfect storm.

MILITARY "REDISCOVERS" CULTURE

Downrange, military personnel quickly recognized that they lacked knowledge about the operational environment necessary to conduct a counterinsurgency or stability operations. Requirements for equipment, such as up-armored High Mobility Multipurpose Wheeled Vehicles (HMMWVs) and body armor, filtered back to the Pentagon, as did requirements for increased knowledge of the people of Iraq and Afghanistan. This process accelerated after the first rotation of divisions redeployed, and individuals who had served in battalions, brigades, and divisions returned to the Pentagon to serve in staff positions. These officers had witnessed at first hand the consequences of inadequate planning for the post-war period and unfounded policy assumptions, and many of them were furious about the unnecessary loss of life due to IEDs and the unnecessary blunders downrange caused by ignorance and ethnocentrism.

Concurrently, the revolt of the generals was in full swing back inside the Beltway. A number of retired, senior military officers and defense officials made public statements highly critical of the war and its planning.[93] Retired Lieutenant General Ricardo Sanchez wrote, "From a catastrophically flawed, unrealistically optimistic war plan to the administration's latest "surge" strategy, this administration has failed to employ and synchronize its political, economic and military power."[94] When General Eric K. Shinseki, Chief of Staff of the Army, testified before the Senate Armed Services Committee in 2003 that several hundred thousand troops would be needed in post-war Iraq, Paul Wolfowitz dismissed his views, calling them "wildly off the mark" and asserting that many fewer troops would be needed, given that there was no ethnic strife in Iraq as in Bosnia or Kosovo.[95] Shortly thereafter the Secretary of Defense named Shinseki's successor, effectively making him a lame duck. Major General Paul Eaton, reflecting on Shinseki's punishment, wrote that "the rest of the senior brass got the message, and nobody has complained since."[96]

The alternative to resigning one's commission and speaking out publicly about the administration's failings was to say nothing and quietly address the problems that could be fixed. Between 2003 and 2006, the frustration and anger in the Pentagon was palpable. Behind closed doors, some senior military personnel complained bitterly about the hubris of the civilian leadership; about the error of de-Baathification and the disbanding of the Iraqi Army; about the arrogance of exporting democracy; about the implausibility of building civil society in a country dominated by a totalitarian regime for thirty years; about US military personnel put in harm's way with inadequate training in counterinsurgency operations; about the fact that McKiernan's call for a declaration of martial law to stop the looting in Baghdad was ignored, and so on. None of this could be expressed publicly. Uniformed members of the US armed forces have restrictions on their civil rights, including the right of free speech. Given these legal restrictions, and the professional ethos of the officer corps where duty is apolitical, public complaining about the administration of a war that was widely seen as unwise and ill planned was not an option.[97] While those military personnel who had hesitations or objections to the war were effectively silenced by their own professional ethos, many members of the officer corps were more than willing executioners of what was obviously a war plan based more on ideology than careful policy analysis.[98]

In the highly charged political environment of Washington DC, the need to improve the military's level of cultural knowledge was a non-controversial, non-partisan issue upon which everyone could agree. Internal criticism about the military's lack of knowledge was acceptable in a way that outright opposition to the war was not: it was bi-partisan, nobody in particular was to blame, and it was true. On October 21, 2003, Dr Stephen D. Biddle of the US Army War College, Dr Andrew Krepinevich Jr., and Major General Robert Scales Jr. testified before the Committee on Armed Services of the House of Representatives about Operation Iraqi Freedom. During his testimony, Major General Robert Scales emphasized the point that "Crucial to the success of combat is an understanding of one's potential opponent as he is, rather than as Americans would like him to be…. Without this kind of political knowledge, which requires immersion in the language, culture, and history of a region, the data gathered by technological means can serve only to reinforce preconceived, erroneous, sometimes disastrous notions."[99]

Major General Scales' testimony inspired Representative Ike Skelton to write a letter to Secretary of Defense Donald Rumsfeld on October 23, 2003. The letter made the case that "… if we had better understood the Iraqi culture and mindset, our war plans would have been even better than they were, [and] the plan for the post-war period and all of its challenges would have been far better…we must improve our cultural awareness…to inform the policy process. Our policies would benefit from this not only in Iraq, but…elsewhere, where we will have long-term strategic relationships and potential military challenges for many years to come."[100]

By 2004, "cultural intelligence" had become a buzzword in the Pentagon. Military journals began to publish articles making the case for the importance of cultural knowledge for military operations.[101] In 2005, Brigadier General Benjamin C. Freakley, an infantry officer in the US Army, published *Cultural Awareness and Combat Power*,[102] followed in 2006 by Lieutenant General David Petraeus' article, "Learning Counterinsurgency: Observations from Soldiering in Iraq." Noting that "cultural awareness is a force multiplier," Petraeus argued that "knowledge of the cultural "terrain" can be as important as, and sometimes even more important than, knowledge of the geographic terrain…. Understanding of such cultural aspects is essential if one is to help the people build stable political, social, and economic institutions. Indeed, this is as much a matter of common sense as operational necessity."[103] After a year's worth of planning, the International Conference on Adversary Cultural Knowledge and National Security took place in Arlington, VA in November 2004. Sponsored by the Office of Naval Research and DARPA, this conference was apparently the first joint inter-agency US government conference on the social sciences since 1962.[104] Various government agencies issued official reports noting the need for increased cultural knowledge.[105] New fellowship programs, such as the Pat Roberts Intelligence Scholars Program (PRISP), were created to support undergraduate and graduate students pursuing studies in critical language specialties, area studies, and technical and scientific specialties.

In October 2004, Secretary Rumsfeld released a memo stating that "foreign language skill and regional expertise are essential enabling capabilities for DOD activities in the transition to and from hostilities." This memo tasked the Secretaries of the military departments to reshape the forces to "provide stabilization and reconstruction capabilities... capable of operating in a range of cultures and languages." In addition, the Under Secretary of Defense for Personnel and Readiness (USD (P&R)) was tasked with developing metrics to identify capabilities and readiness within the force pertaining to foreign language and regional expertise.[106] The following year, this memo became an official Department of Defense Directive, 3000.05, *Military Support for Stability, Security, Transition, and Reconstruction (SSTR) Operations*, on November 28, 2005. The Directive assigned new responsibilities to various DOD elements for planning, training, and conducting stability operations. More importantly, Directive 3000.05 also established a requirement for socio-cultural knowledge, mandating that the Commanders of the Geographic Combatant Commands include information "on key ethnic, cultural, religious, tribal, economic and political relationships..." as a component of their intelligence campaign planning.[107] Official recognition by the DOD of the importance of understanding host nation societies represented a significant shift in an institution that has focused almost exclusively on technology and firepower as force multipliers since the end of the Vietnam War. In addition, Directive 3000.05 created the baseline for bureaucratic action for programs such as HTS that were focused on cultural, regional, and linguistic issues.

Addressing the Shortfall

Recognizing the cultural knowledge shortfall among the operating forces in Iraq and Afghanistan, the DOD and the military services initiated a host of programs and organizations to address the issue. In 2005, the Marine Corps created a Center for Advanced Operational Culture Learning (CAOCL) at Quantico, Virginia with the mandate to provide cultural pre-deployment training, debrief operational units, and provide assistance with doctrine development.[108] In February 2006, the Army opened the TRADOC Culture Center of Excellence at Fort Huachuca, Arizona to develop and disseminate cultural awareness and foreign language training materials for the US Army. By 2007, the Navy and the Air Force had opened culture and language centers. When then Lieutenant General David Petraeus was selected to run the US Army Combined Arms Center, which oversees the Command and General Staff College, the Defense Language Institute, and the training centers at Fort Irwin, California and Fort Polk, Louisiana, he began the process of integrating culture into professional military education, training, doctrine, and language programs. General Petraeus also spearheaded the drafting of the Field Manual 3–24, *Counterinsurgency*. For the first time in 200 years, core social science concepts became part of US Army doctrine.

The military services sought to ameliorate the socio-cultural knowledge shortfall primarily through training. As an organization, the US military places great emphasis on training, both for the purposes of socialization and for combat readiness. The slogan "train as you fight" encapsulates a philosophy of knowledge, emphasizing the concrete skills needed to fire a weapon, drive a tank, or lead a platoon. Philosophers who specialize in epistemology distinguish between this type of skill-based procedural knowledge ('knowledge how'), acquaintance knowledge ('knowledge of'), and propositional knowledge ('knowledge that').[109] Procedural knowledge (which is often tacit, unarticulated knowledge) involves the application of expertise, such as knowing how to fire a weapon. Firing an M-16, for example, does not require knowledge of theoretical physics but it does require aim, concentration, and skill.[110]

When the military began incorporating culture into training programs, it emphasized procedural knowledge (knowledge how) of Iraqi and Afghan society. The goal of most of these early training programs was to inculcate the skills and competencies necessary for troops to complete their missions in a foreign environment. Many early pre-deployment briefings given to soldiers and Marines on their way to war were essentially "sensitivity" briefings, which included advice such as "don't put your boot on an Arab's head" and "do not frisk a female." In the words of Ben Connable, an Arabic-speaking Marine with multiple tours in Iraq, most pre-deployment cultural briefs were nothing more than "Emily Post of Arabia," designed to sensitize soldiers and Marines to the customary norms of the local society.[111]

Inside the DOD, cultural procedural knowledge (knowledge how) came to be known as "cultural competence": "the knowledge, skills, and affect/motivation that enable individuals to adapt effectively in cross-cultural environments... regardless of the particular intersection of cultures."[112] Cultural competence involves a certain level of aptitude, and studies show that individuals with a greater degree of mental flexibility[113] and higher cognitive complexity tend to perform better in cross-cultural situations.[114]

With the military's training focus squarely on cultural competence, what was missing was granular, propositional knowledge (knowledge that) about the culture, society, political system, and economy of local communities. In truth, application of cultural knowledge to operational problems faced by the military requires both knowledge about the local society (knowledge that) and knowledge of how to engage people within the society appropriately, as for example in negotiations (knowledge how). (Ideally, socio-cultural knowledge among military personnel would also include acquaintance knowledge of foreign societies, based on direct experience.)

What kind of socio-cultural "knowledge that" was actually needed downrange? Unless this question was answered, the DOD's S&T portfolio, training and education programs, and databases would be based on nothing more than personal opinions, best guesses, and assumptions. In 2003, representatives from the Army and the Marine Corps came together for a series of informal workshops in Quantico, Virginia to try to develop a shared cultural ontology, breaking down the various elements of a socio-cultural system that were generally common (e.g. religion, social norms, food preferences). A similar process took place for HTS's precursor program, the Cultural Preparation of the Environment, sponsored by the Joint Chiefs of Staff beginning in 2004. A few years later in order to develop a unified field research methodology, a knowledge management system and a revision of the training program, HTS undertook an empirical examination of the type of research requested by military units, based on data we had available through teams down-range.[115] In addition to these initiatives, a variety of checklists existed in doctrine, which were essentially lists of socio-cultural elements with potential operational relevance. The core question for all of these processes was: what elements of culture are of enduring significance to military operations across theaters and over time? How do these elements of culture help or hinder military operations? "Our real, long term, dilemma," noted Brigadier General Benjamin C. Freakley, "is defining the significant military aspects of culture as they might apply in any theater and further determining how these various aspects of culture manifest themselves and might influence tactical operations."[116]

The tendency in US military doctrine to produce lists, taxonomies, and categories results from the need to reduce complexity without the leisure of time. Organization of vast amounts of different types of information requires the imposition of an organizing framework. Checklists and PowerPoint are mutually reinforcing systems of encapsulating knowledge. This information must be comprehensible to all members of the force, which includes privates with a high school diploma and colonels with PhDs. While they are certainly necessary and perhaps adequate for certain domains of knowledge, in general checklists and associated approaches that rely on them are not suitable for socio-cultural knowledge because they neither clarify relationships between elements nor provide explanations. (As Franz Boas once noted, classification is not an explanation.[117] Neither are checklists.) In order to help them understand the meaning of a behavior, ritual, or object within a given context, military personnel need explanations addressing *why*, rather than lists of facts addressing *what*. In the words of USMC General Anthony Zinni, the former commander of US Central Command (CENTCOM) and special envoy for the United States to Israel and the Palestinian Authority, "What I need to understand is how these societies function. What makes them tick? Who makes the decisions? What is it about their society that's so remarkably different in their values, in the way they think, compared to my values and the way I think in my western, white-man mentality?"[118]

The knowledge requirement, as those of us who helped build HTS concluded, was for socio-cultural knowledge about societies, not states. The knowledge the military needed was not yet another 187-slide

PowerPoint on the history of Islam, but knowledge that was grounded in the realities of present time. How do people in Sadr city express their devotion to Allah? How does sharia intersect with the Afghan civil code in the local administration of justice in Khost? The military also needed knowledge about *why* people did certain things, not just a static diagram of *what* the social structure looked like. Why did certain tribes mobilize to defend territory and others did not? Why was there so much conflict between cross-cousins among the Pashtu? US military forces did not need abstract, theoretical treatises on cultural rituals, but rather information that had immediate relevance to their operations. Were all these new gymnasiums in Baghdad just a cover for the insurgency, or were Iraqi men really interested in power lifting? Were Iraqis moving corpses to hide evidence, or was this part of an Islamic death ritual? Enabling US forces to conduct their mission efficiently, effectively, and with less conflict required a deeper, more granular understanding of the population. Yet, this was exactly the type of knowledge that was lacking in the DOD at the beginning of the wars.

THE ACADEMIC/MILITARY DIVIDE DOWNRANGE

As discussed in the introduction to this volume, the original mission of HTS was to "enable culturally astute decision-making, enhance operational effectiveness, and preserve and share socio-cultural institutional knowledge."[119] In other words, HTS was intended to ameliorate the socio-cultural knowledge shortfall experienced by operating forces. During implementation, as discussed in the introduction, HTS experienced a variety of structural and organizational barriers and impediments. One additional issue that caused significant problems for teams and the units they supported downrange was the academic/military divide. This manifested itself within the HTTs, which were composed of both military and civilian personnel, and between teams and supported military units.[120]

Most military operations are group efforts; most academic books and articles are individual efforts. Not all academics, when asked to work in a team, can productively do so. In one case, the social scientist in an HTT in Iraq in 2007 could not adjust to working in a team. He felt that his teammates did not understand the complexity and the timeline for social science research; his teammates felt that he did not understand the operating tempo of an army brigade in combat. "This is not old-fashioned ethnography, where you can just plod along and observe," in the words of one of his teammates. "The military needs it *now*."[121] The social scientist left the rest of his team at brigade, and attached himself to a battalion. Although the battalion commander was very impressed with this social scientist and brought him along on battlefield circulation, this type of split team structure weakened the ability of the team as a whole to support the brigade's decision-making process, which was after all the purpose of the program. After visiting the team and talking to all concerned parties, we realized that this particular social scientist was a "lone wolf" who preferred to work alone, acting as a solo adviser to a commander, rather than spending time sitting at conference tables in brigade headquarters attempting to influence the decision-making process.

Irrespective of seniority or discipline, the "lone wolf" social scientist was a recurrent phenomenon in HTS and seemed to be a function of personality that resonated with the general culture of academia. Whereas the professional ethos of the military emphasizes achieving the overall mission at the expense of individual priorities and interests, the professional ethos of academics emphasizes individual rather than collective achievement. An HTT member in Iraq in 2008 noted that "academics need to take credit for their work, and there's a cultural disconnect there. If you don't put your name on it, you fade away. It's publish or perish."[122] Academics who volunteered to serve on an HTT had to overcome their own individualism and adjust rapidly to the collective work process of the US military in order to be fully effective. As the IZ3 social scientist explained, "This has been a tremendous culture shock.... Civilians often don't know how to course correct—especially professors who are used to being in the classroom, being self-sufficient, being their own CEO, who don't understand the concept of the chain of command."[123]

Another cultural barrier between the military and the academy that caused difficulty downrange was preferred style of communication. The language of academia is ponderous prose; the language of the military is PowerPoint. Civilian academics working on HTTs had to adapt their communication patterns to a more military style, with the "bottom line up front" (BLUF) and a concise set of recommendations conveyed on PowerPoint slides. PowerPoint enforces brevity, linear thinking, and bluntness—anathema to the communication styles of most academics but mandatory for the military. As the social scientist from

IZ3 noted, "I'm trained to leave things open-ended. Here you state the problem, you offer analysis, and then you offer solutions and recommendations."[124] Not all academics, when asked to communicate in bullets, can productively do so. "Not all results translate equally well into PowerPoint presentations," as David Edwards has written; "and one consequence of this fact is that the formal aspects of The Brief inevitably encourage not only a particular kind of communication, but also a particular kind of information gathering that emphasizes immediacy, precision and relevance.... In this context, anthropological research comes off especially badly, given that it tends more often to be impressionistic, anecdotal and inconclusive."[125]

Differences in communication styles between academics and military personnel suggested a deeper variance in their modes of understanding reality. As discussed above, many academics see the world as a series of interesting puzzles to be investigated; the military generally see the world as a series of problems to be solved. Problems are solved in a military context through the military decision-making process (MDMP), which includes seven steps: Receipt of Mission; Mission Analysis; Course of Action (COA) Development; COA Analysis; COA Comparison; COA Approval; Orders Production.[126] The actual, ideal role of the HTT was to provide socio-cultural input to the MDMP, so that problems could be more accurately framed, so that factors affecting the local population could be considered, and so that the solutions the military chose would involve less violence and, where possible, meet the needs of the civilian population. As one HTT member in Iraq bluntly explained, "If you can't feed into the system that a maneuver brigade has, and provide feedback that influences their activities, you should pack your bags and go home."[127] In the MDMP approach to problem framing and problem solving, there is little time or patience for investigating interesting puzzles. If an HTT hoped to influence the final course of action determination, research had to be conducted before the mission analysis stage and input had to be offered as the COA was formulated. Criticizing a COA after the fact has no effect on the military, and only annoys them. As one member of IZ13 noted, "You need to get the cultural knowledge injected into the MDMP so that the CO [Commanding Officer] has the opportunity to choose what he wants to do... When we were able to inject into the process, he chose the COA we suggested. If we had waited for the plan and then commented, it would have had no effect."[128]

While social scientists often approach the world as an open-ended puzzle to be investigated with no clear solution, the military generally approach the world as a problem set that must be solved under time constraints and that may potentially involve the loss of human life. Knowledge about the geographical terrain, the enemy's intentions, weather patterns, and social organization of a local community have value not for their own sake, but because such knowledge is required to solve a problem and/or support the mission. Consistently, every unit that HTS supported demanded operationally relevant information:[129] "while it may be very interesting to know that Arab women henna their hands as part of the marriage ritual, it is unlikely that a research project on this topic would be operationally relevant. On the other hand, a research project on the Arab wedding ritual of celebratory gunfire might be extremely operationally relevant since mistaking non-directed weapons fired to signify happiness for directed weapons fired to signify hostile intent might result in both military and civilian casualties."[130] If the relevance of the research was not immediately apparent, the HTT had to articulate the "So what factor"—what makes input from the HTT important enough to be included in the brigade's deliberations. Civilian social scientists, many of whom had never done applied research (much less applied research in a military context) sometimes found it difficult to adapt to the military's tempo, team orientation, and preoccupation with relevance. Indeed the military's mission focus represents an antithesis to the inductive, experimental methodology most closely associated with anthropology—ethnography.[131]

Even teams that were able to overcome the obstacle of staggered rotation and transcend the military/academic divide experienced difficulties when faced with a highly lethal unit. Each BCT (Brigade Combat Team) and RCT (Regimental Combat Team) has a unique personality, resulting in part from its history, its leadership, its lines of operation, and the operational environment. Some units have a highly lethal focus, grounded in a belief that firepower is the answer to insurgency. One brigade commander I met in Iraq told me, as he smoked his cigar by the fire pit, that his personal ambition while in country was to put a Joint Direct Attack Munition (JDAM) through a building. This kind of statement exemplifies the cult of major combat operations in action. An HTT assigned to a unit with a kinetic focus could contribute almost nothing, since the HTT's own mission was to assist the brigade in lowering the level of conflict in a given area. As the team leader of IZ1 noted in 2008, "It's a question of the psyche of the unit. Our attitude in the Army is often 'go forth and break things.' If the attitude of the unit is that we're going to kill people, the team has to do some serious marketing of the HTT concept." Sometimes the unit was simply not willing to listen. "What crippled us with the CAV," the team leader continued, "is that they'd been here, implementing their plan. Our feedback was counter to their view."[132] Feedback counter to an organization's view of the world will generally be dismissed as irrelevant, and this was a source of frustration for many teams. In 2008, I received a long-distance phone call from a social scientist on a team in Iraq who told me she was going to quit and work for the PRT instead, since the military seemed to have no interest in any of the non-lethal approaches the HTT was advocating.

In short, teams encountered multiple obstacles to their mission. Not least among these impediments was prejudice; academics viewed the military as totalitarian baby-killers, and the military viewed academics as "arrogant, patronizing, and self-righteously indignant"[133] woolly-headed hippies. Yet sometimes, as we saw in HTS, the sacred values of the military and social scientists aligned. As one anthropologist serving on an HTT in Iraq explained:

> It's naïve to say that anthropologists don't have a role to play in the total human condition, which includes conflict. Could an anthropologist stop the war? I'd like to have that answered. I'd like to try, and to be able to say we gave it a shot. There's still hubris in the military, but the Army is now looking for an honorable solution. If this doesn't end well, it will end badly for all of us. As a human being first, and an anthropologist second, I couldn't stand by and let that happen. It's great to argue over a conference table and teach courses, but in the end it was an academic experience. Anthropology has this burgeoning specialization of applied anthropology or advocacy anthropology—I'm advocating for peace.... The brigade asked me why I'm here: so many mistakes are driven by cultural misunderstanding—I'm here to end that, to try to turn enemies into friends. I'm here to get you guys home.[134]

From Policy Relevance to Operational Relevance

Academics often question whether anyone reads what they write, and if so whether the reader finds any value in academic work. As I mentioned at the beginning of this chapter, 40 percent of international relations scholars—whose research should have the most policy relevance—believe that their work has none. On the other hand, the HTS experiment shows that academic research can not only have *policy* relevance, it can have *operational* relevance to the military. As one social scientist serving on an HTT in Iraq noted, "There are real consequences: you may be leaving your career behind, you may die, but you will have an immense effect on what's going on, so much so that it's scary."[135]

As discussed in the introduction, the specific ways in which HTTs were supporting military decision-making included providing socio-cultural situational awareness; providing input to COA development; recommending mitigation strategies; providing effects analysis; supporting the operations process; and providing unit specific socio-cultural training. What were the specific benefits of social science to the operational military? Over the course of the first four years of HTS, military personnel commented repeatedly on the value of social science *and* social scientists for their mission. Of course, not all HTTs delivered quality research or held up under the pressures of working in a war zone. However, when they did, HTTs provided a number of benefits to the military, including accurate data, rigorous analysis, expert knowledge, and reducing the burden on soldiers and Marines by leaving social science to the social scientists, and sometimes reducing the need for lethal force.[136]

One contribution made by many HTTs was providing the military with a unique non-military perspective. HTTs included social scientists from many different disciplines, including political science, social psychology, cultural geography, economics, and anthropology. While each of these disciplines has a different body of knowledge and different preferred research methods, individuals trained in such variegated fields still had something in common: they brought a different perspective to the military. One US Marine Corps lieutenant colonel who worked with IZ13 in Iraq observed, "I can get open source intel, I can get classified and unclassified source—I can throw a problem set for analysis out to internal and reach back assets. What I don't have is [the social scientist] who can tell you about shame and honor... Giving us a different perspective is key. We're military guys, and we're programmed to look at a problem in a certain way. Regardless of education, it's our hardwiring."[137]

As individuals, social scientists contributed a different perspective to the operational military. In addition, social science itself—as an approach to studying human culture, society, and behavior—added value to the warfighter. Understanding the local social structure and the local economy are critical when the mission requires the military to engage with local civic leaders. In the words of the Assistant G3, II Marine Expeditionary Force (Forward):

> In October/November 2008 we took control [of Tripoli, which is the military designation for Ninewa Province in Iraq]. We moved there to focus on the border, because we felt there was a flow of goods, men, material. It's an open border, just desert. It's been a porous border for thousands of years. Smugglers know where to bury the water, bury the fuel... and they make a lot of money. We decided to put some people on problem to find out: who are the sheiks? Who are the tribes? Do they reach into Syria? What are their sources of influence? ... We had to understand the dynamics. Who's going to tell us the truth? Who do I engage? The boundary between Kurd and Arab, that's strategic in nature. The Kurds want buffer between themselves and Syria and Iraq. It's a confluence of all sorts of things. The HTAT is manpower that applies brainpower to research and brings it to commanders and lays out to them who's who in the zoo... With that knowledge, we can set our engagement plan to get bang for the buck—how do we provide security for election? Who should be the police? They also validate the research: here's what I think, let's validate it. If we could have applied that model years earlier, it would have really paid dividends.[138]

Another theme that military personnel consistently mentioned was the value of social science research methods. Most military personnel have not been trained in how to interview local civilian personnel in order to obtain the information they need for stability operations.[139] Soldiers, when required to conduct interviews to obtain information about the local community, tend to rely on rapid-fire questioning which may be counterproductive. As one platoon leader from the 1st battalion of the 112th Infantry Regiment observed:

> The mission now is to go out and talk to people and find the bad guys—work with the IP [Iraqi police], get info on security situation, locate weapons caches, and IEDs. We also do civil capacity—build soccer fields, do road repairs, help medical clinics. It's all about relationships—this guy is in charge of this, and for different things you go to different people. We didn't know that until a couple months ago—that guy can't help you, but this guy can. We [the platoon and the HTT] figured it out together—we just fired questions, but [the HTT] can steer the conversation. [The HTT] doesn't focus on bombs in the basement. They can tell us bigger picture stuff because we are in our own little area... our boundaries are arbitrary—there is a road here, a river there—so you don't have the opportunity to see what's beyond the boundary. That info is nowhere. We started with nothing—we didn't know anything. We went to a police station and asked where the towns were and who was in charge. The S2 [Intelligence Officer] could care less about all that stuff, even civil projects we try to do—it's all let's go

get the bad guys and lock them up. Even now when there are not so many bad guys left.[140]

One of the goals of HTS, as established in the 2006 Iraq JUONS, was to increase the level of situational understanding and thereby to reduce the need for lethal force. Whether HTS had this effect on the units it served would be very difficult to measure, and prone to all the other issues surrounding operational assessment as currently practiced by units in theater.[141] Although HTS was not required to measure its own effectiveness (ideally, program assessments should be conducted by an unbiased, objective body), the subjective opinion of many military units which the program supported was that, indeed, HTTs reduced violence.[142] For example, in January every year, the Shia community celebrates *Ashura*, which commemorates the death of Imam Hussein, the grandson of the Prophet Mohammed. For the Shia, this festival is a demonstration of his sacrifice against tyranny and oppression. During Saddam Hussein's regime the Shia community was not allowed to celebrate because of the holiday's symbolic importance as an expression of resistance to tyranny. After the end of the Hussein regime, the shrine at Katamiya became an alternative festival location for those Shia who could not travel to Karbala. Since the fall of Saddam, the festival had been plagued by ethno-sectarian violence, including a bomb threat that caused an uncontrolled panic on the adjoining bridge in which hundreds of people died. As a mobile training team commander explained, "Based on our understanding of the AO [Area of Operation], we increased security here and decreased security there—they were able to commemorate their religion. Nothing bad happened this year because of our understanding of the situation, which was in part provided by the HTT… It's hard to measure a negative, but I can definitely say that something bad didn't happen."[143]

Having social scientists conduct social science research meant that soldiers did not have to become part-time anthropologists. Soldiers and Marines are selected and trained to do a very specialized task—warfighting. They are not trained to do social science data collecting or analysis, nor is it part of their official duties. In the words of one brigade effects coordinator in Iraq: "We've been working with the USAID [United States Agency for International Development] TCAF [Tactical Conflict Assessment Model] model for atmospherics. The biggest drawback to that model is you need a lot of data. Who's going to provide it? Marines are out doing patrols and interacting with the local populace.

Everyone in your mind is the enemy and you're watching your back—somebody else needs to do it. With HTT, we got into a question about Marines collecting data, but it needs to be a civilian asking the question."[144] Some military critics of HTS have made the argument that, rather than having academic civilians in the battlespace conducting research, this function ought to be performed by uniformed military personnel.[145] However, brigade staffs are highly specialized organizations with a high operational tempo. Every single person already has an assigned task, with no time left over to conduct, analyze, and present social science research.[146] As one brigade deputy commanding officer in Iraq noted in 2009, "I'm glad they're here. 97.5 percent of the brigade has another job—the folks here all do something else."[147]

The HTTs also benefited local civilians. Over the course of a number of years, HTS received and collected what we referred to as "sheikhs' letters." These letters were brought or mailed unsolicited to the HTT or the supported military unit, expressing thanks for the work in the community done by the HTT. The first one we received in 2007 reads verbatim:

> To/coalition force commandary, The respecttable brigader: We are clanse of AL-TAJJY north we present our great falness and apperciation to [redacted] and for all teams members old and new team like colonel [redacted] and Major Phil because the got us assistance to all Iraqi socety and give presentation the American army the costomes and iraqi society traditions and how can get understanding and apperhension and respect the mutual feeling between Iraqi society and American Army. So we recommend to send teams lik this type for all iraqi cities to serve all the citizens, to indicat pretty American face for all Iraqi. As [redacted] has done with his team.

This letter signed by the tribes of North Taji, with all its difficulties in transliteration, had a powerful emotional effect on team members and US military personnel.

HTS seems to have helped US forces, and in some cases directly assisted local civilians. Why was there so much controversy? The answer links back to the discussion at the beginning of this chapter: namely, the same ethical values that made HTS objectionable to anthropologists also tend to foster a "cult of irrelevance" in the discipline.

THE ANTHROPOLOGY BACKLASH

The end goals of HTS, as stated in the official documents that created the program, were to "decrease both coalition force and local national casualties" and "avoid needless loss of life." For those of us involved in the creation of HTS, it was gratifying that US forces in Iraq and Afghanistan recognized the utility of socio-cultural knowledge. The "cult of major combat operations," after decades of dominance, seemed to be yielding to a more nuanced, population-centric approach. Increased socio-cultural knowledge was seen by many segments of the US military as a method to improve decision-making, ameliorate unintended consequences, and reduce the need for violence.

Most external observers, regardless of whether they supported the war on political grounds or not, would tend to agree that providing the US military with the tools and resources to improve their performance and potentially reduce casualties is a good thing. Yet HTS quickly became controversial among its core recruitment base—social scientists and most notably anthropologists. The program was condemned by the American Anthropological Association (AAA) on the grounds that it was "an unacceptable use of anthropological expertise."[148] The Network of Concerned Anthropologists (NCA) sponsored a "Pledge of Non-participation in Counter-insurgency," in which signatories affirmed that they would "not engage in research and other activities that contribute to counter-insurgency operations in Iraq or in related theaters in the 'war on terror.'"[149]

I am frequently asked by uniformed personnel to explain why anthropologists objected to HTS, since the military's need for situational understanding seemed self-evident to them. Why were anthropologists so disturbed that the military was asking for their assistance? Political scientists, sociologists, psychologists, and many other professional social scientists conduct research, provide advice, and deliver training to the military without feeling that they are compromising themselves. Many anthropologists objected to HTS on ethical grounds, including obtaining informed consent; disclosure of research goals, methods and sponsorship; voluntary participation of research subjects; maintaining informant confidentiality; disclosure of significant risks; avoiding harm to the community studied; and so on.[150] However, the moral outrage and the ritual scapegoating occurring in the anthropology community indicated that more than ethics was at stake.

Sacred values, as defined by Philip Tetlock, are those values with "transcendental significance that precludes comparisons, trade-offs, or indeed any mingling with secular values."[151] For many anthropologists, HTS represented a potential violation of the prime directive of the discipline: do no harm to the people you study. According to the AAA Code of Ethics, a "primary ethical obligation shared by anthropologists is to do no harm. It is imperative that, before any anthropological work be undertaken ... each researcher think through the possible ways that the research might cause harm. Among the most serious harms that anthropologists should seek to avoid are harm to dignity, and to bodily and material well-being, especially when research is conducted among vulnerable populations."[152] Like other sacred values, the imperative of "do no harm" allows no trade-offs with other portions of the ethical code, nor with practical research requirements, nor the sponsor's interests. This sacred value even trumps national allegiance: anthropologists' "loyalty to their government has to come after their ethical obligation to the people they study."[153] Hugh Gusterson, a professor of anthropology at Stanford University, believes that it would be unethical "if you study enemies of the United States and then give information [to the US government] that will be used to kill them."[154] According to this absolutist view, an anthropologist who studied al-Qaeda and provided that information to the US government would be acting unethically, presumably even in the case of an imminent terrorist attack.

No other social science demands such a close relationship between the researcher and the subject. Neither the code of professional ethics of sociologists nor that of political scientists calls upon members of the discipline to do no harm.[155] The anthropological code of ethics bears a closer resemblance to the Hippocratic Oath, which contains the admonition to physicians to "abstain from doing harm." In the ethical code of anthropologists, prevention of harm to the research subject may even "supersede the goal of seeking new knowledge."[156] Seeking new knowledge about human culture and society has been the fundamental purpose of the discipline, at least according to the AAA, which defines "anthropology as the science that studies humankind in all its aspects, through archeological, biological, ethnological, and linguistic research."[157] In effect, the sacred anthropological value of prevention of harm may trump the aim of the discipline itself, which is scientific inquiry into human culture and society. Anthropology, one might conclude, has been transformed "from a discipline based upon an *objective* model of the world to a discipline based upon a *moral* model of the world."[158]

HTS also represented an assault on another sacred value of the anthropologists: do not collaborate with the military. For many current anthropologists, the primary threat to the well-being of their research subjects is "the State" in its various forms. Of all the branches of government, the military with its arms and ammunition holds the most potential to harm the subjects of anthropological research. This particular worldview, which posits a sharp, unbridgeable opposition between government and the well-being of indigenous people, is a product of anthropology's unique disciplinary history. Once known as "the handmaiden of colonialism," anthropology was associated with the expansion and exercise of imperial power in colonial territories.[159] By the 1960s, however, the discipline re-cast itself as the "academic wing of the indigenous rights movement, whose role is to advocate the rights of vulnerable cultural minorities."[160] Anthropologists, convinced that ethnographic research could be used to control, enslave, and even annihilate many of the communities that were being studied, avoided conducting applied research on behalf of the government and eschewed government funding. The acceptable role for applied anthropology during the Vietnam period was to assist native people in their revolutionary struggles[161] or through community development in the form of "action anthropology."[162] In the words of Marshall Sahlins, for anthropologists merely to attend a conference sponsored by DOD exemplified "the corrosion of integrity that must accompany an enlistment of scholars in a gendarmerie relation to the Third World. Subversion of the mutual trust between field worker and informant is the predictable next step. The relativism we hold necessary to ethnography can be replaced by cynicism, and the quest for objective knowledge of other people replaced by a probe for their political weakness."[163]

When sacred values are compromised, as Tetlock notes, members of the community will "experience an aversive arousal state—moral outrage."[164] Violation of sacred values may also produce a feeling of contamination, followed by "symbolic acts of moral cleansing that reaffirm their solidarity with the moral community."[165] Among anthropologists, violation of the sacred value "thou shalt not collaborate with the military" has frequently resulted in ritual scapegoating of the perpetrators. Franz Boas, whom many consider to be the father of American anthropology, set the precedent for attacking "collaborators" during the First World War when he argued that some of his colleagues "have prostituted science by using it as a cover for their activities as spies."[166] Gerald Hickey, who advised General William Westmoreland during the Vietnam War, was denied an appointment at the University of Chicago after the war because faculty members were "worried at what 'secret' research you may have been doing for the army."[167] Anthropologists working for the US Army's Special Operations Research Office were subjected to virulent ad hominem attacks during the Vietnam War. One US government official noted that many anthropologists were "the first, the loudest, and the harshest against their colleagues undertaking work for government agencies that have operational concerns overseas."[168] More recently, during a panel at the 2004 American Anthropological Association, one presenter was called a "fascist" by an audience member simply for having produced a study on the wives of enlisted personnel.

Certainly, some of the vehement debate constitutes a legitimate criticism of the role of scholars in public policy. However, the ritual scapegoating of anthropologists who violate sacred values is also part of what has been called a general "culture of accusation" within anthropology, involving denunciation of colleagues for imagined wrongs on the basis of unsubstantiated accusations at the end of which "the targets of the investigation, like biblical scapegoats" are "expelled into the wilderness of anthropology."[169] Needless to say, this "culture of accusation" within anthropology silences debate and discourages dissent from the prevailing consensus of moral right and wrong.[170]

When communities are forced to choose between sacred values, they will make certain trade-offs. One reaction involves "rhetorical redefinitions of situations that transform taboo trade-offs into more acceptable routine trade-offs (one secular value against another, the sort of mental operation one performs every time one strolls into a supermarket)." Another reaction involves "tragic trade-offs (one sacred value against another, such as honor versus life, the stuff of classical Greek tragedies)."[171] Anthropologists, suspended between the sacred value of "do no harm" and the more secular value of publicly sharing research findings engineered a trade-off. The Network of Concerned Anthropologists' (NCA) pledge specifies that signatories "should refrain from directly assisting the US military in combat," but gives permission to "brief diplomats" and "work with peacekeeping forces."

From a military perspective, the NCA trade-off makes little sense. The inter-agency integration that occurs under the national command authority during a conflict belies a firm distinction between "diplomats" and the "military."[172] Furthermore, differentiating "peacekeeping forces" from the "military" does not reflect the reality of current

UN missions. First, UN peacekeeping forces are, of course, composed of military personnel drawn from member nations, including the US. Second, since the 1990s the distinction between traditional "blue helmet" peacekeeping under Chapter VI of the UN Charter (in which an impartial monitoring of a post-conflict ceasefire is undertaken with consent of the parties, where force may be used only in self-defense) and peace enforcement under Chapter VII (in which military actions are undertaken without the consent of the parties, where force may be used in defense of civilians and to ensure compliance) has been eroded. According to the UN, the Security Council "has adopted the practice of invoking Chapter VII of the Charter when authorizing the deployment of UN peacekeeping operations into volatile post-conflict settings…"[173] Following the slaughter in Rwanda and Srebrenica, peacekeeping operations are now routinely given the more robust Chapter VII authorization, enabling the use of military force self-defense, defense of civilians, and defense of mission.[174]

From a military perspective, NCA's trade-off—prohibiting direct engagement with US forces but permitting anthropologists to "brief diplomats" and "work with peacekeeping forces"—reveals some confusion regarding the US inter-agency structure and international law. From an anthropological perspective, however, the NCA trade-off appears perfectly reasonable. Excluding the US military from the list of acceptable clients preserves the sacred value of "do no harm." Simultaneously, by allowing anthropologists to work with the UN and Department of State, anthropologists can claim compliance with their code of ethics, which requires anthropologists to "make the results of their research appropriately available to sponsors, students, decision makers, and other nonanthropologists…"[175]—except of course the military.

Unfortunately, the sacred values of anthropologists tend to encourage disengagement from the policy world, and thereby reproduce the conditions for a cult of irrelevance. Participating in public policy discussions is quite difficult if the only acceptable position is to remain "outside the corrupting sphere of intelligence agencies and government bodies."[176] These days, most academic anthropologists seem to "consider the idea of constructive engagement with national security an oxymoron, if not a horrifying anathema to our ethical code."[177] And indeed, most anthropologists do not participate in any meaningful way in public policy formulation. Few anthropologists actually work for government agencies;[178] only a handful are members of organizations such as the Council on Foreign Relations; and very few teach in public policy schools. Anthropologists have tended to write mainly for other anthropologists, "not for those who have the power to change the world."[179] Reacting to this trend, a few anthropologists have argued that their discipline should have a role in shaping public policy.[180] Roberto Gonzalez in *Anthropologists in the Public Sphere* bemoaned the decline of "civic anthropology," and encouraged anthropologists to share their knowledge with the general public.[181] Catherine Besteman and Hugh Gusterson in *Why America's Top Pundits are Wrong* attempted to debunk the myths of the "punditocracy" and "reclaim Margaret Mead's legacy and find our voices as public intellectuals once more."[182] Yet, when their sacred values were threatened by the prospect of direct participation with the national security community, the strongest advocates of public policy engagement fell back on their sacred values, preferring to criticize rather than participate directly.

CONCLUSION

In 1960, Margaret Mead delivered a lecture at the National Defense University, expressing her hope that anthropology might prove useful to the government: "I ... hope, just hope, that from time to time, in different places, somewhere, either in the technical assistance programs or in our relations overseas or in our diplomacy, a certain amount of material of this sort will be used."[183] The goal of HTS was to use the methods, perspectives, and knowledge of social science to address the socio-cultural knowledge gap plaguing the US military in Iraq and Afghanistan.

In large measure, the dominant warfighting paradigm in DOD—the "cult of major combat operation"—made HTS necessary. The focus on technology, firepower, and platforms meant that other forms of warfare, such as counterinsurgency and stability operations, were bracketed off as "special warfare" and given little attention. Limited investments had been made in the social sciences, and research that was conducted was not coordinated. The necessary pool of in-house expertise did not exist to address requirements for socio-cultural knowledge, and the existing intelligence system was not designed to produce it. The wars in Iraq and Afghanistan did not match any of the contingency plans sitting on the shelf in the Pentagon. There was no "humanitarian army" waiting across the border, ready to follow US troops into Iraq, as President Bush had apparently expected.[184] US and Coalition forces were on their own, lacking the right equipment, lacking the right doctrine, lacking the right training, and lacking the right knowledge. The US military, both at home and abroad, adapted to conditions remarkably quickly and attempted to ameliorate the short-falls that the wars made apparent; HTS was a small but significant element of this process.

In large measure, the Byzantine bureaucracy of the DOD made HTS difficult to build. HTS was built from the ground up inside a bureaucratic system that does not facilitate innovation. As discussed in the introduction to this volume, HTS struggled with a number of structural impediments, including lack of control over its own contracting, lack of control over its own human resources, lack of control over its own budget, lack of staff, and so on. Deploying mixed military/civilian teams to conduct social science research in a war zone in support of US forces had never been done before; there was no manual sitting on a shelf with guidance on how to accomplish the myriad tasks required.

In large measure, integrating civilian academics into military units in a combat environment proved challenging because the worldview, work habits, ethics, and epistemological frameworks of academics and the military differ so greatly. These communities do not often overlap in American civic life and rarely share cross-cutting ties that might ameliorate the misunderstanding, preconceptions, and prejudice on both sides. Moreover, as a number of chapters in this volume discuss, military systems and processes are not inherently amenable to the complexities of social science research. The military requirement for operational relevance tends to preclude open-ended, inductive research methods. The language of PowerPoint (five bullets and "bottom line up front") deters nuanced analysis. The military's operational tempo prevents long-term, in-depth research. The real question, as David Edwards observes, "is *not* whether anthropology could or should accommodate itself to the military; it is whether the military could or should accommodate itself to anthropology."[185]

Excluding cases in which the non-permissive nature of the operational environment precluded any engagement with local civilians, the military did surprisingly well at accommodating itself to social science. Even the cigar-smoking brigade commander (whose personal ambition was to put a JDAM through a building) recognized the value of what the HTT provided. "If someone told me they were taking my HTT," he told me during an interview, "I'd have a platoon of infantry to stop them."[186] Embedding mixed/military civilian teams with military units to conduct social science research and analysis almost always provided benefits to the military. Even when individuals failed to perform as required, supported units still saw the value of social science. In the words of one Navy Seal involved with conducting civil affairs in Al Anbar, Iraq: "In IW [irregular warfare] you're not going to kill your way to victory. The HTT can bring an understanding of economic incentives, what capability is needed, what capacity can be built. We need this long view.... We've been there eight years, but it's like we're just starting. We need the knowledge about how to interact, and what to take into consideration.... Having that capability on the ground is critical. This capability is irregular warfare."[187]

Since HTS was created, the Pentagon has learned what it takes to conduct irregular warfare effectively. Great progress has been made inside DOD with funding, coordinating, and applying social science research. The Minerva Initiative, a DOD-sponsored "university-based social science basic research program," was established in 2008 to focus on "areas of strategic importance to US national security policy" and "increase the department's intellectual capital in the social sciences, improve its ability to address future challenges, and build bridges between the department and the social science community."[188] Also in 2008, DOD established the Human Social Culture Behavior (HSCB) Modeling Program under Director, Defense Research and Engineering to "understand and effectively operate in the human terrain during nonconventional warfare and other missions."[189] The Under Secretary of Defense for Intelligence (USD-I) established the Defense Intelligence Socio-Cultural Capabilities Council (DISCCC) in 2011 to develop and institutionalize socio-cultural capabilities across the Defense Intelligence Enterprise. Also in 2011, the Army Campaign Plan includes "operating and sustaining Human Terrain System (HTS) teams" and "institutionalizing the HTS capability" as Army tasks.

Despite this progress, a significant challenge remains in bridging the academic/military divide. DOD has leaned forward and extended a hand across the gap, inviting participation of civilian academics in both policy-making and operational capacities. Some social scientists have welcomed the opportunity to engage constructively or even participate directly with the military, either through the Minerva Initiative or other vehicles. This type of real experience produces real knowledge, which is the basis for "speaking truth to power." Other social scientists (such as anthropologists) have remained disengaged from the world of national security, impeded by their sacred values and content to criticize what they cannot influence. Such criticism—based on unfounded assumptions, conspiracy theories, and general ignorance— is easily dismissed, while well-informed criticism based on experience is difficult to ignore. The result for social scientists that have chosen to provide direct support of the military in theater is incontrovertible first-hand knowledge and undeniable credibility in Washington DC. Such experiences may someday enable social scientists to actually *make* policy instead of just criticizing it.

3

AN ANTHROPOLOGIST AT WAR
IN AFGHANISTAN

Ted Callahan

"What would you like me to buy for you at the store?" the Afghan National Army (ANA) commander asked, with typical Afghan generosity. We were walking abreast down a rough track that led from the village to a stream and a couple of basic shops. As I was about to answer, I noticed the dust in the road at my feet kicking up, as though large raindrops were falling upon it. In the span of the same second, I heard a number of high-pitched whizzes and, almost instantaneously, the sharp, distinctive crack of a rifle—many rifles—firing. I had the disembodied sensation of movement, though my body seemed to be moving too fast for my mind to be in control of it. I threw myself down, surrounded by the thud of bullets slamming into thick earth. I pressed my body into the ground and furiously crawled using my knees and elbows. I could see a wall ahead of me, and that wall meant safety.

Anyone who doubts the importance of luck in this world has never been in combat. As I crouched behind the wall, wondering what the hell I was supposed to do now, I heard a *thunk, thunk, thunk*—distinct from the staccato gunfire all around me—and watched my interpreter, Rex, roll down towards me like a barrel. I started to run out to him but he frantically waved me away, yelling "Too many bullets." He continued to roll, and then ran to join me behind the wall. I figured he had been shot, since he was crying, until I realized that he was laughing. "Oh, brother, *Allahu akbar* [God is great]! *Allahu akbar*!" For a few seconds, we dissolved into a fit of giggles, like a couple of schoolgirls.

When the ambush began, everyone jumped to the right except Rex and me, who went left. As we were trying to summon the courage to cross the road where we had come—literally—within inches of being killed, to rejoin the patrol, we saw three ANA soldiers coming toward us along the wall, two guys supporting a third.

The injured man, Zalmay, had what soldiers call the "million-dollar wound": severe enough to get some vacation but no permanent damage. A bullet had passed clean through Abdul's upper leg, without hitting the bone or any large blood vessels. I did a quick patient survey and then bandaged the entrance and exit wounds, each the size of a dime. The gunfire began to trail off and we could hear the rapid whump-whump of helicopters inbound. One of the American soldiers ran over and, temporarily deafened from all the gunfire, hollered, "Yo, you guys OK? How's the ANA dude?"

The ANA commandeered a pick-up truck and Rex, a massive, barrel-chested Afghan, deadlifted Zalmay over his head, placing him across his shoulders, and walked to the truck. The Afghan commander came over and apologized, saying that his present to me from the store would have to wait. He pointed out the tree line, about 300 meters distant, where he guessed some ten Taliban fighters had lain in wait for us, with a mix of AK-47s and PKMs.[1] Where, I asked, were the Taliban now? "Bah," he said, spitting on the ground and waving a hand toward the east, "where do you think? Back in Pakistan."

Minutes earlier, our patrol—six Americans and fifteen Afghans— had been talking with a group of sinewy, hard-bitten village elders covered in pine sap about mundane things: how this year's pine nut crop was looking, cross-border economic issues, and restarting the biweekly meeting between Coalition forces and local village representatives. After an hour of productive and friendly conversation, sitting outside a shabby earthen mosque in the center of a sparsely inhabited village, consisting of a number of walled compounds surrounded by emaciated livestock and equally malnourished-looking children chasing them, our respondents begged off—it was Ramadan and they had been hard at work gathering pine nuts without any food or water since dawn, so they wanted to take a nap. The fact that everyone disappeared from the few public spaces in the village so quickly should have alerted us.

Back at the base, our adrenaline still red-lining, the soldiers convened a miniature war council. This is how the conflict in Afghanistan is fought: a group of men in their early twenties, having just been shot at and narrowly surviving, must decide what to do the next day. Their first impulse—and, admittedly, mine as well—was to visit harm upon the village. But for most of these young men this was not the first time they had found themselves in this situation, and the senior non-commissioned officer (NCO) decided that the best thing would be to return the next day, to come again in peace. As Staff Sergeant (SSG) Barnes explained, "We have to show them that we're not afraid, that they [the insurgents] cannot deny us any territory." He grinned at me, adding, "You want to go back, don't you?"

The next morning was not an auspicious one. The weather threatened rain, and low cloud obscured the nearby mountains. The soldiers were told that the air—the ability of aircraft to fly—was likely to become "red" (all aircraft would be grounded), but we still had permission to conduct another dismounted (walking) patrol back to the village, Harawara.

We took a different route into the village, one that avoided coming in by the high ground we had traveled the day before, where everyone within several kilometers had been able to see us coming. Partnered again with the ANA, our patrol of twenty-seven (seven Americans and twenty Afghans) followed the nearly dry riverbed upstream. The tension was more noticeable than it had been before, almost visceral. We sprinted one at a time across open areas, eyes fixed on any potential source of cover from enemy fire. Even the Afghans, who rarely exhibited any anxiety, seemed more alert than usual.

The small villages we nervously passed were all less than a kilometer from the Pakistani border, unassuming in their simplicity yet situated atop the most dangerous frontier in the world, where insurgents freely crossed from the lawless regions of Pakistan to fight in Afghanistan. Composed of several medium-sized single-storey compounds surrounded by high walls and set amidst terraced fields of corn, they exhibited no sign of human life. The mental geography of the soldiers was based on past encounters: "They hate us in this village—no one ever talks to us when we go there. That one over there isn't as bad; at least they talk to us, but they never tell us anything." We passed a couple of farmers out in their fields, who—other than returning my *"Asalaam alaykum"* with a perfunctory *"Wa alaykum as-salaam"*—ignored us.

We reached the store, a ramshackle structure consisting of a large dirt-floored porch and a small, dimly lit interior. In the past the soldiers had found drawings in the store, mostly children's sketches of US soldiers in helicopters, annotated with slogans such as "Long live the Taliban!" and "Death to the foreigners!" They had also found this haunting poem tacked to a wall:

> If you come to my shop then don't talk about the government
> Stay tight at home and don't talk about politics.
> You smile and there is a trick in your smile
> Because you have never smiled at me in your entire life.
> Unlucky *kekar* [a short plant with large thorns] which doesn't bear flowers
> You have seen rose flowers and what do you know about it?
> If you martyr yourself for the honor of Islam
> I will sew a shroud for you with my *zalfi* [long pretty female hair]

We found the shopkeeper, Ghaffar, measuring out firewood for sale. He was an older man, stooped and wizened, with hands like coarse-grit sandpaper, yet he sported a long beard dyed flaming orange, according to the local custom. He agreed to sit down with us and talk. When asked, he disavowed any knowledge of the previous day's ambush, but acknowledged that just across the border, a few minutes away, was "the kingdom of the Taliban." Over the course of our discussion, everyone relaxed—the shopkeeper seemed at ease, there were children walking around, and we figured that we weren't going to be attacked after all. The soldiers bought some grapes and went to the stream to wash them.

There was a loud explosion, immediately followed by the sounds of combat: men yelling, gunfire, explosions. A firefight is, above all, pure chaos, especially when Afghans are involved. I cautiously looked around the corner of the shop. There was a huge plume of dust from the explosion and I could see tracer rounds flying through the air. The Americans were running uphill from the stream, since it was the lowest point of ground and formed a perfect "kill zone." I sprinted 100 meters up a steep slope and caught up with SSG Barnes just as he ducked behind a stone sheep pen, close to where we had been ambushed previously. As bullets clattered against the rock wall, Barnes looked over and, noticing me putting in hearing protection, shook his head and said, "Earplugs? You are such a pussy."

We couldn't raise the base on the radio and, anyway, the air had gone red, so we were on our own. Barnes decided that we would "bound"—leapfrogging singly or in pairs while the others provided overwatch—through the village and link up with the ANA at the far end of the streambed, where they had remained as the ambush unfolded. As we took off running, I glanced at the battlefield: mortars impacting in the forest, people yelling in at least three languages, and gunfire echoing up and down the valley, making it impossible to tell where it was coming from.

We bounded, house to house, rock to rock. By the time we ex-filtrated the village, there was hardly any sound. We rejoined the Afghans, who, having already decided that God had saved them from yet another ambush, were busy collecting their groceries, which they had dropped after the bomb detonated. It had been planted under the soft ground next to the stream, 30 meters from the shop. The Afghan metric of a successful firefight involves how many magazines each man goes through, so the walk back was filled with braggadocio as they debated who had shot the most rounds.

Swilling Gatorade back at the base, the soldiers again debated what to do the next day. This time, there was no trace of good humor, of giddy relief at having survived another day in Afghanistan, the mood that Winston Churchill captured so well, stating "Nothing in life is so exhilarating as to be shot at without result." There was only anger and frustration: "Tomorrow, we go back. Only this time, we're not going to talk about fuckin' pine nuts. We are kicking in doors, looking for weapon caches, and detaining MAMs [military-age males]."

I was scheduled to leave the next morning on a resupply flight, as I was already overdue, so in the morning, once I heard the helicopter approaching, I made my farewells and ran down to the landing zone.[2]

WHAT AM I DOING HERE?

Stories of soldiers being ambushed and shot at in Afghanistan are hardly newsworthy. Except that I am not a soldier. I am a civilian, an anthropologist, and I have no military background or training. How was it, then, that I found myself in the middle of a Taliban ambush near the Pakistani border as part of a US Army patrol?

I was a member of the Human Terrain System (HTS), a proof-of-concept program run under the auspices of the Army. HTS was developed in 2005 in response to the belated realization, two years after the invasion of Iraq, that the US military lacked the cultural knowledge to run a counterinsurgency (COIN) effectively in multi-ethnic, tribal, Muslim societies such as Iraq and Afghanistan.

As initially conceived, HTS would embed social scientists, area experts, and "bi-lingual, bi-cultural" Iraqi- (or Afghan-) Americans with combat forces at the brigade level, enabling the brigade commander as well as his subordinate forces to make culturally-informed decisions. In 2007, six Human Terrain Teams (HTTs), consisting of a team leader, social scientists, research managers, and human terrain analysts, were fielded in Iraq, and one in Afghanistan. The pool of qualified people—those who had either lived in or studied these countries, who spoke the local languages, who had an advanced academic background in a relevant discipline, and who could handle working with the military in stressful and often austere environments—was very small.[3]

I had first heard about HTS in a 2006 *New Yorker* article and was intrigued. George Packer, the author, leaned heavily on anthropology in describing the then-evolving approach to COIN, and cited anthropologist, lawyer, and Pentagon consultant Montgomery McFate's development of a program called Cultural Operations Research— Human Terrain System.[4] I found myself in agreement with McFate that anthropologists seemed to occupy a cul-de-sac in which they were just talking with each other, in increasingly esoteric terms, and had become irrelevant to policy-makers. I got in touch with McFate and was impressed when right away she warned me that any anthropologist considering employment with HTS might be forfeiting a future in academia, given the opposition to the program in academic circles. "It's really amazing, the vehemence," she sighed. I had already heard about the McCarthyish tactics of those opposed to HTS, who hounded anyone willing to break with the comfortable, disengaged orthodoxy of the academy, but still it was depressing that McFate felt it necessary to add this caveat.

During my PhD fieldwork in Afghanistan, I mostly forgot about HTS. One morning, though, while waiting for a flight in Afghanistan, I struck up a conversation with an American soldier who was flying to Farah, in the south-west. He was a member of a Provincial Reconstruction Team (PRT), a civil–military organization tasked with infrastructure development and improving governance. He asked what I was doing and I mentioned that I was an anthropologist. "Anthropologist? Really? Like you study tribes? Man, if you want to get on my flight, we can definitely put you to work."

I asked what the problem was. "We're getting crushed in Farah. We're not supposed to be on offense, but we're fighting all the time. There are these tribal issues in Farah, mostly with the Pashtuns, and we aren't trained to figure it all out. We could really use an anthropologist." As the situation in Afghanistan continued to deteriorate and my fieldwork wound down, I increasingly had the feeling that I was missing out on one of the epochal events of my lifetime, that all the action was passing me by. I got back in touch with McFate and found out that there was a training cycle slated to begin in October 2008, a few weeks after I was scheduled to return to the US.

I had reservations about the program—not least because the contractor's hiring practices suggested desperation—but I decided to participate anyway. The considerable salary was obviously a major consideration, but I also thought that HTS could help not just the US military, but the Afghans caught in the middle of the conflict as well, by giving them a proxy voice in the decision-making process. I was also angered to discover that among the many anthropologists critical of the program, none had bothered to gather any first-hand information, instead mostly relying on rumor and blogs to affirm their preconceptions. The American Anthropological Association Executive Board statement on the Human Terrain System Project, after stating that "it is important that judgments about relationships between anthropology, on the one hand, and military and state intelligence operations, on the other, be grounded in a careful and thorough investigation of their particulars" nonetheless condemned HTS, despite the lack of any "systematic study of the HTS project."[5]

That the most vocal ethical criticism came from American anthropologists in academia was not so surprising. Misled by media reports, they assumed that the program was actually hiring professional anthropologists when in fact—rather oddly—there have been relatively few in the program. Articles such as the *New York Times*' October 2007 piece, entitled "Army Enlists Anthropology in War Zones,"[6] called HTS an "anthropology program," which the critics quickly denounced as "mercenary anthropology."[7]

Perhaps uniquely, anthropologists have an uneasy relationship with the origins of their discipline, a sort of persistent, hand-wringing guilt over its colonial beginnings.[8] Many early anthropologists manipulated their relationship as colonizer to gain access to their colonized subjects, who didn't have much say in the matter, and often their findings were utilized by colonial administrators. That, combined with the fairly left-ist, anti-war bent in academia and especially anthropology, almost guaranteed opposition to HTS.

The academics' ethical concerns revolved around the issues of getting voluntary, informed consent from "research subjects"; the potential for information to be misused for "lethal targeting" (thus failing the anthropological standard of "do no harm"); and the possible branding of all anthropologists as "spies" as a result of the program.[9] Their concerns, if not just their imaginations, were further inflamed by the fact that participants in the program required a security clearance to access classified information.

I arrived in Leavenworth, Kansas in late September 2008. The HTS training was supposed to last four months but dragged on for six. When I began it, I was fit, spoke decent Dari, and had been doing field ethnography in Afghanistan for the past eighteen months. By the time it was over, I had gained 50 pounds, forgotten most of my Dari, and was enthusiastic only about leaving Kansas.

In addition to the first HTT in Afghanistan, AF1 in Khost Province, there were now five more. I assumed I would end up in Bagram or Wardak, since my Dari would be more useful in those places. HTS sent me to AF1, in eastern Afghanistan, along the border with Pakistan, where almost no one speaks Dari as a first language.

AF1 was the flagship team and enjoyed a reputation for producing the best research and setting the standard for the other HTTs. Michael Bhatia, a doctoral candidate at Oxford University who had published extensively on Afghanistan and who was one of the few highly qualified HTS researchers to deploy there, had been working on AF1 until he was killed by an improvised explosive device (IED) in May 2008.[10] Khost had a reputation as one of the worst places for IEDs, something that kept me up a few nights before I deployed.[11]

THE BASE

From Fort Benning in Georgia, I flew to Kabul via Kuwait and from there to Forward Operating Base (FOB) Salerno in Khost Province, Afghanistan. I awoke as the plane banked sharply, "cork-screwing" to lose altitude rapidly and avoid missile fire. The massive rear door opened, the pallets of ammo were unloaded, and we disembarked onto the gravel runway. We were herded to the passenger terminal, where we retrieved our duffel bags, and that was it. The wind blew dust devils along the road just outside the barbed-wire fence of the landing strip. Soldiers sprawled atop wooden benches, languidly chain-smoking cigarettes. I noticed that the air terminal, like almost every other military facility in Afghanistan, was named after someone who had died here.[12]

In addition to Khost, Paktia and Paktika comprised the three provinces that formed our host brigade's Area of Responsibility (AOR). This area, called "Loya [Greater] Paktia" in Pashto and "P2K" by the NATO-led International Security Assistance Force (ISAF), shares a border with the tribal areas in Pakistan. Most Pashtuns, on either side of the border, have tended to ignore it, moving back and forth at will. Today, the leaders of the insurgency in Afghanistan mostly live in Pakistan, where, until the advent of drone strikes, they operated with impunity. Taliban foot soldiers use Pakistani territory for medical care and as a place to rest during the traditional winter lull in fighting—a sort of jihadists' Florida.

Even within Afghanistan it has historically been regarded as "yaghistan," land of the unruly and querulous. The rebellion against the communist government in 1978, which precipitated the Soviet invasion a year later, is often said to have begun in Loya Paktia and many famous mujahideen commanders were native sons. Osama bin Laden had been very active in this area, both during and after the Soviet–Afghan War, and the Taliban had easily gained the support of the population in 1995. Having helped put a Pashtun king back on the throne in 1929, the inhabitants of Loya Paktia were rewarded with a degree of autonomy and were exempted from conscription. As a result, the Pashtuns of P2K are a very independent-minded lot and—more so than the rest of Afghanistan—have had little experience of formal government.

P2K was the battlespace of Colonel Michael Howard, the commander of the 4th Brigade Combat Team (Airborne) of the 25th Infantry Division. When I met him, a couple days after arriving, I was somewhat surprised to confront a fairly unassuming figure who wouldn't stand out anywhere. Howard was tall, whippet-thin, and had reddish hair, which he wore in an extreme crew cut. He had a slightly nasal voice, with a bit of a Southern accent, and was given to homey locutions. Howard was in his mid-forties and his most distinctive feature was his fingers, which were abnormally, almost freakishly long, and constantly in motion. But despite Howard's unmistakably martial bearing, he relaxed in the presence of civilians and from the moment we met he took to calling me "bud." He seemed somewhat amused with the odd mix of people on AF1 and liked to tease us, but he was a staunch supporter of the idea behind HTS.

FOB Salerno was nicknamed "Rocket City," owing to the frequency of mortar and rocket attacks. The base occupies what was formerly a green space outside the city of Khost, which had been nothing but orchards and gardens. It now constitutes one of the ugliest places where I have ever spent six months: row upon row of prefabricated housing, shipping containers, massive "clamshell" tents used as gyms and hangars, blast-proof concrete walls, and gravel walkways. All of this is surrounded by thousands of kilometers of barbed wire and countless HESCO barriers, wire-mesh containers lined with fabric and filled with sand, dirt, or gravel.

An ISAF base is a study in excess. Although the Europeans are allowed to have alcohol, all US bases are dry, since alcohol, as well as sex, pornography, and proselytizing are all forbidden under General Order No. 1. Those are about the only hardships. Mail arrives within a week from the US. The gyms are vast, bristling with various cardio-vascular machines. The dining facilities serve four meals a day—breakfast, lunch, dinner, midnight meal—complete with Baskin Robbins ice cream (four flavors), slices of pie (five flavors), as well as fresh fruits and vegetables. Nothing is sourced locally; everything is flown in. And nothing is recycled. Since all the drinking water comes in half-liter plastic bottles, each day about 30,000 plastic bottles are thrown away (and subsequently burned). Once a week there is "surf and turf" night, with steak, lobster, shrimp, and crab claws. (Though Afghanistan is 1,000 kilometers from the ocean, I ate more seafood there than at any other point in my life.) There are also fast food restaurants (some FOBs have begun shuttering these, due to spiking obesity), coffee shops, and massage parlors.

Most of the workers are "third-country nationals" (TCN), usually from India, Nepal, the Philippines, Eastern Europe, or Kyrgyzstan. Afghans—"host-country nationals"—work on the FOBs as well, but except for the interpreters, most do manual labor: cleaning, construction, dish washing, and laundry. Since the Afghans cannot walk unescorted on the bases due to security concerns, they are always accompanied by a TCN, so while the Afghan worker pulls weeds, a Nepali stands next to him, watching.

Were it not for the host-country nationals and the occasional rocket attack, it would have been easy to forget we were in Afghanistan at all. By Afghan standards, lowland Khost is a fairly prosperous agricultural area, but even so it is crushingly poor. Leaving the well-tended, orderly FOB was akin to entering a different world: the chaotic hustle and bustle of the East, with donkey carts carrying proud men wearing imposing grey or black turbans and their burqa-ed women sitting behind them, and everywhere the dusty, dun-colored Afghan landscape. The troops call it "going outside the wire" but that fails to convey the incredible cognitive shift required to drive outside the front gate. Yes, you were still in Afghanistan, but in a moment all the rules had changed. You were now living in a Kipling poem, where "All flesh is grass" and "The odds are on the cheaper man."

Because of the IED threat in Khost, we were required to travel in Mine-Resistant Ambush Protected (MRAP) vehicles rather than Humvees or pick-up trucks. MRAPs are basically massive blast-resistant boxes set atop a truck chassis. The hull is V-shaped, to disperse the force of a blast coming from underneath the vehicle.

MY FIRST MISSION

AF1 decided that I would learn best by doing, so I was hustled out onto the first mission that came up. We were headed out to some remote villages near the border with Pakistan, populated by Pashtun nomads, called Kuchi, who now made a living selling gas along the road.[13] The newly arrived American soldiers had not had much luck winning over the Kuchi, and security in the district seemed to be deteriorating. A few days earlier three adolescent girls, members of a South Asian gypsy tribe that roam across Central Asia, had been kidnapped, possibly raped, shot and stabbed repeatedly, and their bodies dumped on the barren plain stretching to Pakistan. One of them had been pregnant. The story was that the Taliban had taken credit for the murder, calling them "American spies." Colonel Howard wanted us to figure out whether these problems were a result of criminality, the Taliban, or tribal disputes. He also instructed us to find ways to engage constructively with the Kuchi, as the brigade knew next to nothing about them.

The drive from the combat outpost (COP) where we were temporarily staying to the border region was to take about forty minutes, mostly on dirt roads. As our four-vehicle convoy navigated a rough track, my

Peltor earmuffs—electronic hearing protection—went blank, zeroing out some loud noise. I looked at the saucer-eyed specialist across from me, unsure whether we had hit an IED, but our MRAP was still moving so I figured it wasn't that bad. "No, not us. Look!" he gestured. I glanced out the small window and in the dusk saw a smoking MRAP, the second in our convoy and the one just ahead of us.

The sergeant who had been riding shotgun came back, opened the rear door, and ordered the specialist to take a firing position. I asked what we—the interpreter and I—should do and was told, "Well, do whatever you want, I guess." We decided to hop out and then, well, we just stood there. The soldiers were arrayed along the berm, the defensive ridge of earth flanking the road, waiting for an attack similar to the one that had occurred in almost the exact spot a couple weeks before, in which an IED explosion was followed by small arms fire, or what is called a "complex attack." This being the first SIGACT (or "Significant Action," in anodyne military-speak) I'd experienced, I was keyed up with a mix of dread and eager anticipation, anxiously awaiting whatever was going to happen next. This, after a few minutes, appeared to be nothing.

The guys in the blown-up MRAP were standing around, so we walked over. "Shit. Look at what the fuckers did to my sleeping bag," one of them lamented, holding a fistful of synthetic stuffing. The soldiers tried to tow the vehicle, but the axle was snapped in half and the jagged ends kept digging into the ground. No one wanted to spend the night huddled around the busted MRAP and we all were relieved when instructions came that we should abandon it, since a wrecker was currently unavailable to tow it back to base. We stripped the MRAP, taking out most of the valuable bits, locked the door and drove off to a location the soldiers knew, a few kilometers distant.

After knocking over part of a wall in the dark on a tight stretch of road near a village, we arrived at our campsite—an open stretch of pastureland next to a flyblown Kuchi village, flanked by two small hills where overwatch elements could be placed. The MRAPs were parked in a circular formation and the soldiers, all of whom had night-vision goggles, went about their business. I lay down beside an MRAP, in body armor and all, and fell asleep under the comforting familiarity of the Afghan firmament.

I spent all the next morning watching camel caravans passing through the village and couldn't wait to find out where they were headed. To me, nothing is as evocative of the mystique of Central Asia as a group of nomads, all their possessions lashed to a procession of camels, moving across some desert waste. My romanticism evaporated as our patrol assembled to walk the 100 meters over to the Kuchi: ten combat-loaded infantrymen, two anthropologists, and two interpreters, backed up by two .50 caliber machine guns, an automatic grenade launcher, and other assorted weaponry. It felt somewhat ridiculous. We strolled over to the gas pump located in the center of the village and awkwardly stood around trying to figure out who to talk with. The village was really just a miniature bazaar bisected by the road to Pakistan, with a half-dozen small stores and open-air tea shops, most constructed of nothing more than a tarp strung up to keep the sun and occasional bit of rain off the merchandise.

The Kuchi men—no women were visible—seemed curious but maintained their distance. The inevitable scrum of Afghan children materialized, clamoring for handouts: "Meester, give me pen!" (The pen is a symbol of literacy in rural Afghanistan; highly desirable even for those who are illiterate.) The soldiers fanned out, taking up positions at each corner of the bazaar. Rex and I sauntered over to some men lounging under an awning. I greeted them in Pashto, with my right hand over my heart, shook hands all around, and asked permission to speak with them: "*Khabari, ejaaza?*" My efforts were rewarded with some gap-toothed grins and they invited us to sit and have tea. My Pashto exhausted, Rex took over, explaining that our purpose today was to gain a better understanding of the Kuchi people—where they came from, what tribe they belonged to, how they made a living, what problems they had, and what, if anything, we might be able to do to help them. He added that it was important for the American soldiers to learn such things because Afghan society was so different from that of the West and if the *kharejiyan*—the foreigners—wanted to help the Afghans, they had to understand them first.

This explanation seemed to put the Kuchis' suspicions to rest, as no doubt they were aware of the problems we had encountered with the IED the previous afternoon and likely feared that we had come looking to accost them. Sitting cross-legged in a circle of men, trying in vain to give the first cup of tea proffered to the turbaned elder on my left, I was back in the Afghanistan I knew and, forgetting myself, dawdled on pleasantries and idle chatter. One of the US soldiers shadowing me suggested I get down to business and ask about the murdered girls. No one knew anything about it, even though their bodies had been found just a few kilometers away. I asked about the Taliban but no one knew anything about them either, since "they never come through this area." This line of questioning was going nowhere, so I changed tack and asked about more innocuous things, like trade, agriculture, livestock and where the camel caravans were headed. With Rex's assistance, I explained that I had lived with nomads in northern Afghanistan for a year and so had some sense of how difficult their lives are. The men, warming to the topic, relaxed and a spirited crowd gathered, with the older men talking over one another and tsk-tsking in disagreement. I was able to steer the conversation back towards more sensitive subjects and, having grown voluble, the men catalogued the many tribal disputes afflicting their small community. Whenever I grasped some complicated idea, working through Rex as interpreter, the men raised their hands and said "*afareen*" or "well done."

I tried to use these opportunities to let the villagers ask me questions. They were endlessly fascinated by President Obama's life story, and probably better informed about him than many Americans. One thing they struggled to understand was American society: was it tribal? These soldiers—black, yellow, brown, white—were they all from different tribes? I explained that we had races instead of tribes in America, although I think they just understood that to mean that skin color, rather than lineal descent, was the basis for tribal groupings. "Obama," one man asked, "his father was a Muslim, yes? A *torpost* [black]? And his mother was *spinpost* [white]? Like Dr Abdullah [an Afghan presidential candidate of mixed parentage—half-Pashtun and half-Tajik]."

I had my Army-issue waterproof green notebook out and was furiously writing down the conversation, as Rex translated it. Another man, older and with a vaguely philosophical air, observed, "In America, there must be vast libraries filled with those little notebooks. For eight years, every American who has come here has written down everything we said and then left, never to return."

Anthropology is an inherently muddled discipline, more art than science. Despite various attempts to introduce methodological rigor, at its core it is all about asking the right questions and making sense of the answers. Working for the military made this process a bit more difficult, since I wasn't there to test a particular hypothesis, but the holistic approach that anthropologists pride themselves on was mostly the same. Accordingly, Rex and I raced through the basics: tribal affiliation, number of households, composition and size of livestock herds, crops grown, trading patterns and centers, land rights, degree of contact with the Afghan government, security issues, and a dozen other baseline questions. It was both tedious and stressful. Over six months, I would eventually get very tired of asking the same few things over and over again: "What tribe do you belong to? Is that part of such-and-such tribe? Is there a bigger tribe you are a part of? Is there a smaller sub-tribe below yours? How about below that one?" The stress came from the fact that I usually had just one shot at getting this information and afterwards I would often kick myself for having forgotten to ask or follow up on some point that was obvious in retrospect.

After perhaps two hours, I was told to get ready to walk back to camp. I had not learned anything about the dead gypsy girls or directly about the Taliban, but being able to read between the lines is an aspect of anthropological fieldwork. The disgust the Kuchis expressed toward the government spoke volumes. Like many of the Afghans I would eventually interview, their main concerns were security, justice, and development; they did not especially care who provided it, just so long as *someone* did.

That first mission taught me the central lesson of working with the military: your time is not your own, and no one regards it as a valuable commodity. This was quite a change from academia, where every professor and graduate student greedily hoards his or her every waking moment. In the military, there is no greater truism than the old saw "hurry up and wait." Plus, the Army tends to measure success based on what you did, not necessarily on what you achieved, so there is a corresponding emphasis on quantity over quality.

For example, after a morning of interviews with the Kuchi, we returned to our camp and heard that the battalion wanted to test-fire artillery close to our position. So, that afternoon, we sat around while the soldiers tried to drive a herd of sheep out of the field where the artillery rounds were due to land. Eventually, after a couple hours, the sheep were relocated and the test-fire commenced. Unfortunately, two shells failed to detonate. The battalion instructed us to guard the rounds while waiting for the explosive ordnance disposal (EOD) team. The next day, there was no sign of EOD—they were busy elsewhere. We couldn't go back to the village, or anywhere else outside our perimeter, since the force protection rules demanded that we have a minimum number of soldiers for any patrol. Walking 100 meters to the village next to us counted as a patrol, making a visit impossible since some of the soldiers had to stay behind to stare at the field. With no shade and temperatures were over 100 degrees, to get out of the sun we sat inside the MRAPS. The following day rolled around—still no EOD. Finally, late that night, they arrived, blew up the errant shells, and we decamped. Later, I did some math and realized that during a ninety-six-hour mission we conducted approximately eight hours of interviews, of which perhaps four hours produced useful information. The rest of the time was spent just trying to warm the Afghans up, writing down their answers (after de-conflicting them first), and working through the answers with an interpreter—a ratio of one hour of results for every twenty-four hours of effort.

The hardest part of the transition from training to deployment was learning what the job entailed, since training did nothing to prepare us for the reality on the ground. Most of the academics in the program had some experience with research, even if they had not done actual ethnographic fieldwork previously. All of us were used to having the luxury of time while doing research. I had always been taught that patience was the greatest virtue an ethnographer could possess. HTS was completely the opposite. On an average mission, there would be an hour available from when I exited the MRAP until I had to mount up and leave. In that hour, while taking the necessary safety precautions of establishing and working within a security perimeter, I had to find someone willing to talk to me, introduce myself, identify my purpose, establish some basic rapport, learn something about my respondent, and then, in whatever time remained, ask some focused questions. On a good day, there might be time for four or five interviews, but rarely more.

AN UNCERTAIN SUCCESS

Because we didn't have to observe any sort of grooming standard, I opted to grow a full beard. The Afghans were a little uncertain about foreign soldiers with beards. At one village, a man came up to me and asked, "Special courses?" Unsure, I replied, "Yes, I've taken some special courses, I guess." He shook his head and repeated, "Special courses?" We went through this a few times until he finally got the consonant right: "Special Forces?" The nearby soldiers guffawed, "No, not Special Forces. Hippy. Tree-hugger. Hillary Clinton. Obama." The man walked away, obviously confused.

We had the option of being armed. I ended up carrying both an M9 pistol and an M4 rifle. Initially I had trouble getting issued a M4, as there was a shortage. Five flavors of pie available everyday but a shortage of rifles says a lot about the American way of modern warfare. The rifle was more trouble than it was worth but it made the soldiers supporting me more comfortable, knowing that I could defend myself and, more importantly, support them in a firefight. As one sergeant told me, "Hell, you ain't gonna hit nothin', but at least you'll keep their heads down while we get 'em."

There was a fair bit of ethical controversy in academic circles about civilian researchers being armed. Carrying guns, the thinking went, would coerce Afghans into talking to us, thus making "voluntary consent" impossible. Obviously, none of these people had ever been to Afghanistan, since the last thing that is going to intimidate an Afghan—and especially a Pashtun male—is a gun. The few times I went out unarmed, the Afghans I interviewed invariably asked where my weapon was and, upon being told that I didn't need any since I was their guest, informed me that I was stark raving mad.

The basic disconnect between what HTS was doing and what the critics thought we were doing was that, in the case of anthropologists, they assumed that we were actually doing ethnography—spending time among the Afghans, getting to know them and winning their trust. The reality was that we were doing a sort of drive-by "windshield ethnography," hastily conducted under difficult, dangerous conditions and more akin to journalism than anthropology. It was disappointing, in light of my academic training, my prior experiences in Afghanistan, and my expectations. But given the circumstances, it was about the best that could be hoped for. Yet, while superficial by any standard of scholarship, our research was important because so little has been done in Afghanistan recently. During the ten years of the Soviet–Afghan War, research inside Afghanistan was basically impossible and remained that way during the four years of civil war that followed the Soviet withdrawal. The six years of Taliban rule weren't very conducive to scholarship either. Though the military has been on the ground for over eight years now, their numbers have been so low that even when the country was relatively secure, few systematic studies were undertaken. Now that ISAF is engaged in a counterinsurgency aimed at winning over the support of the Afghan people, in which socio-cultural knowledge is utterly crucial, most of the areas where the future of Afghanistan will be decided are essentially off-limits for any prolonged, serious study. As one Afghan who does human terrain mapping for private clients noted, "Today we have hundreds of researchers in Afghanistan but with no access. If the social scientists had been here in 2001 they would have had a lot more access. Now everyone is interested in the Pashtuns, and the Pashtuns don't want to talk with the foreigners."

Huge gaps in knowledge plagued ISAF operations, and created negative unintended consequences. Determined to do some actual research while I was in Afghanistan with the US Army, most of my six months on the ground I concentrated on the Zadran tribe. The Zadran are the largest Pashtun tribal group in the south-east, living in highland areas generally above the level of productive agriculture. During the war against the Soviets, the Zadran produced some of the fiercest fighters, including Jalaluddin Haqqani, who now leads one branch of the Taliban insurgency, a group of fighters comprising a faction called the Haqqani Network that is credited with introducing suicide bombing to Afghanistan.

Very few Zadran hold government positions and little development had occurred in Zadran areas, which is probably not a coincidence. It doesn't help that most of the "Zadran arc," as their territory is called, is remote, mountainous, and largely outside government control. Colonel Howard realized the problem inherent in having such a large population marginalized and alienated from the Afghan government, and he wanted AF1 to provide a political and economic profile of the Zadran communities. His idea, very much in the COIN mold, was that a better understanding of how the Zadran made a living and how they governed themselves would provide more focused opportunities for engagement and development. The worst thing, in Howard's opinion, would be to wall off and ignore the Zadran—something that had been tried with other tribal groups in P2K prior to his command, with predictably poor results.

My first Zadran port of call was Zerok, a small, poor district in unruly Paktika province, sitting atop several key "rat lines"—supply lines where fighters and materiel from Pakistan moved into Afghanistan. The COP in Zerok was under the highest threat level, so we could only fly in at night. Sometime after midnight, a UH-60

Blackhawk helicopter dropped down into a field while a second Blackhawk (also blacked out) flew in circles above us looking for threats. "OK, this is you. Have fun," the door gunner cheerily told us as he heaved our packs to the ground. A few soldiers pushed past us, climbed in, and immediately the Blackhawk lifted up and disappeared into the blackness. Rex and I walked into the COP, found some empty bunks, and fell asleep.

I got up the next morning and went looking for coffee. Walking out of the sandbagged hooch, I was stunned to see forests stretching off in every direction. With my coffee in hand, I climbed up into one of the four guard towers posted on each corner of the COP. The soldiers did shifts and the young specialist, despite just having begun his, was already bored and happy to have some company. While we talked, a truck filled with timber slowly bounced along the dry riverbed which snaked down from a series of forested mountains. The specialist told me that several of these trucks went by everyday, but he had no idea where the wood came from or where it went.

Everyone on the COP knew that timber was a big deal here, but no one had any details: who owned the forests, how much wood they cut, where the timber was sold, how much they made per truckload, and whatnot. It was an obvious starting point for my research and had the benefit of being a fairly innocuous topic, one not likely to elicit much suspicion.

During one interview with a local villager, I pointed at the uncut forests and asked why they only cut trees further away. "Those are *jalghoza* [a species of pine, *Pinus gerardiana*] forests. No one is allowed to cut the *jalghoza* trees, and if they do, they will pay a fine. Right now, our young men are up in the forests, guarding the *jalghoza* trees." Since the soldiers at COP Zerok had only been here for a few months, and never during pine nut season, they had no clue what this meant. Neither did I, but Rex could see that I was interested, so he took it upon himself to ask the villagers a series of questions. He then explained to me that every fall, the villagers go into the *jalghoza* forests and collect mature pine cones. The women then beat the pine cones with rocks until the pine nuts are disgorged. The nuts (seeds, actually) are gathered, dried, and then transported to the nearest city and from there throughout Afghanistan, where they are sold as a delicacy. For the villagers, pine nuts were an economic mainstay. Knowing this explained why the villagers grew so angry when artillery was fired into the *jalghoza* forests for target practice. The Americans might just as well have been burning their crops.

During the course of my research, I became somewhat obsessed with pine nuts, and this was something of a joke with the brigade. I jumped at every opportunity to visit pine nut producing areas and often watched the soldiers pulling guard duty wilt with boredom as I discussed pine nut minutiae with the villagers. I even delayed my redeployment back to the US so that I could stay for the pine nut season. Researching the Zadran was how I imagined HTS would be, allowing me to go out into remote places and do valuable research. Caught up in my Lawrence of Arabia daydreams, I also took some stupid risks. We nearly lost an entire patrol during two ambushes in Harawara, trying to learn about the pine nut harvest. Another time, while visiting a dangerous Zadran district for the presidential election, I went out with just a couple Afghan policemen (and no radios) as an escort, in violation of common sense as well as the force protection rules.

After several weeks of research in the field, involving trips to more than a dozen different Zadran villages and many hours of fitful, persistent interviewing, I discovered that the Zadran were being approached by ISAF and the PRT as typical Afghan peasants who made a living from farming, even though the average Zadran household only met about 30 percent of its annual subsistence needs through agriculture. The other 70 percent came from income derived from selling timber and harvesting pine nuts, which are specific to the forested mountains where the Zadran dwell. Since the problem with agriculture was that the average household plot was too small to produce much in the way of crops, having been divided over several generations as inheritance, the solution to their economic problems seemed to be in boosting their income from timber and pine nuts.

No one from the military realized how the pine nut harvest worked, or how important it was in the Zadran villagers' economy. During the month of September, entire families would head off into the mountains to collect the nuts, staying out for several nights at a time. Because such camps would be almost indistinguishable from small bands of insurgents, the danger was that the military would mistake the Zadran pine nut gatherers for insurgency and shoot them inadvertently. I briefed the brigade on what the Zadran were actually doing up there in the mountains. They listened and acted on what I had told them: the brigade sent word to all pilots and subordinate units that pine nut season was approaching and that they should be especially cautious not to mistake pine nut parties for insurgents.

The Special Forces team operating out of FOB Salerno got wind of this and asked me to come by and brief them. It was a little unusual, for while the SF guys liked to hang out with the girls on our team—and vice versa—they rarely asked us for assistance with anything. I suspected that this was at least partially due to pride; after all, SF liked to bill themselves as "armed anthropologists" and were perhaps a little unsure about encountering the real thing. I walked over to their compound, easily identified by a sign saying, "If you don't know what this place is then you have no business here." The team leader explained that they were going to be doing night missions in parts of one mountainous district more or less controlled by the Taliban and they were worried about stumbling into pine nut gathering parties. It wasn't clear whether their concern was civilian causalities or having their mission compromised, but I explained how the harvest worked. "So, at night, how are we going to know whether we've got a family or a bunch of bad guys in front of us?" one of them asked. Fortunately for them, the smell of pine sap is overwhelming and a typical group of harvesters would be covered in it. I also described the tools they would be carrying, and mentioned that they would most likely have some donkeys along to use as beasts of burden. They seemed satisfied that any risk of civilian casualties could be mitigated and that was the last I heard of it.

Before leaving, I drafted a basic plan to stimulate an export industry for pine nuts. Similar initiatives, often under the rubric of "alternative livelihoods" to wean farmers away from growing opium, had developed around pomegranates and saffron. I identified the parts of the value chain where value-added processing could occur in Afghanistan and found a few Pakistani pine nut exporters who sourced at least some of their product from Afghanistan. There was great potential. A kilogram of pine nuts wholesaled for $3 in Afghanistan, and retailed for about $5. In the United States, a kilogram might sell for $45.

I worked with the US Department of Agriculture representative to design a plan for the US Agency for International Development (USAID), as well as the brigade's Provincial Reconstruction Team (PRT) and Agribusiness Development Team (ADT), in the hope that they would focus on reforestation. Because rapid population growth combined with a lack of economic diversification had resulted in the forests being overexploited, and already there were large swathes of barren land where all the trees had been cut, reforestation was key to the Zadrans' well-being. I also identified the major areas where timber was transported and sold to merchants from throughout southern and eastern Afghanistan. The paving of the main roads in this area threatened to accelerate deforestation, since better roads would improve market access, a problem that USAID, which was funding the project, hadn't anticipated. The USAID representative just shook her head, mumbling, "In Afghanistan, no good deed goes unpunished."

THE SOLDIERS AND THE NEW WAR

Aside from all the difficulties of doing research in Afghanistan—the insecurity, the remoteness, the jadedness of most rural Afghans—another issue was our parasitic relationship with the soldiers. The HTTs had no life support of their own: no vehicles, food, water, shelter, or, aside from our rifles and pistols, weapons. We were entirely dependent on the unit to support us, in terms of men and materiel. While there was no question that the soldiers in the unit would follow orders and do what they had to, I had been advised by the team to get "buy-in" from the start: find some little vexing issue that had been bothering them and fix it; or quickly figure out something that they didn't know which would be useful.

While this made sense, it was a little surprising, since I had been told essentially the same thing by an anthropology professor about how to ingratiate myself with the community I was studying. "Find some demonstration piece," he told us, "something that will get their attention and illustrate what you are trying to do." It was interesting to conceptualize our relationship this way: we were there to study the Afghans, but since we couldn't live among them as a traditional ethnographer would, we had this intermediary, the military, acting as our host. And, as in most ethnographic situations, we depended upon them for nearly everything, but the relationship was mostly one-sided, since there was not much we could give back. The only currency we traded in was knowledge.

It was not always easy to convince the solders supporting me—often putting their lives on the line—that it was worth the effort and the risk, and, had any of them died during one of my missions, I wouldn't have been able to justify it. I decided the easiest way to convince them was to say something along the lines of "Hey, you've been to this village a half-dozen times and nothing's changed—you guys haven't found out much, there's no rapport, nothing is happening. This time, we'll go out again but instead of coming back empty-handed, we'll have learned something, established a better relationship, and maybe mapped out a way forward." Sometimes I was derided as an idealistic, Afghan-loving hippy; more often, I was given the benefit of the doubt that it might be worthwhile. But always I was worried that something would happen and I would be faced with the question of "What did so-and-so die for?"

That is perhaps the hardest part of COIN. Soldiers are perfectly willing to die to gain or defend some piece of territory; much less so to "win over the population." In a counterinsurgency, however, the population matters far more than any piece of territory and so, in a sense, dying while trying to win over the population is arguably more important than any pitched battle. Still, no soldier wants his epitaph to read, "Died in the service of his country while supporting the collection of social science data to provide a more robust socio-cultural understanding of the human terrain."

Collectively, the soldiers were not hugely sold on counterinsurgency. COIN is often misrepresented in the popular media as a strategy, whereas in reality it is a tactic. The soldiers understood this and regarded COIN in the same way that they did calling in an airstrike: something you do to accomplish your objective. As a result, COIN was viewed along a scale: some people did more of it, some less. Usually it was understood to be talking to Afghans. Despite the myth of the culturally-insensitive American soldier (while undoubtedly true in some cases), most soldiers tried to act respectfully toward the Afghans. Plus, most had experience from Iraq, interacting with local nationals and conducting what the military euphemistically calls "key leader engagements" to describe almost any encounter with the locals. However, the average combat soldier in Afghanistan is probably on his first or second deployment there, knows none of the language and little about the culture, and likely views talking with Afghans more as a chore than anything else. Afghans, attuned to social nuance, pick up on this and as a result the encounters have a very scripted quality: the soldiers ask the questions they're required to, the Afghans politely feign ignorance of any insurgents in their area but mention some pressing development needs, the soldier writes these down, both sides shake hands, and part ways.

113

It was not my place to lecture the soldiers. Their job was far more dangerous than mine and, unlike me, they had no choice where they went, what they did, and when they could stop. Almost every day they were handed stupid, thankless tasks, including escorting me to some village, and they did it mostly without complaint. Interacting with Afghans was not what most of them had signed up for and certainly not what they had been trained to do. If anything, they were far better prepared to kill Afghans than to talk with them. Occasionally, their frustration would boil over.

One day, we returned from a patrol that had failed to generate much useful information about anything—just a series of terse, monosyllabic replies to any question, no matter how basic. The people in the bazaar we had visited were obviously too intimidated to offer much more than a series of curt answers, even to the most mundane questions. One local whispered to our interpreter, "The Taliban are close. They are watching you right now. Be careful." The soldiers were on edge, which made the Afghans more nervous, which made the soldiers even more taut. I, mindful that the presence of our patrol in the bazaar was the problem, suggested that we leave.

Later, sitting in the COP's tactical operations center, surrounded by laptops and numerous monitors showing video feeds from all the cameras outside the COP, one NCO asked me, as we cleaned our rifles (a daily ritual, and a surprisingly social one), "So, did you get anything good today?"

"Um, not really. They seemed pretty scared in that town. No one wanted to talk. Hopefully we can go back again." I answered.

"You see?" he said. "All this COIN stuff is bullshit. It doesn't work. We need to do it like the Russians did." Trying to bait me, he added, "We need to start throwing motherfuckers off rooftops."

"Yeah," another chimed in. "Throw motherfuckers off buildings. That would turn this thing around fast. What do you think about that, Mr HTT?"

"I think I've never seen a building higher than two storeys in this whole province," I deadpanned. "I'm not sure how well that will work."

Since the insurgency in Afghanistan is fundamentally a political problem—in the sense of who gets what, when, and how—there is no military solution. While it might have been more gratifying for these soldiers to try a more aggressive approach—kicking in doors, searching houses for weapon caches, arresting suspected insurgents—the Soviets demonstrated pretty much conclusively that such actions will just galvanize public opinion against foreign forces and generate even more insurgents.[14] Counterinsurgency, with its emphasis on securing the population and addressing their core needs, is how ISAF now intends to approach the problem. In the COIN environment, knowledge is everything, yet most of the maneuver troops in these areas aren't trained to ask the right questions, if they have any COIN-specific training at all. More often, they are mission-focused, but COIN doesn't lend itself to task-oriented behavior. Thus, there are two main issues: convincing the rank-and-file military that COIN is what, if anything, will defeat the insurgency; and equipping them with the tools to do so.

Human Terrain Teams, unlike soldiers, are able to devote their energy entirely toward understanding the Afghan population—and, unlike most soldiers, are actually interested in doing so. HTTs have no other responsibilities and little to distract them from this key task. However, to provide enough value to justify the time and effort required to get them into the field, they too need to be asking the right questions. While HTS invariably requires a huge amount of on-the-job learning, people coming in with no knowledge of Afghanistan or without a basic ethnographic framework spent most of their time trying to develop these core competencies, rather than producing useful research. Many of the HTS reports produced by other teams that I saw were either only slightly more informative than a Google search or else aspired to scientific rigor by couching simple conclusions in long-winded academic discourse.

Given unlimited time and resources, such navel-gazing might not be a problem. But because opportunities to interact with Afghans outside the wire are so limited, there is a huge premium on being able to elicit relevant, useful information in a short time, sometimes just a few minutes. Additionally, a typical HTS deployment is nine months on average, which does not leave a lot of time to pick up all the requisite skills while on the job. Furthermore, a number of people within HTS seemed to have an aversion to going on missions, and invented reasons to stay on-base. Whenever he saw us too frequently on the base, Colonel Howard would casually ask, "How are things coming along? Remember, you're no use to me sitting around this FOB."

Colonel Howard understood our mission and did his best to ensure that we had what we needed. Other members of the military, however, often did not seem to realize that getting the kind of in-depth information they expected us to have requires considerable time, irrespective of expertise. If they were not willing and able to support us, then there was little we could give back to them. Occasionally, on AF1, we could get units dedicated to supporting our missions, sometimes for as long as a few days, but more often we just rode along and used whichever opportunities arose to learn whatever we could about wherever we were.

Even when we were supported, we had to contend with the glacial pace of the average mission, especially if there was any driving involved. First, the mission would have to be conceived and submitted to commanders for approval. Then, on the day of the mission, various preparations would need to happen before we could leave. By the time we got out the gate, I had usually spent about three hours sitting around, and sometimes we would have to drive three more hours just to reach our destination. By this point, the soldiers were often bored and antsy to get back to base for "taco night," meaning less time for interviews. We would drive back, have a debriefing, and then I would type up my notes. A ratio of one hour of interviews for ten to twelve hours of effort is inevitably going to be slow to produce results, but the catch was that without results, getting anyone to approve subsequent missions became less likely.

The inherent paradox of "combat ethnography" is that the longer I talked with the villagers, the more time the Taliban had to set an ambush or plant an IED. The more cursory my conversations were with the Afghans, the less likely it was they would want to talk to me or any other foreigner again, since they were already fatigued from numerous other superficial and unproductive discussions. An Afghan population frustrated by several years of unmet expectations combined with our constrained access meant that we were unable to develop the most crucial element of ethnography: trust. In Afghanistan, trust is only bred from familiarity, and perhaps not even then. In my case, I rarely visited the same place twice and never for any length of time, so I was unable to develop the kind of personal relationships I enjoyed, and relied upon, during my fieldwork in the north. Without these relationships, I was lucky even to begin to understand what I saw around me. Given the rapidly deteriorating security in Afghanistan, it is unlikely that HTTs will be able in the near term to adopt an ethnographic approach involving participant observation rather than just random, cursory interviews. If such an in-depth model were somehow possible, then the ethical concerns of the academic anthropologists would be very valid. But right now, HTS bears as much resemblance to serious anthropology as passport pictures do to photography. Nonetheless, programs like the Human Terrain System hold great potential in a complex and exceedingly unfamiliar place like Afghanistan. Not by enabling a more benign occupation or a more efficient colonization, as critics of the military's relationship with social science would have it, but by trying to bridge two worlds: that of the rural Afghans and that of the international military forces. Without understanding the economy of an Afghan village, it will be impossible to bring material benefit to the people living there. Without understanding Afghan society, it is more likely that well-intentioned but misguided attempts to "win over the population" will fail, to everyone's detriment. For example, during a speech in London, General Stanley McChrystal, then commander of ISAF, noted:

> In Afghanistan, things are rarely as they seem, and the outcomes of actions we take, however well-intended, are often different from what we expect... For example, digging a well sounds quite simple. How could you do anything wrong by digging a well to give people clean water? Where you build that well, who controls that water, and what water it taps into all have tremendous implications and create great passion. If you build a well in the wrong place in a village, you may have shifted the basis of power in that village. If you tap into underground water, you give power to the owner of that well that they did not have before, because the traditional irrigation system was community-owned. If you dig a well and contract it to one person or group over another, you make a decision that, perhaps in your ignorance, tips the balance of power, or perception thereof, in that village.[15]

FAREWELL

I left FOB Salerno in early October. As the military cargo plane lifted off Salerno's gravel runway, just like that, it was gone, my world for six months: the Zadran, IEDs, helicopter rides, Rex, guns, MRAPs, pine nuts. Before I departed, I was given the Commander's Award for Civilian Service. As was customary, I had to give a short speech to the assembled brigade staff, standing next to the imposing figure of Colonel Howard. While he ad-libbed my contributions to the brigade, I felt the most emotional that I had in all my six months at Salerno: relieved to be going home in one piece, disappointed that I wasn't staying longer, guilty that I was free to leave when everyone else in the room had no choice but to stay for another several months, and, most poignantly, acutely embarrassed at being the center of attention in this room full of stern warriors, men (mostly) who ended every meeting with a salute and—in the unselfconscious way that only soldiers could pull off—a collective declaration that "Sparta Lives," the brigade maxim.

I understood the military somewhat by this point—better, probably, than I understood the Afghans—and began with a ribald quotation from Napoleon: "In war, as in prostitution, amateurs are often better than professionals." Once the laughter died down, I explained that even though my job was to impart what knowledge I could gather about the population to the soldiers, in reality they had taught me far more that I had been able to teach them. All I dealt with were facts, things that anyone with a certain amount of knowledge and motivation could have found out. What the soldiers showed me were values, the ideas of sacrifice, valor, and loyalty, as they went about doing a hard, dangerous job with a minimum of drama. As ever with anthropology, it was a one-sided exchange.

4

WHAT DO YOU BRING TO THE FIGHT?

A YEAR IN IRAQ AS AN EMBEDDED SOCIAL SCIENTIST

Katherine Blue Carroll

Serving as a social scientist on a Human Terrain Team (HTT) in Baghdad from April 2008 to April 2009 was the most rewarding and challenging professional experience of my life. When everything falls into place, the work of an HTT social scientist brings together all the best elements of an academic job. In Iraq I taught the soldiers around me through formal briefings, casual conversations, and responses to their many questions. They were attentive students with a compelling reason to be interested in the material, and of course they brought their own fascinating experiences and ideas to the "classroom." I also conducted research for brigade commanders who often acted like good graduate advisors, finding the overlap between my own interests and the gaps in current theory or generating questions from their bird's-eye view of the battlefield and tasking me with answering them. Being on an HTT also gives you thrilling and sometimes overwhelming access to information. Three years after returning from Iraq I am still not tired of talking, teaching, and writing about what I learned there.

This chapter is an account of some of my work as an HTT social scientist. Because each HTT was operating quite differently based on the command culture of their brigade, the characteristics of their area of operations, and their own skills and leadership, I am not suggesting that my experience can be generalized. In addition to describing the types of questions I was asked and the research processes through which I worked to answer them, I have also tried here to capture some of the lessons I learned about how to be an embedded social scientist. The chapter presents three cases of work I did for three different brigades. While I consider these cases to have been my successes, I could just as easily have described and drawn lessons from my failures.

THE QUR'AN SHOOTING

My first HTT assignment was with a brigade located in Baghdad's south-west Rashid district, a mixed-sect area encompassing well-to-do professional neighborhoods (Jihad, Saydiyah, and Doura), poorer enclaves (Abu Dsheir), and farmland (Radwaniyyah). The district had experienced some of Baghdad's worst sectarian violence during 2006 and 2007. Al-Qaeda's struggle to take the neighborhood of Doura was famously bloody, as was the sectarian cleansing of the military and Baathist neighborhood of Jihad.[1] When I arrived in April 2008 the area was experiencing more violence than any other area of Baghdad except Sadr City, where the Mahdi Army militia was winding down its rocket campaign against the International Zone (IZ). In the Rashid district the brigade was targeted by both IEDs and occasional indirect fire, and while al-Qaeda had been suppressed in Doura and Radwaniyyah, the Mahdi Army was still actively intimidating the population in Shi'a areas.

I had deployed early from training and without a team, arriving at the Forward Operating Base (FOB) where the brigade was based at night after an exhilarating ride in a helicopter from the Baghdad airport. "Thank God you are here," my team leader said as we met on the landing zone, and I remember responding "Why?" I was serious. In three months of training at Fort Leavenworth I had learned a lot of acronyms, a great deal about counterinsurgency, some things about anthropological research methods, and a little about how a brigade operated and structured itself on the ground, but while I knew *theoretically* why I might be useful, I had no inkling of how that theory would actually apply.

On my first day in the office my team leader and I met with the brigade commander and explained our team's capabilities. My team leader stressed my background studying and living in the Middle East. We had talked a lot during training about the difficulties of breaking through to the brigade, particularly to the commander, so I remember his response clearly. The brigade commander looked at me skeptically and said, "We had several days of cultural training at the University of Texas before deploying, so I'm not really sure how we can use you." This was not auspicious. The team had been doing useful work, the team leader told me as we headed back to the office, but was not getting real taskings from the staff. This was perhaps, he said, because he was a full colonel, which might make it hard for the staff to direct him.

One morning I arrived to find the brigade headquarters unusually quiet. "Something is up," my team leader said as we sat down at our computers. The brigade's Public Affairs Officer (PAO) stuck his head in our door and told us that one of the soldiers had shot a Qur'an. "What can we do to help you?" we asked. He replied that they had it all under control—but were hoping there would not be rioting or additional attacks. As he left he handed us a copy of the statement that the brigade planned to release. It said something like, "our condolences to the people of Radwaniyyah on this unfortunate incident," as if there were no responsible party. The press release was terrible, but for me it was also terrible that a major cultural incident had happened and the staff had not even considered informing us, much less asking us for help. We agreed that we should re-write the statement, even if it was too late. When we talked to the PAO he told us that they had already scrapped it, but still needed nothing from the HTT.

Throughout the day the facts of the shooting came out. It had happened a day or two earlier on a range outside a police station in Radwaniyyah. The shooter was a sniper and a staff sergeant. He had put the Qur'an up as a target and shot it fourteen times. Then he took it down and wrote something vulgar (either "F#$%^ Yeah" or "F#$%@ You") on it and left it outside the police station for the Iraqis to find. Apparently, local leaders asked for an emergency meeting with the battalion and company commanders in the area, during which they informed the soldiers about the incident and warned them that someone had told the Minister of the Interior and the media. Things, the Iraqis said, could potentially get very, very bad. They stressed that the keys to avoiding disaster would be a speedy apology and real accountability for the soldier. He was ultimately relieved of duty, officially reprimanded and returned to the US.[2]

121

My team leader's view was that this kind of thing happened when soldiers got bored. And in fact Radwaniyyah had been calm for months, as a company commander in the area stressed to me in a discussion after the shooting. Iraqis, he said, were starting to come to the combat outposts in the area to complain, not of al-Qaeda, but that men who had once promised to marry their daughters had since changed their minds and needed a little push from the American forces to live up to their agreements.

The Qur'an shooting was ultimately taken so seriously that planning the response was pushed up to the highest levels at the Department of Defense, though in fact it probably closely followed the course of action that local leaders had advised. A formal ceremony of apology was held in Radwaniyyah involving company, battalion, brigade, and division leadership. The division commander read a letter of apology from the shooter and issued his own apology: "In the most humble manner I look in your eyes today and I say please forgive me and my soldiers."[3] Local leaders were promised millions of dollars of projects, including restoring irrigation canals, building a new government center, fixing a medical clinic and several schools, rebuilding several roads and bridges, and providing more electrical generators.[4] The brigade commander gave the people of Radwaniyyah a new Qur'an, which he presented in the proper way, kissing it and touching it to his forehead, an act for which he was criticized by some on the political far right in the US.[5]

At every level of American–Iraqi contact, apologies were made. Soldiers in Radwaniyyah visited Iraqi checkpoints and even sometimes went from house to house apologizing.[6] The brigade and battalion commanders for the area met with as many other leaders as they could—sheikhs, district and neighborhood council members, religious authorities—one-on-one to deliver personal apologies. Ultimately President Bush even called Prime Minister Maliki personally to apologize.[7]

The brigade issued talking points for soldiers that stressed responsibility and reconciliation. Soldiers were to tell Iraqis that they were sorry for the offensive and disrespectful act, that it went against soldiers' respect for those with different beliefs; that the soldier, having committed a crime, would be dealt with justly and quickly; and that the Iraqis should not let the actions of one soldier damage the positive relationship that the Coalition and Iraqis had worked so hard to build. Flyers distributed throughout the area urged reconciliation and lauded the benefits of presenting grievances in a peaceful manner.

All of this worked. There were protests in Afghanistan in response to the news of the shooting, and three people died, including a NATO soldier. But Iraq, and especially Radwaniyyah, remained calm. Months later in north-west Baghdad, sheikhs would say to me that Americans had learned a lot since 2003 and that the way we handled the Qur'an shooting was especially good. At home, too, the military's quick and comprehensive response was lauded by a diverse set of bloggers and editorialists.[8]

We on the HTT were not told about all these plans to respond to the incident at the time, only that things were under control. But I was determined to find a way that we could contribute. I thought of the soldiers being told to apologize and wondering, probably, what exactly they were apologizing for. Of course they understood that Iraqi Muslims would be upset if someone disrespected their religion and also that to do so put everyone at risk and empowered militias. But for the Iraqis to be so upset over what Americans saw as an act of personal idiocy was doubtless mystifying and irritating to many soldiers. The brigade did not need help with *what* to do, but they needed help in better understanding *why* they had to do it. They needed a better understanding of how the Qur'an shooting made Iraqis feel. I decided that this required an understanding of how the Muslim relationship to the Qur'an as a physical object differed from the Christian relationship to the Bible as a physical object.

I have studied Islam, but I am a political scientist and perhaps not the best qualified person to deal with religious issues. So I began my research on the issue of Bibles and Qur'ans as objects by reading academic articles and book chapters on the subject through my university's library online. The types of cultural, political, and social information that brigades need from their HTTs is normally very local and thus not available outside military sources or discussions with people on the ground. However, for broad cultural or political questions I liked to start with this background reading, which at the very least helped me prepare questions for others. The next step in my research process was to email a colleague who teaches Islam to ask for help. He responded quickly with a scan of Chapter 1 of Farid Esack's book *The Qur'an; a User's Guide* (2005) and his own helpful thoughts on the subject. Afterwards, emailing experts I found by searching academic databases and conference proceedings became a regular part of my research process. To be sure I knew what needed emphasis and what was already widely known about Qur'ans, I also walked the halls of the brigade chatting with soldiers. Finally, I ran a draft of my piece by the brigade chaplain both out of courtesy and also to hear his views on how I had dealt with the Christian relationship to the Bible.

The document I produced from this research, innocuously titled "Muslims and Qur'ans," proposed that Muslim feelings about the Qur'an were more like Christian feelings about the person of Christ than about the Bible. Just as Christ was for the Christian community, so the Qur'an is the charter of the Muslim community, calling it into existence. Christians see Christ as "the Word of God made flesh." This parallels how Muslims see the Qur'an itself, which is the Word of God made text. The Qur'an is not a text tainted by human intervention, but the actual speech of God, perfect in form, style, and language and very, very sacred. (Of course some Christians also feel this way about the Bible, as I was reminded by one of the brigade's Iraqi Christian interpreters.) And many Muslims believe that the Qur'an can intercede for people on the Day of Judgment, as Christians believe that Christ can. When I presented my draft document to the brigade's chaplain, he marked through the line in which I had written that an attack on the Qur'an might feel for Muslims something like an attack on the person of Christ would feel for Christians. "That cannot be true," he said, looking horrified. His reaction confirmed my suspicion that the analogy might help open a window of empathy in the minds of American soldiers, at least those who understood Christianity and were willing to consider what I was saying.

I was anxious as my team leader released the document to the brigade, but the next morning I passed the brigade's main bulletin board and was thrilled to see a copy of my piece posted there with a sign saying that all soldiers in Radwaniyyah were ordered to read it. (If you are not a professor then you probably cannot understand how gratifying it is that people have been *ordered* to read something.) In the office my team leader congratulated me: the brigade was talking about the document.

As a result, we started to get more questions, and the soldiers on the staff began to engage me more about substantive issues. A colleague on the HTT (an analyst) and I were invited to visit each of the combat outposts in Radwaniyyah to give a presentation to the soldiers there. We agreed not to mention the Qur'an shooting unless a soldier brought it up. Instead we updated the soldiers on the current national political dynamics, highlighting the increasing integration of Sunnis into the political process and how this had been made possible by the calm in predominantly Sunni areas like Radwaniyyah. Our goal was to educate and to help alleviate their boredom and frustration by showing them the role they were still playing in the fight to consolidate Iraq's democracy. My team leader and I were also asked to contribute to a presentation on the structure of the Iraqi government and to do an orientation briefing for an incoming Civil Affairs company. A soldier stopped by and asked if I would give a training presentation to his unit on what to expect out in the area of operations. This presentation, called "A Day in Iraqi Life," traced what an "average" Iraqi day had been like before 2003. The research for it drew on information from interviews with Iraqi interpreters and staff on the FOB (especially those who were from the area) and with other Iraqis I talked with on the streets out in the area of operations.

We were still not getting direct taskings from the staff, but a few months later the brigade was faced with the looming status of forces agreement and a resulting shift to warrant-based targeting. As the staff struggled to figure out the Iraqi courts and criminal justice system in our area of operations, I saw an opportunity. This was a job for a political scientist. I went to the brigade's operations officer and offered our services on the project, and he accepted. That same week the staff forwarded a fake draft evaluation of the HTT to us. It said, "The HTT contributes to our mission despite the fact that Professor Carroll clearly earned her doctorate from a Cracker Jack box." This gentle mockery meant that I had been accepted into the brigade community.

I ended up leaving the Rashid district and moving to work with another brigade before I could begin the judicial system project, but the Qur'an shooting incident represented, for me, the foot in the door we needed with the brigade staff. My sense was that my very small contribution opened their eyes to ways that we could be useful and also helped break down barriers between them and me, the new social scientist, especially. Of all the events in south-west Baghdad in the summer of 2008, it would seem that the Qur'an shooting would be the moment when the HTT would be *least* likely to have to find a way to be relevant. But it was the frustration of not being called upon at all at a such an "HTT moment" that made me determined to find a way to contribute, and it also made me willing to go out on a limb and put information out that was outside my direct area of expertise. I knew that the brigade's positive reception of the document stemmed at least in part from the fact that they were in a crisis, taking what help they could get. But I think they also appreciated the empathy that the "why" over the "what" approach showed. I certainly did not want to be the condescending professor who acted as if the soldiers needed me to tell them not to shoot Qur'ans.

The lesson of the Qur'an shooting incident for me as an embedded social scientist was that even when you are not asked to do so, you must find a way to contribute. You want people to feel that something is missing if they have not heard from the HTT. The Qur'an shooting incident also taught me to draw soldiers into our research process wherever possible. This ensured that we did not stray too far from what they, as end-users, needed, but also gave them a vested interest in our success. When I asked a member of the brigade staff about, for example, the kinds of situations in which they encountered Qur'ans, that soldier wanted our final product to be read because his or her thoughts were included in it. I always approached soldiers in my actual status—as someone new to the military who wanted to understand their needs so that I could find a way to help them.

THE PROVINCIAL ELECTIONS

In August 2008 I moved to be the social scientist for an HTT attached to a brigade in north-west Baghdad. A friend from training in Fort Leavenworth was the team leader, so I was happy about the move. The brigade's area of operations, which stretched from the Tigris in the east out to the edge of Abu Ghraib *qada* (rural district) in the west, seemed on the basis of the size and quality of houses there more affluent overall than the Rashid district. But it was also a mixed district whose inhabitants suffered from the same problems as their southern neighbors.

Soon after my arrival my team leader and I sat down with the brigade commander to discuss what I would be doing. After I had introduced myself the commander turned to me and asked, "What do you think you should work on? What do you bring to the fight?" I had recently become interested in the Iraqi police—in trying to understand the social make-up of the various police units in the area and how this affected their vulnerability to militia influence. I pitched this project enthusiastically, but I could immediately see he had other plans. "You are a political scientist," he said. "We've got an important election coming up—the provincial elections—and I need you to work on that." What he wanted, primarily, was for me to map potential areas of violence associated with the elections so that he could allocate his resources on the ground in the best way to keep them secure. Although the US military was working closely at all levels with the Department of State, and although Multi-National Division—Baghdad had many political advisors, information about election procedures was not reaching the brigade quickly enough for my brigade commander. And almost no comprehensive information on the political dynamics of the various personalities and parties was provided to the brigade from any source. Even if this information had been available, its specific implications for our area of operations would not have been clear. The brigade needed someone to pull together a picture of the whole political landscape, including up-to-date procedures, competitive dynamics, and how all this would affect north-west Baghdad specifically. I walked out of the meeting on air: I had been waiting a long time for a direct tasking from someone, and now I had one from a brigade commander.

My team leader and I sat down and developed a research plan through which we hoped to answer the commander's question. To start we would map political party offices, politicians' homes, and other political buildings in the area. My team leader arranged for an order to go out to the battalions to send in locations ('grids,' in military terminology) and photos for party offices and politicians' homes that they knew of. I would also interview politicians and the heads of political parties and ask them how they felt about their security and the competitive environment. The brigade assigned me an interpreter who had been in Iraq with the US military since 2003. Unlike most of our interpreters and HTT analysts, she had left Iraq not in the 1970s but in the 1990s, which meant she had a better understanding than they did of the Iraq we invaded in 2003. I moved to a FOB at the edge of the International Zone (IZ), where she lived, and she and I dug through her wooden box full of Iraqi business cards, pulling out those of politicians and cold-calling them, asking for meetings.

My interpreter and I settled into a rhythm over the next two months. Every day that we could we had a meeting, or multiple meetings, with political actors. Sometimes these were at their homes or party headquarters, and in these cases one of the brigade's units would accompany and secure us. (Once when we arrived for a meeting at the offices of a political party that had evolved from the Sunni insurgency, soldiers who happened to be passing by on the other side of the building told us that as we pulled up in front people were streaming out the back door and running down the street.) More often we met with people at the Rashid Hotel, to which we could drive ourselves. We would set up camp some days in the Rashid lobby having meeting after meeting with the politicians gathered there. Registration was open for coalitions, and so every day the lobby reflected a new constellation of party leaders sitting together hashing out barriers to running on a common list.

When we had a spare moment between our scheduled appointments we would just walk up to people and ask them if they would be willing to chat with us about the elections, their lives, or whatever they felt like. I rarely took notes in these impromptu meetings but used them for "atmospherics," and to expand my network of Iraqi contacts. Eventually people started to approach us and say that since we were talking to everyone else we should certainly talk to them. I began all these meetings by explaining what I was doing in this way: "I work for the American military in north-west Baghdad, and that commander wants to be sure he does all that is needed to help the Iraqi Security Forces make the elections secure, so I want to ask you about threats to your party or candidates that might exist. I'm also a political scientist who teaches at a university in America, and in that capacity I'd like to ask you some general questions about politics and your party's platform and strategy so that I can teach and write about these elections when I go home. Please let me know if it is OK to quote you in some future article I might write."

My research process for the elections involved not only reaching out to the Iraqis, but also to the American community in the IZ. I met with and then befriended someone involved in tracking the election at the Baghdad Provincial Reconstruction Team (PRT), and she helped me attend the Elections Working Group meeting that took place weekly at the US Embassy, which helped me stay abreast of changes in election processes. I also met with representatives of almost all the major organizations involved in the elections, including the International Foundation for Electoral Systems (IFES), which was providing technical assistance to the Iraqi High Elections; USAID's main political officer; the point person on the elections at the United Nations Assistance Mission for Iraq (UNAMI); and representatives of the National Democratic Institute (NDI), which was training parties in how to compete in elections. These people were certainly not interested in helping my brigade find out about the election through unofficial channels (me), but they were often interested in talking to a fellow political scientist or political enthusiast.

As a detailed picture of the provincial elections in north-west Baghdad emerged out of my research, I realized the task I had been handed was monumental. There were fifty-seven seats on the Baghdad Provincial Council, and more than 2,400 candidates were vying for them. Almost all political parties had offices or candidates in our area of operations. The mechanics of the elections themselves were also quite complex. Candidates could run as individuals, as members of party lists, or as members of coalition lists of parties and/or individuals. There were over 100 lists on the ballot in Baghdad, most of them parties. Voters could choose a list, accepting its ordering of candidates and thus their likelihood of actually winning a seat, or they could choose a candidate specifically from that list, which would result in its reordering when votes were counted. This meant that most Iraqi candidates, who were new to democracy and to campaigning, had to run against not only other parties, individuals, and coalitions, but also against their own political allies in their lists. Moreover, most of the political parties taking part in the elections had only recently come into being, and many had emerged from the Sunni insurgency, which in 2008 had made the decision to join the political process.[9]

I gave the brigade regular briefings on the elections, updating the staff on what I had learned of political dynamics, rules, and procedures. About two months before the elections, which were held on January 31, 2009, I gave a larger presentation on my conclusions, which I prepared primarily by going back through the fifty or so engagement reports that were the main result of my months of interviewing. To this information I added what I had found in all the engagement reports from others' meetings with party leaders and candidates that were available on the military's online Combined Information Data Network Exchange database (CIDNE). Finally, I read all the news accounts that mentioned parties and the competitive environment from the news digests published daily by the military. Then I made a list of all the major parties in our area of operations and, based on these three sources, listed their main rivals and the degree of competitive and physical threat that each represented. I assigned a number from one through three to each rival, with three being the highest threat.

I was not far into this process of analysis before I realized my problem: all I could conclude from my research was that the elections would be calm; at least as far as specifically elections-motivated violence went. The interviews pointed to no direct political threats or intense rivalries that seemed likely (according to the Iraqis) to turn into threats. When I had asked party leaders and candidates who might use violence against them for political reasons, most were uncertain. The parties of the Sunni insurgency said that al-Qaeda had threatened to attack them if they participated in the elections, and the Iraqi Islamic Party (Iraq's Muslim Brotherhood party and the main Sunni party that participated in Iraq's initial elections in 2005) insisted that they would be targeted both by al-Qaeda and by those who had objected to their political decisions, especially those involving patronage. But overall the competitive field in Baghdad was too fragmented and complex for the type of clear rivalries that would spark violence to emerge. I had a list of all political entities (parties, individuals, and coalitions) running in the elections, and it showed, for example, at least eleven Turkomen parties and at least five Da'wa parties outside Maliki's running in Baghdad alone. The Sunni insurgents were running in all kinds of new parties. While there seemed to be a great deal of naïvety (or perhaps bravado) by some insurgent parties about their chances, overall apart from a general sense that Maliki's State of Law Party would do well, no one had any idea where they stood with the Iraqi electorate. This, in combination with the complexity of the political environment, meant that if someone were going to try to kill a rival to improve their chances in the elections, it would be difficult to deduce whether this act was necessary or who that victim might be. I was anxious about presenting to the brigade my conclusion that the elections would be peaceful. I was not privy to the type of intelligence that would reveal specific threats, so maybe I was missing something they knew about. And getting up and announcing that the brigade had little to worry about in terms of elections violence might make me seem hopelessly Pollyannaish. In the end I did not have a choice: I had no evidence to base any other sort of conclusion on, so I predicted a calm elections period.

On election day the brigade (a new one that had formally taken over on November 20, 2008) had all its assets outside the wire and ready to respond to any incident. I was back at brigade headquarters holding my breath, but as the soldiers came in from their patrols their faces were serene. "It's like a festival out there," said one of the more jaded members of the brigade staff, "children playing soccer in the streets and running around. Everyone's smiling. This is the best day I have ever had in Iraq." In the end the only SIGACT (significant activity, such as act of violence or found weapons cache) reported in Baghdad on provincial elections day was when two party workers were caught illegally copying the initial tally sheet at a polling station. The polling station workers who caught them made a citizen's arrest and turned them in to the Iraqi police. For the US military, the Iraqis, and the HTT, the provincial elections had been a real success.

Admittedly, it would be impossible to replicate some of the conditions that contributed to what I felt was the success of my work on the provincial elections. Most important was my brigade commander's clear, direct tasking and generous provision of what I needed to accomplish it: a place to live near the IZ, transportation, and an interpreter. His choice to give me, rather than our already-taxed embedded PRT (whose expertise was in any case in economic and development issues), the task of keeping him fully informed about the provincial elections was also a good one. I had been studying elections in the Middle East since graduate school, and while everything in Iraq felt new and different from what I had learned before, my conversations with Iraq's politicians in fact flowed more smoothly because they rested on this base of knowledge.

Having access to the Rashid Hotel and the IZ also made my work much easier, not least because it solved what was for me the greatest ethical problem of HTT work. This was my anxiety about having the military accompany me on special trips to conduct my research. Each time I was taken out to a political party office or a politicians' home, I was terrified that harm would come to the soldiers who were with me and who were only there because of me. The fact that the brigade commander had tasked me to do the work alleviated these concerns a little; each time I sat down to talk to someone I felt that I had to make it somehow *count*, as if our conversation could be worth the risk involved to everyone. I had the same ethical concerns about meeting Iraqis anywhere but near their homes, since traveling was dangerous, time consuming, and often humiliating for them (as a result of IEDs, checkpoints, and traffic). Whenever I could I tagged along on existing missions and tried to squeeze in my interviews or went to meet Iraqis at their homes or in the nearby neighborhood or the sheikh's council buildings. Being able to meet politicians at the Rashid Hotel, where they almost all were anyway, took a great weight off my shoulders during this period of my HTT work.

131

Working with the political side of the human terrain in the capital and close to the seat of power did, however, present its own set of challenges. Sometimes it was difficult to understand my "level" and stay at it. For example, when we called the Iraqi National Congress (Ahmad Chalabi's political party) and asked to meet with them, the party functionaries we talked to initially insisted that Chalabi himself would meet with me. I explained that I was not permitted to meet with him, and although they pressed back hard I was finally able to prevail. In one meeting a sheikh who had just started his own political party and was planning to hold a rally next week asked my brigade commander, who was there, if he could provide security for it. The commander explained that since the sheikh was now a politician he could not offer special help. The sheikh, a clever man who understood how the US military worked, looked at me and said: "Dr Katherine, would you like to come to the rally?" My brigade commander smiled, knowing that I did indeed want to come and that his troops would have to come with me. (I demurred but ultimately was encouraged to go and did attend the rally.) HTT work is a delicate business at any level, but especially at the heart of the political world just before an election where everyone is seeking to maximize political advantage.

THE SHEIKHS OF ABU GHRAIB

Just prior to her death in a bombing, Nicole Suveges, my best friend from training in Fort Leavenworth, called me and said: "My brigade commander keeps asking me to tell him who the 'real sheikhs' are in our area. All these people are coming out of the woodwork telling us they are sheikhs and wanting to work with us, but we have no idea whether they really are tribal leaders. Any ideas?" I was at a loss. *Sheikhs?* She and I were both political scientists, and political science had long ago (and foolishly, I now see) left the terrain of tribes to anthropology. Even that discipline had developed trepidation about the concept of "tribe."[10] How would you find out who was a "real sheikh"? I didn't know where to start, apart from going around asking people and assuming that their response would be accurate.

"Who is a real sheikh?" turned out to be something I was asked constantly while in Iraq. The question was an important one for the US military, which wanted to work with genuine social leaders who could influence the population. But the answer to this question was not just complicated by the fact that a variety of charlatans put on sheikhs' robes to try to access US power and, especially, funds. There are various levels of "sheikhs," which are, ranked in order of their power: confederation, tribal, and clan. Tribal leadership is also fluid to a certain degree. In the 1990s Saddam Hussein, under the pressure of sanctions, began trying to co-opt tribal leaders whose power had previously been suppressed by the Baathist state. When legitimate sheikhs would not cooperate with him, he elevated challengers from within the tribe for the role of sheikh, giving these new social leaders resources to consolidate their power.[11] Iraqis derisively call these men "1990s Sheikhs" or "Taiwanese Sheikhs," but they were not without real influence that came from money and connections to the regime. Finally, moments of crisis create fluidity in tribal leadership, which is based on lineage but also requires merit. Many legitimate sheikhs fled Iraq or were killed during the sectarian violence of 2006–7, and where their heirs were not able to maintain their position new actors who could offer tribal members what they needed rose to the top.

In winter 2009, as the surge brigades left Baghdad and the surrounding belts, my brigade's area of operations expanded to include Abu Ghraib *qada*, which had been a home base for the Sunni insurgency. I was due to leave Iraq in under a month when my brigade commander came to me and told me that he wanted to know the ten most influential tribal leaders in Abu Ghraib. He wanted me to set up meetings for him with them and provide talking points. His goal was to enter Abu Ghraib smoothly with the help of allies and deep situational awareness and to show his commitment to the area by dealing with its main problems immediately. As the brigade commander set about choosing the governance or infrastructure problems, or problems of daily life that he would use brigade resources to tackle in Abu Ghraib, he wanted to be sure that he wasn't responding to special interests but to needs shared by a majority of the community. (It turned out that what the people of Abu Ghraib seemed to want most was the return of their cars which had been impounded by Iraqi security forces, and help from the US military in tracking down family members who had disappeared into the Iraqi detention system.)

I had never been to Abu Ghraib, and my mind was already on my transition home. I think it must be a common phenomenon for those in dangerous situations: you can ignore the risks you take every day until you have an end date in sight, and then you suddenly become terrified you will not make it. Abu Ghraib was the most dangerous place in our area of operations. The commander of the National Guard battalion that had been assigned to the greatest swath of the area and with whom I would be going out had never been to Iraq before. When I told my interpreter about our new tasking she looked panicked: "They are going to kill us out there," she said.

How could the US military have been so uninformed? I knew enough by then not to be surprised that a brigade would rotate out without transferring key information to its replacement. To begin my research process I found briefings and engagement reports here and there on the databases I could access that gave tribal maps for the area and the names of some tribal leaders. Much of this information had been left over from the Marine unit that had been in the area two years earlier. A colonel who had been a battalion commander in Abu Ghraib years before had also just returned to division headquarters, and I made an appointment to talk to him. I already knew the sheikh who was head of one of the largest tribes in Abu Ghraib, and my interpreter and I visited him for lunch at his home (which was outside Abu Ghraib). We visited the governor's representative in Abu Ghraib, the Qaim Maqam, and attended a Sheikh's Council meeting in the Abu Ghraib farming district of Agar Gouf. Every night my interpreter and I called our friends in the political world and other people she knew or that we had met in the Rashid, and these contacts gave us names and numbers of people (supposed sheikhs and otherwise) from Abu Ghraib. We set up meetings with these people where we could, sometimes at the Rashid Hotel. We asked everyone we talked to, "Who are the five most influential people in Abu Ghraib?" and we made a list of the ten names most mentioned from among these lists. This process, we felt, would help filter out bias since it was based on a large sample.

When we met with people to talk about tribal leadership with influence in Abu Ghraib, I explained to them that my brigade was new to the area and wanted to be sure that they understood how things worked in the district and were dealing with the right people. But during my time in the Rashid district I had become interested in tribal law, which sheikhs were using to go after militia members. I began to ask the sheikhs about tribal law, and when I did their faces lit up. Chatting about tribal law relaxed them and encouraged them to speak more candidly about Abu Ghraib's problems and social structure. And those sheikhs involved in tribal dispute settlement were those most respected from an area, so these discussions often turned up names I needed to know.

Our list of major Abu Ghraib tribes and their leaders was fleshing out, but I still needed information. Time was running short. After a particularly fruitless visit with someone from Abu Ghraib at the Rashid Hotel my interpreter and I were dejectedly walking through the lobby. A tall, older man was walking in front of us, his sheikh's robe billowing out behind him. Before I could stop her, my interpreter reached out and tugged on it. He turned around, looking irritated. "Excuse me," she said, "I have a question." He nodded that she could ask it. "Are you a real sheikh?" she said. Horrified, I apologized and tried to tug her away, but the sheikh laughed said that he was, indeed, a real sheikh, and not only that but he was the leader of Iraq's largest tribal confederation, and the one that included the Zobai, the largest and most important tribe in Abu Ghraib. We explained our problem and he told us to be at the hotel the next day at noon. When we arrived we found him sitting with a soft-spoken man who was, we were assured, the tribal historian of the Zobai. He had written several books on Iraq's tribes and had even once had a radio program on tribes and their traditions. The historian pulled a long sheet of paper out of his notebook and handed it to me. It was a chart giving the tribe name, numbers in the tribe, the name of the sheikh and his phone number, and the name of the sheikh's father. I recognized the tribes of Abu Ghraib. Ten lines were marked in yellow highlighter—the most influential tribes in the area.

This information helped me arrange meetings between my brigade commander and the Abu Ghraib sheikhs, both in the area and outside it. I developed resources (PowerPoint presentations, resource books, and documents) for the brigade about the social and tribal make-up of the area, mapping the sheikh's councils, the tribes and their leadership, and the compelling issues throughout most of the area. The brigade used the information these social leaders provided to get a sense of what Abu Ghraib needed, what the Government of Iraq was providing, and how it could best use its own limited resources to bridge the gap. The personal relationship that the brigade commander established with these social leaders also smoothed the path for the soldiers walking and driving the district's streets. If necessary, problems and misunderstandings could be sent up channels on both sides where two personal acquaintances could deal with them.

There are several lessons for an embedded social scientist from what my brigade jokingly called the "Abu Ghraib Sheikh-a-Thon." The first is that HTTs should find more ways to work together to share information that their brigades need. The social networks and security dynamics that HTTs investigate do not, of course, end at the edge of their brigade's area of operations, and it should be easier for HTTs to send each other information. (Busyness and petty jealousies seemed to keep them from doing so, though we did during my time in Iraq have a very successful HTT conference where we all came together to talk about issues.)

The second is that once a relationship was made it should be cultivated. This can be hard to do; after a year in Iraq just calling Iraqis I had met to check on them took many, many hours each week. My interpreter may have been occasionally outrageous, but she was energetic and quite willing to help me make call after call just to say hello to people, or to ask them if they were okay when there had been a bombing, for example, or to gossip with them about some new political news. No one likes to be called only when someone wants something, but when I needed information this cultivated network was important and willing to give it without feeling used. And indeed I cherished these relationships and still try to keep up with my Iraqi friends through email and the occasional call if I can get through. My interest in tribal law, a shared enthusiasm with the sheikhs I talked to, also contributed to my effectiveness. The third is that my interpreter and I both wore civilian clothes and did not carry weapons, so Iraqis felt more comfortable with us, or so they said. Also, and this is crucial, my interpreter and I both enjoyed our work and each other's company, as well as that of almost all the Iraqis we met. My sense was that people did not mind spending time with us.

It probably also helped that both my interpreter and I were women, which gave us the freedom to talk to women as easily as men. When we visited Iraqis in their homes we often went to the women's quarters to chat before leaving, which was fun, familiar, and relaxing. I often wondered and, at first, worried what Iraqis must think of me, an unmarried women living on a military base surrounded by men. Rumors of American licentiousness and drunkenness were rampant. Many Iraqis believed that the Gatorade we drank incessantly was alcoholic. But the Iraqis were unfailingly respectful towards me and most understood perfectly well the role that women play in Western society. (One sheikh asked if he could expect me to become the next Gertrude Bell, perhaps a backhanded compliment.) I quickly realized that there was nothing I could really do about Iraqi suspicions about my virtue, so I put it out of my mind entirely and went on with my work. And overall my sense was that my being a civilian woman relaxed the Iraqis I talked to, or was refreshing for them, and this helped make our conversations more informal.

My brigade was amused to watch me piece together the family and social relationships, competitions, shared anxieties, and real power struggles that tied together the tribal leaders of Abu Ghraib. On the whiteboard behind my desk my officemate, a captain on the brigade staff, wrote: "The Sheikh Lady: An expert in the tribal folk and all the crazy things they do." And after I came home to the US my former brigade's deputy commander emailed me a note saying that the people of Abu Ghraib were saying that the brigade commander was a good man who understood the area well. He gave me credit for this, which was gratifying though surely undeserved. For me the highlight of my time in Abu Ghraib was a visit to the acting sheikh of the Zobai on my last day in Iraq. When I entered his guest room he came to me immediately and said, "Dr Katherine, I have heard about you and have been waiting for a long time to talk to you."

CONCLUSION

The development and deployment of HTTs sparked a debate both within and beyond the US military about whether or not the teams brought anything to the fight that was actually useful or not already available. The scandals and personnel problems that plagued the program aside, I returned from Iraq a firm believer: as an embedded civilian with a doctorate who was only temporarily an employee of the defense establishment, I and other similar HTT team members were able to make unique contributions.

One detracting school of thought on the value of HTTs argues that the funds and energy spent on the program would have been better allocated towards developing cultural competency within the military itself.[12] Certainly the military should invest more in educating its soldiers about how to operate cross-culturally, but there is also real value in housing some competency in an embedded civilian. As someone outside the military's structures and hierarchies, I was free to speak my mind in a way that soldiers might not be. Soldiers are also, as they should be, focused on the successful completion of the mission at hand. Often this mission takes into account long-term success, but a civilian may, again, be more likely to bring a longer-term view of the effects of different courses of action, a valuable perspective. This independence is especially evident if the embedded civilian is only taking a leave of absence from an academic career to work with the military and will not rely on the Department of Defense for significant future employment.

Ideally, an HTT's civilian staff understands the military. This, along with their civilian status, allows them to "represent" the military not only to the local population but also to other civilian organizations on the battlefield that may be initially anxious about cooperating with the military. Of course, embedded PRTs may also serve this bridge-building function, but PRTs, unlike HTTs, do not fall under the direct authority of the brigade commander. This can lead to frustrations if the commander and embedded PRT leader have different priorities.[13] And again, while many Iraqis I met had become quite close to certain American soldiers, they found it interesting and refreshing to talk to a civilian, especially one whose regular job—a professor—they understood and respected. This sped the process of relationship building that is so central to much HTT work.

Finally, while individual US soldiers are doing a marvelous job of recording the conflicts in Iraq and Afghanistan through articles, blogs, books, and videos, there is still a need for a certain kind of analytical recording of what is happening on the battlefield. This HTT function benefits not only incoming units, but also military and civilian decision-makers in the long term. There is certainly also a need for teachers who are outside the military but who can speak from experience about these wars. Again ideally, former HTT social scientists are uniquely prepared to become these critical witnesses, recorders, analysts, and teachers.

HTTs can contribute in many ways to their brigades' work. Yet despite what I consider to have been some real successes during my time in Baghdad, my primary thought as I left was that I wished I could go back and do it all over again and do it better. Although I extended my deployment from nine months to a year, when I left I was still learning something new every day about how to conduct research in a battlefield environment and how to present that research credibly to soldiers. The research processes I have described here and the lessons I learned about communicating with the military seemed hard-won at the time, but looking back I can now see that they all rested on the relentlessness and hard work of maintaining a positive attitude in the face of suffering and folly. We must all bring these characteristics with us to our work to some degree, but I believe the secret to success on an HTT requires the conscious cultivation of these attitudes. This is not easy. During my time in Baghdad I was often filled with righteous indignation at people who did things I considered stupid. I was also sometimes physically exhausted and/or excruciatingly sad. But over time I learned to manage those feelings and do my job.

Maintaining the energy needed to keep up with a deployed brigade's needs and rhythms and a positive attitude while doing HTT work is especially challenging since the results of your efforts may be frustratingly intangible, or at least much less tangible than we were led to believe they would be in training. "What am I even *doing* here?" I asked a member of my brigade staff on a particularly bad day at the end of my deployment. "Am I even helping you at all?" His response was, in part, what led me to teach a class on the War in Iraq at my university and to keep writing about what I learned during my year in Baghdad. He said that the brigade considered me to be an investment that would pay off over the long term. The HTT experience was certainly that for me.

5

PLAYING SPADES IN AL ANBAR

A FEMALE SOCIAL SCIENTIST AMONG MARINES AND SPECIAL FORCES

Jennifer A. Clark

The key to success if you are working as a female civilian adviser to a military unit in combat is: show no weakness and always lend a hand. This is often difficult to do; just carrying the standard pack weight can be exhausting. For the average mission, I had a large Mole (pronounced Molly) pack with a plastic frame, one large compartment, and two small side sacks to fit my three uniforms, underclothing, shirts, a work-out outfit, a pair of tennis shoes, my field journals, camera, pens and pencils, toiletries, and three light-weight novels. In my small bag I carried my computer and other notebooks and a few CDs with extra data. My body armor was 45 pounds not including my Kevlar helmet. All in all I was carrying a load of 90–100 pounds on my 5 foot 6 inches, 160-pound reasonably athletic body. Up until my deployment I had no idea I could carry all of that weight and still walk fast enough to keep up with the unit.

In this chapter, I discuss some of the challenges of my work in Iraq with both the Marines and the Special Forces, especially the process of integration with various units and some of the differences between them. The civilian–military divide remains large in our country, but as a civilian working with the military I was able to bridge that gap, come to understand military culture and motives, and appreciate the difficulties of life for our servicemen and women in a war zone. Learning about the military and integrating with them was the pre-condition to doing my actual job: researching local communities and helping the military make decisions more in harmony with the local culture. In this chapter, I discuss some of my research on Sunni, Kurdish, and Yezidi communities in Iraq. Although I had worked in Iraq before, it was through my work with the Human Terrain System that I was able to utilize my skills as a social scientist to assist the military and indigenous population understand each other better.

PROFESSIONAL BEGINNINGS

When I began studying anthropology as an undergraduate degree at Cleveland State University, I was positive that I wanted to study Native American populations. After fieldwork with the Sioux and Cherokee and an amazing class on human osteology, I switched to physical anthropology, specifically forensics (with a double major in art history). I also became certified in Craniofacial Reconstruction,[1] a forensic technique that uses clay to sculpt and rebuild the facial features of a skull for identification. In graduate school I studied bioarcheology, a mixture of physical anthropology, archeology, and cultural anthropology while conducting fieldwork in Oaxaca, Mexico. In Mexico, working on the El Palmillo Project from 2000 to 2004, I excavated hundreds of burial sites and became very experienced with fragmentary remains and remains with extensive violent trauma. I had earned my Master's degree and finished all my PhD coursework and research when a traumatic injury during fieldwork caused me to leave my studies.

In 2005, while recuperating from my injury, I was asked to join a team of forensic anthropologists, archeologists, and osteologists to excavate and analyze the clandestine graves of victims of the Hussein regime, with the intent to prosecute Saddam and his administration for war crimes. The team was stationed in Baghdad and excavated multiple graves under the direction of the Army Corps of Engineers, the Regime Crimes Liaison Office,[2] and the FBI. I spent three years on and off in Iraq with the Mass Graves Investigation Team (MGIT),[3] mostly stationed at the lab in Baghdad, but also in the field in northern and

142

western Iraq. I became friends with the local Iraqi merchants and contractors who came to the base, and many of the American and multinational service members who passed through the base and our labs.

On the MGIT I worked as an osteologist, then managed the Pathology Lab, and finally became the Evidence and Case Files Manager, handling all the incoming and out-going evidence and case reports. During my tenure on the MGIT, I re-created the faces of Kurds and Yezidi-Kurds for identification, enabling the team to make positive matches between faces and identification cards, based on my reconstructions. As result of this experience, we became well versed on the plight of the Kurds and the al-Anfal Campaign of the late 1980s.[4] I learned a lot about their culture and history, their dress, jewelry, traditions, and physical attributes. I also learned much about how so many of them died.

In late 2007 the mission ended, Saddam was prosecuted, and we had repatriated the remains of over three hundred Kurds. I was coming home feeling a little disjointed: sad to see the mission end and yet glad I had been a part of such an important team, and uneasy about leaving behind all of the military friends I had made. I still wanted to help but I had no idea in what capacity I could, until I heard about the Human Terrain System. I applied for the program and after months of waiting was called to join the program as a social scientist in August 2008. I flew out to Fort Leavenworth and completed several months of training on counterinsurgency, Army culture, Iraqi history and culture, the military decision-making process, course of action development, and various social science analysis programs. We underwent field exercises and interviewing techniques, and learned all about our teammates.

INTEGRATING WITH THE MARINES IN IRAQ

I was scheduled to deploy around Christmas for Baghdad, Iraq. I was initially scheduled to embed with Army units south-west of Baghdad at a small forward operating base (FOB), called Falcon. However, while waiting for deployment at the Continental United States (CONUS) Replacement Center (CRC) at Fort Benning, Georgia, I got a call from HTS management telling me that I would be joining the Human Terrain Analysis Team (HTAT) at Marine Corps Division Headquarters in Anbar Province. The rationale for the significant change was that the team there was having some difficulties with the

Marines, had no social scientists, and needed someone who had been deployed before and was strong-willed enough to deal with the somewhat difficult Marine Corps culture.[5] Later that day I received an email from our team leader welcoming me to the new team and advising me that the I MEF Marines (1st Marine Expeditionary Force) did not like the HTAT. I was told to expect problems.

Throughout training we had received a lot of information on working with Army units, military culture, and chain of command, but nothing on other military branches. I was entering a military culture blind, but enthusiastic. Before heading to Iraq I also read what I could; my favorite book was *Generation Kill* by Evan Wright.[6] What I learned was that Marines have a tradition of being tough and versatile, unified by one ethos with a strict set of values. However, there is a duality to their nature: although they see themselves as the ultimate warriors who are always prepared to fight, they are caring, giving, and gentle when dealing with the injured, sick, and young. Infantry Marines revel in their masculinity and express a level of machismo that is at times difficult to tolerate. They are incredibly professional and yet can be the rudest, crudest, most childish people I've encountered. The Marines say "every Marine is a rifleman," meaning they are all the same, yet the infantry distinguishes itself in every way it can.

I arrived at al Asad airbase late on a rainy winter evening. The trip into Anbar was relatively uneventful and we quickly settled into our rooms. These were made of shipping containers called CHUs (containerized housing units). Typically two people are housed within each room, but because of our pay grade I and the other team's social scientist were given our own rooms. Although certainly not large, it was great to have some privacy. Aside from a single cot and a metal wardrobe, they contained no furniture. Our team leader was resourceful though, and had met up with a local contractor who provided us with internet antennae and connectivity, and we were able to scrounge in the dumping area for any discarded furniture. Every time a unit rotated out, there would be a mass dumping of bedding, locally sold furniture, rugs, and other various goodies. Before the end of the week I had a mini-fridge, a desk made from a huge piece of wood and two filing cabinets, a dresser, and a massive Persian rug that covered the entire room, donated to me by some out-going Navy guys.

After we had stowed our gear and had chow, we met our new team and were briefed on the difficulties the team had been experiencing with the Marines. They were specifically told to "sit in their office, eat donuts, drink coffee, and keep out of the way." Apparently the team had not been able to produce materials of use to the Marines, which was not their fault per se. The I MEF was leaving and not doing a lot of off-base missions, the Marines were unhappy with housing Army civilians, plus the social scientist we replaced had allegedly been ego- tistical and did not integrate well with the unit. Basically, the situation did not look good, but I had no intention of spending my deployment sitting around. I had come to help, to do research and fieldwork, and be operationally necessary. We just had to prove that this was a new team, a new start, and that we were prepared to contribute. The team immediately began brainstorming in order to formulate some research ideas, and by the end of the session we had a plan. I would handle short-term immediately relevant research and inquiries, and our other social scientist would work on the Legacy Project, which was a long- term project that tracked the various tribes and entities within our area of operations. Together we would plot out tribal culture and any sig- nificant issues they were experiencing that were relevant to the Marines over time, so that a consistent cultural database would exist for all in- coming units.

Our next step was to integrate within the unit and to advertise our expertise and skills in a clear and concise manner, so that the Marines would understand how to use our capability. It was not easy. We were immediately asked how we differed from their Civil Affairs (CA) teams, or the Provincial Reconstruction Teams (PRT), or the Intel and Psychological Operations (PSYOPs) guys. We were labeled as "egg- heads" and "eaters," euphemisms denoting useless contractors who drained base resources. We had to come up with quick sound bites that described our capabilities and skills, hoping to catch the attention of a decision-maker.[7]

Eventually we gained a foothold with the Information Operations (IO) officers, who asked us to join in on a working group tasked with creating culturally sound and sensitive messages for the Iraqi people. The 2009 elections were looming and the Marines were concerned about stability and security in the region. We were asked to help cre- ate radio messages, pamphlets, fliers, and talking points for the Division and for the lower brigades and battalions. The working group included IO personnel, PYSOPs, a PRT representative, Civil Affairs, and us. We made some great friends in that group and they introduced us to their colleagues up and down the chain of command. It was a starting point.

After a month into the deployment, the Marines conducted a Relief in Place/Transfer of Authority (RIP/TOA) with the II MEF Marines, commanded by Lieutenant General Richard Tryon. We were concerned about the RIP because we had no idea whether the new Marines would embrace us or disregard us, causing us to have to start at square one with the introductions. We got lucky. The Marines from I MEF who had worked with us in the IO working group told their relief officers about us, and within a week of their coming to al Asad the II MEF Marines were visiting our offices. We quickly integrated with the II MEF and continued our work with IO, so were asked to develop short papers and briefings on our expertise and capabilities, as well as our assessment of the area of operations (AO). We also had our team leader introduce us to a special staff section called Assessments. Although it was neither our job nor our mission to conduct assessments, our team leader felt it was the best way to get us integrated with the new staff sections. The Assessments team would take information from all the various staff elements, along with surveys and research from the various contracting agencies that were conducting local surveys and opinion polls, and put the information together for the evening briefings to the Commanding General. We would help by providing any cultural information we thought was useful.

Integrating with Marines in a combat theater was not easy. For example, I was given a lot of grief by the Master Sergeant regarding my appearance. He was about six feet tall and broad-chested, with a weathered face that reminded me of a young R. Lee Ermey[8] and a voice that sounded like sandpaper. Instead of getting upset at his comments, I asked him to teach me how to fix whatever offended him. He began by telling me how to lace my boots properly, and how to place my dog tags so that they did not make noise or catch light, which could easily be seen by the enemy. He told me it did not matter that we were on a larger base, that Marines were always diligent. I pointed out that I had seen many Marines with their dog tags bright as day, shining in the sun, and was rewarded with a few expletives and commentary about what he'd do if he was *their* NCO. As he railed, I changed my laces and tags. He also told me about uniforms and how a Marine's uniform would never be messy like an Army uniform (which was made with Velcro pockets and wrinkled easily). Furthermore, the Marine Corps did not hand out their uniforms to civilians like the Army. I knew it was pointless to argue or defend, so I observed instead. What he was telling me was that the Marines are an elite military organization that requires more than just enlistment to belong; there is pride in being a Marine that is unique to the Corps.

I learned over time that there is an estimated five-minute window to prove one's competence, and after that a Marine will write you off as useless. They prepare for readiness to an extreme that sometimes translated into inane absurdities (like issuing infraction notices for wearing reflective belts in a non-standard manner). They are not fond of academics who try to pull rank just because they hold a certain pay-grade. On the other hand, Marines liked to see you working out alongside them at the gym, pitching in to help without asking, and attempting to blend in even if you are not really one of them. The base Marines were exceedingly polite, immaculate in presentation, and very professional. At times it was difficult to imagine any of them as elite killing instruments of war.

I later came to find that the Marines who were forward deployed and operating at the small bases (mostly infantry) were radically different from the Marines at al Asad. While all Marines shared an overarching organizational culture, smaller sub-cultures within the Marine Corps differed quite a bit. For example, forward deployed Light Armored Reconnaissance (LAR) Marines reveled in and embraced the worst-case scenarios and horrid conditions found in the remote forward deployed combat outposts (COPs), as I discuss later in the chapter.

The Hit Hospital Study

The other team social scientist and I continued working with IO, but I also linked up with the team leader of the Iraqi Advisor Task Force (IQATF). Although the IQATF team considered us competition, the team leader and I felt that HTS and IQATF could work in tandem to strengthen usable cultural products for the Marines. While they mostly conducted atmospherics and gauged the population's perception regarding certain subjects, HTS conducted social science research and provided course of action development based on cultural considerations. IQATF was set to conduct a series of hospital assessments throughout the region and I was asked to join the mission as an extra set of eyes. I drew up a quick research plan to investigate the hospital's resources and any challenges they might be facing with security and supply levels. It was an ephemeral research question, which quickly changed once I began talking with the director of Hit Hospital (pronounced *heet*).

Accompanied by Marines from the Medical Division, IQATF, and a PRT member, we were given a tour of the hospital and then were scheduled to have lunch with the hospital administrative staff. I was fortunate enough to get a few minutes with the hospital Director, who was forthcoming about the challenges facing the hospital. He said that supplies were limited and not enough for the population he was serving, danger and threats were ever-present, and there were no security personnel on duty to protect the hospital. Additionally, they could not serve the women in the community because there were no female nurses available who would work at the hospital. This left a large portion of the community without health care. His information caused me to switch my research question entirely on the fly, focusing on two questions: 1) Why are female nurses not prevalent and how can we encourage women to attend nursing college? 2) What is the distribution of black market medical goods, and is the black market the most applicable means for locals to acquire medical services, medicines, and goods especially in the rural areas that are far from the big city hospitals?

I discovered that the MEF Medical Division and the State Department's PRT wanted to build a nursing college for women in Hit because there were so few female nurses. The women in Hit and the surrounding cities could not get the care they needed because to be seen or touched by males outside of their family would be dishonorable. Building a college and training nurses seemed as if it would solve the problem. However, once I began interviewing the hospital Director and the only two female nurses at the hospital, I realized that there was a cultural stigma against female nurses. Being a nurse would entail talking to and touching people, including males, who were not a part of their family.[9] Additionally, there was a local perception that only disgraced "fallen" women sought out the nursing field. It was acceptable for women from "good" families to become nurses only if they attended the prestigious nursing school in Ramadi, a four-year course that was unaffordable to most Iraqi families.[10] I wrote a quick paper on my findings and suggested a longer-term research effort that would investigate the viability of a college in Hit if no local females would attend, and whether or not better education could create the perception that a nursing college in Hit was as prestigious as the college in Ramadi.

The second research question regarding the black market was disconcerting because it posed a potential ethical challenge. The MEF and PRT provided much needed medical supplies to the hospitals, and those supplies were getting funneled to the black market. Was diverting supplies a legitimate practice for supporting the community or a response to Saddam-era policies? Or was it a break down in governmental functions during the reconstruction phase (post invasion) and something that could be fixed? Or was it plain and simple corruption? Regardless, I wanted to figure out how best to inform the Marines of the problem, while also providing several solutions or "courses of actions" (COAs) for them to consider. The Hit Hospital mission and branching research topics were a way for me show the Marines that our team was "value added" and not "eaters."

The Hit mission became a full-fledged project under the request of the II MEF Medical Director. He asked that we continue to do assessments of the hospital and then create a survey that would interview patients and families about service and care, local remedies, transportation and cost issues for care, and any factors we thought would improve health care for Iraqi women. I wrote the first survey and then our team leader passed the project to the social scientist from Regional Combat Team (RCT) 8 when I became overloaded with requests for support from other staff sections. Overall the Marines considered the Hit research useful, and therefore a success. When I left Anbar, the nursing college was being built, but I do not know if it was ever finished.

Preparing for Tripoli

While conducting the Hit missions I heard that the Marines were going to take over an area of operations (AO) code-named "Tripoli" that encompassed the north-western section of Ninewa Province. The Marines already controlled the entire province of al Anbar and now would assume control of another very large section of real estate to the north, but without any reinforcements. They also had little cultural knowledge of the area aside from the basic Sunni–Yezidi–Kurd ethnic breakdown and a geographic assessment highlighting significant actions (SIGACTS) (e.g. violent enemy attacks).

I began sifting through intelligence reports and operations reports from the field and sorted it all into folders on my desktop. I then acquired a huge map of Ninewa from the print shop and began writing out tidbits of information that looked important, or useful, onto colored sticky notes, placing them on the map generally or at the actual location of the event. Over time a pattern emerged. I sifted through hundreds of documents multiple times to make sure I caught every event of tribal, political, cultural, or criminal significance (at least what I thought was significant) and cross-referenced them with any reports found on the internet or found by our analysts back at the Research Reachback Center (RRC). I then found the Marines and analysts who had written the intelligence and operations reports and spoke with as many of them as I could in order to gather as much information as possible on Ninewa. My massive map covered in multi-colored sticky notes became something of a circus attraction for the Marines. They kept coming in and pointing at the map then asking me to explain why I was doing the investigation when no request had come to me for assistance. I would simply say, "You're going to need this, just wait. I'll be here when you get extended in Ninewa." They thought it was a joke, but I had hit the nail on the head.

The II MEF Marines were extended in Tripoli about a month after I had started the map. True to my word, they began coming to my office asking to see the map and to look at my files in preparation for heading north. I sat with them and talked about what I did and did not know, and I always asked for follow-up meetings once they returned from missions so that I could update my files. At the same time I found a recent report that outlined why Ninewa would be of interest geographically to the Kurds.[11] I was disturbed by the findings in the report and began looking into the up-coming Kurdish constitutional vote (repeatedly re-scheduled) and the allegations of Kurdish expansion prevalent in the Iraqi news. Both Sunni and Shia accused the Kurds of trying to claim lands south of the Kurdish autonomous zone, to include Kirkuk on the grounds that these areas had been part of their homelands prior to the al Anfal Campaign of 1986 through 1988.[12] Baghdad argued that Kirkuk had always been a multi-cultural city, with a largely Shia and Turkoman population, which legally belonged to Iraq and was therefore under Baghdad's control.[13] What confused me was why the expansion, interpreted as legal by the Kurds under the provision in Article 140 of the new Iraqi Constitution,[14] would include the Sahl-Sinjar Mountain and the Sinjar Valley, which was a Yezidi territory.

After much reading and mapping, I wrote a report for the Marines that highlighted the pattern on my map in correlation with my hypotheses about the Kurdish expansion in Ninewa. I outlined what was documented, where there were gaps in knowledge, events that might affect stability in the region, and several courses of action, including sending me to Ninewa to conduct field interviews with the locals. I wanted to hear from the Iraqis about whether or not they would welcome or refuse the Kurds (and Kurdish government control) in their area. I expected the report to get little to no notice from the Marines, but instead I was given a lot of face time with the head of the Division Intelligence office (known as the G2), as well as the Economic, Political, Intelligence Cell (EPIC), Psychological Operations, Information Operations, Civil Affairs, the PRT, and a host of other departments. Marines and State Department officials filled my first briefing to maximum capacity.

I wanted to go out to Ninewa, and the man who would make that happen or completely kibosh my plan was the division G2. He was a full-bird colonel, six feet tall, dark in skin tone, bald, with a friendly and yet intimidating smile. He had a reputation for being difficult. When I was first introduced to the G2 my back was turned and my team leader and I were exchanging barbs. I was mortified to realize that the G2 was standing right behind me, and had heard me telling my team leader off. Smiling and chuckling a bit, he pulled out a chair next to him and told me to ignore the forty-plus people in the room while I explained my paper and the map he had been hearing so much about. I unrolled the map and briefed him, as if it were just the two of us, on everything I had learned and suspected about activities in Ninewa. He asked me what I wanted and I told him I needed support to go into the field.

The G2 told me he would support my request, but two months later I was still waiting and assumed some red tape was holding up the research mission. One day I was sitting in my office and a very tall, older Marine walked into our office. He was very quiet and came towards my desk a bit sideways, which prevented me from seeing his rank on his collar. He asked if I was the "girl doing the Tripoli Project." I responded that I was the social scientist researching northern Ninewa and he launched into a barrage of rather colorful language, declaring that I was stirring the pot and causing grief for his Marines, getting them worked up over an area that would probably be handed back to the Army within weeks. That is when I saw his stars. The Commanding General of II MEF was personally chewing me out! He gave me an order to stand down and then told me that I would never amount to anything within the Marine Corps. I was pretty upset, but figured at that point I had little to lose. I had been studying the Marines closely and had a few ideas about their culture, so I responded: "Sir, with all due respect, you are wrong. You can put me on a plane, but you are staying in Tripoli; I know this through my own contacts, and you will need my research. You will need me. So if you have me leave, you will lose your Ninewa expert, and you will be sending your Marines north with their heads up their asses, flying blind, with no cultural understanding whatsover, and it will likely get some of them killed." Personally, I was shaking in my combat boots. I figured I had just seriously screwed up, was taking a major risk in saying what I did, but I also thought that I had to act tough and stand my ground or I'd be labeled as weak, an "eater," and would lose all the credibility I had earned. It was a massive gamble, but it paid off. The General smiled, gave me a barely perceptible nod, then turned and left.

I immediately went to my team leader and told him what had happened. Some Marines who overheard the ass-chewing told my team leader I had "huge brass" and to expect my orders to leave within 24 hours. I was near tears, but managed to explain my rationale for acting the way I did. One of the Marine colonels sitting nearby began laughing and commented about how the CG was probably so surprised by my vehement response that he had no idea how to react. We called the G2 and told him what had happened and that we were afraid the Tripoli project was going to be stopped. He told us to proceed. The G2 also told me not to worry about the CG; that I was to take my orders directly from him from now on. He said that he would find out what was causing the delay and issue a FRAGO (fragmentary order) if necessary.

Two days later I was given orders to fly to Ninewa, along with a team of RCT 8 Marines to conduct fieldwork in the Sahl Sinjar basin and mountain range. I briefed RCT 8's commanding officer (CO) the next day, and he was not happy about receiving a FRAGO from Division Headquarters to take a civilian social scientist on what he felt was a sight-seeing tour. After the briefing, though, we compromised and I promised him he would have our briefing at the same time as the G2 so that he would not feel he was second in line. Before I left he asked me to do something odd. He wanted me to evaluate, unofficially, how his new lieutenant performed in the field. I told him I'd provide honest feedback when I returned, and we scheduled our mission for the next day.

In the Field

The team flew up to Sahl Sinjar airfield after planning, drills, prepping, and waiting. There is a saying we all knew: "Hurry up and wait," and it applied to our little unit as we sat around in the out-going area of the flight line. As I pretended to read my book, I noticed the Marines in this unit were playing cards. I got up and made my way over to see what game was most popular. Spades. I was in luck. I played this game regularly with my friends and knew I could hold my own. Just as I was about to ask to join in we were called to the flight line. We all had to load our gear onto pallets. Many of the Marines looked at my colleague and me as if we'd ask for help. We didn't. We grabbed our heavy packs, which easily passed the 50-pound mark, and hoisted them out to the pallet area, then helped the Marines load the rest of the packs that were there. We received nods in our favor, which was the goal.

On board the C-130 (a massive plane that is the primary carrier for troops in Iraq) we all filed in and sat down on tiny mesh seats, packed in like sardines with our knees compressed against each other. We were all supposed to wear our Kevlar, but instead held the helmets in our laps, falling asleep in whatever position we could manage. It was incredibly loud, as there are no buffers on the plane, so ear protection was mandatory. Despite the discomfort, the tightness, the heat (there was AC but no one felt it), the noise, and the smell, most of us managed to sleep. We were told to drink at least one bottle of water, but frankly none of us wanted to risk having to pee in those conditions. Again, I took the time to observe the guys with whom I was on mission. Many were considerably younger than me, barely out of school, and yet all had seen combat. I wanted so badly to talk to them and hear their stories and hoped that I'd have time in between my own mission objectives.

We landed on a long patch of asphalt laid out in the middle of nowhere. It was dark and the powdery sand had been kicked up so we could only see the faint light of a Marine's flashlight ahead of us. We were told our packs would be at our tent area, but we had to "hump it" over there, which was about a "click" away (a kilometer). The man speaking was a young staff sergeant with a booming voice. He was exactly the picture of a Marine: stout, muscular, with cropped hair, and he began to give a rousing speech to get us geared up, including plenty of expletives and references to the male genitalia. At one point he passed by me and realized a woman was in his lines (there were two actually—me and the RCT 8 social scientist). He immediately began to apologize for his references to manly body parts and turned the brightest red I have ever seen. I assured him I was not offended and offered that "mine were as big as his" to which he laughed heartily and relaxed. We began our brisk march to the camp to an equally, if not more offensive, cadence that had us all laughing so hard it was difficult to breathe.

My colleague and I were given our own tent at the end of the row of men with two spaced-apart cots and a small heater. We went and grabbed our gear and unpacked, talking to each other about our experiences and what we thought we could expect on this mission. She had done a lot of other projects and had been deployed with HTS longer than I had, but I'd had more overall downrange time than her. Her background was journalism and counterterrorism, and she had worked in the Middle East before. She was cheerful and enthusiastic, and asked great questions. I was the lead researcher, so I discussed a few of the guidelines I had planned for the fieldwork. She had research questions she wanted to explore as well, so we came up with a set of ten standard questions and ten alternative questions to ask people, depending on time. We also agreed upon the wording for our informed consent and how we would interview people. We decided that if waylaid by groups of people we'd split responsibilities: one would ask questions while the other observed and took notes. The observer would be able to identify the most powerful individual in any group; and any perceived threats to cause us to close the interview, or anything else that would help us to understand the situation.

The next day we woke up, grabbed a power bar and a can of coffee and went to find the CO of the 3rd Light Armored Reconnaissance (LAR) Marines stationed at Sahl Sinjar airfield. The colonel did not really see the reason for our being there on his base, but understood we had orders and said that he would accommodate us as much as possible. He asked for consideration in reporting; that we brief him first after each mission, to which we agreed. He then briefed us on his area of operations (AO) and we spent a few hours with him and his intel guy going over the towns and areas of interest. We planned on moving out the next day with some of our Marines and some of his Marines. Our objective was to reach the small Sunni towns and perhaps some of the Yezidi[15] towns just north of the base and south of the mountain.

The colonel told us that we would have to come back each night instead of doing a continuous mission because of "gender issues." I was a bit taken aback when I heard that. I told the colonel that my colleague and I had no issues with "roughing it" and were fine with doing a continuous mission in order to cover more area. He replied that the consideration was for his Marines, not for us. That having females around, who had other "bathroom considerations" was unsettling for his men and he did not want them to get "unwound." So, we would instead spend upwards of fourteen hours a day travelling to and from base trying to interview as many people as we could, while driving 25 miles per hour or less in three large Mine-Resistant Ambush Protected vehicles (MRAPs). For me personally, it was maddening and frustrating. I had this impression about Marines being so tough, and yet they were afraid of using the bathroom in front of two girls. Although I can understand there was a fear of accusations of sexual misconduct, it was still upsetting because we would waste so much time that could be spent talking with locals.

The next day, we started out at a Sunni village where women were making bricks. We stopped and talked, then moved on to another village. As we went from Sunni village to Sunni village we realized that the residents felt isolated and cut off from services. They had no clean water, no access to medical services, and a nasty bout of chickenpox was spreading through the area. Additionally, they believed they could not pass through the city of Sinjar because it was being held by the Kurds. I took notes and added a few research questions based on this new information. I felt horribly for these people. They lived in small huts and had been greatly affected by drought. The winds had beaten down the walls of their homes and the women had infected sand-flea bites all over their legs and arms from making mud bricks. They seemed weary and cautious about speaking with us, so I kept our interviews very brief and repeatedly asked for permission to talk to them. I assured them we would contact the PRT and the AO commander and try to get water out to them as soon as we could, which we did as soon as we got back to base.

At one location there was a very large gathering of people. The group was Sunni and they were having a wedding. We asked them if they would like to talk, or prefer that we leave. They politely and warmly invited us to tea inside the sheikh's home and we were led into the comfortable main room covered with carpets and pillows and a small heater for the tea. While the women stayed outside, men of all ages followed us into the room, and we knelt on the rug in front of the group. We removed our helmets and gear (as much as we could) and gratefully accepted the scalding sweet chai offered to us. We explained who we were and what we were researching, and that we were genuinely interested in hearing what they had to say regarding the government, rule of law, Kurdish expansion, access to health care and clean water, etc. We told them to speak as freely as they wished and they voiced their concerns about unemployment and being blocked by the Kurds from going into Sinjar. They also told us how they fought with us in the Awakening and now they had no representation in the government. After about an hour of talking, we thanked them and told them where they would be able to find my report. I also told them I would make sure that their concerns would be heard.

We headed further north and delivered some barbed wire and supplies to a Yezidi household on the western side of the mountain. We planned to be there for a few hours, and while there the owner, a Yezidi-Kurd, had his wife prepare a feast for us. The house was quite large with a garden at the back, a small pipe of water from a deep well, a few sheep and goats, and a large patio. The family brought out tables and chairs and we feasted outdoors. While the women cooked, we talked to the men about health issues and the Kurdish expansion, and various other issues facing the Yezidi people. The father told us about life under Saddam and how hard it was to get work under the new Shia government. He also told us about the cell tower and radio station he had at the side of his house. He was a Kurdish Regional Government (KRG) party leader and had a self-declared responsibility to the Yezidi in his community. He told us that he made sure they had seeds and grain, water, and buses to take the children to school. He also told us that the Yezidi south of Sinjar were not really Yezidi, that the Yezidi were actually Kurds, and that the others were liars and false about their loyalties. It made me wonder about the divide in the Yezidi community between their declared origins. Were they Kurds or weren't they? We had an enjoyable afternoon but then loaded up the MRAPs and continued north.

We visited two more Yezidi-Kurd settlements and conducted brief interviews before heading back down the mountain and back to base. What I came to realize is that many of the interviews we conducted that day would likely be disregarded. We had a faulty interpreter who I realized had been threatening to the interviewees, and the Marines themselves had potentially created some bias due to their extremely close proximity to me and my colleague during interviews. Afraid that we might be harmed, the Marines wanted us close enough to touch with their boots. Therefore, I could in no way guarantee that the Iraqis felt safe in talking with me. Overall I noted my fears in my notes and pulled the data from my sample. The only group of notes I saved were from the Yezidi-Kurd who hosted us at lunch. I was very frustrated.

The next mission took us further up the mountain to the very top. Although we only got to interview a few groups, we did get to see a 600-year-old Yezidi shrine and all of the enclaves of Yezidi traditionalists who were embedded in terraces within the mountain. I was able to interview the caretaker at length about life under Saddam. The Yezidi had been fierce fighters and highly educated, but were also seen as outcasts and often targeted by the regime. They had legends and prophecies about white warriors with blue eyes who would save them from persecution. To the Yezidi, the Marines fit the description and so they had a particular fascination with Coalition forces, often taking jobs as interpreters and aids. The caretaker told us about the shrine and how the Yezidi prayed, and why the shrine was built in the particular design that was special to all Yezidi shrines. He told us it was called "The Shrine of the Forty Warriors" because it was built on the site where forty brave warriors had died hundreds of years ago defending the Yezidi families.

On our way back down the mountain it began to rain rather hard. The captain with us was very strict with his men and rarely smiled. As we stood on that mountain overlooking the valley he seemed to relax and smiled a few times at my sarcastic comments, but once back in the MRAP his face became stone. Once the rain hit, visibility disappeared and the night fell, making everyone a bit tense. The Marine manning the turret was in the worst spot, facing the beating rain and getting completely soaked through with the icy droplets. Although the captain chastised his men for taking pictures ("this is not a sight-seeing tour!") the lance corporal in the turret secretly took our cameras and snapped pictures for us when the captain wasn't looking. For several hours he stood, moving from side to side inside the turret in order to shield us from the rain that was pouring into the MRAP. When we got back to base, the soaking lance corporal had a smile on his face and thanked us for letting him help out on this mission. It was then that I realized there was something very special about the LAR Marines—something very different from the Marines stationed back at al Asad, and I really wanted to learn all I could of this sub-group's culture.

The next day we had a break and the RCT 8 Marines we had been on mission with were doing minimal tasks and playing cards. I started watching them and eventually one asked if I knew Spades. I said yes and he dealt me in. What they played was not the traditional game but rather "Marine Spades." Some rules were pretty off the wall, such as dealing two cards face up and passing two cards to the left to your opponent, or giving up the little joker to the opponent. It took a bit of getting used to, but once I caught on, I won. I won every game. Whoever partnered with me won. So it became a huge contest over who could rattle whom, who could smack-talk the worst, and who could tell the bawdiest jokes. This small group of guys had accepted me. I learned everyone's names, their home location, marital status, why they had joined the Marines and how much they absolutely loved their jobs. They all did. Granted, there were things they did not like, but overall it was a brotherhood of guys in bad situations and they reveled in it. I learned that they initially feared me because they thought that I was some high-level CIA "spook" doing collections, and they were afraid I'd rat on them for any misstep. I laughed pretty hard at that, but explained to them what my role was, and how I could help them understand the cultural environment.

The next day we went on mission with the Marines from RCT 8, to a series of small Yezidi villages that had been targeted by al-Qaeda recently and in the past. Our intent was to follow up on allegations of Kurdish expansion, false arrests and imprisonment, and genocide. On the way we got lost, misread a map and wound up in a wadi (a dry riverbed created by massive but sporadic seasonal rainwater) and broke a mine-roller, bounced over dunes and berms, broke all the radio antennae on all the Humvees, got stuck in a small alley in a Yezidi village, and tore apart a soccer field. It was not a good day for us. Realizing we were pretty handicapped by the broken mine-roller and antennae we met up with another unit, got supplies and ate some Meals Ready to Eat (MREs). While waiting for support I called the 5th group Special Forces Operational Detachment Alpha (ODA) that was stationed at COP Nimr. I had been corresponding with their team leader for a couple of months while at al Asad and he knew I'd be on mission in Sinjar. I explained our situation and asked them if we could hitch a ride.

They showed up seemingly out of nowhere and jumped out of their vehicles in mismatched Army uniforms and T-shirts with a range of equipment. The Marines hung back while I spoke with the ODA team leader. I jumped in his Humvee, and the ODA escorted the Marines back to their base at Nimr. The base was very small and was actually inside a relatively large Kurdish Peshmerga base. In order to get to the ODA base we had to navigate through a maze of Hesco walls (cardboard and wire boxes filled with dirt stacked on top of each other to form walls) and two checkpoints manned by local Yezidi men.

When we got to the ODA base, we all jumped out of the vehicles to assess the damage to the Marines' vehicles. While waiting for the ODA's cook to prepare dinner, I watched the reaction of the very young Marines. They were enthralled with these quiet, serious men. Many asked "Who are those guys?" I told them jokingly, "They're Delta secret squirrels" and many of the young Marines believed me. One of the Marines asked, "Can you ask the team leader how I can become a Delta?" I smiled and told him I'd find out. Without any experience with the Special Forces, the young Marines were easy to pick on. Eventually I explained to them how I knew the ODA and their activities in contrast to the LAR Marines at Sahl Sinjar.

The Special Forces guys invited my colleague and me to stay at Nimr and my team leader ordered me to stay in the field as long as possible, so it was a mutually beneficial arrangement. As the LAR Marines got ready to leave Nimr, my colleague and I grabbed our gear and were escorted to a shipping container at the back of the base that housed two dusty cots and a door that barely closed. They said it was about standard for their housing, and we were completely fine with the austere conditions. When we went back to say goodbye to our Marines, we found them loaded to the gills with sweets, sandwiches, sticky buns, Rip-It energy drinks, and other junk food. The ODA had raided their personal supplies, filled the guys up, and fixed their radios; but they could not fix the mine-roller. We hugged our Marines and promised card games when we saw them at al Asad. Despite all the trouble, we had had a great mission and assuaged their fears that we'd tell their superiors they had failed in any way.

As the Marines flew back to their base, I reflected that integrating with the Marine infantry had been difficult because of my gender and because I had not gone through their training. Within the Marine Corps, the infantry is an excluded occupational specialty for women.

The infantry throughout its history has developed a tight brotherhood that does not easily accommodate women; their jokes, their songs, and even their general conversation would be considered sexist by most standards. Knowing these things about them helped me develop a persona that was at times open, honest, and funny, at other times crude and rude. When necessary I became the hard professional who would not allow smart comments during a mission planning brief. Although I technically held no rank, I made it clear that I was senior and was not there to screw around.

AT THE SPECIAL FORCES OUTPOST

I thought that integrating with the ODA would make working with the Marines seem like child's play. I was pleasantly surprised to discover that I was very welcome in the ODA compound. I had been speaking with their team leader via phone and emails and had exchanged several papers with him before we met. He had taken a few anthropology classes in college and was interested in how social science could aid military understanding and potentially decrease kinetic operations. Unlike many of his colleagues, he felt that kinetic operations, although sometimes necessary, should not be the first choice and should not be the primary focus of the operator's mission. In his view, the ODA was the best choice for counterinsurgency operations because of their ability to study the indigenous culture and to rotate in and out with a partner team for years on end, which allowed for institutional memory and continuous education on the area of operations. It also allowed networks to be built and fostered over time. Considering that Arab culture is largely network-based and information is largely spread by word of mouth through a hierarchical system in Iraq, his assessment about the usefulness of ODA teams appeared sound.

Special Forces teams are composed of small groups of men, each with a specific task and occupational specialty. Although they are all effective operators, there is little overlap in their responsibilities. Their small size and daunting mission objectives force teamwork and efficiency, cohesion, brotherhood, and trust.[16] The Special Forces teams that have worked together a long time will often involve their families, creating small civilian communities. As these soldiers told me, Special Forces are so integrated that some teams will discuss whether or not a prospective marriage might interfere with team dynamics.

Based on their own level of unit cohesion and my prior experience with SEAL (Sea, Air, Land) teams in Iraq, I had not expected to be accepted by the ODA. The Army Special Forces teams I embedded with were nothing like the SEALs I had met. They accepted me immediately, with the exception of the sergeant, the second executive officer (XO). The XO was very wary of me, believed me to be a "leftist hippie peace-loving culture-freak" who was likely to be "anti-military and trying to find some way to bash them and their mission." Laughing, I told him, "Don't worry. I'm a Republican, love the military, want peace but believe in military action when necessary, and have no intention of bashing you unless you do something bone-headed worth bashing." After that, he became my primary guard. On every mission he was right next to me. He sat with me at chow. He sat in the common area whenever I was writing up notes. One day I finally asked him, "If you hate me so much, why are you always around?" He told me he was making sure I didn't get into trouble. The truth was, he and I had somehow become friends.

The first day at the compound I spent with the team leader going over what we did and did not know, and met the Yezidi guards who watched the base gates. The team also put us through practice lanes so we would know how to get in and out of vehicles in case there was an attack. They threw flash-bangs down to see how we would react to noise; they shot near us, and then had us move through rooms as they practiced clearing. They kept asking us if we wanted weapons, but we declined. There was no reason for us to have weapons, especially when talking to locals. In fact, I made it clear that I'd prefer that they stay as far away from us as possible while I interviewed. They were happy to comply. Unlike the Marines, the ODA stayed easily 15 feet from me at all times while I talked with people, and many times I entered gated compounds while they stayed in the street. There was a level of trust and understanding with the ODA that I did not have with the Marines. They understood the local culture far better and knew how much leeway to give me, and as a result I was able to acquire far more detailed interviews, longer in length, with a much healthier understanding of the communities than I had with the prior missions.

The ODA team I was with was an amazing team. The locals knew them, the politicians trusted them (although they did not share that trust), the local merchants always had good produce for them, and their professionalism was apparent in everything they did. They worked out together, shared clean-up duties and watched movies at night like a big family. By the second evening I was doing the same, including cooking a few meals for them. However, they already had a local cook who lived with them and I did not want my job to become "Lady of the House." Unfortunately, the Yezidi cook (named "Cook") did not believe in hygiene or refrigeration. He would cook a meal, place it on trays, and leave it out on the counter-bar for us to eat whenever we came back from mission. We rarely knew how long it had sat out and it was rarely covered with lids or plastic.

Given these conditions, it was only a matter of time before one of us got sick. Me. Being sick in Iraq is an awful thing, but being sick from food poisoning, especially when you are a lone woman in a group of men (by that time the RCT social scientist had returned to al Asad), trying to do a mission, is exceptionally bad. I am pretty sure it was Cook's baked chicken that did me in. We came back from a morning meeting with the Sinjar Mayor and had lunch around noon. After lunch, we had arranged an interview with the Peshmerga.[17] The meeting was intended to be with the enlisted men, a relatively casual and mostly get-to-know-you type meeting. However, when we arrived there were several vehicles out front and two rows of soldiers lining the front entrance.

As soon as we took our seats uniformed men filed in and stood in front of their chairs until a stately man with a very impressive moustache entered and walked behind the large desk. Once he sat, the rest of the room followed suit. He was introduced as one of the generals in the Kurdish Army of Peshmerga, and he had come down from northern Sinjar to speak with us after he had heard about our meeting request. We assured him our intentions were just to meet our neighbors, but he waved his hand to silence us and began telling a story of how the Pesh and the American soldiers had shed blood together to topple Saddam's regime. He said that once blood is shed with the Pesh, the two forces become brothers. He told me he knew who I was, and asked, "Why are you inquiring about the Yezidi?" I told him I was trying to learn about their culture. Considering many of the interviewees feared the Pesh, I did not want to provide details that might get people into trouble. He smiled and the officer to his left handed him a piece of paper. He unfolded it and began to read my list of interview questions. He raised a bushy eyebrow at me and the room began to tilt.

I was sweating heavily, my breathing was rapid and, feeling sicker by the minute, I squeezed the hand of the Special Forces guy sitting next to me. I looked the Peshmerga general in the eye and told him that it was apparent that he had ordered the Alsayeish (Kurdish Secret Police) to follow me. "I applaud you," I said; then continued, "If we are to be 'brothers', please explain why the Pesh have moved so many forces to the Iraqi Army-controlled areas and built numerous new forts in areas that are not Kurd-controlled?" He looked at me and said, "It's for the protection of the Yezidi, to protect them from al-Qaeda, and themselves. The Yezidi are unsure of who they are, and are politically split, so the Pesh are making sure that no hostilities occur."

Considering the Yezidi were openly afraid of the Pesh, claiming the Pesh were making false midnight arrests, and the Yezidi were being threatened with revocation of basic services like food stamps and water deliveries if they did not publicly claim to be Kurds, I sincerely doubted that the Pesh were securing the communities for their "own good." I was not there to start a fight, and desperately wanted to vomit, so I tried to change the subject. I was shaking in my seat and the room was spinning when the General said, "you are as white as a ghost." The ODA guy on my left quickly escorted me outside, where I fell to my knees, vomited everywhere, and passed out. I woke up fourteen hours later hooked up to an I.V. in my little trailer at the back of the base. The medic who was changing out my I.V. bag with fluids and Zofran, a medication that prevents vomiting, said that everyone was talking about the meeting, not just because I had passed out, but because I had held it together long enough to go head to head with the Peshmerga General. I was feeling that I had messed the meeting up, had failed in some regard, and was mortified at having passed out, but instead the Special Forces team was praising me.

IN CONCLUSION

During my HTS deployment at al Asad, I had the daunting task of understanding the various indigenous peoples and the primary socio-cultural issues that would be of critical concern to Coalition forces. In my case that meant having to learn about the Iraqi Arabs (Sunni and Shia), the Kurds, the Yezidi, the Army, Marines, the Infantry Marines, and the Special Forces. The geographic range I needed to understand during my tenure was Anbar and Ninewa Provinces, and eventually the city of Mosul. I also had to learn how to work with and integrate with the non-governmental (NGO) personnel and the Department of State

Provincial Reconstruction Teams who often had a vested stake in acquiring the information I had collected.

But perhaps the most critical knowledge I had to acquire concerned the culture of the military. Each service branch is inherently different; soldiers and Marines go through different training systems and bond in different ways. Their shared experiences and histories vary by branch as well. In addition, there are subcultures within each branch with experiences and histories unique to their groups. The LAR infantry Marines out in the field had a cohesiveness that was not shared by the Marines at al Asad. Whereas Marines from the infantry were more open, honest, crude, relaxed, and bonded, the Marines at headquarters struggled with red tape, rules, a lot of officers, routine, and desk jobs.

These different military units handled local people differently and approached cultural learning differently. Unlike the ODA whose mission often required them to work closely with local nationals and whose training and education often included substantial regional components, the infantry Marines did not learn about the culture of Iraq. They relied on the officers and the intel department to tell them the snippets of information they'd need to conduct their missions. Once I was there, I provided the necessary information for success without requiring them to take the time (that they did not have) to read manuals and books about Iraqi Arabic, Kurdish, Yezidi, and Chaldo-Christian customs.

No matter how well integrated, I was always an "other," an outsider. Of course, I was a desired asset with critical cultural knowledge and therefore was not an "eater." However, at the time when I was with HTS none of the service branches felt that advisors were essential to mission success. (They were willing to accept "good enough" which often meant muddling through deployments while making huge and at times disastrous cultural mistakes.) But the most significant factor of my "otherness" was that I was a civilian and female.

In order to meet my HTS mission, I had to develop a toolkit of various integration techniques that worked with a wide range of people in a short period of time. Knowing how to play cards helped because it opened doors and built rapport, and so did being professional without ego about my education or pay grade. Being prepared, being knowledgeable about the research, maintaining my ethical standards, and maintaining my honesty helped me to integrate with the military. I also stood my ground with the military units I served and with the local nationals when necessary. Perhaps integration lessons or cultural clues could be printed on decks of playing cards, so they can be learned while throwing down a hand?

6

THE FOUR PILLARS OF INTEGRATION

HOW TO MAKE SOCIAL SCIENCE WORK IN A WAR ZONE

Kathleen Reedy

While I was in Afghanistan, there was one question above all others that would make me wince: "What exactly are you doing out here?" While most military units deploy knowing how to incorporate Civil Affairs, Military Information Support Operations (MISO, formerly Psychological Operations), and even Provincial Reconstruction Teams, an HTT with its social scientists is not something they train to use or expect to have. Military leaders do not always understand what a socio-cultural perspective offers them, and doctrinally an HTT does not have a natural "home" or method of employment in the host unit. This dynamic means that every team must prove its usefulness with little or no direction while negotiating where, how, and why it should fit in. Such flexibility can allow leaders to tailor the structure to meet their needs, but when combined with a situation where neither the team nor the unit understands how such research should be conducted or used, it can also create gaps where an HTT does not function effectively.

Based on experiences with HTTs in both Iraq and Afghanistan, I suggest there are four key elements to applying social science in a war zone. Each is essential for truly integrating this kind of information into the

167

military decision-making process and contributing meaningful research to the counterinsurgency effort. Social science should lead to: short-term recommendations on issues of immediate concern; medium-term analysis and measurements of a unit's effectiveness; long-term identification of local and national social issues leading to insurgency; and most importantly, successful integration into the unit to ensure recommendations are actionable and "actioned." This chapter will examine case studies of each pillar in order to illustrate the importance of socio-cultural knowledge in conflict zones, what it offers to deployed units, how getting and applying it rests on the HTT really being a part of the team, and what adaptations it requires an anthropologist to make to her standard research to fit into a military environment.

PILLAR ONE: SHORT-TERM RECOMMENDATIONS

The first and perhaps easiest use of an HTT is in dealing with short-term issues that are population-centric. Typically, HTTs were tasked to explain and map the local tribal situation. Teams could produce quick turn-around social network displays and identify powerbrokers, as well as gather accounts of the history of tribal disputes and alliances in the area. Providing such background information, especially if it is new rather than regurgitated, has its place, but interpreting or analyzing the data so as to offer actionable recommendations is essential to getting a unit to trust and rely on you.

Zadran Unity

When I was first sent to work with 1–33 Cavalry Squadron (hereafter 1–33) in Afghanistan, my assigned task was exactly this sort of tribal study. The Zadran tribe covers nine different districts in three provinces and is one of the major tribes in Khost, Paktika, and Paktia Provinces.[1] They were of interest to the military primarily because the main insurgent group in the area, the Haqqanis, belonged to the Zadran tribe. The unit wanted me to "find out" about the Zadran, just as every unit who had occupied the area as far back as the British had done. No one was entirely clear on what they wanted me to uncover, but I figured I would look for local leaders who could mobilize the population, historical alliances, blood feuds, and general attitudes toward the government.[2]

I quickly discovered that the Zadran live in a very rural, mountainous area in eastern Afghanistan. They did not see themselves or act as if they were some kind of unified social entity; they had no tribal leaders with the ability to mobilize the population, and people were not likely to support someone in the insurgency or the government just because they shared a last name. Real authority and influence rested at the village level (and most of these villages were small, with maybe five to ten families), not at some higher, largely imaginary tribal level.

Merely recommending that the brigade stop worrying about the tribal issue was not really useful for making positive steps. Explaining to the unit that the information implied that support for the insurgents was largely passive and so could be combated was much more "actionable." The prerequisites for insurgency include a vulnerable population, a lack of local leadership, and a lack of effective government.[3] There was not much we could quickly do about the remote and impoverished status of the area or about the Zadran leadership. A lack of effective government, however, was an issue we *could* influence in various ways. Rather than just providing cultural background, I was able to steer the unit away from one course of action (engage the tribes) and offer them a practical alternative (develop the local government) in order to reduce support for the insurgents.

Paving a Road

Offering a tangible recommendation for action, rather than merely dismissing the tribal issue and telling the unit to stop obsessing over it, earned me some credibility with the unit's leadership. Being seen as a contributing team member allowed me to tackle problems that were less obviously "socio-cultural" in nature, because I had proved I could combine population-based information with COIN theory and offer solutions that the unit could actually enact. When 1–33's successor unit, 6–4 Cavalry Squadron (hereafter 6–4), came in, they inherited me along with their Area of Operations (AO) and continued to incorporate me to an even greater extent than had their predecessors.

Several months into their deployment, the Provincial Reconstruction Team and their partnered Afghan officials decided to stop funding a local road-paving project because it was deemed too expensive and too insecure after workers on the road were attacked. The commander of 6–4 initially lacked strong opinions on the project, but I was already out in that portion of the AO and the troop commander in charge there was concerned. He could not give me a specific reason, but he felt it was a bad idea to stop the paving. A new teammate and I decided to do everything we could to offer the troop commander some support, or at least allay his concerns. We managed to visit almost a dozen villages in the surrounding area over the next few days and discovered that the troop commander's hesitation was well-founded. The population living near the planned road was, by and large, economically very vulnerable and lacking in any real local leadership. In addition, they felt abandoned by their government as they had received almost no development projects in years. They had looked forward to the road as it would offer both short-term employment for contractors and long-term economic benefits by making their valley more accessible. In addition, we could see that it would generate support for the government by showing that their officials had finally prioritized their remote little area.

Working closely with the troop commander and his staff, we quickly drafted a joint report to send to the squadron commander, recommending that the project be continued, even if that required cutting funding from more stable and secure areas. Upon reading it, the squadron commander quickly agreed, saying he had never realized the greater implications, and he became a strong advocate to continue the paving.

In these immediate-need situations, the HTT can offer much more than social maps and identifying leaders. They have the ability to penetrate into the deeper social, political, economic, and even security-based issues that lie at the heart of seemingly simply matters in a relatively short period of time and convince the military to "do the right thing."

PILLAR TWO: MEDIUM-TERM MEASURES OF EFFECT

Uncovering the underlying concerns in an AO is time-consuming. Thus, experience and continuity in a battalion-size AO were part of what allowed an HTT to offer meaningful medium-term analysis and assistance to units.

Term Assessments

One of the hardest things for a deployed military unit and its civilian partners to do while in the full swing of things is to step back and make a real, holistic assessment of what they have accomplished. The daily pace of running missions and operations, such as meeting quotas on how many people to fingerprint, and figuring out where and how to spend development money quickly, consumes every waking moment. Commanders do not have the luxury of convening a regular round-table meeting with all the soldiers and leaders who are out on the ground and then sitting back to consider the bigger picture before making an informed assessment. Further, the baton-pass between the incoming and outgoing units is far from smooth. The HTT, in theory, does not change out at the same time as the unit, and so can provide consistent analyses. Even more importantly, team members regularly operate between the tactical and decision-making levels, spending time on the ground with line platoons getting the deep perspective, and then working with commanders and staff to incorporate this information into broader goals. This continuing ability to occupy different levels means that the HTT is in an ideal position to serve in a role that few else in the unit can: the HTT can offer real insight into what, if any, impacts a unit is experiencing over time.

HTT continuity is particularly important at the unit's halfway mark, when they have had enough time to initiate projects and programs, but also have enough time left to alter their strategies if things are not work-ing. Offering recommendations at this point does not particularly require new research, just an understanding of how the entire AO looks and has looked over the course of several months. It basically involves looking at the region, seeing what has changed (or not), why, and what can be changed to achieve the desired effect (if anything).

When 6–4 hit their halfway mark (six months), the squadron com-mander called together his troop and platoon leaders, as well as all the staff and enablers, to have an open discussion on what they had achieved so far. It was an awkward and uncomfortable moment. The commander had drawn up a list of questions he thought were relevant, but no one wanted to speak up with negative comments, so it was not as useful as it could have been.

Afterward, I sat down and decided to put some thought into it. Having spent several more months in the AO than the unit and having talked regularly with command, Afghans, and line soldiers, I had a pretty good intuitive sense of how things looked at the moment com-pared with when I had first arrived. I therefore set out to write a mid-term assessment. I gave each district—the smallest political unit we worked with—a quick "better, the same, or worse" assessment, then broke them down into various topics with more detailed explanations and recommendations on how to go forward. Some of the topics were patterned on the strategic priorities of the military, but some were just ones that seemed relevant according to my experiences.

For instance, local governance[4] was a major focus for high-level decision-makers. My approach was to assess whether the efficacy of and local opinions about governance had changed, and then whether that change had anything to do with what the US military had done. In one district, everyone agreed that governance had actually improved, but it was because a new district governor had been appointed and people liked the new one more than the old. Initially, it seemed improvement in local perceptions of governance had nothing to do with the unit's actions. However, there was more to the story, as 6–4 had changed its patrol patterns in the area when they arrived, making an effort to be regularly present on the main roads in much the same way that state troopers are on highways in the US. Though that presence had not entirely eliminated the violence, especially in remote areas, I knew from interviewing local Afghans that these patrols created an improved sense of safety, making people feel more comfortable going to the district center and engaging the new governor. They knew, if nothing else, that they would be safe on their way to and from the district center. The unit's background actions, then, had enabled governance to improve by making it more readily accessible. This impact would not be visible unless one spent several months talking to people as I did; only then would it be apparent that people felt a little safer than they had before.

Measures of Effect

Underpinning my analysis were my own measures of how well the unit was doing. Though I tried to separate them out into distinct lines, overall they were based on my personal, highly qualitative, and often intuitive understandings of a place. For most of the daily village assessments I wrote, the first section I included was one I called "atmosphere," for lack of a better term. In this section I tried to encapsulate the sense or vibe I got from a particular place, which could be very hard to put into words, but was, in my view, one of the best and most effective measures of local attitudes toward the military, the government, and the insurgents. But as useful and helpful as this qualitative data was for me, it was not exactly something that military leaders, or even other civilians, could put on their progress reports.

What they needed were clear, distinct, and consistent measures. But numbers of violent actions, "bad guys" captured, or dollars spent were not always really informative about the reality on the ground. To their credit, the military acknowledges this fact and generally considers these figures to be "measures of performance" (e.g. bad guys captured) as compared to "measures of effect" (e.g. reduced insurgent influence).[5] While I was with 6–4, it came down the pipeline that everything we did was required to have thought-out measures of performance and effect. The trouble with that was that even if we said the measure of effect for a road-paving project would be "increased approval and support of the local government," there were always so many other factors involved in that support (reported corruption, change in officials, insurgent activity, and so on) that tying an intended effect to a single cause was unreasonable. Nor was there any effort to establish some kind of baseline against which we could measure any future impacts. The military system is just not used to dealing with qualitative data on such a large scale.

Social scientists often strive to make qualitative information more comprehensible and to integrate it with quantitative measures. My time on the ground, as well as my dual qualitative/quantitative perspective, helped me provide a baseline of recommendations as to how various efforts were likely to impact the population, and what kinds of questions line units could ask in three or six months' time to assess the effects. I could also make plans to have my team carry out more detailed research to supplement their efforts, so we could bring our expertise to bear in trying to tease out causal relationships.

For example, another battalion I briefly worked with was considering where to start a new initiative to build and train a local police force. Their initial thought was to put it in a district along the Pakistani border, which was generally peaceful and did not have a permanent American base. I argued against it, saying that there would be no way to assess the measures of effect quantitatively or qualitatively because there was almost no insurgent violence in the district and the local government was relatively popular. If anything, adding a new American presence might cause insurgent activity to increase and make it look as if the plan to put in a police force had not just failed, but been detrimental to the population.

It was, in fact, often difficult to get units to see past attacks as the prime measure of effect. It took an HTT's qualitative eye sometimes to see beyond this measure. While I was at a combat outpost (COP) for yet another battalion, there was an unfortunate incident where part of an American illumination round (an artillery round attached to a parachute that provides an intense light for people to see by at night) fell into a nearby wheat field and set it alight. The area had been hostile to Americans and the Afghan government to begin with, so the platoon and I went out first thing in the morning to apologize and pay for the damages. Ultimately, the local farmer was overpaid; not because of our naïvety but in hopes of showing that the Americans were more interested in being good neighbors than in getting the best deal. A few nights later, the outpost received nearly a dozen rounds of incoming mortar fire, making it look like a negotiation failure. A purely quantitative analysis left soldiers and commanders feeling that the gesture had been wasted. I urged patience, and when I had to leave the outpost, I asked unit leadership not to keep track of the attacks on the base, but to get out into the population and assess the atmosphere. In the months after the reparation payment, the previously cold and distant population had warmed somewhat and engaged more readily with the Americans on patrol. A qualitative measure of effect showed an improvement. Attacks on the base continued, but what seemed like a negative quantitative measurement actually confirmed that the American gesture had won some local support. Feeling threatened, the insurgents had to increase their attacks to compensate for that development. A simple, short-term quantitative measurement would have made it seem that the act of paying reparations was a waste of time, but my ability to combine it with longer-term qualitative measurements that soldiers could carry out themselves revealed a different picture.

PILLAR THREE: LONG-TERM ANALYSIS OF SOURCES OF INSTABILITY

The long-term perspective is perhaps one of the most difficult perspectives for a military unit to incorporate into their daily planning. Realistically, over the course of a nine- or even twelve-month deployment, considering the time it takes to get into place, find the rhythm of things, and prepare to come home, units really only have a few months to focus on accomplishing anything. Despite all attempts to make transitions smooth, battle handovers from one unit to the next rarely provide for a consistent operating environment. Trying to achieve long-term effects is nearly impossible. Big projects and ideas often get lost.

One of the major consequences of unit rotation and time constraints is that while higher-echelon strategic planners may have some kind of long-term plan for the entire country, these are not readily translated into long-term initiatives and plans at the local levels. But in counter-insurgency operations, getting buy-in and support at the local level is the most important aspect to defeating insurgents and creating stability. When COIN theorists talk about uncovering the prerequisites and root causes of insurgency, it is with the understanding that these can vary from one village to the next. This gap between strategic and tactical realities is what creates a situation like the one in Afghanistan where, despite hundreds of thousands of military troops, the most optimistic estimates suggest that only half of polled districts have a functioning government presence and many of those continue to face security risks.[6]

HTTs can once again play a role here, with their big-picture/little-picture approach and their team continuity over time. Between and around the small, immediate projects that units request, the HTT can focus on uncovering and monitoring the underlying sources of instability and support for the insurgency (or at least lack of support for the government). They can then recommend short- or even longer-term projects that units can undertake to address these concerns, which they might otherwise have overlooked. Interacting with the population with an eye toward strategic goals is something the HTT is better prepared to handle than platoon leaders (who are focused on immediate needs) or even other enablers like intelligence officers (who are focused on finding individuals and networks) or Civil Affairs (who are often overwhelmed with overseeing more finance-based projects).

Getting Out as Good Governance

While out conducting patrols in the rural and mountainous areas of Afghanistan, I often asked people what they thought about their local government. If counterinsurgency happens at the local level, the existence of a government is essential to encourage people to support the government instead of an insurgent group. I found people tended to answer my questions regarding one of the most influential local figures, the district governor (DG)—who is appointed rather than elected—in one of two ways: either "he's great, he does a lot for us," or "he never comes here."

People would rarely condemn a local official outright. Instead, they would complain that he did not come to visit them. It did not take long for me to realize that *was* their way of saying they did not approve of their DG.[7] People's concern over lack of visits ran a lot deeper than wanting someone to come in for a photo opportunity. Consultation is one of the most highly valued aspects of leadership for Pashtun Afghans. Whenever they have a major dispute, an elder will take charge, but all of the men from a village or area will get together and have an opportunity to speak their mind in what is called a *jirga*. Ensuring everyone has a chance to speak his piece is central to getting community buy-in for any decision, and this foundation is as true for government officials as for elders.

Many districts hold semi-regular *shuras* (council meetings) to allow villagers some kind of informal advisory input into governance, most often concerning development funding. However, most villagers complained that only elders were invited or allowed to go to those *shuras*, leaving the majority of men out of the consultation process. That system was, they felt, a slight to their honor. As a result, they all too often were not invested in the *shura's* decisions, especially since the DG was appointed and so had no formal accountability to the population.

American military and civilian leaders recognized the importance of interaction between the population and the local leaders, but many did not realize how essential it was to go beyond just including the elders in consultation processes if they really wanted to develop local buy-in for the government. The impacts would be slow to accumulate, but it was crucial for developing lasting legitimacy. To that end, our HTT recommended that units make an extra effort to encourage local DGs to actually visit the villages in their districts, ensuring everyone had the opportunity to speak to them, not just the elders.

In the end, recommending that the DGs get out more, and perhaps providing security for them to do so, was not a huge or onerous task, but it was not something a commander usually put on his PowerPoint slide as an accomplishment for that week. The effects were hard to quantify, especially in the short term. But my team was able to present that information in a way that was straightforward and intelligible to a COIN-trained military audience, and to offer recommendations that they could implement in the short term, even if they might not be around to see the end results. Understanding the cultural dynamics, then, and how they translated into ways the military could make small changes that would have a real impact on long-term stability was exactly the role for which HTTs are suited. In addition, though units may come and go, ideally the HTT will be around to measure the effects and help provide the continuity to carry projects and plans across a span of time longer than a single deployment. When they inherited me from 1–33, 6–4 embraced this idea and used my expertise to tailor the entire second half of their deployment to the tactics, techniques, and procedures that I had recommended, based on the preceding unit's effectiveness. Their approach led to continued improvement in the local area, and when I left to return to the US, they were so convinced that this long-term vision was essential to their mission that the commander insisted he have an instant backfill for me to continue the process.

PILLAR FOUR: INTEGRATION WITH THE HOST UNIT

Conducting analysis and making recommendations aimed at improving short-, medium-, and long-term effects are thwarted if an HTT is not fully integrated with the host unit. Over the course of participating in two Program Development Team assessments of deployed teams and deploying twice myself, a good half of the teams I observed were failing in some way. Some of these instances were due to operational inefficiency on HTS's part. I was on one team that, for several months, consisted entirely of three social scientists. It had no team leader, research managers, or human terrain analysts. We had trouble getting our timesheets validated, much less doing effective research. There had been no accidents or emergencies, it was just that the "Stateside" planners had failed to do their jobs correctly and left the team and our host brigade without the promised support.

Personality is also a major factor in whether a team is successful or not, especially the personality of the team leader. If he or she does not mesh with the host unit, the teams are quickly sidelined or ignored. Of course, the host unit's attitudes and personalities also play a role; I have seen brigades that were so focused on the "killing bad guys" aspect of their jobs that they largely ignored anyone who was not involved in lethal activities, including members of their own staff such as Civil Affairs or information operations. All of these staff elements, along with the HTT, were basically dumped in a room together and allowed to do whatever they wanted as long as it did not require any assets or resources.

In some ways, though, these two problems are fairly straightforward and easy to address if higher management is willing to step in. Far more common and more difficult to fix are teams that are sidelined because neither they nor the host unit really knows what to do with them. While conducting the assessments, I had numerous staff officers and commanders tell me that while they liked the individuals on the team, they really were not sure what they did or whether they were useful. In these instances, teams often chose or were assigned to focus on what I called "cultural fluff"—topics that were interesting but were not truly useful or operationally relevant. Topics like the aforementioned tribal studies were all too often put into this category if the HTT did not make an active effort to highlight how and why they were relevant to the daily lives of soldiers conducting counterinsurgency.

Full integration into a host unit, then, is essential if an HTT is going to be able to offer useful and actionable analysis and recommendations. Teams have to be fully staffed; personalities have to be vetted, or at least put aside so that working relationships can develop; the unit has to be receptive; and everyone has to know the HTT's actual capabilities. There is a handbook for commanders on how to employ teams, but it offers a wide range of possibilities without much detail, and most commanders do not have the time or energy to spend reading booklets while deployed. Since there are still many commanders who do not know what an HTT is and more who do not know whether they will have one or not, they do not waste their time reading booklets before deploying. Thus, it is largely up to the team to sell itself. Established teams need to approach an incoming unit with strong examples of previous or on-going research and its impacts. New teams need to offer a strong research plan that gives explicit examples of the short-, medium-, and/or long-term recommendations that will come out of their work to make a good first impression and earn the trust of the unit.

Organization

One of the most important aspects of developing a functioning team with strong research capabilities (and also one of the first things a brigade will ask about) is how the team is or should be organized. Most units have a set procedure on how to organize themselves. Different staff sections all know what areas fall under their responsibility. Established enablers, like Civil Affairs or Psychological Operations, have been around long enough that everyone knows what they do and where they fit. But HTTs, being newcomers to the game, do not have a natural or doctrinal home. This unspecified role is intentional, as it allows a degree of flexibility for units to employ them as they see fit. When you get a proactive team and an open-minded host unit, this arrangement can be ideal. Otherwise, teams may slip through the cracks or get subordinated to a staff unit that might limit their full potential.

I have seen many forms of team and unit organization that have worked under different circumstances. Commonly, the HTT resides at brigade (or equivalent) headquarters and moves out en masse to address specific problems that arise. While flooding the zone may allow teams to collect a lot of data in a short time, it limits them to immediate issues and eliminates the possibility of conducting research and analysis at the medium- and long-term levels that are the core of counterinsurgency. Enabling teams to develop familiarity and expertise with the population and their vulnerabilities requires a more distributed approach to HTT staff integration. The best organization I have been a part of had team members individually embedded at the battalion level. In many ways, the brigade's role is to support battalions, and that is where much of US military strategy is actually executed. Any HTT that wants to conduct research in an area has to coordinate with the battalion leadership anyway, so it makes sense to live and operate at that level. Rather than working under the nebulous label of "special staff," as happens at brigade level, an HTT member at battalion level becomes just one of the team with greater access to the battalion commander than ever happens at brigade level. For example, I embedded with several battalions and in each was welcomed and encouraged to walk into the commander's office whenever I wanted. In fact, my position as a civilian whom they did not have to rate often made me seem more like an equal with whom ideas could be regularly shared.

Working as part of a smaller staff at battalion level meant that I was closer to the action and more easily incorporated into all parts of the planning and analysis cycles. Like other staff, I was actually responsible for writing part of the commander's weekly report up to the brigade commander. I built working relationships with everyone, which established trust in me and my judgment. Those foundations allowed me to make practical and relevant recommendations to the staff and command because I knew what they were doing, what they could do, and how to frame my ideas. And because I was part of the team, my recommendations often did not come in the form of long-winded papers, as some HTTs produce, but in informal conversations or emails, or as part of my slide and briefing spot in the daily Commander's Update Brief. (And if there is anything that indicates you are a part of the team, it is having your own CUB slide.)

Working at battalion level also made getting out on patrols much easier. From a battalion staff, I could quickly and easily get down to the company and platoon level, who interact with the population every day. The much smaller size of the battalion AO meant that I could feasibly visit all or most of the AO and make regular trips back to the same villages. I did not always have a specific problem or issue in mind; I would just go out regularly to assess the medium- and long-term issues that were really at stake. This familiarity with an AO was what ultimately gave me the background to make judgments about the real population vulnerabilities in different areas and how we were impacting them.

Ideally, at least one HTT member would be embedded in each battalion (two for the larger ones), while the team leader and a social scientist would remain at the brigade headquarters to receive and coordinate research at that level. This enables a brigade's research taskings and priorities to be relayed to teammates already embedded in the relevant battalion AO. Such a set-up actually facilitates travel outside the wire by lessening resistance to having an unknown entity tromp about in their battlespace and eat up their resources. Granted, not all HTTs have the numbers to organize like this, but even in Iraq when I was part of a four-person team, we were able to embed two teammates with the battalions (determined by the brigades according to their priorities), while the team leader and I stayed at brigade. With strong information sharing, I could organize research to meet the brigade's interests while my teammates helped the battalions with their needs.

Top to Bottom Integration

Too often, HTTs (and other civilian and military enablers) focus only on the brigade or battalion commanders and staff and use the company and platoon levels as ways to get out and conduct research. I have seen many instances where platoons grow to resent these intrusions and having to "baby-sit" or "nerd-herd" some HTT. Some platoons went out of their way to make it difficult for outsiders to get a seat on their patrols because they resented being treated as inferior and did not see a lot of value in social science research.

The first key to ensuring that an HTT has regular and easy access to patrols (and therefore to research participants in the host nation population) is to engage and interact with the platoons. When they learned that I was not uppity, that I could take a joke, and most importantly that I could take direction in an emergency, platoons were often willing to take me out. Instead of waiting for a commander to assign a platoon to escort me outside the wire, I asked platoons to take me out on missions. Asking them, and being willing to take "not today" for an answer, won me a lot of approval. After a while, some platoons independently put me on their missions and later informed me that I was coming along. Data collection was a lot easier that way.

Another civilian once asked me how I got the soldiers to like me so much on a professional level. I asked a company commander what he thought and he replied without hesitation, "You give back to us. Most enablers only write their reports and give feedback to the higher-ups, but you give feedback to my soldiers, platoons and me first. We get to see your reports and hear your ideas before anyone else, you offer useful suggestions, and you listen to ours. No one else does that. Plus, your reports aren't 20 pages long."

After patrols, I would often sit down with the platoon and company leaders and give them my thoughts, including any recommendations that were useful to them. I would sometimes even take notes for them, since I was doing it for myself anyway. This process helped me vet my information before passing it on. Interviewing soldiers and getting their insights and observations added a lot to my analyses.

Finally, I did not write long papers. While doing the assessments, many units complained that a forty-page paper describing an issue that came up a month ago was of little or no use. It was already out of date and few people had the time to read something that long. Writing for your audience is pivotal, and the deployed military audience generally wants its information short, sweet, and in five bullet points or less. The longest papers I wrote in over two years of being deployed were no more than ten pages (with pictures), and the first page of each was always a few bullets that summarized the entire thing and offered relevant recommendations. An HTT can write longer papers in their own time, after the short report has already come out or by request, but to avoid being dismissed information had to be brief and to the point.

Last but not least was "actionability." A critical aspect of research for the military was offering recommendations that a unit could actually carry out. In Iraq, our HTT discovered that corruption was unexpectedly a much bigger local concern than security and violence. "Eliminate corruption" is a nice idea, but not a practical recommendation that a military unit can actually implement. However, I have seen HTT papers that offer just that kind of broad and vague advice. Instead, our team chose to say, "conduct workshops with Iraqi journalists and [the American journalism professor who conveniently was doing a month-long embed] to help educate the Iraqis on how to do more effective investigative journalism into corruption." That was something tangible the unit could do, so they jumped at it and it earned us a lot of respect.

THE HIDDEN FOUNDATION: ADOPTING A NEW STYLE

Underlying all these pillars is the unspoken requirement for a social scientist to rethink her own way of "doing business." Anyone who decides to work in an applied setting rather than the often highly theoretical one of academia (particularly in fields like anthropology) must make a transition. My first concern was ethical in nature. The anthropological community's debates regarding the Human Terrain System[8] were always a serious concern of mine. When beginning work with a new unit, my first step was to clarify what I did and did not do, both in terms of research topics and actual data collection. Some of my directions included: I would not go into someone's home unless for a pre-planned meeting; I would not talk to anyone who did not choose to speak to me of his or her own free will (and I was to be the judge of that); I was not an intelligence gatherer; all of my information was unclassified; I would not record or hand over any names aside from known public officials; I would not ask about insurgents or supporters; and most importantly, my data was protected and while I would share my final analysis, the raw information was strictly my own. Army intelligence sections can be a little possessive of their turf, so were usually relieved that I was making an active effort to stay out of their lane. Soldiers on patrol never minded that their jobs actually got easier when I came along: all they had to do was keep an eye on me, and since I only talked to people who came out into the streets (which sometimes meant I did not talk to anyone at all, if we were in an area that was not very supportive of Americans), they did not have a lot to worry about.

Maintaining an ethical stance as part of an HTT was not much more complicated than my graduate research in Syria in 2004. In both cases, my primary worry was protecting my research participants from harm, which meant taking great care in choosing who to interview and how to control and disseminate my information. In each case, I was surprised by how simple that process really was. On patrol, soldiers were always responsive to whether or not I would interview someone, and I took notes on my personal computer that was not connected to the military network. I would email my final, scrubbed analysis to my unclassified work email and disseminate it from there. No one ever asked for more than I chose to give, nor did anyone I had interviewed come to harm. Though I keep it private to protect anonymity, all my research data is and will remain unclassified. Copies of my reports were sent to the classified system because those computer systems were more reliable and this was standard operating procedure in a war zone,[9] but they retained their "unclassified" labels and I maintain copies of them on my personal, unclassified system.

My research methods in an HTT were different from my grad school experience. At no point did I conduct ethnography as part of an HTT,[10] as compared to having spent thirteen months conducting fieldwork in Syria. Rather than living with the population, my time was limited, so I relied on semi-structured qualitative interviews that would usually last about an hour. On a bad day, I might find myself cut short after fifteen minutes because of unforeseen events. After a few weeks spent in one area, I could get a good sense of what was important and how to tailor my interviews, but the first few patrols were always tricky as I tried to develop a reputation in the community and figure out the locals' major concerns.

Working for a customer rather than for the sake of the research itself also distinguished HTT research from traditional anthropology. When I first started working with a particular unit, they would generally have a list of things that they thought they wanted to know about the "local culture." It took time for me to build rapport with them before they trusted me enough to let me be the one who decided what questions they should be asking. Even when I got to that point, though, it took an adjustment on my part to work to a timeline and produce those "actionable" recommendations. When I went out on a patrol, units would expect some kind of instant report on what I had learned, preferably broken down into three to five bullet points. They automatically expected instantaneous and easily quantifiable results to justify why they had risked people's lives to take me outside. This attitude was not so much because they did not understand that social science is qualitative and takes time, but because they expected this of everyone who went outside the wire. To fit in, I had to balance my ideals with theirs: I would give them quick observations, but always with the caveat that it would take time and repeated trips before I could offer anything of real substance or solid recommendations. When I left Syria after thirteen months, I felt that I still had a lot more information to gather before I would *really* have a grasp of what was going on. That feeling was magnified significantly in a deployed environment where the aphorism "perfect is the enemy of good" reigns supreme. Learning to accept and work with extremely limited timelines was a major challenge, but continually coming up with practical recommendations was perhaps the most difficult adjustment. Anthropologists are skilled at identifying and assessing social inequities and power dynamics, but often do so from the big-picture perspective and with the intent of raising awareness rather than offering immediate, easy-to-follow suggestions on how to alter or improve the situation.[11] Learning how to do that, but then rapidly turning those observations into small-scale changes that a commander could effect on the spot, took some trial and error. All in all, getting used to a very condensed timeline, non-ethnographic research methods, and producing regular recommendations rather than just high-level analysis took some time and active effort on my part. However, without my willingness to recognize and make those adjustments, I would never have been successful at living up to the four pillars of incorporating social science into the military mindset.

CONCLUSION

To be truly successful at integrating social science information and methods into the military process, an HTT must move beyond providing cultural background material. HTTs have a lot to offer in the way of practical and actionable recommendations that account for both short-term issues and drive towards long-term counterinsurgency goals. Their ability to make critical assessments about operating in and melding the tactical, operational, and strategic needs of a host unit makes them an invaluable source of insight for decision-makers. But the unit itself will rarely understand how to employ a team, so the members must be proactive and take the initiative in demonstrating their capabilities across the short-, medium-, and long-term pillars of research and analysis. As with their research participants, HTTs must develop rapport and credibility with the military units they support and work continually to maintain that status as a reliable entity. The fourth pillar of integration, then, is the base on which all the others rest. Knowing the customer, what kinds of information they want, and how they want it presented is what allows an HTT to be successful in any endeavor. True to the tenets of social science, this system, as any other, requires a strong working relationship as its foundation, as well as understanding one's role and the changes one has to make to fit in.

7

INVESTING IN UNCERTAINTY

APPLYING SOCIAL SCIENCE TO MILITARY OPERATIONS

James Dorough-Lewis Jr.

In the summer of 2009 I embarked on my second deployment to Baghdad. During my first tour I had been mobilized as an Army human intelligence collector and Arabic linguist. From debriefing to interrogation to managing informant networks, human intelligence (HUMINT) collection involves a host of activities where people serve as sources of information in response to gaps in knowledge. The bulk of us who were human intelligence collectors (or HUMINTers) had been required to learn a foreign language as part of our initial entry training—although, strapped for personnel, the Army temporarily suspended that requirement for many HUMINTers. From working with professors at the Defense Language Institute in Monterey, California (who were native speakers), we had learned the value of competence in cross-cultural communication. In conflict environments where partnerships with local populations make the difference between success and failure, many of my colleagues and I already felt the need for a "cultural revolution" in terms of how the US military incorporated the worldviews of Iraqis, Afghans, and other foreign nationals into its decision-making processes.

And we were not alone. Across the contemporary operational environment, the military was coming to the realization that victory in a counterinsurgency could not be achieved through the tactical attrition of low-level gun fighters. Effective counterinsurgency was not about winning on the battlefield as much as it was about seizing the premise of the battlefield itself, and reshaping it into an environment that deterred insurgent forces. Doing so required an intimate understanding of the interests of local populations, the distribution of power within them, and the ever-evolving indigenous social mechanisms in place. Because culture constitutes the meaning-making force constructing the multiple, overlapping, and even mutually exclusive realities of the battlefield itself,[1] without an ability to incorporate culture as a key decision-making factor, the military was at a loss.[2] With this awareness, the US military has come to face a paradigm shift unlike previous shifts it has undertaken over the course of our nation's history. The military as an institution began to realize the importance of cultural knowledge in fulfilling the goals of counterterrorism, stability, and humanitarian operations. Leveraging a practical (as opposed to a theoretical) understanding of culture has taken a new place at the forefront of mission planning and resource allocation in the contemporary operational environment.

When a friend mentioned that the Army was experimenting with a new program that sought to infuse the military decision-making processes of units on the ground with the knowledge they needed to negotiate the complexities of local cultures, I could not resist. So, three years after having left as a uniformed soldier and HUMINTer, I again found myself in Iraq's capital province, though now as a civilian social scientist and doctoral student in the field of conflict analysis, supporting the US Army's Human Terrain System (HTS).

Drawing from these experiences, this chapter explores the influence of the US Army's approach to contemporary operations through the guise of my experience as a HUMINTer and as a social scientist. It looks at how the influence of the traditional military decision-making process sometimes works against the military's success. And it argues that establishing an embedded capacity for social science research and analysis holds promise for facilitating the military's evolution to meet the challenges of the increasingly complex environment in which it must operate. This chapter outlines my own meditations on several years of attempting to reconcile these two apparent competitors for policy-makers' attentions. It is the result of a reflection as much about myself as the outside world.

RECONCILING INTELLIGENCE AND SOCIAL SCIENCE

One of the key mantras espoused during my HTS training at Fort Leavenworth, Kansas was "We don't do intelligence." So important was the idea of what we *didn't* do, in the HTS's group identity, that it more often than not substituted for what we *did* do, which was, theoretically, social science research to help military commanders make better choices on the ground. Once I arrived in country I found the role of intelligence as something HTS did or did not do in the field was far more complicated than the bumper sticker version.

A number of terms are much harder to define in practice than one would think, starting with "intelligence." My military training had taught me that decision-makers (be they politicians or military commanders) do not always have sufficient information to do their jobs as well as needed. Missing pieces of the puzzle are prioritized as they are identified, and then restated as questions tasked out to intelligence collection professionals who may be able to provide all or part of the answers. Collectors report responses to whichever questions their sources can answer, and intelligence analysts synthesize all the responses into a final report that informs decision-makers, enabling them to make wise choices. New missing pieces are identified as they emerge and the process repeats itself. Granted, this is an oversimplification of the activities undergirding a rich community of constantly evolving members and capabilities, but it is essentially what intelligence professionals know as the "intelligence cycle." The collated, collective response analysts produce is referred to as "intelligence." Going into it, it seemed as if HTS's sensitivities about being associated with "intelligence" really had nothing to do with the nature of intelligence itself, as I understood it. What was wrong with giving information to decision-makers so that they could make better decisions in the name of the American people and those they were trying to support?

Objections within HTS to *doing intelligence* appeared to spring from two major lines of thinking. First, the intelligence community has a long history of violating basic American values. As one of my former commanders cautioned us more than once, intelligence professionals in general have historically demonstrated stronger intestinal fortitude to complete a mission in spite of its challenges than moral courage to do the right thing in spite of pressures against it. Some of course would say that values shift over time and an entire community of professionals cannot be held accountable for being unable to predict how citizens of the future might interpret their activities. Point well taken. But if a shroud of secrecy over current operations means that the public learns about abuses committed by the intelligence community well after the fact, then the public has little recourse but to assume that the intelligence community's scandals of tomorrow are being carried out today. At the same time, the history of social science is not exactly free of its own transgressions. Laws and policies governing research within the United States were enacted in response to a string of violations of basic American values, as well. From my perspective as a social scientist "on the shop floor," so to speak, HTS's phobia about being associated with "intelligence" stemmed from not wanting to be thought of as an organization that failed to inform and respect those who agreed to participate in its research.

The second line of thinking might have been the least well understood, judging by the comparatively few times it was explicitly articulated within the organization. At that time, HTS was a proof-of-concept project with an as-of-yet undefined fit within the grander scheme of military operations. It was not within the best interests of HTS's long-term survival to compete against already well entrenched functions of the military system. As we were frequently reminded during our HTS training, the Army already had intelligence collection, analysis, and management assets, as well as assets to liaise between military units and the civilian population (civil–military operations), assets to develop programs to influence the population (information operations), and so forth. HTS was to be a synthesizing agent at the level of unit commanders that made all these other assets function better—in military terms, a "force multiplier"—by connecting military commanders with the wealth of knowledge and insight stashed away in ivory towers. As with academic researchers, intelligence professionals spend years honing their craft, developing their voice, and acquiring their credentials. They are required to meet stringent training and certification standards to be fully vested members of the intelligence community. HTS team leaders, social scientists, research managers, and human terrain analysts (the four duty positions in HTS at the time) were not so credentialed to collect, handle, or disseminate classified information.

As one of only a few social scientists who had been an intelligence collector before joining HTS, it took constant vigilance to separate the lines between my duty position with HTS and the duty position of my past. Once in a deployed environment, away from the scrutiny of HTS's central leadership, and under pressure to achieve results for units who did not always understand what social science could contribute to their operations, it was a challenge to keep from wandering beyond HTS's organizational mandate. The ideal within HTS seemed to be that if we distanced ourselves from intelligence, and brought to the military decision-making table what could be incorporated from the social sciences while leaving intelligence personnel to perform their own functions, then we could avert an inevitable clash of interests.

Even now, social science's relationship with intelligence has yet to reach a state of mutual respect, which is unfortunate because the two have much to learn from each other, especially through the lens of HTS's diverse and sometimes contradictory experiences. It is my firm position that social science and intelligence offer distinct but complementary contributions toward achieving the objectives of peace and stability in a conflict environment. The most disconcerting aspect of my experiences in the fields of social science and of intelligence has been the lack of clarity regarding how each community defines and evaluates the other. The social science/intelligence debate usually begins with how social science serves the interests of the intelligence community and why that may be a desirable or undesirable relationship.[3] In some respects this is a moot point—there *is* an enduring relationship. The American intelligence community counts "Open Source Intelligence" (OSINT) as one of its five primary intelligence gathering disciplines. OSINT collectors answer intelligence requirements by culling sources of information generally available to the public or through the open market.[4] Mark Lowenthal, who served as the Assistant Director of Central Intelligence for Analysis and Production and as the Vice Chairman for Evaluation on the National Intelligence Council, specifically includes "conferences, symposia, professional associations, academic papers, and experts"[5] as components of OSINT. If the potential that a social scientist's work might be incorporated into the intelligence process is reason enough not to engage in the research endeavor, then no social scientist should ever publish anything, ever. Clearly, the position that social science should never contribute to the intelligence mission is reactionary and uninformed. On the other hand, we still have no definitive answer as to whether or not the unique processes and perspectives of social science research can be of use within the intelligence community at all. It has been argued that the postmodern movement in British social anthropology in fact sprang from a period of intense self-reflection on the compatibility (or lack thereof) of the needs of private businesses and government agencies for concise, objective results on short deadlines using ethnography's traditional methods of lengthy participant observations and thick, subjective description.[6] And yet applied ethnography, if ethnography is any indication of the social sciences as a whole, has experienced notable growth as a viable, non-academic career approach in industry and government.[7]

A more interesting question than what social science can or should contribute to the intelligence community may well be what social science can learn from the intelligence community about informing the policy-making process. One of the first things I learned as a HUMINT professional was that my service to my commander did not extend in all directions, at all times, and for every whim. Members of the intelligence community are subject to national oversight mechanisms implemented through a chain of directives and policies. As a HUMINTer, I cannot, for instance, conspire to engage in assassination, conduct the waterboarding of a detainee, or knowingly retain information about a US person for more than ninety days.[8] HUMINT is a military career field carefully controlled by a robust set of laws and regulations that supersede the orders of military commanders.

Any organization tasked with providing social science research and analysis to military decision-makers should take a page from HUMINT on how to stay within one's lane without alienating oneself from those one is meant to support. This advice extends well beyond the legal considerations of conducting social science research, which echo many of the same underlying prerogatives as those governing intelligence activities.[9] Discussed in more detail shortly, social science does something unique from any other activity in the military or intelligence system, and relies upon a set of assumptions that may seem foreign—or even fanciful—to military and intelligence professionals. Ontologically, an effective social science capacity operates from the assumption that reality is multiple and subjective. Epistemologically, effective social scientists seek to dismantle the barriers between themselves and their subjects and represent their subjects' interpretations. Axiologically, the value of a social scientist rests in his or her ability to acknowledge biases and to identify how they shape decision-makers' perspectives of their operations, rather than pretending biases do not exist or do not matter. Rhetorically, the efforts of social science should always lead to a product that speaks the military's language and references its priorities *without* surrendering social science's unique voice and vision. Methodologically, social science that is worth the military's investment should never mimic the military's way of doing business since the military can do that itself without such an investment.

Generation after generation of social scientists have been developing methods for elucidating the relationships that characterize social systems, and it is in everyone's best interests for the military to have access to the wisdom of that legacy. Military intelligence professionals have already written a template for how members of an organization such as HTS might explain what they can and cannot do for military commanders. HTS and anyone like them should heed the lessons others have learned.

Members of HTS often debated whether or not the organization should establish a standard format for reporting findings, or adopt a reporting structure that fitted the unit's needs. On one side were those who felt that a top-down approach would undermine a team's loyalty to the unit it was assigned to support. Contrary to what may be popular belief, military units each have their own culture, communication styles, power brokers and gatekeepers. Some Human Terrain Teams argued that if they had to choose between developing their own way of doing business in the context of their unit or introducing their unit to a reporting structure imposed by HTS leadership back in the States, the unit's interests would win out every time. On the other side were those who felt that the social science community had already developed a template for reporting research findings. From field notes to published research articles, they pointed to the basic documents that most social science fieldwork produces and argued that if HTS is a social science organization, then it needs to produce standard social science products. Trends within the intelligence community reflect a splitting of this difference that perhaps HTS or similar organizations should observe. Though the specifics of intelligence reporting are generally classified, most intelligence organizations mandate the core reports and their formats that communicate intelligence to its consumers. Much as publications within the social sciences share a common template, intelligence reports constitute the language of the intelligence community and the measuring stick for productivity. At the lowest levels, however, commanders and other military decision-makers have almost free rein to specify what they want to see in their briefings, from the content to the colors. In the intelligence community, consumer-tailored briefings are produced based on a standard product repertoire, not the other way around.

Aside from report formatting, HTS debated the report's customer or audience. Those on teams at the lowest levels argued that they worked directly for their commander and that higher echelons within HTS had no right to dictate how teams allocated their time, up to and including time spent submitting reports through HTS-specific communication channels. Higher echelons in the field, however, argued that their mandate was to aggregate reporting from teams at lower echelons and analyze the results to answer requirements particular to commanders at higher levels. Meanwhile, HTS leadership argued that unless teams at all levels submitted their reports to a central database, team products would evaporate into the ether when the unit the team supported re-deployed to the States. In fact, much of HTS's work over the years has been lost through nothing more than a lack of knowledge management.

If HTS suffered from a dearth of centralized knowledge management systems, the intelligence community is swimming in them. Many of them serve niche functions, but all have processes that allow for the dissemination of reporting to any authorized party with a valid reason to have the information and a security clearance commensurate with the report's classification. I cannot tell you the number of times that I as a HUMINTer received requests for further information on my reporting originating from intelligence analysts across the globe with no predictable relationship to my own unit. Additionally, as a HUMINTer, I never conducted the evaluations of my own reporting or the validation of my sources' truthfulness and accuracy. Within the intelligence community, the producers of intelligence are often considered the least capable of determining its worth. Likewise, HTS's social scientists, if no one else, should understand how knowledge emerges from the collective efforts of a community of inquiry, rather than from a magic bullet that solves every problem and leaves no question unanswered. It is clearly within the best interests of the military that the producers of its social science be responsible to a community of evaluation and validation, the more formal the better in both the short and long runs.

UNDERSTANDING VARIATION IN MEANING

Given the fear of being associated with intelligence and the inclination of so many former military professionals within HTS's ranks to go about business as usual, tension between "intelligence" and "social science" was a constant feature of working for HTS. Standing with one foot in both worlds, it became clear to me that the divide was deeper than maintaining the line between one Army function and another, touching instead on core understandings of the nature of things. One key distinction seemed to be the definition of "security." As an Army HUMINTer I had no reason to question the meaning of "security." "Security" was the absence of active, hostile resistance to state-centric directives of control. When bombs were not exploding, assassinations were not being carried out, and armed militias were not setting up checkpoints on roads to identify and slaughter members of supposedly rival ethnicities, we had achieved "security." Social scientists do not have the luxury of such an obvious definition. The nature of our inquiry (not to mention the indiscretions of our collective history) requires us to ask, "security for whom?" For a social scientist, the military does not hold a monopoly on the meaning of "security," something that service members who have devoted their careers to fulfilling the military's security mission understandably do not enjoy hearing. "Security" to me had become a contested term, and I no longer had faithful answers to the question of "security of whom?" Without a ready-made definition of "security," everything was subject to scrutiny in a way that, at least on the surface, seemed to put a drag on the expedience with which the Army prefers to carry out its operations. The easy path is simply to yield altogether and to adopt unquestionably the military's definition. It is my fervent position, however, that—in the way of most avoidant approaches to conflict—doing so denies the military access to the very diversity of understanding that it sorely needs.

There is value in raising the military's awareness of definitions of security outside those of its traditional paradigm. A women's health project in which the Human Terrain Team I was on was involved is a case in point. Developing the health services infrastructure had been identified as a key line of effort to sponsoring stability in a volatile region where I was assigned as a social scientist. Investing in a local hospital was one element of this line of effort that military units along with the State Department's Provincial Reconstruction Teams (PRTs) supported. The health of women, seen as a particularly vulnerable population, served as one measure of success, but reports were filtering down that some women in what had formerly been known as the Sunni Triangle were still not getting the care they needed. On paper it looked as if there should not have been a problem. The area had been on the front lines of sectarian violence in 2006 and 2007, but with the emergence of local security initiatives, a comparative quiet had come about. In part because it was easiest to keep tabs on one location at a time, the Army selected a single hospital as the primary focus of its attention, coordinated through its Civil–Military Operations and Medical staff. The hospital itself was in a geographically central location and at the nexus of all the major highways of the area. Judging from population estimates, the Army provided it with enough supplies and equipment, and it was sufficiently staffed to meet anticipated demand.

The unit had asked if we would meet with some local women in the Sunni area about their access to medical care. In almost every case the women to whom we spoke had the same thing to say: the hospital in which the Army had invested was not appropriate for Sunni women. Accessing the closest hospital required traveling through the area where the women had lost husbands, brothers, and sons, and many explained they would rather go without medical care—even in cases of emergency—than pass through a district that had become aligned with their own personal traumas, as well as a trauma for their community. In practice, the Sunni women felt as though they had no choice but to travel to a different hospital at least an hour further away. In many situations this trip was simply untenable, and women went without treatment at all. For these women, the "security" problem remained relevant to their lives well after the Army had considered the crisis basically resolved. By the accounts of every PowerPoint presentation and Excel spreadsheet available, the right resources were in the right place. The soldiers' meaning of "security" had been met, and the Army had since engaged the task of investing in a hospital using the most efficient calculations possible with the intention of reaching the widest number of people with the least chance of duplicating efforts. Had HTS not built relationships of trust with those women, and represented the women's alternative meanings of security with fidelity as well as in a manner digestible to the unit's military decision-making process, then the unit would not have been able to make sound decisions that in the end moved toward meeting the interests of the women, the community, and the unit.

Another key distinction between my perspectives as a human intelligence collector and those as a social scientist regards the nature of information. For a HUMINTer, information resides in the mind of the source. It is the task of the HUMINT collector to tease that information into the light so that an intelligence analyst may process that "intelligence information" into fully evaluated intelligence. As a HUMINTer, I mined for the raw materials that would later be fashioned into a finished product of the intelligence industry. As a social scientist, I recognized instead that information was a co-production between the collector and the source. The questions a HUMINTer asks do not just define the parameters of what will and will not be collected; they imbue that information with value, and filter that information through the mind of the HUMINTer, molding it into mechanisms through which it will be communicated to the next person, who then takes it through the same process from his or her standpoint. The lines between when a HUMINT source answers a question from his or her fallible recollection and when he or she consciously fills in the gaps to satisfy the collector's prodding are not nearly as firm as my HUMINTer self understands. What I hear as a HUMINTer can never be independent of my biases, or my mood, or even my linguistic limitations, which often force the source's original message to be dragged through the biases, moods, and limitations of an interpreter. My social scientist self would confidently say that the very interaction of the HUMINTer and the source (not to mention the interpreter) creates, not reveals, what is communicated up the chains of command as a result of that interaction. As a HUMINTer, I of course recognize that even my most truthful sources misunderstand, edit, and distort recollections of their experiences, but these are dynamics I have to sort through in search of some ultimate set of objective "facts." Even as I have grown comfortable with the presence of ambiguity in my HUMINT work—as I've often told my HUMINT students, in our business the 60 percent solution *is* the 100 percent solution—my efforts still strive to access something independently real behind that shroud of uncertainty. Either such-and-such a country has or has not acquired a certain piece of technology. Either such-and-such a person does or does not make improvised explosive devices. These are "facts," and they are what my HUMINTer self pursued. To generalize, HUMINTers, like much of the population at large I dare say, are positivists at heart.

During my first tour in Iraq I debriefed victims of kidnapping who had escaped or been released from captivity. The process included talking the victims through their ordeals to acquire the most details possible about what they had survived. An essential element to completing the debriefing was managing the emotional state of my interviewees, which frequently involved my holding their trembling hands, hugging them through bouts of sobbing, and telling them everything would be all right. I recognized that they had suffered traumatic experiences, but it was neither within the scope of my mission nor my training to provide counseling—that was someone else's job. My job as a HUMINTer and a soldier was to collect the information, and my personal sympathies with the victim's situation were irrelevant to the final product, no matter how long after coming home I could still see their faces in my dreams.

As a social scientist, I would later work with military personnel to trace these influences and to call them toward a critical evaluation of how they impacted the "facts" supporting the unit's decision-making process. In one case, the unit I was supporting had constructed a dizzying diagram of a business organization whose activities were significant to achieving one of the unit's goals. The diagram used lines drawn between names of the organization's members to show relationships between them. The first stage of my contribution involved using social networking analysis software to measure the influence of different people in the network based on different definitions of power. The use of the software itself is nothing that a proficient analyst could not leverage on the unit's behalf. But in an interpretive sense my real value came from being able to point out that the lines themselves held more information than first met the eye. Consider, for instance, a line drawn between a man and woman indicating they are husband and wife. In the United States, husbands and wives historically share privileged relationships characterized by the ability of one to serve as next of kin for the other, protections against one being compelled to testify in court against the other, as well as joint custody of property and, often, offspring. Not every culture, however, distributes those benefits in the same way. In many cultures of the Middle East, such privileges pass from a husband to his brother and from a son to his (male) cousin. Keeping track of how this unacknowledged information influenced the military's decision-making process—which more often than not simply required articulating it aloud—was within my capacity as a social scientist, but not as a HUMINTer.

RECOGNIZING THE LIMITS OF MILITARY EPISTEMOLOGY

I brought to my mission as a social scientist a familiarity with several of the Army's standard processes for identifying goals, allocating resources, and monitoring progress. They had made sense to me as a soldier at a gut level and I had seen them transform large undertakings into digestible tasks. Now, however, I recognized that while the Army's traditional approach worked brilliantly for complicated projects, it could not capture the complexity of the Iraqi social context. I use the terms "complicated" and "complex" distinctly. A complicated system is one made up of diverse parts operating in tandem, but it cannot adapt to change. A complex system is also made up of diverse parts operating interdependently, but the system can adapt to change, sometimes in remarkable and surprising ways. To adapt a borrowed analogy, a watch is complicated but will cease to function if even one part is removed or damaged; while an ecosystem is complex as, up to a point, it can accommodate the removal or damage of some of its components.[10] The success of the modern military mission depends on the military's ability to interface with complex systems—cultures, economies, and political systems—from which unpredictable, bottom-up phenomena emerge. The operational concerns regarding the dynamics of complexity have forced the military to attempt to harmonize its assets, especially where they concern operations for stability and reconstruction.

The effects-based approach to operations (EBAO) attempted to meet those concerns by providing a framework for holistically assessing the influences that converge toward an environment's behaviors and capabilities, and then modifying those influences to adjust behaviors and capabilities to correlate with desired outcomes.[11] EBAO's intent was to serve as a tool to analyze the military's allocation of its lines of effort across all disciplines at all levels, and to redirect the focus away from end-states themselves and onto the effects that lead to those end-states. Bringing complex systems into line with the military's traditional targeting mentality ideally meant that the military could develop methods of dealing with complex systems using many of its traditional mechanisms of coercive force but through the guise of harnessing the system rather than attempting to control it. A thorough understanding of complexity brings with it several advantages. First, not every system is a complex system. Some problems are quite simple, such as the standard number of bullets soldiers need during initial combat training to qualify on their rifles. With some experimentation and bit of number crunching we can identify the optimum answer. Some problems are complicated, rather than complex, such as maintenance procedures for large weapons systems. Problem solving in this case becomes an exercise in keeping one's eye on learning curves in order to reach the optimum response among several possible, and the costs of transitioning from one way of doing business to another that promises more advantages. The military does not always deal with complex systems, and often its traditional mechanisms of problem solving do the job just fine. A second advantage is that when working with complex systems, the military can maintain its awareness of their non-linear, unpredictable nature. The adaptive characteristic of complex systems notoriously masks signs of a major problem until it is too late. All seems well until suddenly and all at once the system reaches a tipping point where everything exponentially changes in a way that could not have been predicted. We might understand tipping points as the place in the system where one or more of its key characteristics (diversity, connectedness, interdependence, or adaptation) have either increased too high or decreased too low.[12] Under the concept of EBAO, military targets—be they individuals or processes—were continuously re-conceptualized into their essential components whose dynamic, evolving, and non-linear characteristics require an understanding of each target as a complex system. In other words, pre-EBAO concepts of operations treated the subjects of their concerns in an "anti-social" manner that EBAO intended to correct.[13]

During a 1993 televised debate on the military and foreign policy sponsored by the Center for Defense Information, the late American strategist Colonel Harry Summers argued adamantly, as he had done in many other forums, that the mission of the military is and always will be "to kill people and destroy things in the name of the United States."[14] The US military by then had already established a long history of deployments domestically and abroad in missions having little association with proficiencies hailed by Col. Summers. In 2006, military planners had designated over 500 humanitarian projects in almost 100 countries.[15] The long-awaited Army Field Manual 3–0, *Operations*, joined the realities of counterinsurgent operations with the Army's recent experience to state that in the field of engagement non-lethal actions are the companions of success against any enemy. FM 3–0 put the term "non-lethal" into full effect in the military vocabulary, explaining its characteristics in civil support operations (i.e. law enforcement), information operations (i.e. propaganda), the application of non-lethal weapons (e.g. tear gas, etc.), and intelligence collection, all of which are tools at the commander's disposal to achieve the desired end-state.

From the meeting point of my experiences as a soldier and as a social scientist surfaced new insights about vulnerabilities to the military's approach to counterinsurgency, stability, and humanitarian operations rooted in its underlying assumptions about the nature of society and analytical tools reflecting those assumptions. In terms of the processes it brought to bear on its mission, the Army frequently relied upon "maturity matrices" to track the progress of its efforts over multiple lines of effort toward a grand vision of where it wished to go. A maturity matrix generally consists of a spreadsheet listing on one axis the major components of a particular goal of a unit's mission. The other axis lists descriptions of the components at the start of the mission and at the end of the mission, with interim milestones in between. The description of each interim state informs the unit as to what interventions it needs to focus its resources on achieving. In counterinsurgency and stability operations, the goals of a unit's mission almost always involve a complex system—cultures, economies, or political systems— which means that the activities that units engage in to achieve their interim objectives are in essence social interventions: psychological operations to shape the population's perceptions, micro-grant programs to encourage small businesses, or election-monitoring to ensure the integrity of the voting process, and so on. Through the guise of a maturity matrix, these social interventions are the products of basic decision theory, which responds very strongly to standard frameworks of military problem solving.

In traditional decision theory (with variations as exchange theory, network theory, and rational choice theory), the vision of an end-state is broken down into its components, the current state of each component is assessed, gaps between current and envisioned states are analyzed, and resources are allocated along lines of effort corresponding to each component in order to transition its state from that of the current to that of the envisioned.[16] So if a unit's mission is "To provide a stable environment in the area where we've been given responsibility so we can transfer legitimate governing authority to the Government of Iraq," we might say that achieving the goal requires (1) the selection of government officials viewed as legitimate representatives of the people, (2) the development of a sustainable economy, and (3) the development of an infrastructure that at least satisfies the population's basic needs. We would then break down each of these goals into its component parts. Taking the first goal regarding the legitimacy of government representatives, we might say that we would need (1a) to invest in a valid process for electing officials, (1b) to sponsor the technical competence of an independent judiciary, and (1c) to encourage a positive reputation for a professional police force. A fully formed maturity matrix would list (1a), (1b), and (1c) as the headings for three rows on a spreadsheet. The first column would describe the state of (1a), (1b), and (1c) at the beginning of the mission. For instance, the description of (1a) might say, "Political parties control access to polling sites, voters cannot cast ballots in secret, and the population does not view official ballot counts as representing ballots cast." The last column for (1a) might say, "Access to polling sites is politically neutral, voters can cast ballots in complete secrecy, and the population views official ballot counts as accurately representing ballots cast." In between would be a list of incremental steps leading from the description of (1a) in that first column to the description of (1b) in that last column.

Such a matrix—and herein lies the problem with the military's use of maturity matrices in general—reduces highly complex and interrelated social processes, institutions, and players into discrete lanes of activities. Since military goals in asymmetric environments of counterinsurgency and stability operations are fundamentally social goals, the use of maturity matrices rests upon a basic assumption that society is composed of the sum of its parts. This approach requires that certain aspects about society must evolve from one state to the next, when a more responsive approach to operations would provide room for the dynamic, unpredictable, and even revolutionary change inherent in complex systems. Despite persistent challenges to meet deadlines set forth in maturity matrices and other decision-making tools emphasizing the gradual progress of societies toward equilibrium, the military continues to operate under the unspoken assumption that while the details of political and social development may change from country to country, the underlying structures and institutions are common. Furthermore, it is assumed that deciphering how those common structures operate would allow the military to maneuver social structures and institutions in one direction or another.

The effects-based approach to operations did, at least nominally, address many of these issues and appeared, if only at the level of theory, to have begun the task of raising the military's awareness about how contemporary work on complexity and complex systems might assist in the military decision-making process. Successes, however, were fleeting, sporadic, and easily contested. In 2008, the Commander of the US Joint Forces Command published guidance directing that EBAO was no longer the active approach to planning and decision-making because it "has been misapplied and overextended to the point that it actually hinders rather than helps joint operations." His list of specific concerns included that EBAO promised "a level of unachievable predictability; cannot correctly anticipate reactions of complex systems...calls for an unattainable level of knowledge of the enemy; is too prescriptive and overengineered; [and] discounts the human dimensions of war (for example, passion, imagination, willpower, and unpredictability)."[17] From this point forward, EBAO as an approach to military operations fell into decline, but officers and planners who lived through the experiment remain influenced by its tenets.

Perhaps no better example serves to illustrate how the military's persistent understanding of society as engaged in a linear, predictable evolution failed to predict seemingly spontaneous change than *al-Sahwa*, also known as "the Awakening." I was deployed as a soldier to Iraq in 2005 when we got word of a new movement taking place in the heart of what we believed to be the solidly anti-Coalition province of Anbar, west of Baghdad. Soon after the earliest days of the Iraqi insurgency, al-Qaeda had made strong headway with the Sunnis in Anbar, who were afraid of what the future of a Shi'ite-controlled Iraq would mean for their way of life. Al-Qaeda's representatives penetrated Anbar, made their case against Coalition forces, and found safe haven in many communities. From our perspective, the Sunnis were fighting to restore the Baathist regime, which would transform Iraq into the stronghold of al-Qaeda that Afghanistan had once been. The de facto rule of thumb quickly became that Sunnis were insurgents, and working with us ran counter to their perceived best interests; whereas on the whole it was easier to make friends with Shi'ites, since they would essentially end up running the country in a majority-run democracy. We had more optimism for building relationships with Jaysh al-Mahdi, the militant arm of the Iranian-backed cleric Muqtada al-Sadr, who would later prove to be a staunch adversary of our interests, than we did with this new Sunni group. And we were wrong.

At some point, al-Qaeda had mistakenly convinced itself that its relationship with the Sunnis of Anbar Province was something more than an alliance of convenience. As much as Sunni leaders did not like their prospects in a new Iraq, they liked the idea of non-Iraqis telling them what to do even less. When al-Qaeda killed a couple of Sunni sheikhs to make it clear to everyone who was really in charge, several Sunni tribes shifted allegiance. In a movement that seemed to spring from nowhere and build into a national force, Sunnis drove al-Qaeda out of their communities.[18]

I returned to the States in 2006 as Coalition forces were still struggling to figure out what had just happened. It was to my amusement that I later heard military spokespersons commenting on the Awakening as if it had been a stroke of American genius. Once I had returned to Iraq as a social scientist, the Awakening had developed a full-fledged military program supported by American forces and ostensibly operated in service to the central Iraqi government. American forces had hoped that members of the Awakening, now called the Sons of Iraq, could be incorporated into a responsible plan for demobilization, demilitarization, and reintegration, but the dynamics of Iraqi society once again proved an enigma. The Shi'ite-dominated government apparently feared that if the Sons of Iraq remained intact, they would force the central government to make accommodations for groups—primarily Sunnis—to whom it would rather not have its policies beholden. The last project I conducted for HTS found members of the Sons of Iraq disheartened at their prospects for the government jobs they had been promised in exchange for their service against al-Qaeda.

The Sons of Iraq ended up being an armed force led by tribal sheikhs who exerted control over the rural territories constituting the majority of Iraq. For this reason, the central government seemed to believe that it needed to dismiss the Awakening from the "legitimate" political landscape, much as it had tried (unsuccessfully) to do to the tribes entirely. This anti-tribalist position, however, was a clear echo of an American posture from the beginning of its intervention into Iraq, which seemed to assume that the future of a "modern," "civilized" Iraq had no place for "backward" tribes. Because the American government had failed to account for the role of conflict in reshaping key components of the social environment, it had precious few mechanisms to facilitate the incorporation of tribal dispute resolution processes into overall national reconciliation strategies, of which the tragedy of the Sons of Iraq was merely one symptom. In fact, tribes continue to play essential roles in managing conflict in rural areas where the hand of the Iraqi government holds little influence,[19] something that American military commanders at the lowest levels recognized early on and used to their advantage.[20]

Returning to Iraq years later, the tribal system appeared to offer solutions to many counterinsurgency problems that the central government lacked mechanisms to manage. In one case when I was serving as a social scientist, the unit to which I was assigned requested that my team and I decipher an incipient conflict among members of the local population. The Army was having difficulty determining whether tribal politics, civil rights, or counterinsurgency operations were at issue. The local Sons of Iraq commander had gone into a village and rounded up a list of suspected insurgents. During the operation, several villagers were killed and at least one home was burned. The village's tribal sheikh was declaring the matter to be a tribal conflict between the tribe to which members of the village belonged and the tribe to which the Sons of Iraq commander belonged. Meanwhile, family members of those affected had brought a legal suit against the Sons of Iraq commander, claiming that he had violated their relatives' due process. For his part, the Sons of Iraq commander staunchly defended his actions, claiming that the village was a well-known hotbed of al-Qaeda and that the operation was one in a string of counterinsurgency offensives. When I met with the tribal sheikh and his entourage, they indeed described the conflict in terms of a tribal dispute. The sheikh was calling for the intervention of neutral mediators to settle the dispute between the two tribes, but when I gathered a list of who was involved I found that the parties were not divided along tribal lines. Based on the tribal names, one would never have guessed that it was a tribal issue at all. The families of those who had brought the lawsuits all stated that if the issue was taken to tribal mediation, they would drop their legal claims. And speaking with the Sons of Iraq commander, he agreed that tribal reconciliation was the quickest mechanism to bring the conflict to a conclusion, all the while insisting that he was only doing his duty as a security professional.

As it turned out, the area had experienced problems similar to these since well before the arrival of Coalition forces. With the fall of Saddam Hussein, al-Qaeda had come to the area and attempted to build a constituency among the population, but they quickly rejected the leadership of the foreigners. A conflict between parties broke out, dividing generally along the lines of past conflicts, concerning who would lead the local version of an anti-Coalition insurgency. Around this time, the Army had proactively delegated decision-making authority and access to resources to commanders at the lowest possible levels. The local American military commander imported the Sons of Iraq concept to the area. One of the groups that claimed leadership of the insurgency then switched sides, receiving their "charter" as a branch of the Sons of Iraq. Thus, one group had been blessed off as a "legitimate" force, while the other was still an "insurgency." Then, the members of the "insurgency" approached US forces asking to be their own Sons of Iraq unit. They were denied because resources were only authorized for one unit in the area. When the commander of the new Sons of Iraq group initiated his "counterinsurgency offensive," his motivations were highly debatable, but the results were that the members of the "insurgency" side of the conflict took their fight to the courts. When the legal process proved difficult to negotiate (mostly because it was still in its formative stages) the local tribal sheikh re-narrated the conflict as one between tribes in order to access alternative dispute resolution mechanisms available within the tribal context. The American commander in the area saw the value of encouraging tribal reconciliation, even though this meant that the legal system would not be able to use the highly visible case as an opportunity to bolster the legitimacy of the Iraqi government through formal trial proceedings.

The delegation of power to the local US commander was intended to give him authority to make changes according to the vision of higher echelons, ideally with the minimum amount of direct intervention from above. The reality of operations in complex environments, however, often leads to unanticipated consequences that may contradict national security strategy. In this case, instead of supporting the central government, US forces unintentionally promoted tribal leadership in Iraqi society in direct contradiction to the strategic vision. This example provides a case study for how a failure to appreciate unintended consequences in a complex environment can and did lead to poor outcomes. Identifying and communicating how the underlying narratives had been used to deconstruct and reframe the conflict stands uniquely within the purview of a social science approach to the subject.

GRASPING THE ETIC/EMIC DISTINCTION

All social science data involving human subjects essentially boils down to the intersection of a subject and the environment. The United States government has invested many resources developing a massive intellectual, physical, and cybernetic infrastructure devoted to managing data about key personalities, organizations, communities, processes, etc. The vast majority of this data comes from an etic perspective, meaning that it is drawn from scientific inquiry and direct observation. An etic perspective would lead the military to believe that economy of effort can be achieved by investing in a centrally located hospital and ensuring that investment in resources meets the average needs of a population of a certain size. This paradigm supports the data management needs of multiple lines of effort, such as civil affairs, civil–military operations, and military intelligence, all engaged in missions contributing to the end-state objectives. Etic approaches represent the logic of the scientific method, claim to represent universal truths from an outsider's observation, and focus on linear, causal relationships. By contrast, emic approaches represent the meanings of experience, claim only to represent the particular from an insider's observation but do so faithfully, and focus on intentions over behaviors.[21] The military in general, and military intelligence in particular, understand the etic. No fully incorporated Army element, however, has the responsibility for including emic data into the pool of information and for making it digestible to commanders on the ground using a substantive, mindful, and coherent methodology.

Emic data is that which represents the experience of local peoples in their words and context.[22] It records their narratives and has the potential to express the whole of what can be communicated about the human experience. The narrative approach to mediation, for example, relies on the way people's stories of their world explain the construction of that world. The path of communicative discourse, then, opens the door to reconstruct interpersonal relationships in a new, joint experience that reformulates each party's interests into those that are mutually sustained.[23] Categorizing etic data is an arbitrary undertaking tailored to the needs of each mission using the data to satisfy its planning and monitoring requirements. At a gathering of HTS social scientists we once attempted to define the categories of ethnographic research as a tool to assist Human Terrain Teams in the field with a common way of organizing information. In that case we used a qualitative data analysis technique known as pile sorting, which is a method for aggregating how a group of people view the differences and similarities of elements within an overarching theme. I later adapted the results of this exercise to arrive at (in order of priority for my team): (1) what my commander determined to be the drivers of instability in our area, (2) demographics, (3) economics, (4) environment and infrastructure, (5) conflict and conflict resolution, (6) the population's needs and aspirations, (7) social organization, and (8) patterns of life. So how does one arrive at a definitive taxonomy of human experience? One decides what it is and adjusts according to the contingencies of its usefulness.

The military has no problem wrapping its mind around etic categories, regardless of how they are specifically constructed. The military already uses various taxonomies, depending on the mission at hand.[24] If the Army needs to understand the categories of cultural context, the etic categories we came up with at HTS, the specific ones I developed for my own team, those used by Harvard University's Human Relations Area Files, or any other mindfully constructed, informed taxonomy would serve as an equally effective starting point. Besides dividing information up in a new way, however, etic categories alone would offer nothing more to the military than what the military could develop independent of an embedded social science capacity. But if the etic categories were cross-referenced with emic data, then the meaning behind the lived experiences of the local population, which constitutes the center of gravity in a counterinsurgency environment, could be represented in a way that informs the military decision-making process while respecting the intentions of the population. This in turn could facilitate the military's redefining the term "we" as one encompassing the military and the population, while marginalizing spoilers.

On my team, we assumed the position that as the unit's social science capability we alone among the staff functions were charged with the responsibility for representing the population's perspectives of its own context. How did they view themselves? How did they view us? And how did they view others around them? We adapted this three-pronged, emic approach to cross-referencing our etic categories from the first, second, and third person categories used in many languages to define a comprehensive representational system of experience. We then went about cobbling from various sources (such as direct observation, media outlets, research data collected from members of the local community) any information we could find about how the population viewed, for example, the state of its own economy, the role of US forces in the local economy, and the local population's economic relationships with its neighbors.

Programs to translate social systems as networks of culturally imbued relationships into digestible information, such as has been the intent of the Army's Human Terrain System, may ease the military's level of discomfort with developing the contextual fluencies required for mission success amidst the contingencies of polyvalent cultural "realities." Such programs only have their worth, however, if they are actually delivering concrete, validated results through the social sciences. Neither the military nor any other agency needs to fund an internal social science capacity that either will not or cannot do social science. One of the hurdles facing HTS is how to bring the right subject matter experts in the right applied social sciences to answer the right questions at the right time and place, communicated through the right language and medium. Social scientists operating too close to the military are in danger of becoming a duplicative function. Social scientists operating too far from the realities of a military engaged in real-world unified land operations are in danger of becoming useless.

FINDING THE MEANING OF "SOCIAL SCIENCE"

The search for striking this balance begs a further question: When we say "social science," to what are we referring? I've saved this question for last because, besides the administrative challenges of developing an independent social science support mechanism, it rests at the heart of the problem. As a HUMINTer, I was in the business of human relationships where they intersected with threats to the military mission. Who is the enemy? What are they doing to threaten the mission? How are they going about it? When will they do it next? Where are they? And, perhaps most importantly, why are they doing what they are doing? As a social scientist, my job was not to reiterate what I could already do as an intelligence professional, but to offer military decision-makers clarity about the broader stage on which the drama of counterinsurgency and stability operations takes place. This underlying premise is not about mitigating threat, but facilitating cooperation requiring a multidisciplinary insight on human relations across time and space. As individuals, my colleagues and I represented the fields of anthropology, conflict studies, political science, economics, history, and several others. As an organization, HTS's efforts were initially classified under the guise of anthropology, and then later under the umbrella term of "social science," but a more accurate nomenclature would be "applied human geography."

Improvements in a broad array of data collection and analysis techniques developed within the social and information sciences, such as agent-based modeling, social network analysis, complexity theory, and geographic information systems made further advances in communicating social science findings to military commanders when elucidating the particulars of a geographic area. As merely a means of communication, maps hold much more explanatory power for the military than, say, the thick narratives of interpretive ethnography. The arrival of geospatial intelligence as a fully anointed "INT" bodes well for the military's ability to capitalize on sophisticated analysis and visualization developments in the field of human geography for transmitting complex information more efficiently up and down the chains of command. Within the Department of Defense, the institution with the highest demonstrated proficiency for developing these products is the National Geospatial-Intelligence Agency (NGA). As one of my former graduate professors and his colleague have outlined, the definition of geospatial intelligence is still emerging from the experience of a community focused on describing the spatial relationships of human activity, partly through the worldview of intelligence, partly through those of physical and human geography.[25] As the fog clears on this definition, the military would be well advised to house its social science capabilities in the NGA as an organization pre-equipped to support technical analysis and primed to support human geographic research without confusing it for intelligence, but where actionable results always serve as the litmus test for the value of its efforts.

The distinction between social science research and intelligence collection that I have sought to delineate are not intended to be all-inclusive, but rather to represent points of departure salient to our understanding of these two threads of activity as I have experienced them. Social science cannot and should not attempt to do what intelligence does, and vice versa. That is not to say that the two cannot or should not communicate. They do and should because both threads are integral to the success of military operations where the traditional mission of "killing people and destroying things" simply does not achieve the desired results of peace and stability. The effects-based approach to operations and the processes it spawned sought to dispel the prejudices and misconstructions of the military's previous operational dogmas as if the reductionist light of the Scientific Method could solve them. Nevertheless, the assumptions these processes carried with them degraded the military's ability to do exactly what it has increasingly understood to be the primary factor of success for counterinsurgency and stability operations: harnessing uncertainty.

But the story does not end there. The social sciences continue to offer new and innovative perspectives on how civilian populations negotiate violent conflict, how social structures and institutions contribute to stability or the lack thereof, how communities process the dynamics of post-conflict environments, and how the distribution of resources—including power—meets perceived needs and interests, to name a few. Meanwhile, the field of applied human geography frames these insights in a time and a place for which military commanders are assigned responsibility. If these perspectives receive serious consideration by military and civilian decision-makers, it will be because their thoughtful application has found root in a sincere attempt to aid in the success of long-term strategies in every area of operations. As the involvement of American forces abates in Afghanistan as it has in Iraq, nothing in the future of US military missions indicates a reduction in the intimate connection between understanding complexity and operational success. EBAO made sense as a starting point, but it could never have fulfilled its promise of facilitating the military's success in complex operational environments without mechanisms that bring to the decision-making table ways of identifying and processing information that the military cannot foster from within itself. Remedying this gap in capability is the promise of applied social science, and one worth the investment.

8

ALLIED CIVILIAN ENABLERS
AND THE HELMAND SURGE

Leslie Adrienne Payne

The 2009 US military surge in Helmand Province, Afghanistan—a southern province wracked by Taliban violence—involved not only the withdrawal of British forces and the insertion of 33,000 US troops, but also the addition of scores of civilian enablers whose purpose was to act as force multipliers. The Human Terrain Team (HTT) to which I was assigned was one such force multiplier. Together, the US military and its many civilian enablers had to contend with two interlocking challenges: understanding the complex dynamics of Helmand Province and knowing how best to work with allied components, particularly the British, in order to achieve operational success. Tackling the latter challenge proved particularly difficult for my team, as we were woefully untrained in the nuances of allied collaboration.

Although British military forces transferred battlespace responsibility for Helmand Province to the United States Marine Corps, many British civilian components remained in order to drive the capacity building agenda. Our British civilian counterparts looked like us: ostensibly, they talked the same talk, walked the same walk, and my team respected the institutional knowledge they had amassed on Helmand Province. Naïvety led us to believe that collaboration would be effortless. But instead, we experienced something between stone-walling and reluctant cooperation, leading us to theorize about how best to achieve success within the International Security Assistance Force (ISAF) Coalition framework. My team and I tried looking inward rather than pointing fingers: "Was it something we were not doing or failing to understand about our allied enablers?"

What we finally realized was that a British military imbroglio in Basrah, Iraq, directly preceded and foreshadowed much of what occurred in Sangin, Afghanistan. When examined together these campaigns showed a pattern of societal engagement that can best be described as elite-centric rather than population-centric. This difference in approach proved critical at the tactical level of warfare, where civilian enablers must interact closely with each other on major war efforts like capacity building. Collaboration with allies proved difficult because my HTT's practice of grass-roots, population-centric research diverged with the British preference for working with higher-level power brokers, many of whom were disconnected from the ordinary public. We were both trying to understand how best to help Helmand Province, but we approached this problem from different, irreconcilable directions.

BASRAH AS A HARBINGER

British forces were in Basrah from 2003 to 2007. Compared to Baghdad and other kinetic areas of Iraq, the British perceived Basrah to be a relatively calm and manageable situation early on. On account of this, they drew down their peacekeeping force over the summer and autumn of 2003 from 40,000 to 12,000. By the end of the year, their force level was down to 8,000 persons for all of southern Iraq. British soldiers were commonly seen patrolling the streets of Basrah in soft hats and relaxing over coffees and hookah pipes in the city center. Peacekeeping patrols were conducted in unarmored vehicles and it was not uncommon to see British soldiers on bicycles, riding along as they chatted with Basrawi children.

This soft-line approach to security is not to be conflated with population engagement. British forces were enjoying what they perceived to be a semi-permissive security environment; they were not canvassing the locals and engaging with the community to determine needs, wants, and concerns of the population. The reality at that time was that local Shi'a militias were quickly consolidating power, death squads systematically hunted former Baathists and law and order was quickly disappearing across the whole of Basrah. All of this happened unbelievably quickly. By 2004, the British were unable to build a local government that could forestall the radical Shi'a militias. By 2005 British troops saw their movements restricted throughout the area, with their casualties mounting and morale dissipating. By the end of 2006 Basrah had essentially been lost to the Shi'a groups; and by 2007 Muqtada al-Sadr's Jaysh al-Mahdi (JAM) had succeeded in reducing Basrah's Sunni population from 15 to 4 percent in just a few years. By 2006, when British Army General Sir Richard Shirreff took over command, he reported that there was "no security." Of the 7,000 soldiers under his command, only 200 were available for patrolling Basrah's streets. The rest were "fixed to their bases...this was not what I had been led to expect."[1]

What ensued in Basrah over the next few years was an intensive effort to broker deals with the many Shi'a groups. For example, the British negotiated their own security with the elite Shi'a leadership in these powerful militias. The local population, the majority of which had been victimized by these militias, was fully aware of the British strategy and wondered why commensurate attempts were not made to assess their needs and fears, and provide for their security. "The view prevailed that looting, intimidation, rape, kidnap and murder were essentially Iraqi problems—of which they certainly were. No one, however, was interested in what the Iraqis wanted or needed—or in how Iraqi (here specifically Basrawi) wants or needs related to the mission in hand. The British force existed not to protect the Iraqi population of the city: it existed largely, indeed almost exclusively, to protect itself."[2]

There were British civilian officials in Basrah, but they rarely left their military bases after 2004. Working with the community and population was not within their remit of responsibility. Instead, the military took on this task. In order to wind down the campaign in southern Iraq and transition to southern Afghanistan, British forces in Basrah stepped up their co-opting efforts with militia elites. They had used this strategy over the years to obtain security gains, only this time they were negotiating their own peaceful retreat. British forces ended up releasing detained JAM activists in exchange for a three-day cease-fire in the city, during which time they left their military bases and relocated to Basrah airport. These brokered deals with the militia elites paid dividends. British forces were guarded by their enemies on their way out of Basrah; and thereafter, if British patrols wished to enter Basrah city, they could do so only after agreement from JAM.[3]

Before my tour in Afghanistan, I spent thirteen months on an HTT that eventually wound up in Basrah after the British forces pulled out. My team spent our first nine months in provinces north of Basrah, where we queried the local population and provided analysis to various battlespace commanders. When told of our impending move down south, we wondered how stable Basrah would be and what we would find upon arriving. The British passed little cultural data to US forces and my HTT during the transfer of authority process. What we did obtain lacked analytical insight and depth. While there was some information about local tribes and militias and many maps and charts depicting neighborhoods and key areas, there was an absence of insight on the grievances, hopes, aspirations, and cultural nuances of local Basrawis.

My team drew the conclusion that when faced with mounting levels of violence, British forces chose to focus the bulk of their effort on warfighting and security, rather than population-centric research. Because of this we spent the last four months of our tour helping US forces and the United States Agency for International Development (USAID) understand the population in an important subsection of Basrah called Al-Hayyaniyah. We produced an ethnographic study on Al-Hayyaniyah that provided analysis on the impact of internally displaced persons, local expectations of government officials, and parallels between Sadr city and Al-Hayyaniyah, and so on. It was the type of robust population study that could probably have helped the British in their struggle to control and hold southern Iraq.

In *Losing Small Wars*, Frank Ledwidge, a former British naval reserve military intelligence officer, argues that the British fell into a pattern of poor planning, misunderstanding the insurgency, over-aggressiveness, and not positively engaging with the population in southern Iraq. During the years of Britain's presence in Iraq, "no real account had been paid to what the people of Basrah actually wanted. The consequence was that the people had been lost long before the city had been sold to the JAM."[4] Reflection shows that while engaging militia elites in Basrah may have been militarily useful, engaging the broader population would have helped with human security and quality of life challenges. For example, a more population-centric approach could have solicited input from local Basrawis on how best to staunch the violence. Constructive dialogue could have ensued, with different peace approaches tried out in earnest. Instead, favor was curried amongst powerful militia elites, resulting in fewer British casualties but an increasingly fearful public.

I am not sure if it is a blessing or a curse, but my two deployments with the Human Terrain System (HTS) happened to be in the very locations where unsustainable combat losses resulted in the recent withdrawal of British forces and their replacement with American military units: southern Iraq (Basrah) and southern Afghanistan (Helmand Province). That serendipitous connection allowed me to see how the elite-centric approach the British took in Iraq was reproduced in Helmand, Afghanistan. While the Helmand campaign was designed to recoup losses sustained in southern Iraq, the British brought with them the combat-intensive, elite-centric approach they had applied in Basrah. However, they ignored pertinent lessons about community engagement and population security, the leveraging of which may have improved their odds in Sangin and throughout Helmand.

BLOOD-CURDLING SANGIN

A few months after leaving Iraq, I deployed to Helmand Province, Afghanistan. I had begun to hear the horror stories about Sangin during the summer and fall, and finally arrived on the ground there with my team in October 2010. We were based out of FOB (Forward Operating Base) Delaram in adjacent Nimruz Province, but all of our missions took place in northern Helmand. From the FOB it was a twenty-minute flight to Sangin via rotary wing aircraft. Our team conducted a total of four field research missions in Sangin during my thirteen-month deployment. Each of our missions there lasted an average of four to six weeks and entailed us interviewing sixty to ninety local villagers. We learned about Sangin the traditional and hard way, by talking to as many locals as possible—face to face and in person. We asked about their history, current plight, and future aspirations. It kept us very busy, and on edge.

Sangin was a dangerous place. From 2009 to 2012, Sangin was the "killing field" of the Afghan theater. Helmand Province was the hub for opium production and distribution in southern Afghanistan, and the Taliban were fighting an intense battle to keep it. Sangin, arguably, was the epicenter of it all. The district of Sangin is located in the northern part of Helmand Province. Through it flows the Helmand River, which irrigates the driest of landscapes, giving rise to the regional moniker "the Green Zone." In 2010, its population was estimated to be 50,000–65,000.[5] Years ago, Sangin's reputation was that of a wide open city with a sprawling bazaar. The bazaar still exists today, and while impressive, now serves as a highly productive narcotics processing market. In Sangin, the drugs business was the Taliban's cash cow and they protected it tooth and nail. Most of the world's opium comes from Afghanistan, and Helmand Province produces much of it. In Sangin one found the ungodly marriage of poppy harvesters; drug barons who controlled production and the related facilities; and the Taliban who inserted themselves at various junctures of the process and reaped many of the benefits. The Green Zone, with its irrigated lands flanking the Helmand River, allowed the drug enterprise to thrive.

Compounding this drug situation was a series of violent and protracted tribal clashes that had dismantled the social structure of the district, resulting in debilitating security and leadership vacuums. Locals in Sangin segmented time into categories of before and after the 2007 tribal conflict. That year, a massive tribal uprising irreparably damaged relations with the British and resulted in the total disappearance of tribal leadership and civil order. Many tribes exist in Sangin, but the two most dominant and populous have been the Alikozai and Ishaqzai. The Alikozai had had been embraced by the Government of the Islamic Republic of Afghanistan (GIROA). They were considered more elite, better educated, and they had many political connections throughout southern Afghanistan. The Ishaqzai tribe was quite the opposite and had been more aligned with the Taliban. The Ishaqzai always maintained that their alliance with the Taliban resulted from Alikozai oppression, and the Alikozai always denied Ishaqzai allegations of maltreatment.

After persuasive urging from the International Security Assistance Force (ISAF) in Helmand, consisting primarily of British forces, to mount an offensive against a newly developed Taliban–Ishaqzai faction in the region, the Alikozai did so and sustained heavy losses as a result. ISAF never delivered the assistance it had promised beforehand as a quid pro quo for standing up to the Ishaqzai. In the aftermath, more tribal battles ensued. Tribal leadership fled to the provincial capital, Lashkar Gah, in order to escape the violence. Meanwhile, the Taliban slipped in and took advantage of the security and leadership void. Thereafter, many Sangin locals came to resent the British on account of their broken promises.

Helmand came right on the heels of Iraq and the British transitioned to that conflict without conducting a thorough lessons-learned process of what had and had not worked in Iraq. In 2006–7, British strategy was moving in multiple directions. Whitehall was insisting on a reduction of forces in Basrah, British troops in southern Iraq were still pursuing battlefield success, and meanwhile the British strategic priority was shifting to Helmand.[6] Indeed at one juncture operations were being planned in both theaters simultaneously.[7] "While it is certainly true that Iraq was a war of choice at the strategic level, the armed forces were more than willing to enter Helmand. From the start, Helmand was intended to 'make up for' the disaster of Iraq."[8] This lends insight into how the British dealt with the horrors of places like Sangin and Musa Qal'eh.[9] They built precariously held forts, enduring wave after wave of Taliban attacks, while indiscriminately bombing the surrounding villages in order to ensure their survival.[10] To be fair, these environments were violent and kinetic from the start, and population research and engagement understandably took a back seat to security.[11] In describing how the British coped with the Taliban threat in those early stages, Ledwidge (2010) says:

> On several occasions platoon houses came very close to being over-run. This was prevented only by dropping heavy bombs on the villages concerned and by subjecting them to gunfire and missiles by the Apache helicopters. Rather than "taking the fight" to the Taliban, the army became involved in engagements that it had not expected and for which it had not prepared, but in which the Taliban was only too ready and willing to participate. The army had, in fact, lost the initiative…The heavy bombing resulted in trashed town centres—such as Sangin, which became a huge problem for the hugely reinforced British stationed there over the next four years—and, most seriously, in the thousands of displaced people. Sangin in particular acquired something of an iconic status for the British land forces, the army and marines. The appropriately named "break-in-battle" was intensely bloody and savage.

In May 2006, British troops from 16 Air Assault Brigade arrived in Helmand and initially deployed to the provincial capital and a city to the north. They were undermanned from the start. Most of the 3,500 in the brigade were support personnel, leaving only 650 men who belonged to the 3rd Battalion of the Parachute Regiment (3 PARA).[12] But the battle group was also saddled with support requirements, and only 168 men of the 650 were actual combat troops. Indeed, they were spread thin.[13] In May–June 2006, 3 PARA had pushed north and established garrisoned "platoon houses" in Sangin, Musa Qal'eh, and

Now Zad amongst a sea of Taliban fighters. The platoon houses were attacked immediately and many died on both sides. More importantly, many innocent civilians were indiscriminately killed, further hardening an already embittered population. As Ledwidge notes:

> The British had played perfectly to the Taliban's strengths. They had dispersed in small numbers, used very heavy weaponry to make up for numbers, destroyed several town centres and created the perfect human environment for rebels to thrive. The consequences of the military misjudgments of those early months are with the mission in Helmand still. Whether by luck or design, the Taliban had succeeded in diverting the British paratroops from what they saw as "counterinsurgency" to fighting a high intensity battle, destroying and depopulating town centres. In so doing, the British had fulfilled exactly their historic role as most Helmandis saw it—that of aggressive and destructive invaders.[14]

Similarly, in "Understanding the Helmand Campaign: British Military Operations in Afghanistan," Anthony King describes a company within 3 PARA as saying:

> No real thought is going into what we are doing and why. We have done next to zero "pacification ops" amongst the people and these we must do if we are to win the people over. Our resources are limited and so we should keep ourselves to an area that we can influence in a coherent manner rather than spreading ourselves about the Province in an incoherent, uncoordinated and not mutually supporting way.[15]

Over the next two to three years, intense fighting continued. British soldiers struck various deals with tribal and village leaders to keep the Taliban away. Some of the deals worked, some did not; some were scrupulous, others apparently less so. Communities in Afghanistan are tightly knit, and the locals learned of every deal, advance, and retreat made by the British while simultaneously bearing the brunt of the fighting.

In late 2010, when the British pulled out militarily and handed the reins to the Marines, they left behind a destructive legacy pockmarked by indiscriminate violence, heavy-handed tactics, and tacit neglect of the Afghan population and their needs.[16] Irrespective of the veracity of such claims, this was how many Afghans interpreted such events.

CONTINUING THE PATTERN IN AFGHANISTAN

When I arrived in Sangin as part of an HTT supporting the US Marine Corps, the security situation was in total disarray. As a social scientist,

I never thought it mandatory to carry a weapon until I came back from our first mission in Sangin. I never understood how truly ferocious the Taliban were until Sangin, never saw my first dead or limbless Marine until Sangin, and never truly saw the face of this ugly war until Sangin. Sangin was such a mess and so dangerous, in fact, that the USMC Regimental Combat Team commander in Delaram delayed our first mission for months because of the blanketing violence. During that first mission to Sangin in October 2010, the Marines were still clearing areas beyond the Sangin District Center and so we were only allowed to operate within the urban area very close to the District Center for safety reasons. Security slowly improved as the Marines steadfastly sorted out the aftermath and continuing mayhem.

During our fourth mission to Sangin in summer 2011, our team was engaging communities in the most remote areas of Sangin District. By that time the exceptional warfighting, diplomatic abilities, and population-centric approach of the Marines had expanded Sangin's "security bubble," resulting in my HTT being able to interact with a larger portion of the population. The Marines' counterinsurgency (COIN) strategy in Sangin was simple and sound: fill the leadership vacuum by instituting a functional and legitimate district-level government and convince locals to divest themselves of the Taliban's shadow government. At its core, the strategy was population-centric and revolved around gaining the trust of locals in Sangin. The Taliban's shadow government was reputed to be swift and decisive at dispensing justice and arbitrating disputes. The Marines knew that the absence of real leadership and real justice in Sangin equated to the strengthening of the Taliban. My team was tasked with obtaining first-hand information about who the locals wanted to lead Sangin; however, this task was predicated on our ability to move around the area safely and talk with many people. The expansion of Sangin's security bubble allowed this to happen.

My team and I learned about the British experience in Sangin when we began interacting with villagers in their environments. Not sure if the Marines were fully aware of the intense emotion and anger being harbored by the locals toward the British, but convinced of their need to know given their operational responsibilities, my team began reporting to the Sangin battalion commander and staff what we heard on the street. From the Afghan perspective, the British had come to their country three times without an invitation and "had been ejected on each occasion with ignominy. That this perceived story of almost constant British defeat was not entirely true does not matter: the Afghans of the south believed it."[17] In short, locals blamed the dismal state of Sangin on the British forces, whose roughshod approach to the violence in central and northern Helmand (in the view of Afghans) had exacerbated the security situation. The result was a flood of information requests from the Marines asking my team to ascertain the depth of hostility and whether locals were appropriately differentiating between USMC and UK military tactics. We learned that anger ran deep and that locals were aware of, and grateful for, the sensitivity of the Marines.

CIVILIAN ENABLERS

In Sangin, just as at almost every other FOB where military personnel are stationed, there was an evening meeting, a commander's update brief that was called the "O&I" (operations and intelligence), where the battalion staff briefed pertinent information from the day to the commander and talked about the enemy threat situation. One night during the O&I someone announced that the British flag had been stolen from atop their FOB bunker, an act that truly incensed them. They were angry and insulted over it, and I wondered why such a thing would happen in the first place. What satisfaction would someone get from stealing their flag, or what kind of message was being sent? To add insult to injury, the flag was never recovered, nor was an explanation unearthed that identified the perpetrators or their motive. Although it was never proven, theories at the time revolved around young and mischievous Marines who were eager to let off steam and vent their frustrations about the war. Emotions towards their British predecessors were mixed, with some Marines harboring anger over the violent state in Sangin and others leaning more towards apathy. Rather quickly, more pressing matters stole the spotlight on the FOB.

About two weeks later, my interpreter and I were trying to talk to a group of Afghan villagers in the bazaar, and stonewalling the discussion was a barrage of vitriolic questions about my nationality. "Is she Russian, British or American?" they demanded of my interpreter. The conversation would have shut down immediately had the answer been anything other than "American." Hatred for Russians still runs deep in Afghanistan due to the destructive nature of the Russian–Afghan war, but the British military and their civilian "enablers" were also despised by common Afghan villagers. Both of those incidents raised a couple of questions. First, if the British pulled out militarily, why are so many "civvies" (a colloquial term for a civilian working in a military war zone) still here? And second, why do Afghans dislike these "civvies" as much as they disliked the uniformed British military?

In answer to the first question, everyone wants to leave Helmand with his or her head held high and feeling a sense of accomplishment—the British are no different. With the wars in Iraq and Afghanistan, the British were fighting a public relations battle identical to that of the US: people both wanted out and wanted victory—not a moral victory, but a geopolitical one that confirmed the potency, competence, influence, and political reach of the UK. For the British civilians in Sangin, especially at the time when our paths crossed, this was doubly important. The civilian capacity building entities, such as the British District Support Teams (DST) and Provincial Reconstruction Teams (PRT), were there to ensure some kind of victory for the British government even though military forces had departed. The answer to the second question lends insight to the political savviness of locals in Sangin, as interviewees often mentioned British civilians who were rumored to be building a puppet government without soliciting local input from villagers. Despite the fact that the DST rarely left the FOB, local Afghans were keenly aware and unsupportive of the DST's political machinations.

The DST's lack of popularity among the local people was partially a byproduct of their engagement strategy. Either military forces, civilian enablers, or a combination thereof can engage the population. While British military forces conducted the lion's share of population engagement in Basrah, in Helmand British civilian teams came on the heels of the military forces with the express task of building capacity with the local population. Thus, DSTs were first introduced to Afghanistan in 2009. They can be thought of as first cousins to PRTs, which were introduced in 2002 to assist with governance, reconstruction, and capacity building endeavors at the provincial level.[18] Many DSTs were US-led in areas where the US military exercised operational command over an area of operations. The teams were led by, and primarily staffed with, civilian government capacity building specialists. Most teams consisted of three to five individuals.[19] Their utility was based on their ability to live and work with forward-deployed military units that operated at the district level.

In Sangin, the DST was led and staffed by British civilians. It directly worked with the USMC battalion commander at FOB Jackson, was well integrated with the battalion staff, and occupied an office in the basement of the abandoned mansion that served as the battalion Command Operations Center (COC). It made sense that the few British-led DSTs in Afghanistan were concentrated in Helmand Province. The British were the first ISAF element to push into Helmand in 2006. They had amassed the most information over those four years before relinquishing control of the province to the Marines in 2010, and all involved were starting to recognize the imperative of preserving the "continuity of information." The British thought they were the best suited to help with the government capacity agenda, so their civilians stayed to get the job done even as their military left.

In September 2010, when my team was first informed that we would soon be going to Sangin for a mission, we immediately began combing through the massive amounts of electronic data the DST had amassed on Sangin. To their credit, they had done their homework. Scores upon scores of detailed village maps, geographical and topographical maps, tribal lists, infrastructure charts, and much more existed. I was immediately impressed and wondered what more my team could learn about Sangin if the British had apparently unearthed everything. The USMC regimental combat team intelligence shop, the S2, talked it over with my team in late September and we all decided that data validation was the way to go. The British had seemingly learned everything about the city, people, tribes, and dominant religious figures in Sangin, but how accurate were the data? And maybe we could elicit more and different information from the locals.

Before our team of eight arrived in Sangin on October 7, 2010, we sent the DST our research design and expressed our enthusiasm to learn and work with them. Courtesy and common sense told me that was the correct thing to do. Also, we had been forewarned that the DST considered themselves the pre-eminent "brains trust" on all things related to the people, government, and culture of Sangin. Understanding academic territoriality and sensitivities all too well, I was even more determined to finesse the situation as much as possible.

We arrived at FOB Jackson, Sangin, shortly after midnight on October 7, 2010. Based on the horror stories I had heard, I remember thinking our helicopter would never make it past the insurgents' ambush that was likely to happen as we were landing. Oddly, despite the dangers of Sangin, my team slept peacefully that night, but the first order of business the next day was to meet the DST. We incorrectly assumed that DSTs functioned like PRTs and they would fill whatever information gaps we had about Sangin. I am pretty sure they, conversely, were well versed on HTTs and what we hoped to accomplish. Plus, they had our research design, which spelled out our field research plan in detail.

There were three of them, including a carbine-toting, body-building mute, who served as both their private security detail and a Schwarzenegger body double. They were extremely polite but wary, and probably saw us as a menacing group of eight individuals intent on reinventing the wheel. That first morning, we met for an hour and sat quietly as they explained the complex intersection of Sangin's tribal, district government and security situation. We understood that every day their job entailed working with the fledgling district government in some way, in conjunction with the USMC battalion commander. We told them that *our* job would entail going out into the bazaar and neighborhoods and talking to the people. They wished us luck, pledged their support, and we promised to share with them all that we learned.

I am not even sure if my team and I actually knew what function the DST filled at that time. It was the first of such teams most of us had come across. Usually, there were so many different civilian "enablers" trekking through the area of operations that it was hard to keep track of them all. If the truth be told, civilian enablers were so ubiquitous and had such similar missions that it was miraculous that territorial clashes did not happen with more regularity. Most of these missions fell under the category of "combat support missions" and had traditionally been performed by military personnel in previous conflicts. In Afghanistan, these combat support missions generally consisted of equipment maintenance, logistical support, and intelligence gathering and analysis. There were also non-combat support missions such as administrative positions within the joint task headquarters; and capacity building missions parallel to the Chief of Mission effort to improve Afghan security institutions.[20]

The personnel mix could definitely be confusing to anyone unfamiliar with ultra-modern counterinsurgency warfare, which was characterized by "Coalition-centric operations" and non-traditional (i.e. civilian) actors in the battlespace. There was even a term for this unprecedented influx of civilian actors: the "Civilian Surge." According to the 2012 United States Government Accountability Office report on the civilian presence in Afghanistan:

> In March 2009, the President called for an expanded U.S. civilian presence to build the capacity of the Afghan government to provide security, essential services, and economic development with limited international support. In this expansion, U.S. agencies were to deploy civilian experts under the authority of the Chief of Mission beyond the U.S. embassy in Kabul to the provinces and districts to create more of an impact on Afghan lives by building the capacity of local government institutions. Housed with military personnel, these field-deployed civilians were to coordinate with their military and Afghan counterparts to integrate their capacity-building activities into the larger counterinsurgency campaign.[21]

The Department of Defense (DOD) reported that its civilian presence in Afghanistan grew from 394 civilians in January 2009 to 2,929 in December 2011.[22] Unlike previous wars, there were simply too many critical jobs central to the war effort and too few military personnel to do them. The need for US civilian augmentation in Afghanistan was indisputable. But throughout Helmand, the British civilians took the lion's share of the capacity building effort. By the time my team reached Sangin, it appeared to be a foregone conclusion that the DST had the lead voice on district-level governance issues.

We soon learned that they rarely got out amongst the people or canvassed the community. To be fair, their job was to help build capacity with district government leadership, not to do field research like us. But as locals began to tell us about earlier British military practices (which involved a lot of shooting and defensive driving, but not much community liaising and bridge building), we learned that they also rarely got out and talked to people about their needs and desires.[23] It seemed to be a pattern, especially given my prior experience in Basrah: the British were focused on elites rather than the ordinary locals.

People often assume that narratives in war zones rarely change: ask locals about their community dynamics and they will invariably respond by asking for essential services and complaining about meddlesome Westerners. It does often unfold like that, but things were much more nuanced in Sangin. In Sangin, everyone wanted to talk about how unfortunate it was that their tribal system was broken. The few tribal leaders left alive—those who had survived the 2006–9 bloodshed—fled Sangin to Lashkar Gah. All the major tribal leaders who had influence, trust, respect, and the savvy to navigate the intricacies of Sangin felt it was too dangerous to come back and wrench the city from the Taliban's grip. We heard this story dozens and dozens of times from farmers, bakers, teachers, carpet sellers, shoe repair men, mechanics, bazaar patrons, pharmacists, and everyone else we managed to talk to. Locals revered these men in Lashkar Gah as the ideal leaders that Sangin desperately needed, and they agonized over their absence.

Something did not click here, and I started reaching for the disparate pieces that I was hoping would complete the puzzle, Sangin's crazy puzzle. When talk of "rescuing Sangin" ensued, locals kept mentioning names different from those I had heard discussed by the Marines and DST back at the FOB. Why were the locals and the DST identifying different purported community leaders? My team had arrived in Sangin with a list of six or seven social issues that the regimental commander wanted us to look into. Sangin's "leadership dilemma," which was inseparably connected to the tribal problem, emerged as the premier field research issue due to the frequency with which locals brought it up. So, midway through our first mission our focus shifted to the essential leadership issue based on the direction in which locals were steering us. The problem was that the DST was doing the exact same thing, but they were querying political elites already in power rather than common villagers.

Local villagers were telling us who they wanted to run their government. They pointed to men that were far away (yet still in contact with their tribes and villages) in Lashkar Gah, and even some that were still in Sangin but frightened to assume leadership roles due to threats issued by the Taliban. Taliban vengeance was described as merciless. Stories were told of the tribal leader who was noosed to a car tailpipe and dragged about the streets of Sangin during the 2007 tribal uprising, howling for his life as his body was slowly shredded. Because of stories like these, community leaders stayed hidden in the shadows, practically underground and out of reach. Every day the British and Marines were working with the government officials who claimed *they* would save Sangin. However, these were different men from those we heard about on the street from passionate rank and file locals. Many of the government officials were not native to Sangin and were reputed by the locals to be of ill character. Something did not ring true. If the goal of capacity building was to establish a government that was legitimate, representative, and accountable, then why weren't we listening to what the people wanted? What about representative government?

After deciding that our efforts should squarely focus on Sangin's leadership dilemma, I drafted a new research design for my team. We disseminated this to the battalion commander and his staff, in addition to the regimental commander back at Delaram. With full consensus on our way forward, we began to execute our plan. We cast a wide net and solicited input from different social strata, but our efforts were always constrained by the tense security situation in Sangin. At the outset we decided on a four-prong approach that entailed conducting interviews with locals who worked on the FOB, locals who visited the FOB, shopkeepers and patrons in the bazaar marketplace, and farmers at a wheat seed distribution event. Because of the primacy of tribal issues in Sangin, we also made sure to speak to people from many different tribes. We soon learned the intrinsic value in each type of interview. For example, we were able to conduct longer interviews with locals who came to the FOB for business reasons because it was a secure environment. Yet, shorter interviews conducted with locals in the marketplace allowed my team to contextualize conversations by also observing the sights, sounds, and bustling activity of Sangin. Overall, we were able to conduct eighty-six interviews during that first trip to Sangin: fifteen key leader interviews (government and security officials), forty in-depth interviews (interviews that lasted about an hour), and thirty-one marketplace interviews where we talked to locals when patrolling with Marines in the bazaar. We also managed to interview locals from seven of Sangin's main tribes.

Soon after we started, our research began to adopt a cataloging dimension due to the amount of data we were amassing; we were hearing about so many different people and had to keep track of them over the course of our three missions. We created a comprehensive Excel spreadsheet that tracked the names (the ideal leaders) we were hearing about, their tribal affiliation, how often they were mentioned, why people claimed they were influential, where interviewees lived, and other important information. Trends in the data became apparent, and we soon noticed a handful of men who were repeatedly mentioned as being ideal leaders for Sangin. They had all fled to Lashkar Gah during the heavy violence a few years back. We briefed results as we went along to make sure Marines at the company, battalion, and regimental combat team levels had the operationally relevant information they needed. But, it was between our first and second missions to Sangin that I believe our team really put our money where our mouth was.

We returned to FOB Delaram in Nimruz Province, analyzed our field data, wrote an analytic report and conducted many briefs in support of our conclusions. It was late November 2010, two weeks before we were to return to Sangin for our second mission (and barely home from the first), when a researcher on my team stood up during one of our HTT morning meetings and dramatically proclaimed, "We must go to Lashkar Gah and find the leaders mentioned by those in Sangin." The idea seemed too ambitious, especially given the logistical difficulty and limited access, and I immediately shot it down. He was angry with me, and I soon understood why. In many ways the credibility of our data rested on the veracity of these claims made by Sangin locals. My researcher claimed that our "bottom line" would resonate with the Marines that much more if we performed the due diligence and found these very men, the political exiles, who populated our spreadsheet. He was right and I was wrong.

SEARCHING FOR THE EXILES

After a few weeks of planning, two of us went to Lashkar Gah and managed to locate and interview eight of the ten men we were hoping to find. Unfortunately, we also managed to anger the PRT while there. The Lashkar Gah PRT was closely linked to the Sangin DST, and news of our probing activities quickly spread. The assistance provided us by the PRT was nil, and they candidly opined that our efforts were in vain. Their perspective was that Sangin's exiled leaders were comfortable with their new lives in Lashkar Gah; had put the horrors of Sangin behind them; and were of marginal importance to those back home. This sounded like a plausible interpretation of the situation, but the PRT lacked the empirical data to back it up. Although the Lashkar Gah PRT routinely met with government officials and various local elites in the capital, population-centric research and analysis was not their bread and butter. They worked with higher-echelon, provincial-level leadership, not displaced leaders from places like Sangin. By contrast, such fieldwork was the mainstay of HTTs, and our research methods had to be scientific and credible, with empirical data supporting our claims. We wanted to be correct in our assessments and be able to brief the Marines with confidence and credibility on the leadership dilemma during our next trip to Sangin.

Our findings substantiated the claims made by locals in Sangin. The exiled tribal and community leaders with whom we spoke lamented their inability to return home. Despite being so far away in the provincial capital, their knowledge of local events and political maneuvering in Sangin suggested they were highly connected to the goings-on there. All spoke of having something akin to a personal assistant who lived in Sangin. These assistants would pass guidance and edicts from the exiled leaders in Lashkar Gah to their tribes and communities in Sangin. We also learned it was not uncommon for Sangin locals to visit these exiled leaders to ask for help with tribal mediation—a far drive over very difficult terrain. Essentially, these leaders were legislating and leading from afar, and many back home still felt intimately connected to them. Practically all interviewees said they would return to their native Sangin if security improved and the Taliban were less of a threat. In the end, we felt vindicated by our results from Lashkar Gah, which detailed what it would take for these leaders to come back to Sangin and assume leadership positions.

CHRISTMAS IN SANGIN

While our second and third missions involved working with the population on a number of issues deemed operationally critical by the battalion and regimental commanders, the main focus remained the leadership question. Meanwhile, our British DST counterparts reluctantly welcomed us back to Sangin in December after learning of our activities in Lashkar Gah. Since we were spending Christmas and New Year in wintery cold, bare bones Sangin, I was hoping for easy collaboration, not a rehashing of our earlier competitive relationship. However, they made it clear that they disapproved of our mission to seek out the Sangin exiles in Lashkar Gah. While we were away, they had continued their daily task of supporting and professionalizing the men who made up Sangin's district government. All of these men hated their rivals in Lashkar Gah, with whom we had just met, and vehemently denied their power and popular appeal within the local Sangin population. Essentially, each team was vying for the ear of the battalion commander, and the more I tried to justify support for these revered exiled Sangin leaders, the more my team was marginalized by the DST. We understood their reaction, but we also knew that if the goal of counterinsurgency was to persuade the community not to support the insurgents, a key step in this process must be helping the people build the government *they* wanted, not the one that was easy for us.

Christmas and the day after brought a welcome surprise that both vindicated our hypothesis and incensed our British colleagues even more. In mid-December the North Sangin Peace Process took place, a multilateral effort by Afghan and US government officials to bring influential Alikozai tribal leaders and local Taliban to the bargaining table. Peace agreements throughout Helmand fail with regularity and enthusiasm is often tempered at the onset of these negotiations. However, there was widespread optimism this time around. Everybody hoped that if the peace process was successful in the north, it could then be tried in the Ishaqzai-dominated south, which boasted a much stronger Taliban presence.

My team learned that in order to facilitate the peace process in the north, serious star power had to be brought in from Lashkar Gah. Ma'mur Sulayman Shah, the most popular and renowned exiled Sangin leader, legendary in the eyes of most locals, was asked by Afghan provincial leaders to travel to Sangin and lend credibility to the peace process. In addition, two other former Sangin leaders were asked to return. Just a month earlier, we had interviewed these same men in Lashkar Gah about their willingness to return to Sangin and assume leadership positions, an experience that left us buoyed about their ability to positively effect change in the district. We were ecstatic after hearing about their return, an enthusiasm that was shared by many locals throughout Sangin.

Ma'mur Sulayman Shah's mandatory presence at the negotiating table spoke volumes about his influence and prestige compared to the current district governor and other DST-supported officials. A few days before Christmas we arranged to interview these men once again, only this time our interviews were to take place in their native village of Sangin, not Lashkar Gah. I conducted a two-hour interview with Ma'mur Sulayman Shah on 26 December 2010. As a renowned leader and former mayor of Sangin, his demeanor was electrifying and his influence was convincing. One felt it immediately and it became evident why so many in Sangin revered this individual.

A few days later we briefed our assessment to the battalion commander and the DST. We explained that Ma'mur Sulayman Shah's return to Sangin after a five-year absence underscored his influence, and that he was critical to the success of both the peace process and the future of Sangin. Every morning of his visit about 400–500 villagers gathered outside his compound waiting to shake and kiss his hand and discuss security in Sangin.

The DST downplayed the significance of the interview from the beginning. They offered a counter-argument that pointed to his unsuitability to lead, due to his remote status, his inability to fulfill the educational requirement for the district government position, and the unavailability of vacant positions in Sangin. They emphatically told the battalion commander that the current government in Sangin was established, well tested and familiar. Ma'mur Sulayman Shah was an unpredictable gamble. Yet, the DST never attempted to meet with or interview him, which could have better informed their perspective. Nor did the DST ever interact with locals and canvas the community about Ma'mur Sulayman Shah's desirability and appeal. The DST also disregarded USMC reports that locals viewed District Governor Sharif (who had been endorsed and informally mentored by the DST) as an unconnected outsider. In Afghan culture, and particularly in the Pashtun-dominated south where camaraderie and kinship are key, locals cast a wary eye on outsiders. District Governor Sharif was from the northern area of Kajaki and his tribe was a minority faction in Sangin. In the eyes of Sangin villagers, these facts alone meant he was a poor fit as district governor.

Our nightly O&I brief frequently involved the DST steadfastly denying the potency of these exiled Sangin leaders, while my team argued just the opposite. British military and civilians, after accumulating years of experience in Sangin and other Helmand districts, were convinced of the veracity of their beliefs. Our limited time in Sangin limited our credibility with the DST and worked against us. After debating it amongst ourselves for months, we concluded that both the Marines and the DST preferred to support the current cast of characters rather than gamble on the exiled leaders. The emphasis was on bolstering the politically savvy elites in power, with little time dedicated to understanding what the local people actually wanted.

STAYING TRUE TO OUR BELIEFS

After Christmas, our team kept plodding away and canvassing the Sangin population, trying to figure out which leaders people wanted at the village and tribal levels and why. Each time we returned, Sangin was a bit safer and we were able to get further out and talk to more people. By the third mission (April–May 2012) we divided the team into three groups of two and worked from remote patrol bases for four weeks.

The results were insightful. That final report was entitled "Northern and Southern Sangin Leadership: A Human Terrain Team Population Assessment Report." It was our best work and also the most controversial and there was an entire section entitled "The Preference for Ma'mur Sulayman Shah." Accompanying the report was a quantitative product, "Influential Leaders Field Data Spreadsheet," with responses from our 165 interviewees. In actuality, the spreadsheet was a map of what the people in Sangin wanted and why. The passage below is from our final report, which articulated our bottom line to the Marines:

> The security vacuum in Sangin, the extensive reach of the Taliban, the inability for consecutive peace processes to take root, and GIRoA *tashkiel* [table of authorities] shortages all have a common denominator in the absence of indigenous and effective leadership. Although Sangin's District Governor (DG) and other government officials are considered competent and cooperative with Coalition Forces (CF), locals consistently mention the nonrepresentational nature of GIRoA and the District Development Shura (DDS). Locals prefer these positions to be staffed by individuals they want and trust. The ideal situation is one where individuals that are both genuinely popular and appropriately powerful are occupying leadership positions that affect change in Sangin. Until that happens, locals may not directly rebuff GIRoA officials and elders in positions of authority, but if those individuals do not resonate as the people's choice then locals may question the motives and authenticity of the Marines—who are perceived by locals to financially and militarily support GIRoA. If examined through a security lens, failure to support representative government may make the Marines and GIRoA appear disingenuous in their attempt to move Sangin in a better direction, and incite anger and despondency amongst the population.

THE HEART OF THE MATTER: CONCLUSIONS

Generally, one refrains from dissecting a conflict when right in the middle of it. Reflection and analysis often come later. At the time one is just trying to make it through the confrontation. After I left Sangin for the last time in the summer of 2011, I thought a lot about how our team was probably branded as "those pesky meddlesome kids" despite the positive results of our studies. I came to understand why the DST had been such difficult civilian allies and why they were so emotionally invested in their mandate. But, I also spent some time wondering about the other civilian enablers in our battlespace. For example, would we have struggled so much had we partnered with teams of USAID or Department of Agriculture members instead?

Introspectively, I was also compelled to question the functionality and efficacy of my team. Did Sangin's pressure-cooker environment inadvertently affect my team's demeanor and objectivity? Over the years I had witnessed many situations where people and teams morphed for the worse under stressful circumstances by becoming ultra-aggressive, or conversely insular and uncompromising. Perhaps the passion with which we pursued the Sangin leadership challenge was too passionate. More importantly—but much more difficult to consider—perhaps my drive to communicate the peoples' needs and desires was operationally superfluous. After all, the Coalition's capacity building objective in this phase of the war was to build governance, not establish a representative democracy per se. Did we push too hard? As field researchers, was our job merely to learn about the community and report the results, and not to become passionate advocates during the process?

In the end, I realized that our clash with the British was not a reflection of my team's shortcomings. In fact, it was the opposite. The British led the effort to rebuild the government of Sangin (and other districts throughout Helmand), and success on this front would have minimized disappointments on the military front. Everyone wants to end their deployment with their heads held high and feeling a sense of accomplishment. The core of tension was that the DST's end-state was far different from ours. They wanted to build, support, and mentor a district government in Sangin. Helping Afghans establish stable and functional district and provincial governments was one of many ways in which NATO was characterizing victory in Afghanistan. They wanted capable and reliable people to staff this government, and they were cognizant of the limited timeframe bracketing all efforts. The British felt close to creating this end-state in Sangin, and the last thing they wanted was for my team to suggest that the government they supported was the wrong one. Our end-state revolved around a core pillar of HTS's mission: we wanted to research and learn about the people of Sangin and relay this information to battlespace commanders so that they could make an informed decision about what kind of government to build. Only after I left Sangin for the last time did I finally understand why we were so unwelcome. Our mandate as field researchers was different from their mandate of capacity building. I mistakenly assumed that the DST's mandate should shift to resemble ours, and that local population-centric research was the preferable method for reaching that end-state. But as a social scientist tasked with understanding the cultural milieu of Afghanistan, I should have known that that was my vision, not theirs.

So, what happened in the end? Honestly, there is no Hollywood ending here. We submitted our findings, conducted many briefs, and did what many do when deploying and redeploying to Afghanistan: prayed that our analysis resonated with someone. To our knowledge, none of the exiled leaders with whom we met were incorporated into Sangin's local government after our departure from Sangin. We also lost visibility on political developments in the district as the months wore on and we were tasked with other missions. We certainly did not expect our population studies to usher in a whole new government in Sangin, but we hoped that all involved gained a better understanding of the criticality of representative government when rebuilding a war-torn community during a COIN campaign. In such an environment, building effective governance is predicated on securing the trust of the people. The population must believe you have their best interests in mind and are committed to actualizing a better state of affairs. Anything less can lead to a reversal of fortune, with the population instead cozying to the insurgents. We hoped that the British understood that we were just doing our job of community engagement and liaising. And finally, we hoped that coupled with that understanding was their own revelation: that missteps in Basrah and struggles in Helmand could maybe yield successes in the future when dealing with precarious, war-torn populations, wherever that next encounter may be.

9

ASSESSING THE HUMAN TERRAIN TEAMS

NO WHITE HATS OR BLACK HATS, PLEASE

Carolyn Fluehr-Lobban and *George R. Lucas Jr.*

Ethics discourse in American anthropology has been generated, for the most part, in times of historic crisis. These crises have reflected the political tenor of the times, most often when the country has been at war: the declared First and Second World Wars of the twentieth century and the undeclared wars in Vietnam, Afghanistan, and Iraq. Professional anthropology found its conscience in the wake of the Second World War with the first formal code drafted by applied anthropologists in 1948 by the Society for Applied Anthropology (SfAA). The first code of the mainstream, four-field American Anthropological Association was born in the tumultuous days of the Vietnam War amid allegations that a few anthropologists had been involved in counterinsurgency and intelligence work in Southeast Asia. This followed earlier, less explosive revelations in the mid-1960s of anthropologists' alleged involvement in counterinsurgency research in South America in a project known as "Camelot." That anthropologists were again immersed in a blame and shame ethics discourse around the wars in Iraq and Afghanistan was not surprising but predictable.

Controversy in anthropology over ethical, professional, and political issues has swirled around the employment and deployment of anthropologists in a variety of contexts in the "global war on terror" after September 11, 2001 and the subsequent wars in Afghanistan and Iraq. It has been said that the First World War was the war of chemists, the Second World War of the physicists, and that the Third Word War (the emerging current global insurgency context) is the war of anthropologists. This latter characterization refers to the importance of anthropology and the role of culture in counterinsurgency in the present era. During this period the most controversial "engagement" of anthropologists was with the Human Terrain System (HTS) that embeds social scientists, including anthropologists, with military units as socio-cultural advisors. Although few anthropologists were actually a part of the HTS teams, the deaths of three non-anthropologist social scientists added deadly consequences to the mix of compelling moral and ethical issues.

ANTHROPOLOGY'S LITANY OF SHAME

How should we finally understand the contentious disciplinary and professional debate surrounding the development of the US Army's Human Terrain System program?

One approach, grounded in comparatively recent discussions concerning the discipline's Code of Ethics,[1] is that the specific controversy regarding HTS is merely the latest chapter in a larger narrative framework, from the perspective of which the broader discipline of anthropology has unconsciously come to view itself.[2] From this narrative perspective, our wider understanding of what anthropology is, and what anthropologists do (and, just as importantly, what they will not and should not do), encompasses much more than a mere factual history of its origins, or a hagiography of its great figures (from Herder and Dilthey, to Malinowski, Boas, and Levi-Strauss). On the face of it, this history may be told as the sequence of incidents of systematic abuse and betrayal by certain anthropologists, in the recent past, of their professional responsibilities towards colleagues and research subjects.[3]

A plausible, if unconscious, subtext of this narrative revelation of the hidden disgraces buried within anthropology's history, however, characterizes it more problematically as a highly selective and ritualistic ceremony, solemnly intoned by the collective community: the ritual recitation of a "litany of shame."[4] The characterization of this "historical telling" or "performance" of anthropology's history as a "litany" captures the unconscious, unreflective, ceremonial, indeed cultic manner in which principal elements of the factual history are highlighted, recited, and collectively renounced in their entirety by the disciplinary community.

More precisely, anthropologists themselves (on this interpretation, at least) tend to define both themselves as professionals, and the core commitments of their present practice, largely through periodic, repeated re-enactment of this community ritual—one that seems to entail a collective repudiation of a succession of morally abhorrent things that past anthropologists have said and done (or, more accurately, that they stand accused by anthropologists in the present of having said or done in the past). While the repeated performance of this largely unconscious and unreflective ritual goes mainly unnoticed by members of the discipline, it is perhaps the first and most striking feature of their collective life witnessed by any visitor or newcomer in their midst. It pervades their collective discourse, their public pronouncements, and the disciplinary rhetorical stance of their written documents, from introductory textbooks to scholarly treatises. By exposing and deconstructing this hidden subtext, however, observers may come to understand the manner in which the discipline or profession of anthropology attempts to define itself at present primarily through this ritual *negation*, or ceremonial repudiation, of that shared past.

Significantly, this negative litany of repudiation is itself set within a vague and, at best, poorly documented, partially substantiated, and highly interpretive historical context, within which anthropologists of the even more distant past are accused of having collaborated with the colonial and imperial powers of previous centuries in the oppression, subjugation, and exploitation of indigenous peoples throughout the world.[5] Despite the factual record's support of something more like a mixture of opposition and resistance to, as well as collaboration with, governing elites in the exploitation of indigenous peoples, this pre-twentieth-century history is likewise formulated by contemporary anthropologists more as a mythology than as a factual history. The mythology is constructed to convey a moral stance and commitment, rather than an authentic historical investigation intended to discern and distinguish acceptable from unacceptable past practices in the origins of the discipline.

In the annals of the history of science, there is simply nothing with which to compare this remarkable disciplinary self-loathing, save perhaps in medicine.[6] Even there, by contrast, the instances of intentional malfeasance are concrete, fully documented, and certainly, in their most grotesque and abhorrent features, not nearly so dependent upon disputed or highly prejudicial interpretations of the key events in which they are grounded. The Nuremburg and Belmont Codes, for example, arise from the reflection by health-care professionals on specific and well-documented acts that abuse or defy the core values of the profession—they are not taken as the essence, even the past essence, of the profession itself. In the history of medicine, additionally, the acts of intentional abuse and deliberate, wholesale malfeasance are largely limited to the twentieth century, where they are distinguished clearly from the earlier details of a mostly venerable, patient-centered history—one that is admittedly littered (as with most other histories of scientific disciplines) with quaint, archaic, and scientifically mistaken practices to which, even though they were sometimes unintentionally harmful, no collective moral disapprobation is attached.

As opposed to its mythological pre-history, anthropology's own explicit "litany of shame" is, in one sense at least, similar to medicine's recent history, in that it is likewise grounded explicitly in terms of recent, quite specific, and decidedly negative historical milestones drawn from the twentieth century. About these selected and "ritually forefronted" historical episodes, quite remarkably there appears to be widespread and largely uncritical consensus among these scholars and academics who, as a matter of principle as well as customary practice, agree with one another on little, if anything, else. These recent historical milestones include: the censuring by the American Anthropological Association of its principal founding figure, Professor Franz Boas of Columbia University, for accusing and denouncing unnamed colleagues of having engaged in espionage during the First World War,[7] the collaboration of Margaret Mead, her husband, Gregory Bateson, her colleague and close friend, Ruth Benedict, and other anthropologists at the time with the OSS during the Second World War, and subsequently with its successor agency, the CIA, and military intelligence services during the Cold War;[8] and, most centrally featured in this litany, "Project Camelot," a social science research project funded by the US Army Office of Research in the mid-1960s,[9] alongside "Operation Phoenix" in Vietnam, and ultimately the so-called "Thailand Affair," involving a research project focused on rural populations, funded by the Defense Advanced Research Projects Agency (DARPA) in the early 1970s.[10]

To label this collective historical discourse within the profession of anthropology a "litany" is to draw attention to the fact that the resulting narrative entails almost universal agreement on the part of a vast majority of members of the discipline on the historical details included, in the order in which they are recited, and in the normative meaning or interpretation to be attached to each. And, in sharp contrast to the recent history of medical malfeasance, this interpretive consensus within the discipline appears to be forged despite substantial evidence of the historical inaccuracies in, the rampant inconsistencies among, and finally, the highly questionable interpretive significance of, each and every detail included within the narrative.

The Role of Shame in the Human Terrain

Almost from its inception, HTS was wholly subsumed within this larger narrative, pre-empting any impartial assessment of its legitimacy or effectiveness. The program was instead beset with hostile and skeptical questions concerning its professional probity and seemingly unquestionable hostile intent.[11] HTS itself was denounced by a majority of the profession as yet another example of what both the larger factual history and the litany of shame depicted, well before there was even a shred of concrete evidence, one way or another, concerning how the program itself would work, and what its participants would be expected to do (let alone whether it would in fact prove to be yet another episode in this unfortunate historical narrative). Instead, all of these potential expectations were refracted through the lens of anthropology's dramatic, historical litany. As a result, anthropologists themselves were exhorted to abjure any association, affiliation, or participation in this program, almost as if, by doing so, they would threaten to violate a ritual taboo.

To be sure, HTS was hardly immune from a variety of legitimate and justifiable concerns (as the various accounts by HTS participants included in this volume bear witness). Important questions and concerns were generated, even by guarded supporters of the initiative, along the lines of its practicality and operational feasibility.[12] Would the effects of the program justify the considerable financial investment required to sustain it? Would "academic anthropologists" really be all that useful in the field? Would the program be able to attract and retain the requisite caliber of knowledge and talent, in light of the rigors and the very real risks to be experienced in the course of duty? Was the program itself well organized and competently administered? Then subsequently, after the program had gotten underway and the first HTS teams began to be deployed in Iraq and Afghanistan in 2007, concerned critics (including rank and file members of the US military forces themselves) began to wonder what measurable impact it was having, in terms, say, of increasing the rate of overall mission effectiveness, or lessening incidents of cultural conflict, let alone, most importantly, in helping to reduce the rate of non-combatant casualties.[13] These appeared to be properly framed questions regarding administrative and organizational features of the actual program in operation (in marked contrast to the speculative hypotheses grounded only in anthropology's core principles, rather than concrete evidence). As such, these questions and others like them were fully amenable to empirical study and data-driven investigation.

The vast majority of complaints, however, continued to come from outside the program itself, primarily from members of the community of academic (rather than "practice") anthropologists, who complained that the program itself inherently constituted a violation of the discipline's Code of (professional) Ethics.[14] Some critics worried that baseline professional principles, such as informed consent, or the strict injunction to "do no harm" to research subjects, would be inherently compromised by the work that anthropologists would inevitably be expected to perform for military forces in the field of combat.[15] Others suggested that the information gathered about local populations might be used to deliberately harm them, by telling military forces (in the words of one critic) "whom to kill," thus "weaponizing" anthropology.[16] In these respects, critics feared the program would emulate the worst excesses of prior, infamous social science experiments undertaken in cooperation with the military (such as the aforementioned Operation Phoenix, Project Camelot, and the Thailand Affair).

Still other critics thought the chief objection to be an inherent conflict of interest, common to all forms of "practice" or practical anthropology, that must inevitably confront any anthropologist drawn to participate in this program: between, for example, the client commissioning and funding the research on the one hand, and the trust, confidentiality, and welfare of the subjects of the anthropologist's research on the other. This conflict would be especially pronounced if the "classified" or clandestine nature of the field studies undertaken was to be kept secret, or otherwise partially or wholly withheld from the academic community at large.[17] Finally, external critics also worried that suitably qualified personnel to take on so difficult and complex a mission would be difficult if not impossible to recruit. And to add to the confusion, as the program deployed its first HTS teams to the field in 2007, critics objected that the program itself was poorly organized and mismanaged—in effect, a bungling, misconceived waste of government resources.[18] Partly as a result of this wave of criticism and controversy, a resolution approved by the Executive Board of the AAA in October 2007 flatly asserted that participation in HTS "constituted a grave breach of professional ethics, and an unacceptable use of disciplinary expertise."[19]

Commissions on the Engagement of Anthropology with the US Security and Intelligence Communities

Following the Executive Board resolution, the American Anthropological Association established two Commissions on Engagement of Anthropology with US Security and Intelligence Communities (CEAUSSIC I and II). These commissions, which extended over a four-year period (2006–10), sought to investigate a range of issues associated with military engagement during the wars in Iraq and Afghanistan. However, despite their broad charge embodied in the lengthy title of the commission, their ultimate preoccupation was with the Human Terrain System, in which only a handful of anthropologists were employed.

The formation of the first commission was a response to a 2007 front-page story in the *New York Times* by David Rohde that featured HTS in Afghanistan. The article referenced the assistance that HTS was providing to the military during humanitarian operations, such as medical clinics and training programs for Afghan widows. The front-page headline of America's premier newspaper, "Army Enlists Anthropology in War Zones," signaled the alarm within the AAA and demanded action.[20] Fluehr-Lobban was consulted in the early "what should we do?" conversations that took place among the AAA leadership and Committee on Ethics. The balance of these conversations was that David Rohde's article did not recognize the potential harm which social scientists might cause to Iraqi and Afghan people (or potential harm to the profession of anthropology). The article's focus on anthropologists deployed in war zones evoked the primary fear of anthropologists, that of potential harm to the discipline.[21]

The first report of the commission, devoted as mentioned to "military anthropology" more broadly, was brief and almost entirely devoid of specifics.[22] It lacked details concerning the HTS program, and was not careful to distinguish this from the broader scope of military anthropology generally. In the absence of any concrete evidence of wrongdoing, moreover, it relied for its conclusions upon hypothetical case studies that were amateurish, poorly designed for their intended purpose, and in any case largely irrelevant to the concerns of professional ethics otherwise cited in that report.[23] It showed the combined effects of absence of evidence, and of the commission itself being forced to operate in an atmosphere of controversy and crisis, far from their collective comfort zone or domain of expertise. The first CEAUSSIC report had revealed absolutely no recognition whatever on the part of members, for example, that HTS employees were in fact, at the time of writing, private military contractors, rather than military personnel, thus rendering the HTS program and its employees vulnerable to a score of independent moral and legal objections raised regarding the growing public–private partnership in combat zones, and the uncontrolled growth of private military contracting generally. (This oversight was corrected in the second report.)

The final report of the first commission raised so many issues and questions that a second two-year period was designated by the AAA to examine these in more depth. The second phase of CEAUSSIC focused exclusively on the Human Terrain System, resulting in a lengthy report in 2009. Although the second CEAUSSIC report of 2009 in many respects represented a substantive advance over its predecessor, neither of the commissions over their four-year term met as a full committee with HTS personnel or their sponsors to interrogate the realities of this program or others where anthropologists were working with and for the military. Rather, a few members of the commission conducted interviews that were summarized in the final reports issued by the commission that were neither written nor fully reviewed by the full commission. Voices that favored dialogue with the military HTS personnel, and possible refinement, modification, or reformulation of the program were not encouraged. A proposal initiated by Fluehr-Lobban within CEAUSSIC II to host a meeting of HTS personnel at the United States Institute of Peace was jettisoned within the commission on the basis of a criticism that the USIP was "not a neutral venue."[24] Thus an historic opportunity to examine broadly and critically the major professional and ethical issue of the day, engagement with the military during a time when the nation is at war, was essentially lost for the profession.

The second commission report contained copious details on the founding, funding, structure, and administration of that program. Despite repeated allegations infusing both reports that HTS activities would inevitably involve spying and secret research, the gathering of covert military intelligence, and the intentional harming of research subjects, neither of these two reports, nor any other subsequent factual accounts of HTS, documented any actual incidents of this sort. The report contained no concrete descriptions of actual professional malfeasance, nor could any of its allegations regarding HTT members engaging, or being asked to engage, in espionage, intelligence activities, or colluding in doing harm to research subjects be independently verified. Instead, it chiefly cited concerns about obtaining the appropriate informed consent of research subjects proposed for study. Interestingly, the second report acknowledged the earlier paucity of evidence concerning actual HTS practice, and stated that research into such activities had only recently begun to be undertaken. In claiming this, however, the commission's members strangely chose to overlook extant published findings that had been extensively peer-reviewed by the anthropological community (including by some of the commission's own members). Instead, as evidence of the "new research" being undertaken on HTS, the commission randomly cited un-refereed editorials, blogs, and online opinion pieces by members of the commission themselves, along with a single, self-published book by a self-styled journalist and outspoken critic of the program.

Such oddly unprofessional conduct might have been overlooked had it resulted in any new light being shed on actual practice. Instead, for all its detail, the second report marshaled, as evidence for its findings against the professional propriety of the HTS program, what at the time were still largely unsubstantiated complaints of mismanagement, excessive expenditures, and overall ineffectiveness. These were surely legitimate questions and concerns to raise, though on that basis one would be obliged to dismantle most of the government bureaucracy, not to mention universities and professional organizations like the AAA itself.

Alongside the claims of ineffectiveness, incompetence, and financial mismanagement, the remaining objections pertained to the danger inherent in this kind of fieldwork. Three social scientists (though, significantly, no anthropologists) lost their lives while engaged in HTS activities, while a fourth member of the program was apparently kidnapped. Tragically, in the cases of two team members (Michael Bhatia and Paula Loyd) killed in Afghanistan in 2009, the testimony concerning their extraordinary professional competence, dedication, relevant expertise, and performance in the field were all uniformly exemplary.[25] It thus seemed wildly inconsistent, as well as professionally inappropriate, for journalistic critics and CEAUSSIC commission members to cite their deaths as an argument against the program, in light of the universal and undisputed testimonials to their competence and effectiveness in the field, and to the exemplary nature of their work in this program while they were alive. Those testimonials seemed to constitute powerful counter-evidence to the array of charges lodged by critics against the program itself.[26]

Debate Concerning "Military Anthropology"

Notwithstanding these unfortunate casualties, the furor over HTS continued to plague the discipline of anthropology for several more years, and in the process swept up a number of other distinct practices that might be said to have fallen within the domain of military anthropology, but which had little or nothing to do with this Army-specific program to employ social scientists in combat zones. Some of the most vociferous HTS critics angrily denied that they, or any of their colleagues, had ever routinely conflated or denounced these other activities included within the broad scope of military anthropology. Such protestations of innocence and lack of generalized prejudice were countered, however, by explicit testimony from those engaged in these harmless and benign activities in a military setting, who, with one voice, testified to the near-universal and indiscriminate abuse heaped upon them by their colleagues, merely, it seemed, for the sin of accepting a paycheck from the federal government.

So confusing did the debate become that it was sometimes the case that even knowledgeable participants could not distinguish what specific practices were being denounced, nor determine to what degree it might be inherently wrong for social scientists to collaborate or serve as employees with the government or military in any sense.[27] Were other practices that fell under this large umbrella, such as teaching military students, compiling cultural data and information for their orientation to new cultures before deployment, or carrying out anthropological eth-nographic studies of military cultures themselves all properly subject to professional disapprobation? At one point, an anthropologist engaged in the seemingly innocent and scientifically significant exploration of indigenous archeological sites and the repatriation of Native American ancestral remains discovered on federal land (in part to assure faithful compliance with the terms of the Native American Repatriation Act of 1990) found herself and her work sharply denounced by colleagues as unethical and unprofessional, simply because her employer was the US Army Post at Fort Drum.[28] The discussion among anthropologists glossed over the different types of military anthropology, as if it were cut from the same cloth. As Lucas noted, types of military anthropology include: (1) anthropology *of* the military; (2) embedded anthropologists, such as HTS; and (3) anthropologists as subject matter experts and as educators of military personnel.[29]

These additional ethical issues, and the features of routine practice within the other forms of military anthropology, are the subject of a recent ethnographical analysis.[30] The contributors to that volume offer details concerning the lives and work of several anthropologists rou-tinely engaged in their profession. Their diverse efforts are seen to encompass the study of ancient indigenous cultures and the repatria-tion of Native American burial remains on federal land, teaching a wide range of intellectually challenging courses to diverse students in a variety of university classroom settings, conducting highly specialized field research in foreign locales, and providing valuable support to international humanitarian aid, peacekeeping, and development proj-ects abroad. Indeed, the only thing that demarcates these individual scholars from their colleagues and peers in the discipline is simply that they are employed, in all these otherwise mainstream pursuits, by branches of the US military. Some are even uniformed military person-nel. These factual accounts of their individual lives, motivations, and daily work, however, both underscore the inherent value and legiti-macy of that work and decisively refute the spurious charges of profes-sional betrayal lodged against them by colleagues in their discipline. They certainly demonstrate that academic anthropologists within this broadly defined sub-field of "military anthropology" are not secretly engaging in "espionage and clandestine research," nor are they betray-ing the confidence and risking the welfare of their research subjects.

Notwithstanding, the senior editor of the study documents charges from colleagues in the AAA that, simply by engaging in such activities, these anthropologists are guilty of breaching the most fundamental ethical canons of acceptable professional practice, and ought to be denounced as "war criminals."[31] The individual accounts by these anthropologists of the ignorance, bigotry, and prejudice with which they are frequently met by colleagues, simply for their involvement in these otherwise conventional professional pursuits, together with the shocking revelations by Professor Rubinstein of brutal and cruel professional malfeasance committed by leading scholars against other contributors to this volume, lay bare a shameful and deeply rooted pathology within the disciplinary culture that threatens the collective integrity and, indeed, the very future of anthropology itself.

This volume, somewhat in contrast, proposes to engage in similar historical, ethnographical, and personal narratives of participants in the HTS program itself. We have shown that a great many of the criticisms above are speculative suspicions, involving matters of principle, rather than direct observations of alleged perverse practices. Most such claims are therefore inherently falsifiable, in that they would require support in the form of evidence that, at the time, no one possessed. The motivations and professional qualifications of the participants, the ethical conundrums they may have faced or the unethical orders they may have been given, together with the effectiveness of the program and the competence of its administration, all should be determined either through scientific field studies or through peer review. Time and again, it was seen to be a characteristic of the most vociferous and vitriolic complaints lodged against the HTS program (and against those who deigned to participate in it) that any underlying evidence supporting the charges against both them personally, and against the program itself, was wholly absent. As many commented at the time, this evidentiary under-determination seemed an especially inappropriate situation for a self-described community of scientists with a strong positivist tradition.[32]

Although reliable data and concrete evidence concerning the HTS program were admittedly difficult to come by in the earliest years of a new program, details about it did begin to trickle in slowly over the ensuing years. Reliable public press reports in the *New York Times* and the *Washington Post* that attempted to offer balanced and fact-based assessments of the impact of the program were, however, denounced by critics as inaccurate and one-sided, and otherwise dismissed as part of an "orchestrated campaign" through which (in the words of David Price) "HTS has been given an uncritical free ride in the press."[33] The deaths in quick succession of the three social scientists mentioned above, for example, were once again seized upon as proof of mismanagement, poor training, bad administration, and a general lack of qualifications.[34]

SURVEYING THE HUMAN TERRAIN

The debate left the matters of fact about the program undetermined, while empirical questions capable in principle of being run to ground through systematic, scientific investigation were left unpursued. Despite the two AAA CEAUSSIC commissions on "engagement," HTS had not been objectively assessed by the official anthropological community charged with this historic responsibility. The initial commission in 2007—just prior to the election of the anti-war candidate Barack Obama—was politically charged and the HTS program, in which anthropologists were allegedly involved, was a target for possible self-righteous anti-war action. Although little was known of the actual operation of the HTTs on the ground, condemnation was swift and complete. Adding names to the "Litany of Shame" was in full swing. Since neither of the two commissions ever met as a whole with HTS personnel—despite promises to do so and an effort to convene such a meeting at the US Institute of Peace—the commissions lacked the knowledge needed to make an assessment of HTS from the standpoint of professional anthropology and its code of ethics. As the controversy over HTS unfolded, the professional community was in fact labeling "good" and "bad" anthropologists, the latter being those few anthropologists who worked professionally with the military or openly with the intelligence apparatus.[35]

A more balanced, fact-based treatment of the issues regarding anthropologists and the military is needed, across the spectrum of the full range of possible engagement, the decision-making, and the consequences of decisions. On the one hand, the ethnographies recorded by participants in this volume aim, at minimum, to provide a database of actual experiences, versus hypothetical speculation, on what HTS participants are actually called on to do, and how useful or effective their actions have (or have not) proven to be under the specific sets of circumstances that each of these authors describe. On the other hand, and to ensure breadth and scope coverage, it seemed incumbent to interview other participants in the program who were not themselves contributors to this volume, in order to gauge their motivations for participating in the program and their experiences while deployed, including whether or not they themselves either initially experienced ethical qualms about joining the program, or subsequently were asked (or even ordered) to engage in activities that might be characterized as professional malfeasance.

Carolyn Fluehr-Lobban was provided with contacts of persons who had served with HTTs through her work as Adjunct Professor of African Studies at the Naval War College in Newport, RI. Ten former HTT members responded to a questionnaire (reprinted in the Appendix) and eight of these persons were interviewed by phone. Every person contacted responded and none refused; indeed, several indicated that they were glad to have the opportunity to discuss the realities of HTS as they were experienced on the ground. All of the respondents but one agreed to disclosure of their identities.[36] Nine of the ten HTS respondents interviewed were male. All were aware of the controversies within anthropology regarding HTS and two indicated that although they were opposed to the war in Iraq, they felt that working on an HTT was a way to ameliorate its negative effects. Lachlyn Soper, for example, indicated that her "main personal concern was my opposition to the war in Iraq."[37]

HTS began to work in Iraq in 2007 and the narratives of various former members extend from this year to 2012. Half of the respondents held either an MA or PhD in the field of Political Science or a sub-field; four held MA degrees in International Relations or International Studies. Additionally there was an MA in Library Science, with extensive Middle East experience; a West Point graduate specializing in military intelligence; a National Guardsman; and a former US AID worker. Six were deployed only in Iraq between 2008 and 2011, and the other four were deployed or worked exclusively in Afghanistan during the same time period. The periods of deployment ranged from seven months to two years with an average of ten months. The US AID worker worked in Afghanistan for a total of eighteen months between 2011 and 2013. The impressive backgrounds and credentials of the respondents counter the assertions that HTS personnel were generally newly minted, unemployed MAs and PhDs desperate for work. Most were seasoned analysts with prior experience in intelligence in government or military agencies and several expressed an attraction to the "hands on" experience that HTS offered.

Although all the respondents were keenly aware of the controversy surrounding the HTS program, they were glad of the opportunity to set the record straight, from their perspective, regarding the realities on the ground of the HTS. Thus, they were willing to go on record with their personal assessment of the program.

Motives for Joining HTS

All of the seven who responded to the question regarding their motives and reasons for working with HTS mentioned harm reduction or "doing some good" as the primary motive.[38] This was usually related primarily as prevention or lessening of harm to Iraqis or Afghans, but also to US and allied soldiers, seeing HTS as a significant harm reducer in both respects. The respondents' discussion of harm reduction emphasized the explicit non-lethal nature of the HTS program and the mission of HTS workers as cultural advisers rather than as military personnel.

"Enhancing cultural understanding" as an important way of reducing harm was emphasized as a major motive for joining and serving on HTS teams. Serving as cultural advisors gave practitioners a sense of serving both military commanders and Iraqi or Afghan people.

> "I wanted to help the mil understand the cultural environment to avoid mistakes, avoid bombings of large social gatherings in Afghanistan as HTS was advertised. This first-hand experience on the ground was not remote or theoretical and I got the first taste of the local environment in central Asia, although I had studied in Russia and worked out of the embassy."[39]

> "I wanted a chance to help out first hand, to make sure that the soldiers are not at risk; to supply more effective operations locally; to engage in harm reduction. When I first heard of HTS my first thought was how I really could have used something like this in my first deployment. I was looking for a way to use what I had learned to prevent the blunders of ignorance and inexperience that delayed progress and mission accomplishment."[40]

David Southworth commented on the value of HTTs for harm reduction in local cultural–religious settings. He related an incident where a large Afghan crowd had gathered to celebrate the Shi'ite high holiday of Ashura (tenth day after the end of Ramadan) celebration. The local US Army leadership immediately thought it was an anti-American demonstration. HTS personnel intervened with the appropriate cultural explanation, and instead of breaking up the crowd the religious celebration continued without incident.[41]

Preparation for Work

Most respondents were trained at Fort Leavenworth and received several weeks to five or more months of training, especially in language and culture and basic cultural sensitivity, so as to be able to operate more effectively and not offend. Lachlyn Soper was among the first to be deployed in 2007 and she indicated that the language training in Pashtu was limited, with only three weeks of study. In the field she used two interpreters. The fundamentals of anthropological research methods were used as the main framework for this training. Lachlyn Soper described two training blocks which included basic research methods that she indicated "were new to me, such as interview techniques, basic ethnography, or network analysis. Each training [block] lasted a week."[42]

Several respondents indicated that they would have preferred to have more training in the culture of the military itself, to learn their language in order to communicate more effectively. Ironically, while generally satisfied with their preparation for foreign cultural difference with the goal of working with and among Iraqis and Afghans, along with some limited linguistic training (the assumption being that HTTs would be primarily working in English through translators), some respondents felt better prepared for working with their foreign allies than with their domestic compatriots.

Types of Engagement

The work described by the respondents is varied and reflects their diverse backgrounds and areas of expertise. For example, before joining the HTS program Larry Katzenstein was a community organizer in NYC working on stabilizing and racially integrating neighborhoods and on violence reduction. He found that "the teams in NYC and Baghdad had a great deal in common."[43] Former CIA employee Eli Corin described his experience:

> "I had one [HTS] deployment out of Bagram, Afghanistan along with four others to help explain who we were and how we are part of civil affairs and not mil ops [military operations]. The senior social scientist had been a journalist during the Russian occupation. He taught anthropology in Denver. Our first op was with a French convoy with an interpreter. Our job was to advise on culture and how to talk to people. The other Americans all wore beards so as to blend in better, but we went out in civilian dress without beards but with

body armor. We used informed consent and started this at the top with the hierarchy. The mil let their presence be known in our missions but we were able to talk because the presence of weapons is so normal."[44]

Michael Albin described the goal of HTS work in both Iraq and Afghanistan as promoting good governance:

"Anti-corruption programs were a key part of our tool box and this was linked to values study. The Iraqi police still needed work so we placed corruption in the context of war and social disruption. Some earn their living by skimming; others were just surviving and our studies showed how the system and process works. In Afghanistan the program worked better. We had no teams in Syria, Iran, and Libya where they would have done some good in earlier stages of conflict."[45]

Work products produced by HTTs are also illustrative of the types of engagements the teams experienced. An unclassified HTT report on the Sangin region of Helmand Province in south-western Afghanistan, near the Pakistani border and one of the persistent locales of the Taliban, is illustrative.[46] For this report, the HTT conducted interviews with fifteen key leaders, both governmental and non-governmental; forty in-depth interviews with participants in an informal Claims Day court adjudication on Forward Operating Base (FOB) Jackson; interviews at a local food distribution center; and opportunistic interviews while on patrol and in the local bazaar. The key findings of the report focused on local "tribal dynamics," leaders and local ties of drug trafficking and Taliban actions alleged to be tied to the former. The report emphasized the security of the local population, especially as enhanced by the Afghan local police. Signs of "normalcy" were noted, such as the local population's access to cell phones and the functioning of government schools (which were not open). The recommendations were all related to inter-ethnic conflict mitigation; the support of legitimate local leadership; proving security in smaller areas so that locals could participate in their own defensive initiatives; the sidelining or co-optation of drug traffickers; regular meetings with local leaders; countering Taliban propaganda; having competent local religious scholars reference Qur'anic verses to counter advocates of violence and the drug trade, and so on.[47]

These are clearly military–strategic goals and recommendations, and are neither ethnographic nor anthropological analytical statements. While the method of interviewing members of a local population is recognizable social science, the end purpose of improving cultural analysis and providing the military with information is clearly linked to human security and harm mitigation as it relates to a counterinsurgency strategy. If the goal of the HTS is improved intelligence and cultural understanding with the intent of harm reduction, even though clearly related to military–strategic ends, can it be morally or ethically opposed? If HTS within a military anthropology is no more or less problematic than a business or development anthropology, why does it represent a special case?

Ethical Codes

Perhaps one of the most harmful yet ultimately effective allegations made about HTS was that its intent and execution were lacking in ethics and morality. HTS seemed to be tied so closely to generally unpopular wars: in the case of Iraq, a "war of choice" initiated by unfounded charges by President George W. Bush that Saddam Hussein possessed "weapons of mass destruction"; and in the case of Afghanistan, a supposedly "right war" widely viewed as unwinnable. Professional ethics may have been confused with some anthropologists' personal opposition to these wars, such that any seeming collaboration on the part of anthropologists could be viewed as unethical or even immoral if the anthropologist was viewed as abetting those working at or near the "tip of the sword." The memory of the Vietnam War loomed large and the inevitable condemnation and shaming were soon to follow.

Only one of the respondents was an anthropologist, and this individual was aware of and consulted the AAA code of ethics. Others indicated that their discipline or field of study had no relevant code of ethics to consult or study in advance of deployment. However, all respondents indicated that discussion of ethics was part of their advance training, and that in several cases specific study of the AAA code of ethics was incorporated in their training. They reported that emphasis was placed on harm avoidance and reduction and on informed consent.

Those who responded to the survey were keen to discuss ethics, professionalism, and the balance of causing harm versus doing some good. Many HTT personnel consulted a professional code of ethics for guidance, often from their own discipline. Michael Albin related that he consulted ethics codes/statements for the AAA, the American Library Association, the American Political Science Association, the Middle

East Studies Association, and the Associations for Asian Studies and African studies. He noted that "some of these have only rudimentary statements, but the exercise was useful in that awareness of ethics gave all HTS staff a common ethical framework and vocabulary."[48]

The political scientists, however, uniformly responded that they had no professional code to consult. Larry Katzenstein reported that the American Association of Political Scientists has a policy of using Department of Defense ethical standards.[49] Eli Corin reiterated that there was no code in International Relations, but "we did spend a day on the anthropology code of ethics and consideration of the AAA concerns. Half of the class was military and they have their own strict code of ethics, but for the IR people and those doing applied work, we borrowed codes from other fields to study."[50] Phil Carlson also indicated that he did not consult any ethical codes, but that there was much discussion about targeting, confidentiality, and the obligations of team members to one another.[51]

Lachlyn Soper reported having no ethical or moral concerns. She read the AAA code of ethics and studied it in training. "We studied the ethical issues that the anthropologists had and we understood the red line drawn at any lethality." She was most concerned to protect the local interpreters and various local assistants as well as intelligence sources. Although she had no appropriate code in her field of public policy, she nonetheless followed the protocols of ethical engagement, including protection of local sources. In her view, not talking to someone was preferable to placing a person in harm's way by talking to them.[52]

Purported Lack of Review

The AAA was said to have attempted to engage HTS management on ethics matters, without success. According to Montgomery McFate, the anthropologist most closely associated with HTS: "The AAA never tried to contact us officially, for example, about ethics at any point. The first we heard about their views was when they issued their condemnation in 2007."[53] There is no independent confirmation of whether an attempt was made by the AAA to contact the HTS program ahead of the formation of the first commission authorized in 2005.

One of the key arguments of the AAA reports on the HTS program was its lack of Institutional Review Board or peer review. According to McFate, discussion of appropriate review for HTS began in 2007 when the program was initiated and centered on whether the program was exempt from Title 32 CFR 219.[54] HTS requested the US Army Training and Doctrine Command (TRADOC) Judge Advocate General (JAG) to provide legal review. A 2010 memo from the JAG concluded that HTS human subjects research complied with the exemptions in 32 CFR 219. The Army Human Research Protections Office (AHRPO) disagreed with the JAG memo. However, after reviewing years' worth of research projects, AHRPO determined that HTS was actually in compliance. HTS then began working collaboratively with AHRPO to establish an IRB process, following AHRPO's general rule that if the research was brigade-initiated, then it was considered an "operational request" and was not subject to IRB (amounting to 85 percent of the research conducted by HTS). Then in 2011 AHRPO determined that all research was exempt on the grounds that it was in support of operations.

Nevertheless, McFate reports that HTS independently maintained a process for peer review of research, informed consent, and ethics training, consistent with what the interviewees report. In a personal communication she wrote,

> Since we had no resolution on exemptions from 32 CFR 219 from the JAG and recognizing that there was no single ethics code that applied to such a diverse group of social scientists, we began in 2008 to draft our own Guidelines for Professional Practice (GPP). We called it "guidelines" since the military is already bound by a code of regulations, the Uniform Code of Military Justice. The HTS GPP was signed in 2010. The GPP prohibits engagement in lethal targeting activities, participation in interrogations or interviews without full consent, and encourages publication of research results. The GPP bears similarity to the AAA and other social science ethics codes in that it requires HTS personnel to "avoid initiating or facilitating harm to the people and cultures they study" and requires that HTS personnel "seek to mitigate harm whenever possible." The GPP also requires that HTTs provide informed consent and that they respect interviewee/interpreter confidentiality. What makes the document unique and different from social science codes of ethics is that it requires HTS personnel to balance their own situation as researchers with the larger military imperatives. Thus, HTS personnel are required to "comply with the UCMJ and the Rules of Engagement of the supported unit" and to "report imminent or on-going threats and criminal activity to the responsible authorities in order to safeguard life and property." The Guidelines also give HTS personnel their "right to self-defense while acting within theater escalation of force parameters." (What this means is that if someone is shooting at an HTT, the HTT may shoot back.) The Guidelines also require that HTS personnel "not knowingly jeopardize the supported unit's safety." In addition, the

Guidelines try to balance the desire to publish results with the requirements for operational security of information, which might harm either local nationals or military security. This requirement for complex ethical balancing is summed up in the section on "multiple stakeholders", which notes that "HTS personnel will recognize their obligations to multiple stakeholders, including their supported military units, local nationals, and fellow HTS personnel. HTS personnel will act in good faith toward these various communities, while seeking to balance the interests of all parties in a fair and thoughtful manner."[55]

Lethal Targeting

As part of the overall harm discussion, several respondents were keen to point out how HTS was misrepresented by some of its early academic critics as involved with lethal targeting. "Personally I never understood the targeting concerns; HTS was not about targeting; this is not something that the mil needs help with."[56] Michael Albin was clear that "ethics cannot involve targeting but that intelligence can use the tactic to penetrate private spaces and targets." He continued, "I was a cultural adviser and never was involved in targeting discussions."[57] Larry Katzenstein emphasized that he had no ethical problems in the field and that there was no kinetic targeting by HTS personnel.[58] In the words of Fred Chapman, "There was no lethal targeting."[59]

Some respondents noted that their own ethical boundaries came into conflict with normal military processes and procedures. For example, Michael Albin noted that "HTS was put into Ops Orders that are subject to Division Command execution. Social scientists refused to go on the mission because of the wording in the command that went beyond the ethics of anthropology, a lightning rod wording."[60] Although HTS fell under the umbrella of the non-lethal targeting cell (as opposed to lethal targeting performed by the intelligence staff, whose job involved identification of "bad guys") along with Civil Affairs, provincial reconstruction teams, etc., DS2 observed that "it quickly became apparent that the Army leadership on the ground did not know how to use us, and so had us working on projects that would indirectly serve to provide lethal targeting information. I'd prefer not to go into further detail on this."[61] When HTTs were asked to join missions outside the parameters of the program (known as "mission creep"), there was resistance by team members. David Southworth reported that he turned down any "5 a.m. or night raids as they are typically culturally invasive and involve house searches where women are involved."[62]

Identification of Self to Informants

Some of the respondents offered observations about the manner in which they identified themselves to interviewees in the field. According to Michael Albin, "We introduced ourselves as cultural advisers who advise commanders and were welcomed as such."[63] As Lachlyn Soper noted:

> We were surrounded by a company of 40 armed twenty-year-olds and the soldiers are the first out. I was usually with the platoon leader and a village elder. Officers gave me the lead in discussions with locals with a typical scripted introduction: "I am an American civilian here to learn about your political and social needs to convey these back to command." However, my own view is that the locals viewed us as part of the military and did not perceive us as neutrals.[64]

Secrecy/Classification

The fact that HTS was perceived by anthropologists to be part of US intelligence and was thus by definition not fully transparent was a key factor in the opposition to HTS. This central criticism was continuous throughout the period under review. The ethical problem of secrecy was part of both CEAUSSIC reports on HTS. The issue of the inherent problem or violation of ethics that secrecy represents was directly taken on by the respondents.

Much of the confusion within the CEAUSSIC reports stemmed from a lack of understanding about the nature and process of classification in the US military. In a downrange military working environment, almost all communication flows over an internet system called the Secure Internet Protocol Router network (SIPR). The SIPR system used by networked military computers is a classified system, meaning that access to the system is restricted to individuals with a security clearance. Much but not all of the information stored in or transmitted through the system is itself also classified. Thus, for example, a document containing information about troop movements marked "secret" would be transmitted through SIPR. However, an unclassified document about local agriculture would also be transmitted through SIPR. In other words, the classification of the document is a separate issue from the classification of the security system in which it resides.

Because HTTs worked in a downrange military environment, all their reports had to be transmitted and stored on SIPR. Many of the reports themselves, however, were unclassified as per HTS policy. Some documents produced by HTTs were marked For Official Use Only (FOUO), as per Title 5 of the United States Code, section 552. FOUO documents are unclassified but not releasable to the general public, and often pertain to the internal rules and practices of an agency; to geological data such as maps; to personnel and medical files, and so on. Interestingly, however, when the reports contained information concerning local nationals whom HTTs had interviewed, these reports were marked classified as per Executive Order 13526. From a military perspective, releasing the names of "sources" might potentially endanger military plans and operations. From a social science perspective, releasing the names of sources might result in harm to those very same "sources" should they be targeted by armed opposition groups. Thus, Lachlyn Soper was keen to point out that "secrecy is practiced for the protection of local contacts. The social media went to even greater lengths to protect the identities of their sources for the purpose of harm prevention. Trust and mutual respect are the greatest harm reducers. The main thing is the information and not the source."[65] Michael Albin made a similar observation: "At first we used names [of local nationals in our HTS work] but then stepped back from this as the main thing is the information not the source."[66]

The original policy of HTS was to have teams conduct unclassified research. However, the need to use SIPR (and the difficulty of moving unclassified information off a classified network once it is there), combined with the desire of both the military and social scientists to protect sources, led to a tendency toward unnecessary classification. As Michael Albin notes,

> Classification was a big mistake. By 2009–2010 HTS was more militarized, away from their original model...TRADOC ended the McFate/Fondacaro era and military folks were appointed who lacked the knowledge and history of the purpose of the HTS program. The attempts to bring social science more into COIN have been shunted aside to a bureaucracy.... Reneging on the non-classified nature of the program was my greatest disappointment. The original idea was for research to be shared inside and outside defense. It was clear early on that HTS backed off of this and open sourcing went out the window. As to why this happened it is Army practice to keep all this zipped up. It is easier to be on the secret side than the messiness of openness. The military viewed [the ethics debate surrounding] HTS as an academic problem not a practical one.[67]

Integration with Supported Units

Many of those interviewed pointed out difficulties experienced in integrating into their assigned military units. William Post was a US AID
worker in Afghanistan (deployed July 2011 to March 2013) based in
Sangin in Helmand Province. As an outsider to the HTT he commented
about their relative position within the overall command structure:[68]

> The HTTs really have to struggle to gain legitimacy with their work out
> here. The problem is that they suffer many of the same travel limitations
> that I do so their reports are limited to a dozen or so anecdotal interviews
> with people. Another challenge is that the military just doesn't know how
> to use the HTT's. I think that if they were tasked with specific questions or
> analysis they could produce a valuable product. Unfortunately, this doesn't
> happen. It would be a frustrating job.

As the above quotation indicates, HTS teams were dependent on the
military units they supported and had to hitch rides in order to get to
the villages they sought to contact.

Another issue the respondents identified in working with the military concerned the time necessary for research. Fred Chapman reflected
that "I ended up doing mostly staff work as we never had the sufficient
team to do the promised work."[69]

Some of respondents noted problems with other team members. As
Fred Chapman noted:

> The teams were dysfunctional, full of young inexperienced kids. For some,
> HTS was their first real job. We worked with Arabic translators who were
> viewed as cultural specialists, but they were really just translators. There's
> a big difference. The military in a war zone views culture as a tactical rather
> than strategic issue. They wanted answers immediately. We seldom had
> enough time to conduct the sustained fieldwork necessary to provide the
> Army with a truly useful product.[70]

Another recurrent theme concerned military expectations for what
HTTs could provide, which were not always matched by reality. DS2,
a political and cultural analyst who worked in support of DOD studies related to irregular warfare, commented:

> Expectations for what the HTT could deliver were out of step with reality.
> The brigade leadership on the ground thought we were ALL anthropologists
> and Iraqi tribal experts who could deliver immediate products detailing the
> ins and outs of the local population. This wasn't the case. I was the team
> social scientist (there was high turnover on the ground) and had only just
> arrived when my team leader went on leave for a month. So instead of

studying up on the local area and getting to know my new colleagues, I had many administrative tasks to deal with: dealing with the army leadership, disciplining poorly performing team members, etc. When the team leader returned we had additional administrative issues to deal with, including the arrival of new team members, including a trained anthropologist/ethnographer who, unfortunately was not helpful, due to personality conflicts. We were left on our own to determine a good way ahead for how we could support the brigade.[71]

In addition to difficulties integrating with supported units, some personnel experienced difficulties with HTS. According to DS2, issues also concerned pay "in conjunction with poor support from headquarters personnel, who seemed to have little idea of what we did on a daily basis, hurt morale and distracted us from our primary mission of supporting the military to find non-violent solutions to local problems."[72]

Shunning

Academic shunning was experienced by the only anthropologist to be interviewed. Fred Chapman, an anthropologist/archaeologist formerly from the University of Wyoming, said that initially it was the HTS controversy that attracted him. He intended to feature HTS as a case study for a public sector class he was assigned to teach. After he decided to join HTS, most of his colleagues at the university were either indifferent or generally supportive. However, a few cut off contact with him.

He compared the vocal non-support of the AAA leadership and some members of the anthropology community to how many academic archaeologists responded to the National Historic Preservation Act (NHPA), which requires federal agencies to consider and mitigate effects to important historic and prehistoric sites. Due to ethics concerns, the lack of research orientation, and tight completion timeframes, many archaeologists chose not to be involved with fieldwork mandated by NHPA, and consequently lost a crucial opportunity to shape how and to what standards applied archeological fieldwork was conducted.[73]

THE FUTURE OF HTS

Montgomery McFate and Steve Fondacaro have said that HTS could be most useful at "phase zero" conflicts, before the shooting starts.[74] Some of the survey respondents agreed with this assessment. David

Southworth concluded that: "Overall HTS was and is a great idea and needs to be retained as socio-cultural teams with new commands like AFRICOM. The US would be wise to keep programs like HTS around for the future in a context of inter-cultural dialogue, not the clash of civilizations."[75] Similarly, Larry Katzenstein predicted that the program will end once US forces withdraw from Afghanistan, and will be taken up by USAID or some conflict resolution group.

Other respondents felt that the military's focus is shifting away from a focus on human beings, back toward technology. In the words of Michael Albin: "My overall observation is that DOD's interest in the program is waning; my view is that making social scientists part of the military was an error. Human intelligence is generally waning and the HTTs are disappearing."[76] Although HTS was vindicated by the Arab Spring of 2012, times are changing in the DOD. "By the Arab Spring we showed our value and earned a seat at the table," in the words of Michael Albin, "But by then the decision had been made that there was no more need for social science and no time to invest in the lengthy social-cultural research it involves."[77]

CONCLUSION

As we reflect upon this period and issue, we may wonder what motives or fears drove the opposition to the HTS program. Was it primarily the unpopular wars begun by President Bush but continued by the popular President Obama? Was it another echo of the Vietnam War, where non-Europeans were again the target instead of the Second World War "good war" among Europeans and Euro-Americans? Was it opposition to the targeting of Muslims in the post 9/11 world? Was it another period of atonement for the role that mainstream Boasian anthropology played in the control and management of American Indians? Or was it the personalities and public posturing of the main actors?

There are no easy answers, but there are some counterpoints to be made. The wars in Iraq and Afghanistan, while unpopular among average Americans, were not opposed with the passion of the anti-Vietnam War movement. The fulfilled promise by President Obama to withdraw from Iraq and follow a timetable for withdrawal from Afghanistan defused further opposition. Anthropologists do work with non-European populations across the globe and are sympathetic to their conditions, but their collective support on their behalf has not been a major part of organizational activism. Anthropologists working in government have been acknowledged in the profession for decades, but have not been specifically criticized by the AAA except for the cases of Vietnam and HTS. The over-production of anthropologists with PhDs has been noted and new job opportunities touted. There has been a generally uncritical acceptance of anthropologists in development working for the World Bank, International Monetary Fund (non-government organizations), or US AID (a government organization) when many of the policies of these institutions have been sharply criticized as harmful to non-European peoples they are intended to benefit.

Intelligence gathering is not anthropology. But if this distinction is true, renowned British social anthropologist E. E. Evans-Pritchard (who openly gathered intelligence for the British among the Nuer in South Sudan and in Cyrenaica in Libya) was not an anthropologist. Nor were Robert Lowie or Ruth Benedict, who openly and patriotically worked in intelligence for the war efforts against American Indians and the Japanese. In retrospect we can understand the possible motives of these anthropologists, but sorting out any universal good or harm in these cases is problematic both historically and absolutely in ethical and moral terms.

Are these cases of anthropologists consulting for governments cases of them not *doing* anthropology? This seeming dichotomy between so-called pure research and applications of anthropology was resolved, or at least set aside, when the Society for Applied Anthropology (SfAA) was formed in the post-Second World War years as an affiliated professional organization. The SfAA has been joined by other professional organizations, such as the National Association of Practicing Anthropologists (NAPA). This was also controversial at the time for its seeming emphasis on contract anthropology exclusively.

At the heart of the HTS controversy is anthropology's continuing identity crisis. Clearly "anthropology *is* as anthropology *does*" will not suffice in this case, as anthropologists doing intelligence work have been judged by some as *not* anthropology. Anthropologists are clearly neither imperial agents nor social workers, but on occasion they may appear to be a hybrid of one or the other. While only a small number of HTS personnel were/are anthropologists, all understood and responded in some way to the criticism leveled by professional anthropologists.

Could the profession not have a military anthropology as the psychologists have a military psychology? Can contemporary American anthropology accept this new sub-field? The gold standard of ethics—"do no harm," though in many cases unattainable even so—is nonetheless met by the non-lethal essential goal and intent of the HTS program. This is clear in theory and in the practice reported by the respondents interviewed for this chapter.

Some anthropologists are pacifists; others may have conscientiously objected to military service. Others are employed by the military.[78] If acting as a cultural advisor in US military operations is a violation of anthropological ethics, then how and in what contexts is this the case? Both authors are unconvinced that the emerging sub-field of a "military anthropology" is different from what is already being practiced as anthropology, or that is a violation of anthropology's professional ethics. Since there is no sanctioning body in anthropology's main professional association, anthropologists will continue to do as they have always done, which is to respond to questions of ethics interrogated by special Task Forces, such as CEAUSSIC I and II. Absent any quasi-legal process, alleged violations of ethics end up being used mainly for pedagogical purposes, which is how they are best used. Undoubtedly, this will be the case for the "HTS Controversy" and may this time inform future debates, but past history does not ensure that this will be the outcome.

10

TANGI VALLEY

THE LIMITATIONS OF APPLIED ANTHROPOLOGY
IN AFGHANISTAN

Brian G. Brereton

When the Department of Defense (DOD) announced it was starting a proof-of-concept project based on social science called Human Terrain System (HTS), I was immediately intrigued. I had recently completed my PhD at Cornell University's Anthropology Department and felt that serving as a social scientist on one of these teams might be a good opportunity to investigate whether—contrary to popular opinion—the US was competently conducting operations in Afghanistan, and attempt to assist as an anthropologist.

Of course, fresh from fieldwork conducted in China and Taiwan, under the close scrutiny of Cornell's Institutional Review Board for Human Participants, I was worried about violating the central tenet of my discipline, "do no harm." Two vocal critics of the HTS program, Roberto González and David Price, state, "Assisting counter-insurgency operations stands to violate relationships of trust and openness with the people with whom anthropologists work."[1] Yet to me, doing nothing to mitigate the effects of potentially destructive military forces on a local population equally served to violate these relationships. Rephrased, I felt "do no harm" should never be used as an excuse to "do no good." When presented with the opportunity to work in HTS, I felt it would be better to understand and attempt to shape the US intervention in Afghanistan than ignore or feebly protest a decade-long effort.

From 2009 to 2010, I deployed to the eastern Afghanistan provinces of Wardak and Logar to assist the US Army's 10th Mountain, 3rd Brigade—and later 173rd Airborne Brigade Combat Team (ABCT)—as a member of a Human Terrain Team (HTT). A week after arriving at Wardak Province's Forward Operating Base (FOB) Airborne, I had the opportunity to travel to the Tangi Valley, where I ended up conducting the bulk of my research while in Afghanistan. Wardak's Tangi Valley, occupied by US forces from 2009 to 2011, became notorious for the number of US troops killed there. Attacks in the Tangi Valley include the biggest single-day loss of US lives in Afghanistan, when insurgents shot down a Chinook helicopter carrying thirty Americans and eight Afghans on August 6, 2011.[2]

This chapter begins with a discussion of the potential efficacy of applied social science in Afghanistan, framed by my time conducting research in the Tangi Valley. I then turn to the limitations of anthropology in Afghanistan and discuss problems of participation, difficulties in designating HTS efforts and personnel, operational constraints and their effects on research, and the inhibiting mindset of some traditional military officers. In conclusion, I offer a case for the continuation of applied anthropological efforts under a proposed Department of State (DOS) program.

THE MILITARY VALUE OF SOCIAL SCIENCE

My time in Afghanistan demonstrated to me there is a clear need for applied social science in conflict settings; a need that was similarly recognized by the US military through its recent re-emphasis on counterinsurgency. The US Army's *Field Manual 3–24: Counterinsurgency* states that intelligence preparation of the battlefield in counterinsurgency operations "requires personnel to work in areas like economics, anthropology, and governance that may be outside their expertise. Therefore, integrating staffs and drawing on the knowledge of non-intelligence personnel and external experts with local and regional knowledge are critical to effective preparation."[3]

This need for applied social science in a military context was underlined by my first week in the Tangi Valley. Our HTT was invited by military leadership to support a census of local residents led by our Counter Improvised Explosive Device (CIED) team. Members of this team asked several basic questions to determine household name and size before allowing others, including our team, to ask additional questions. While my HTT attempted to conduct a focused and systematic query, one particularly belligerent US Army staff sergeant took this opportunity to harass local citizens. He interrogated each head of household with his two favorite questions, "Why are you supporting the Taliban?" and "How many times a week do you have sex with your wife?"

When it became apparent his unit commander did not plan to intervene, I sat down with this soldier to ask why he selected this line of questioning and to explain how it was harming our relationship with local residents and hindering our ability to conduct research. He stated that most local citizens in the Tangi Valley supported the Taliban, and he was asking about sexual relations because he had recently read that President Hamid Karzai had passed a law requiring wives to have sex with their husbands every four days at a minimum. Additionally, this law allowed a man to withhold food from his wife if she refused his sexual demands.[4]

I explained that our HTT also wanted the answers to these types of questions: "Why do local populations decide to support the Taliban?" and "How do national laws impact citizens in the Tangi Valley?" However, there are far more subtle ways to elicit a better response from a potential interlocutor. Additionally, by insinuating Taliban collusion and discussing a village elder's spouse, many Pashtun men in the Tangi Valley were being deeply offended. In fact, in some cases, these questions may elicit a delayed, violent response (such as attacks on US patrols) based on the Pashtun code of justice, *pashtunwali*. After I had explained some alternative ways to approach some of the same topics more tactfully, this soldier stopped his antagonistic questioning, allowing our team more time for research. This staff sergeant later became one of our team's biggest advocates, frequently emailing to invite us on subsequent patrols.

While we may not agree, as social scientists, with the pre-emptive nature of our recent international interventions, we can still assist by mitigating the impact on civilian lives. By refusing to participate, we are not hurting the US military or government but local populations, such as those in Afghanistan's Wardak Province. While certainly not always philanthropic, the US military is often well-positioned by virtue of its location and resources to implement social scientists' population-centric recommendations. Indeed, as Montgomery McFate states, "The use of military for humanitarian disaster relief, peacekeeping, and counterterrorism operations means that the military will be increasingly forward-deployed in hostile, non-Western environments."[5]

It seems negligent for academics to imply—in numerous critiques bemoaning social science's misuse—that the military (and local populations it comes into contact with) could benefit from academic knowledge and methodologies, but then willfully withhold that information. McFate and Andrea Jackson explain that military commanders, generally unfamiliar with ethnographic methodologies, are often left with "inadequate—and sometimes wrong—information."[6] This was certainly my experience, as I found that military commanders, such as those in the Tangi Valley, were almost completely unaware of basic socio-cultural facts about their respective areas of operations. When our team discovered that the majority of citizens in the Tangi Valley were Wardagi Pashtuns, except for a single town of Durrani Pashtuns, recent acts of intra-Afghan violence immediately made sense to our military leadership in this newly discovered cultural context. These commanders were then able to institute a series of civil affairs projects to address perceived imbalances between these groups, perhaps stopping some future local, tribally motivated violence.

Military units who decide to conduct their own social science research often stumble along, making serious yet basic research mistakes. US Army Lieutenant Colonel Jack Marr describes his need for socio-cultural information while deployed to Iraq. Marr quickly realized that understanding the "human terrain" was paramount to the safety of his soldiers and the stability of the area under his direction. Marr directed the entire unit to focus on "collecting and collating ethnographic information," including religious boundaries, key economic structures, mosques, important personalities, tribal boundaries, local demographics, and data about personalities who were known to be supporting insurgents.[7] Marr states that this process only took about two and half months because "human terrain mapping" questions were asked during "intelligence-driven raids, cordon and searches, and attacks."[8] Marr reveals that his teams would question as many military-aged males as possible to get answers to these socio-cultural information requirements, and after the raids this information would be analyzed in a "census-like" compilation of data.[9]

This example of ad hoc research demonstrates the enormous need for social science methodology among US military units determined to conduct socio-cultural research (which pales in comparison to the need of a military unit unaware of the relevance of socio-cultural research). An anthropologist could easily formulate solutions to some of the glaring methodological problems with Marr's well-intentioned research design. These solutions include addressing a lack of informed consent, the combination of lethal action and socio-cultural data collection, no trial questionnaires or iterative design process, misinterpretations of research terminology such as "census," and a lack of standardized sampling or research methods. These simple solutions could have drastically improved the reliability of the socio-cultural information collected and led to more holistic solutions that, for instance, could have included input from local women (not just military-aged males). Yet despite the improvements which could be introduced by a trained social scientist, there are limits to what applied anthropology can accomplish in a combat zone.

THE LIMITATIONS OF APPLIED ANTHROPOLOGY

Military members, media pundits, and academics billed applied social sciences, such as anthropology, as *the* solution to the war in Afghanistan; whether mapping the human terrain, comprehending a counterinsurgency, or defeating improvised explosive device (IED) networks. Felix Moos, a professor at the University of Kansas, stated that in our current counterinsurgency efforts, "Only social scientists...can give the military the knowledge it needs to complete that task with a minimum of violence."[10] Similarly, US Army Lieutenant Colonel Fred Renzi has stated, "Because EI [ethnographic intelligence] is the only way to truly know a society, it is the best tool to divine the intentions of a society's members."[11] Jacob Kipp, who as the former director of the US Army Foreign Military Studies Office assisted in the founding of HTS, has written, "There is broad agreement among operators and researchers that many, if not most, of the challenges we face in...Afghanistan have resulted from our failure early on to understand the cultures in which coalition forces were working."[12]

Likewise, the *New York Times* published several glowing reviews from military commanders and civilian leaders describing the HTT effort in Afghanistan. Colonel Martin Schweitzer, commander of the

US Army's 82nd Airborne Division, said that the unit's combat operations in eastern Afghanistan were "reduced by 60 percent since the [social] scientists arrived."[13] Other unnamed US military officers called the advice from HTT members "brilliant," and explained that it helped them to see their operations from an Afghan perspective. Western civilian officials such as Tom Gregg, the United Nations chief for southeastern Afghanistan, also praised the use of anthropologists in Afghanistan, which he saw as an indication that the US military was "going through an enormous change" and starting to focus its efforts on areas long neglected by traditional military interventions.[14]

Unfortunately, these optimistic sentiments confuse two separate arguments: that the US can achieve its stated goals in Afghanistan, and that it can pursue its stated goals more expeditiously using social science. The first argument is far too complex to deliberate in this limited space; however, the second argument will be considered in this chapter. While socio-cultural information can assist the US military to achieve or redefine some of its objectives and mitigate a portion of the violence meted out on local populations during overseas operations, it is not a silver bullet that can instantly cure the whole situation in Afghanistan. There are real limits to the application of anthropological theory and methods in Afghanistan, including participation of practitioner and interlocutor, designation of efforts and personnel, operational constraints on research, and the mindset of some traditional military officers.

Participation

Applied anthropology—anthropological techniques and knowledge leveraged to solve a specific problem—is limited first and foremost in Afghanistan by participation. These participatory constraints apply to both practitioners and local interlocutors. Many knowledgeable local interlocutors have been killed or displaced by Afghanistan's thirty years of war. While working in one Tangi Valley village, my HTT discovered only ten families out of over 100 had not relocated in the last thirty years. The vast majority of those who chose to leave were educated, relatively wealthy, and had social networks outside their own villages. In discussions, the remaining village elders would often apologetically shrug at our questions and explain, "The person who knew that is no longer here."

After thirty years of war, there are also few anthropologists who have had the opportunity to conduct long-term ethnographic fieldwork in Afghanistan or study its predominant languages, Dari and Pashto. The lack of practitioners with relevant linguistic and local knowledge severely limits the application of anthropology in Afghanistan. Foundational American anthropologist Dell Hymes famously stated that language skills were as central to anthropology as the practice of ethnography, anthropology's primary research methodology, itself.[15] Afghanistan's thirty years of war limited consistent access by foreign researchers to the country. In practice, HTTs are seldom staffed with the "experienced cultural advisors familiar with the area in which the commander will be operating" that were once envisaged during the program's conceptualization phase.[16] Instead, social scientists with thematically relevant fieldwork experience from other parts of the world are forced to rely on a pool of local interpreters contracted to work for the US military.

This distance between practitioner and interlocutor frequently plagued our HTT while working in Logar and Wardak Provinces. Our team employed two to three Afghan interpreters on a rotating basis and we would regularly rehearse and refine typical questions asked while conducting research. However, when traveling to various research locations there was often not enough transportation for our researchers and HTT interpreters and we were forced to rely on interpreters attached to local US military units. These local interpreters sometimes hindered the research process by serving as a linguistic and cultural barrier between social scientist and source. These interpreters occasionally did not speak much of the local language, as interpreters were often ethnic Tajiks from Kabul who spoke limited Pashto, and frequently expressed open disdain for the rural, Pashtun population we worked amongst.

In one instance, I was asked at short notice to conduct some research in the Tangi Valley and was unable to bring an assigned HTT interpreter. Upon my arrival at Combat Outpost (COP) Tangi, I was assigned an ethnic Hazara interpreter from Bamyan Province. When interviewing local citizens concerning their religious practices and beliefs, I noticed a hesitancy on the part of interlocutors. Before deploying to Afghanistan, I was given limited Dari training and—after listening closely to the interpretation of my question, "Do you visit local religious shrines and pray there?"—I noticed something amiss. The Hazara interpreter, a practitioner of Shia Islam, was using the word "*haram*," or forbidden, to describe local religious practices, immediately making most local people reluctant to discuss religious participation. Unfortunately, there were probably innumerable instances of impeded research due to linguistic, ethnic, and demographic differences introduced by interpreters that I failed to notice or correct.

In addition, the discipline also imposes its own limits on members, which further constrains the number and role of potential researchers. Many anthropologists in the US have voiced their concern at practicing anthropology in Afghanistan, a region still entangled in war. This trepidation is outlined in an American Anthropological Association (AAA) executive report detailing concerns with the HTS program, and includes: difficulties that anthropologists may have in distinguishing themselves from the military units to which they are assigned and in articulating what they are doing; responsibilities to US military personnel that may conflict with obligations to the people they study; problems ensuring informed consent, and risks that information collected by anthropologists may be used in the short or long term to target specific populations or individuals; and possibilities that anthropologists working elsewhere may be identified with US military operations.[17]

The first AAA concern is the difficulty in distinguishing anthropologists from the military unit they work alongside. Before deploying to Afghanistan, everyone in the HTS program is outfitted with a full array of military apparel and gear, including the standard US Army uniform. In addition, team members are free to bring as much civilian clothing as they can carry (or have shipped to themselves). Because each operational environment is different and each military brigade has its own rules about whether attached civilians can wear uniforms, HTS's policy was to allow teams to make their own determination in conjunction with their supported unit. Our team often debated the pros and cons of collecting socio-cultural information in military uniforms versus civilian clothes. These debates covered the safety, comfort, and ethics of different types of clothing. From a safety perspective, military clothing is a good idea because it is flame retardant. From an ethics perspective, military garb visually informed potential interviewers that they were talking to a representative of the US military. Yet I often felt that the military uniform might limit the desire of local residents to talk to yet another military member. My HTT felt that civilian clothes were acceptable, as we always traveled with US troops and introduced ourselves before soliciting information.

In the end, clothing decisions were usually determined by our operational environment and the preference of the military unit we worked alongside. When working alongside US troops during my first week in the Tangi Valley, we camped each night near local villages. My HTT had decided to wear civilian clothes and once, while walking around after dark, we were mistaken for local villagers. After this incident, the commander of the CIED unit asked us to wear our military uniforms on any subsequent patrols where we would be out at night.

The second AAA concern is that anthropologists working for programs like HTS might find themselves caught between conflicting responsibilities to US military personnel and the people they study. In this scenario, researchers might be asked to betray the trust of local populations by gaining their confidence and then sharing sensitive information with military leadership who mean them harm. Our team attempted to mitigate this potential problem by introducing ourselves as members of the US government and asking questions focused on non-lethal topics. My HTT had a series of semi-structured interviews that could be employed, depending on interlocutor and the amount of time we had for questions. I almost always began with the query, "What is the most important issue that you and your family face?" This allowed our HTT to establish a baseline for what mattered most to local populations in a specific area. Additional questions for a limited interview included: "If you have a problem, where do you go to get it resolved?" "What are your primary security concerns and how can we help you resolve them?" "What do you think about the current economic conditions in this location?" "Have there been any changes in the village population over the last year?" "How do you get news and entertainment?" and "What does your village need more than anything else?"

In the rare case that an interlocutor shared information with immediate military implications, such as knowledge of insurgent activity, US military personnel took over the conversation to ensure that proper protocols were met. In this case, soldiers usually asked a series of follow-on questions to determine if danger to US troops existed or could be mitigated. Although our military uniforms, introductions, and focused questions usually allowed interview participants the opportunity to self-censure, when one family mentioned that their father regularly traveled to Saudi Arabia (possibly portending terrorist ties) military personnel stopped our interview and began their own. After answering several questions about their father's company and producing a business card, US troops were satisfied that the father posed no threat and my HTT was allowed to continue its research. Although these military personnel did not explain that their questions had potentially lethal consequences, the topic and tone of their questions probably alerted family members to their intent.

The third AAA concern is that anthropologists working with the military cannot ensure that an interviewee had given true informed consent. Critics of HTS maintain that interviewees surrounded by armed personnel are not free to decide for themselves if they want to participate in a study. Yet I found that the majority of Afghans—after decades of conflict—are comfortable expressing divergent opinions or staying silent around groups of armed men. I regularly had whole villages refuse to talk or answer specific questions that they felt were too revealing. In one instance, a local taxi driver from Wardak Province's Saydabad District felt comfortable answering all of my team's initial questions. However, when I asked about road safety—particularly how improvised explosive devices (IEDs) impacted his ability to work—and typical Taliban taxation on those in his profession, he quickly stated that he did not feel comfortable talking about these topics. I tried, later in the interview, to come back to these questions, but he remained reluctant to answer and I moved on to find another potential interviewee.

While some HTTs attempt to secure written consent from everyone interviewed,[18] literacy rates among Afghans in Wardak and Logar Provinces were as low as 20 percent.[19] I felt that in this environment, written consent would not mean much. Instead, my team began with a detailed introduction and asked for verbal consent before proceeding. My HTT would introduce ourselves as representatives of the US government and explain that our information would be given to—and used by—the US military. As one of the few forums where rural Afghans could air personal grievances to international forces, our team found that even after this detailed introduction and description of data usage, local citizens clamored for the chance to discuss their lived realities and would regularly line up to talk when we walked through a population center.

For example, when we were in the Tangi Valley's Joyzarin village we began asking local residents about recent Afghan National Police (ANP) interventions in their village. Our discussion began with several village elders who complained about general abuses, including illegal road blocks, taxation, and search and seizures. After several minutes of discussion, I looked up to see a crowd of nearly 100 people, all asking for the chance to discuss their issues concerning local ANP abuses. Despite the presence of US military troops and Afghan National Army (ANA) soldiers who were providing protection for our team, local citizens felt comfortable enough to explain in detail the grievances suffered at the hands of the ANP, including itemized lists of stolen property they wanted returned.

The fourth AAA concern is that information provided to HTS anthropologists can be used to identify and select populations as military targets. González and Price ask, "If anthropologists on HTS teams interview Afghans or Iraqis about the intimate details of their lives, what is to prevent combat teams from using the same data to one day 'neutralize' suspected insurgents?"[20] It should be noted, first, that the US military also practices "non-lethal targeting," such as outlining which communities need humanitarian aid after a natural disaster and how best to deliver that aid. Second, HTS personnel are civilian employees working for the DOD and the information they collect is the property of the US government. However, there are some key points that preclude HTT data from being utilized in the military's lethal targeting cycle.

First, as a rule, HTTs are never tasked with collecting lethal targeting information; unit commanders have dedicated intelligence personnel who are trained to locate, analyze, and track that type of data. Second, although our HTT interviewed individuals, we never asked for names or included personally identifying information in our reports detailing a local population's perceptions. The one exception to this general rule was "personality profiles" on key provincial and local leaders. This effort, separate from our public sensing reports that included no individually identifying information, only commenced if a key public figure agreed to talk with our team. Self-censure was also encouraged with our interviewees through structured interviews that were designed to focus on culturally relevant areas of people's lives which they felt comfortable discussing with foreign strangers. Even so, it was not uncommon during an interview to have military personnel tack on an interview question they imagined was germane to the conversation. These questions, often blunt interrogations like "where is the Taliban?", were never answered by interviewees (and my team attempted to curb this type of behavior whenever it occurred).

For example, while talking with a group of village elders in Wardak Province, we asked if they preferred living under Soviet, Taliban, or Government of the Islamic Republic of Afghanistan (GIRoA) rule. Each stated they vastly preferred the Taliban, giving us multiple reasons: better governance, swifter justice, and a safer environment. One of these elders explained that during Taliban rule, if a thief was caught in the village of Jalrez, his hand was immediately cut off and he never stole again. Now, thieves regularly go free after paying local judges miniscule bribes. Another elder explained that, under Taliban rule, land disputes were quickly resolved by local Taliban leaders who were from the area and knew both aggrieved parties. Now, it takes months for a GIRoA court to hear a land dispute case and they often find in favor of the richest plaintiff. We passed this information to US military leadership but, despite its relatively sensitive nature, the 173rd ABCT did not want to know who these elders were, just how they could improve local perceptions of GIRoA.

In the long term, it is difficult to predict how information collected by HTTs may be used by the US government or military. This socio-cultural data may be aggregated with similar information from other sources to develop disaster relief plans; facilitate natural resource extraction; or be utilized to predict emergent behaviors and target terrorist organizations. This third option appears, to many anthropologists, to be the most overtly harmful. Commenting on HTS data and its use in simulation and modeling programs, González states: "These programs focus upon modeling and simulation, but it is not difficult to imagine that in the near future, agents might use cultural profiles for pre-emptive targeting of statistically probable (rather than actual) insurgents or extremists in Iraq, Afghanistan, Pakistan or other countries deemed to be terrorist havens."[21]

Although it is certainly possible to imagine data being used this way, the US military is often hesitant for purely pragmatic reasons to use lethal force. This is evidenced by General Stanley McChrystal's discussion of what he termed "insurgent math," where for every innocent civilian killed we create ten insurgents.[22] Indeed, if military leaders do utilize HTT data in social system simulations, the information seems more likely to encourage a shift from lethal to a range of unconsidered non-lethal options. For instance, instead of deciding to immediately occupy an area through military force or initiate a lethal drone strike, US military Civil Affairs teams or the US Agency for International

Development (USAID) could be sent to provide economic opportunities and address the underlying causes of terrorist actions.

That this ethnographic information could be utilized to harm local populations is still a very real issue for many anthropologists and interlocutors in Afghanistan and remains a concern that cannot be completely alleviated. To my knowledge, none of the socio-cultural information my team produced was incorporated into the lethal targeting process. My team infrequently worked with our battalion's S2 (the designation for an intelligence staff section) occasionally providing cultural context to intelligence questions when requested. As one member of my team stated, "I really enjoy this job because we always get to be the good guy. Whenever we talk in brigade or battalion meetings, we always get to stick up for the local population."

In fact, sometimes the information my team gathered was utilized to disrupt the lethal targeting process. In interviews with local citizens, my HTT learned that during the hot summer months many rural farmers irrigate their fields at night to mitigate moisture loss due to evaporation. These details were passed to unit leadership, who thought that these farmers were coming out at night to emplace improvised explosive devices (IEDs) underneath local roads. After receiving this information, military leaders stopped actively targeting these previously suspected insurgents and directed our HTT to learn more about irrigation practices in the region and whether there was anything the US military could do to assist with agricultural processes. In this study, my team determined that water allocation was highly regulated but that storage facilities after harvest were lacking. This led our counterparts in USAID to explore agricultural programs focused on cold storage for the region's apples.

Classification

Another limitation for applied anthropology in Afghanistan is classification. By classification, I mean both the designation of efforts to collect and apply socio-cultural information and the categorization of the data collected.

By labeling these efforts "social science," HTS raised an unrealistic set of expectations and opened itself to a host of criticisms. Some anthropologists, like Carolyn Fluehr-Lobban, exclaimed, "At least call it something else. Call it open-source intelligence. This is not something that we comfortably recognize as anthropology."[23] Anthropologists do not recognize the efforts of HTS personnel as social science, due to the rapid, sometimes superficial, and often uncorroborated nature of its research. Yet just as anthropologists in academia are uncomfortable labeling HTS personnel "social scientists" or "anthropologists," many HTS members also felt uncomfortable with these labels and the academic rigor they implied. Many participants in the program would rather be called something else: perhaps "socio-cultural advisor" rather than social scientist or anthropologist, to avoid association with any strict disciplinary standards.

This problem of designation, what these types of practitioners should be called, has been reflected in similar problems related to what can—or should—be done with the information they collect and analyze. HTS, at its inception, remained hopeful that its research could remain unclassified. Previously, the HTS website stated, "HTTs are assigned staff to the BCT [Brigade Combat Team] and support the commander with open-source, unclassified socio-cultural analysis, performing a non-combat support role."[24] Despite this emphasis on unclassified information, all HTS personnel are required to apply for—and maintain—security clearances while employed by the program. This is necessary because most military information systems and work spaces are classified, even if much of the information carried on the systems and discussed in certain locations is not. Not having a clearance would prohibit HTS personnel from going to meetings and using computers. This is the nature of the military environment.

These initial conceptions of unclassified cultural information were picked up by academics external to the HTS program eager to use its data. Barry Silverman states in an article titled "Human Terrain Data—What Should We Do with It?" that "human terrain information is open-source derived, unclassified...information."[25] If HTS data could remain unclassified, the information would be available to a broad community of interested researchers—inside and outside the US government—who could access, utilize, and collaborate on projects using this information. If, in the future, Afghanistan becomes stable enough for academic anthropologists to conduct research, they could read, verify, and build off the knowledge in existing HTS databases.

However, while working in Afghanistan much of my reporting was either classified or placed on classified systems accessible only to US government employees. While the collected data remains benign, the reference to any ongoing US plan or operation mandates immediate classification. For instance, while working in Wardak Province we collected information focused on social interactions in one of the local markets near a US base. Because this US base was scheduled to close—operationally relevant information we included in our final report—the entire article was classified. Although this base has since closed, rendering the classified information no longer sensitive, the final report will remain classified for at least ten years, the US government declassification standard for "secret" reports. This classification of socio-cultural information severely limits the ability of future anthropologists to learn from, or build off, previously collected data.

Operational Constraints

In addition to limitations related to participation and classification, there are also serious operational constraints that impede HTS research in Afghanistan, including security concerns, military standard operating procedures (SOPs), inconsistent and incompatible technological capabilities, and military rotation schedules.

Security concerns limit the ability of HTTs to collect research. As Matthew Arnold and Anthony Vinci explain, "Current efforts are generally dependent on working with conventional military units…This tends to raise their profile to such a degree that they cannot necessarily obtain the unbiased and truly local information that they require."[26] My HTT sometimes encountered reluctance from local populations to discuss sensitive issues, particularly when discussing village leadership or insurgent involvement. Once, when talking to village elders from Durrani in the Tangi Valley, our team was making excellent progress through the series of semi-structured interview questions. Our questions included: "How do you perceive GIRoA, Afghan National Security Forces (ANSF), and Coalition Forces (CF)?" "What do you think of the present security situation in Afghanistan?" "What do you think of the present political situation in Afghanistan?" "What are the biggest challenges facing your family and your community?" and "What do you want to see happen in the immediate future for your community?" However, once locals saw our team and its military escort in the center of their village they began to gather. What began as a promising interview quickly devolved as these village elders stopped sharing sensitive details about life in Durrani, because of other locals nearby.

The bias that can sometimes result from the presence of uniformed military personnel while an HTT is conducting an interview is just one security-related limitation. Another concern in the constant tension between classic ethnographic methodologies and the unstable Afghan environment is the amount of time researchers are typically allowed for an interview. My HTT generally utilized brief, semi-structured interviews loosely based on the Rapid Assessment Procedures or Rapid Ethnographic Assessments Procedures.[27] However, an emphasis on force protection meant that my HTT was often limited to around ten minutes per interview, which was never enough time to elicit answers to all of the questions in even our shortest semi-structured interview. When talking to a local farmer in Wardak Province's Chak-e District, we began with our standard questions concerning the most important issue he and his family faced. This farmer was eager to talk and began outlining his entire social network and its history through Russian and Taliban rule. Just as the conversation began to yield real research results, we were forced to continue our presence patrol through the valley because stopping in one location for too long increased our risk of attack. These security concerns frequently curtailed my HTT's time conducting research in Afghanistan.

This same issue of force protection has recently been addressed by military leadership in Afghanistan. While soldiers in Iraq were often prevented from interacting with the local population because it was imagined to be unsafe,[28] US military leadership has agreed that this isolation actually made them more vulnerable and has since encouraged troops to live among local Afghans, walk on patrols, and buy goods from local markets.[29]

Military SOPs also limited our ability to collect quality socio-cultural information (and, to be fair, also kept us safe). To avoid being targeted by insurgents, US military units operating in Afghanistan designed their patrols to be "systematically unpredictable," meaning they never developed recognizable travel patterns.[30] While this occasionally presented the opportunity to conduct research in new areas, it often precluded classic methodological techniques, such as follow-on interviews. This systematic unpredictability also sometimes meant avoiding the local population entirely, as our unit would travel through uninhabited mountains or fields to avoid potential IED emplacement sites. When leaving COP Tangi, we often avoided populated areas by walking out the back of the base, through the uninhabited valley behind our location, and then down into a specific village. There was also little chance we would be visiting that location again in the near future.

When my HTT did engage the local population, it was not always under ideal interviewing circumstances. For example, I often attended medical events where US military personnel provided free health care to Afghans in need. Unfortunately, local citizens were sometimes sent by the US military to talk to our team post-procedure, while in a medically incapacitated state. We politely declined interviewing these potential interlocutors and explained to our military counterparts that we needed individuals who could lucidly answer questions. Similarly, in Wardak's Saydabad District, I once had the opportunity to visit a local school and observe classes with representatives from the DOS and USAID. Our military escorts asked if we wanted to begin interviewing children and they could not understand why we declined. My HTT tried to explain that it was not appropriate to interview a child without first talking to their parents and obtaining consent, but our military escorts viewed this as an excellent opportunity to collect socio-cultural information.

Military SOPs sometimes meant that what needed to be studied could not be, and what did not need to be studied was. Our HTT was often asked for operationally relevant input to solve a specific military task. For instance, we were once asked to identify the village most receptive to working with the US military within a specific district. I designed a detailed semi-structured interview to gauge local receptivity to US military engagement. Our team systematically visited each nearby village, but after our decision was researched and rendered, we were told that according to military SOPs the village we had selected was too far from the nearest US base. Since there was only one village within the mandated zone, the "choice" of a receptive village for US military civil engagement was determined not by the ideal socio-cultural features, but rather by pragmatic military considerations.

Another operational constraint hindering socio-cultural research efforts in Afghanistan was the inconsistent and often incompatible technological capabilities. HTT research managers—tasked with collecting, storing, and distributing research notes and finished products—were constantly distracted by unsuccessful and inconsistent database systems where submission standards and formatting conventions changed weekly. These research managers were asked to upload notes and products to multiple databases—CIDNE, TIGR, MAP-HT, and the HTT's Research Reachback Center—each with their own submission rules.

Although technologically advanced programs are designed to ensure institutional memory as US military units rotate into and out of an area, this lack of standardization means that information is often difficult to locate or utilize. These new technologies are also designed predominantly for quantitative data points, which made it hard for our HTT to input rich, contextualized qualitative information. For instance, CIDNE was primarily designed to track acts of violence and has limited data fields, making longer qualitative reports difficult to upload or search.

Another operational constraint to socio-cultural research in Afghanistan is the military rotational schedule. Military units often rotate in and out of the country every six to twelve months and some are rotated internally at a much faster rate. For instance, some 10th Mountain, 3rd Brigade companies moved several times within Wardak Province during their twelve-month deployment. Once, our team was told to prepare a product on violent conflict between Kuchi migratory tribes in eastern Afghanistan and settled Hazara residents. After weeks of preparation and research, our team was told by military leadership that the study was no longer needed because they were rotating troops out of the area. Although this data would have been useful to subsequent military troops operating in this location, units often expressed a lack of interest for work initiated by their predecessors.

HTS was designed to bridge the information gap between the rotations of an outgoing and incoming military unit in Afghanistan by establishing a "knowledge base." As McFate and Steve Fondacaro explain in an article on the origins and early years of HTS, the US military signed a Joint Urgent Operational Needs Statement (JUONS) in 2007 to create the HTS program. This JUONS stated that HTS was designed to help "avoid needless loss of life that has occurred due to lack of a systematic process and systems to enable transfer of human terrain knowledge during unit Relief in Place/Transition of Authority."[31] Yet HTS itself suffers a very high turnover rate, particularly for individuals on HTTs in the field, and often retains little institutional knowledge at the team level. This, coupled with the technological issues outlined above, meant that crucial socio-cultural information was often lost when its producer redeployed back home.

Mindset of Some Traditional Officers

The final limitation to socio-cultural information collection efforts in Afghanistan is the mindset of some traditional military officers. After

Vietnam, a conflict marked by an increase in US government and military cultural skills and linguistic abilities, the US military adopted tactics based on Cold War threats and lost many of the cultural and linguistic skills it had acquired. An emphasis on Cold War skills meant that traditionally trained officers were predominantly focused on "order of battle" intelligence, the number of forces, weapons, and military capabilities in an enemy's forces, and countering these classic military threats with lethal force. Even today, traditionally trained intelligence officers often share this same Cold War-inspired myopic focus. Arnold and Vinci explain that the Intelligence Community "still lacks the consistent ability to understand the local social, political and economic realities below the level of the nation-state with any real methodological rigor or success."[32] This traditional mindset, which can negatively impact HTTs in several ways, includes an obstinate embrace of Cold War military tactics, an unwillingness to deal with complex social problems, and a fundamental misunderstanding of HTS and what it can provide. (These problems rarely apply to the US military's younger officers. Marr echoes this sentiment with the statement: "Today, however, most Soldiers with multiple tours in theater understand that U.S. forces must consider the population first in everything they do operationally.")[33]

Examples of these Cold War approaches include anachronistic codes of war, such as never giving up ground that has been won. For example, after a period of exhausting research in the Tangi Valley, my HTT presented its findings to a group of mid-level military commanders attempting to determine the next course of action in that area. Our team, along with DOS and USAID personnel, successfully convinced this group that the best course of action for the US military was to withdraw from the Tangi Valley, as our presence there was both antagonizing the local population and putting them in greater danger. Although this group of mid-level military officers wholeheartedly agreed with our recommendations, when they presented these findings to their superiors they were told we could never surrender ground taken with US lives. This same anachronistic stubbornness plagued US efforts in Afghanistan's Korengal Valley.[34]

The transition from Cold War mentality to counterinsurgency has not always gone smoothly, as some officers remain unwilling to grapple with complex socio-cultural issues. In Afghanistan, unit commanders are often forced to play a very difficult and nuanced role. On the one hand, they must be responsible leaders and ensure the safety of the soldiers and citizens entrusted to their care. On the other, they must earn and maintain the respect of the young American soldiers under their command. Here, the Cold War persona, a strong warrior focused on an enemy's capabilities and how to exploit them militarily, is sometimes viewed as the key to earning and maintaining this respect. This type of attitude rears its ugly head in frequent statements from US military leadership, like the comment from a battalion commander: "If there weren't so many Afghans it would be easier to kill them all." An HTT can attempt to address some of the negative habits within a brigade or battalion by clearly demonstrating the efficacy of non-lethal action, but the onus is truly on military leadership to encourage a more socio-culturally savvy attitude within military units.

Unfortunately, cultural information is sometimes treated as banal and unimportant by some military commanders. Major Robert Holbert, one of the first HTS researchers in Afghanistan, recounts his experience attempting to convince a military unit that searching a village at 4 a.m. on a Friday morning, an Islamic holy day, may not be the best course of action to bolster community relations.[35] Often, a college-educated US Army captain is well aware of these basic niceties but is forced to walk a delicate balance between the safety of his troops and antagonizing the local population.

This tension was present when I interviewed the agrarian residents of an isolated valley and learned that they were extremely upset that US military troops were walking through their fields and trampling their crops. I took this information to the company commander but learned that his sergeant major had recently been killed (and he himself had personally been injured) by IEDs emplaced on local footpaths. This commander was certainly aware he was antagonizing the local population by trampling through their fields but, as he stated to me, "We will stop walking through their fields when they stop blowing us up on well-traveled paths." In trying to implement a successful counterinsurgency strategy, the US military is forced to walk a careful line between the safety of its troops and the well-being of local populations.

I had the opportunity to interview this same company commander a week before his departure from Afghanistan, to collate any "lessons learned" for incoming personnel. He expressed his appreciation for the socio-cultural information my HTT had collected and disseminated, but ultimately felt he had failed the troops under his command due to the US military's emphasis on cultural sensitivity, counterinsurgency, and restrictive rules of engagement. He stated that he would rather have known nothing about the Afghans he worked amongst and had the ability to treat the local population more harshly if it meant keeping his subordinates safe. In the end, he felt that socio-cultural information was at odds with his ability to conduct an offensive, lethal military campaign.

Collecting socio-cultural information in Afghanistan was also limited by a fundamental misunderstanding of HTS and what it could provide, particularly among traditional officers. Despite HTS products like the conveniently labeled "Commanders Handbook" and the countless capability briefs our team delivered, HTTs were sometimes nevertheless viewed as external, unknown, and unproven entities. This can create difficulties in an environment where the unit commander is comfortable with their proven assets and believes that an HTT has been tasked to fulfill the same role as existing personnel. A brigade/battalion commander controls a sea of acronyms: Civil Affairs (CA), Foreign Area Officers (FAO), Provincial Reconstruction Teams (PRTs), Information Operations (IO), Psychological Operations (PSYOP), and Human Intelligence Collection Teams (HCT). As Marr explains, "Patrols were reinforced with civil-affairs teams, human-intelligence collection teams, psychological operations teams, or additional medical personnel. These military specialists provided specific areas of expertise to assist the patrols, and the [Task Force] used their skills to enhance the perceived importance of the tactical unit."[36] Often lumped together with HTTs as "enablers," these teams fight for similar resources at headquarters and in the field.

We sometimes received taskings from senior military leaders that were far outside our area of expertise. For instance, our HTT was once asked to provide a product that plotted IED emplacements and explosions on a map of the Tangi Valley. This misallocation of tasks frequently occurs as busy military leaders ask for products from anyone within shouting distance. My team simply recorded the request and passed it on to our Joint IED Defeat Organization (JIEDDO) representative, who had the tools and expertise necessary to complete this IED-focused product. However, as with any staff environment, some elements accepted tasks they lacked the ability to complete competently in order to curry leadership's favor. In our case, the brigade's Civil Affairs team and Chaplain often felt that research concerning humanitarian assistance and religion were their respective provenances. My HTT explained that research was not a zero-sum game and frequently shared information on these topics in order to overcome this sentiment and behavior.

THE CASE FOR SOCIO-POLITICAL ADVISORS

While both anthropologists and military units agree that anthropological knowledge can be useful in locations like Afghanistan, they disagree over what the efforts to collect this information and its practitioners should be called. Some authors, such as Renzi, have proposed it should be labeled "ethnographic intelligence."[37] Ethnographic intelligence, defined by Anna Simons of the US Naval Postgraduate School, consists of "Information about indigenous forms of association, local means of organization, and traditional methods of mobilization."[38]

This definition is problematic for two reasons. First, ethnography is held to very high disciplinary standards. Laurel Richardson explains that the five criteria she employs to evaluate ethnographies include: substantive contribution, aesthetic merit, reflexivity, impact, and expression of a reality.[39] Operationalized intelligence collected from a conflict zone rarely includes all of these components. Second, intelligence generally connotes a body of knowledge not open to academic collaboration and public consumption.

"Human terrain" is another misnomer that sounds strangely clinical or nefarious. In discussion of the term "human terrain," González states, "The unusual juxtaposition of words portrays people as geographic space to be conquered—human beings as territory to be captured, as flesh-and-blood *terra nullius*."[40] Yet this, ironically, is precisely what HTS seeks to avoid through its detailed research and population-centric suggestions.

"Socio-cultural advisor" better expresses the actual role of a social science researcher assisting the US military, whether in HTS or any other similar program. Who is best qualified to fill this position of socio-cultural advisor to the US military operating overseas? While those who collect this information typically have backgrounds in either academia or military intelligence, neither background is completely adequate. Socio-cultural advisors have the difficult task of straddling two epistemological worlds. They are tasked with condensing complex socio-cultural information into succinct yet operationally relevant datasets.

Academic social scientists and anthropologists possess many of the basic skills necessary to conduct socio-cultural research in Afghanistan. Unfortunately, those who decide to participate in applied social science are often unprepared for the rapid pace, focused nature, and physical rigors of the research. US military intelligence officers are well prepared to provide rapid and focused information, but are sometimes unprepared to articulate the depth and complexity present in social systems. Intelligence personnel also are not trained to collect socio-cultural information utilizing methods that enhance research efforts through objectivity and statistical relevance. For example, while military Foreign Area Officers (FAO) often learn the language of an assigned nation and execute requisite political or strategic level readings, "Few FAOs are ever subjected to deep cultural immersion totally outside the military structure, most do not develop real cultural and social expertise."[41]

Based on my experience working for HTS and the DOD, a program supporting socio-political advisors would be most successful if run by the US Department of State and associated with its existing Foreign Policy Advisor (POLAD) program.[42] At one time, there were almost 100 POLADs serving as policy advisors to DOD division headquarters and brigade staffs throughout Afghanistan. If provided with an adequate budget, the DOS could conceivably create a parallel Socio-cultural Advisor Program staffed by government and contract personnel. Qualified Socio-cultural Advisors—with advanced social science degrees and experience conducting overseas research—could be recruited from academia, the US government, and private business and spread amongst the division headquarters and brigade staffs throughout Afghanistan.

This proposed DOS Socio-cultural Advisor Program could dodge some of the difficult ethical conundrums facing HTS personnel currently working in Afghanistan: issues with participation, classification, operational constraints, and a traditional military mindset. For instance, this program could provide Socio-cultural Advisors with permanent office space near division and brigade leadership (such as those currently afforded to POLADs). Where Human Terrain Teams are sometimes marginalized by military leadership, POLADs are taken very seriously and often have unparalleled (for civilians) access to US general officers and the military decision-making process. The DOS could assign dedicated interpreters to Socio-cultural Advisors and arrange travel for both to assigned research locations. The DOS also possesses the resources needed to schedule lengthy, repeated interviews with local interlocutors, much as they presently do with political leaders in Afghanistan. This research could be kept, produced, and disseminated on unclassified DOS systems and sent to researchers interested in collaboration. Finally, while HTTs are currently composed of Team Leaders, Social Scientists, Research Managers, and Assistant Social Scientists, a DOS Socio-cultural Advisor position would be more manageable—and less prone to contradiction—by limiting socio-cultural advising to a single individual.

This proposed program certainly would not be perfect. Most notably, DOS Socio-cultural Advisors might have restricted access to DOD missions and might be viewed as perennial outsiders. Additionally, the DOS has its own sets of institutional concerns and impediments. However, when working in Wardak's Tangi Valley, the POLAD at FOB Airborne often came on extended missions and was given the same access to potential interlocutors as my HTT. In fact, in the previously referenced conversation concerning the proposed departure of US forces from the Tangi Valley, it was our POLAD who most ardently argued against a continued US presence. This proposed DOS program could provide Socio-cultural Advisors who could articulately explain cultural nuance and forcefully argue for a population's needs.

CONCLUSION

In outlining some of the basic realities of conducting research in Afghanistan, I have shown that applied anthropological knowledge—while not the solution for the war in Afghanistan—can substantively assist both the US military and local citizens.

On April 8, 2011, US forces withdrew their permanent presence from the Tangi Valley. Military leadership stated that this action was impelled by the impending drawdown of US forces from Afghanistan, a desire to allow ANSF to take the lead for regional security, and a shift in focus to more populated areas in Wardak Province.[43] Most likely influenced by numerous security, political, and economic considerations, I would also like to think that my HTT—along with our DOS and USAID colleagues—had something to do with the genesis of this decision. Although US military forces still occasionally conduct operations in this area, as evidenced by the August 6, 2011 Chinook crash, the local population is less frequently affected by military operations or interventions.

Vocal critics to efforts such as HTS have proclaimed anthropologists should "reaffirm our democratic values, our professional autonomy, and our social responsibility by refusing to participate" in these types of efforts.[44] Yet this sounds anything but democratic or professional. Despite the many limitations to anthropological (or anthropologically-inspired) efforts in Afghanistan, ignoring an opportunity to assist a local population does not seem more ethical than wholesale boycotts or uneducated critiques of these efforts.

Many of the critiques leveled against anthropologists who decide to work in Afghanistan apply equally to those who decide to pursue work in academia. González proposes that economic incentives and blind veneration of the military are somehow enough to convince anthropologists to participate in programs such as HTS.[45] However, salary and academic adoration similarly motivate many professors. González and Price suggest that anthropologists who decide to conduct open-source intelligence "are not free to share the results of their work with local people who participated in the research."[46] Yet how often does an average anthropologist conducting ethnographic research share their work or positively impact a local population? Most anthropological writing is theoretically focused and crammed with jargon. In some ways, serving as an analyst and liaison between a military unit and the local population is the ideal platform from which to attempt a positive influence on groups of interlocutors, both locals and the military.

The manner in which anthropologists, individually or collectively, decide to address this issue may determine the future of the discipline itself. Hymes anticipated many of the problems that still plague the application of anthropological knowledge today. He explains, "The issue is not between general anthropology and fragmentation, but between a bureaucratic general anthropology, whose latent function is the protection of academic comfort and privilege, and a personal general anthropology, whose function is the advancement of knowledge and the welfare of mankind."[47] As my experience shows, anthropologists can participate in the advancement of knowledge and the welfare of humankind as buffers between a foreign military and local population.

Horrific tales of abuse and images of Afghan women disfigured for disobeying patriarchal or religious decree have met with academic calls for cultural relativism. Yet as Chris Hedges stated, "Liberal institutions, seeing tolerance as the highest virtue, tolerate the intolerant."[48] While some anthropologists will decide to participate in these efforts and others will not, by indiscriminately ostracizing our colleagues and dismissing their efforts, anthropologists are missing an enormous opportunity to mitigate human suffering and assist in the expansion and application of our discipline.

11

THE HUMAN TERRAIN SYSTEM

SOME LESSONS LEARNED AND THE WAY FORWARD

Janice H. Laurence

As earlier chapters discuss in detail, the Human Terrain System (HTS) was catapulted into existence by urgent operational needs for socio-cultural knowledge to inform the irregular warfare missions in Iraq and Afghanistan. After Operation Anaconda in Afghanistan in 2002 and the "shock and awe" invasion of Iraq in 2003, the US military required something beyond technology and superior lethal force to accomplish their morphing missions. By 2005, deployed forces were engaged in counterinsurgency and stability operations. While the continued presence of al-Qaeda and the Taliban would require continued kinetic combat capabilities, engaging the local population and cooperating with Coalition partners to stabilize and support Afghanistan and Iraq would require a different (or at least an additional) set of tactics and skills. Unfortunately such socio-cultural capabilities were in short supply within the military. The rapid acquisition of "in-house" socio-cultural knowledge was unfeasible; and so HTS was created by the Army.

This chapter reviews the socio-cultural knowledge requirements that resulted from the wars in Iraq and Afghanistan, noting the limitations of the military's in-house capabilities, and the resultant need for

HTS. As an experimental program, HTS needed a flexible, adaptable management structure that could accommodate the evolving nature of the program and enable control over personnel and human resources to produce Human Terrain Teams (HTTs). Unfortunately HTS lacked such a management structure and instead faced obstacles and obstructions both from its higher echelon command, TRADOC, and the prime contractor. Despite these obstacles, the HTTs did add value to the military units they served, as demonstrated by both internal and external assessments of the program.

AN URGENT NEED

While the US military is heralded for its technical, tactical, and warrior competencies, there are critical deficiencies in cross-cultural competence. That is, US forces lacked the capacity to perceive, monitor, manage, understand, and employ socio-cultural information to guide reasoning and action. Although US officers proved to be effective leaders of their own troops in more traditional combat operations, US military leaders were vulnerable with regard to building trust and cultivating relationships with local nationals in their areas of responsibility.[1] Cross-cultural interactions are often stymied by differences in language, religion, behavior, values, beliefs, social organizations, political systems, economic systems, education, history, law, customs, and social controls.[2] Furthermore, as discussed in the Introduction to this volume, the brigade combat team (BCT) and regimental combat team (RCT) rotation schedule and process further exacerbated the socio-cultural deficits. Just as a brigade was making some, albeit limited, headway in getting to know the local community leaders and area needs, it was time to depart. Thus, a new brigade with its own priorities and methods would start from scratch on each rotation.

This socio-cultural gap established the requirement for HTS, especially its core component, Human Terrain Teams (HTT). Indeed, the brigades wanted and needed social scientists to help them understand the target area culture and its impact on operational decisions.[3]

In addition to combat specialties, the US military includes a host of service and support occupations to which military members are assigned. Indeed, behind the "teeth" of the military is a huge "tail" of technicians, clerks, administrative associates, mechanics, computer specialists, high-tech equipment operators and repairers, health care specialists, and other workers. Additionally, well trained and disciplined soldiers are led by a smaller cadre of capable professional officers. Practically all officers have a college degree and a multitude have credentials beyond the bachelor level.[4] And while US military officers have a background in a variety of academic disciplines—to include the behavioral and social sciences—there is a bias towards engineering, the "hard" sciences, and certain segments of the humanities (e.g. history, geography, English).[5] Generally speaking, military officers are proficient engineers and technocrats who take command and seek great precision and control. But in the counterinsurgency and stability operations in Iraq and Afghanistan, the traditional military skill sets around precision guided munitions, firefights, cordon and search operations, and patrols proved to be inadequate to the task at hand. Military operations other than war require a different mindset. In "traditional" combat it is perhaps counterproductive to get to *know* the human terrain. Dehumanizing the enemy—Krauts, Japs, Gooks, and Hadjis—reduces the moral and spiritual repugnance about killing.[6] In counterinsurgency, however, understanding the local population is critical.

Although the warrior role is far from narrow, the military's missions have grown well beyond warfighting, to include peacekeeping, disaster relief, deterrence, reconstruction, and now counterinsurgency. Because of its size, structure, and organization, the military must often undertake assignments as an agent of American security and diplomacy that might otherwise be functionally more fitting for another government department or agency. Although the military might have been stretched thin and be unprepared for the complexities of counterinsurgency, they did not waste time whining but saluted and got on with the mission. But a warrior spirit and a "can do" attitude were not sufficient for the volatile, uncertain, complex, and ambiguous (VUCA) situations that prevailed after the shock and awe phase of the wars in Iraq and Afghanistan.

Existing Capabilities

While the military has uniformed professionals in seemingly relevant career fields like intelligence, foreign area officers (FAOs), civil affairs, and military information support operations (MISO, formerly called psychological operations), neither their availability nor their skills sets were congruent with the need for operationally relevant social science expertise to provide understanding of the human terrain so as to optimize the military decision-making process. As discussed in McFate's chapter in this volume, intelligence officers, for example, were certainly "in the fight" but they were focused on the enemy. FAOs had languished owing to severe staffing shortfalls and a lack of organizational support.[7] Similarly, although Civil Affairs (CA) with its core of reserve professionals (e.g. doctors, lawyers, engineers, farmers) had relevance for reconstruction and development projects, they were in short supply.[8] These officers and soldiers had other assignments and duties that precluded them from adopting the particular mission of social science support. Those who argued for using in-house capabilities[9] such as FAOs or CA failed to consider that FAOs are assigned to higher echelons or to US embassies, and were not available to fill this capability gap. Using FAOs and CA to fulfill this role would have taken many years to recruit, educate, train, and deploy them, leaving an immediate warfighter requirement unfulfilled. In response to a capability shortfall identified by deployed military units at all levels, HTS had to be created from scratch three years after the war began.

Things typically move s l o w l y in a bureaucracy and the Pentagon is no exception. But the need to understand the human terrain was urgent and required immediate attention. As discussed in the introduction, HTS had to recruit, train, deploy, support, and sustain a dedicated, embedded social science capability so as to conduct operationally relevant research and analysis. Further, it had to develop and maintain a socio-cultural knowledge base, in order to preserve and share the accumulating socio-cultural knowledge. This was far from easy, especially under the "needed it yesterday, so give it to me NOW" mentality engendered by Operation Enduring Freedom (OEF) and Operation Iraqi Freedom (OIF). Shortly after the need was identified in 2006, the first HTT deployed to Afghanistan in February 2007. Another was slated for Afghanistan and three for Iraq by early 2008. The demand for teams from the senior leaders of both combat theaters steadily increased. By 2009 HTS had fielded twenty-seven teams with a demand for a dozen more at the brigade or higher levels of command. This warp speed pace was truly remarkable for the defense establishment.

Conducting an Experiment

HTS was experimental, and thus the whole HTS program, especially training, was meant to evolve. As a learning organization, HTS adjusted in response to experience on the ground as the organization learned how to serve the military mission better. Training was iterative; the composition of teams was iterative; human capital strategies and program and personnel management practices were iterative. One might even say that the whole war was iterative. Even the behemoth of bureaucracies, the Pentagon, recognized that continuous change was necessary in the face of uncertainty. The need for flexibility and adaptability were explicitly called for in the 2006 Quadrennial Defense Review (QDR) and reinforced in the 2010 QDR.[10] US forces were required to adapt to the conditions in their Areas of Responsibility (AOR)—the specific regions in Afghanistan or Iraq. Having a one-size-fits-all HTT would not have worked. HTS understood this and embraced this second-order flexibility into its design.

Especially early on, HTS was not in a position to make a clear definition of the mission in training. As Callahan's chapter notes, research access to Afghanistan and Iraq had been limited or non-existent for thirty years, and thus detailed information could not be included in the HTS training curriculum. Furthermore, HTT research had to satisfy the brigades' operational needs rather than the scientific curiosity of the team members. Because the brigades were in the "you don't know what you don't know" quadrant of the Johari window,[11] operational relevance of certain research topics could not be pinpointed. Thus, training was tweaked periodically on the basis of formal and informal feedback from the field. As part of the assessment team for the original HTS proof-of-concept experiment, I sent feedback to the training director and deputy program manager before leaving the field and long before the assessment report was published internally. Such assessments continued with the Program Development Team (PDT). Information was accumulating from what the military required and what teams actually did in the field. This prompted a total overhaul of training that began early in 2009 and was fully implemented in 2011. In addition to changing content and emphasis, training redesign included separate modules for civilian social scientists and the military students. For example, the military trainees did not need to sit through the basics of military culture and the social scientists did not need to sit through social science research methods 101. Another key training improvement was replacing the British Aerospace Systems (BAE) contractors with returned team members as trainers.

Not only was training adjusted, but so too was the HTT structure. For example, team structure and placement within the BCT structure were assessed. Team size was also examined. Teams in Afghanistan needed to be larger, with nine members rather than five. The vastness of a BCT's area of responsibility led to teams being split up. More team members with the right skills were required. In addition to growing the number of HTTs, Human Terrain Analysis Teams (HTATs) were added to synchronize research and facilitate integration of social science research and analysis products at division level. Theater Coordination Elements (HTS-TCE) at the corps level provided programmatic support to teams and coordinated HTS operations at theater and combatant commands. HTS also contracted for Social Science Research and Analysis (SSRA) support in both theaters, thus necessitating an SSRA Research and Analysis Management Team (RAMT). And although not detailed here or elsewhere in this volume, there were other program elements that were adjusted as needed. Among these elements were the Research Reachback Cell (RRC), the Subject Matter Expert Network (SMEnet), the Program Development Team, and the database toolkit (Mapping the Human Terrain—MAP-HT). None of this expansion represented empire building. Rather, the additional elements were either requests from brigade, division, and corps levels or proved necessary to run the program.

As this discussion shows, HTS was designed to respond to urgent and unfolding operational needs. In turn, the innovative nature of HTS required a flexible, adaptable management structure that could accommodate the adaptive program. Unfortunately, HTS did not have such a management structure, a topic we will return to soon.

Amalgamating a Team

Building the HTS organizational infrastructure was hard enough, but the toughest part was building the HTT, the embedded social science capability. As mentioned in Chapter 1 and detailed in Chapter 2 of this volume, the military was not comfortable with social science, let alone those practitioners who conducted interviews and observed interaction. And, truth be told, social scientists (especially PhDs from the academy) were not comfortable with the military and the need for "fast action" research. Yet somehow these diverse professions had to be melded together.

As discussed in the Introduction, qualitative social scientists with field research skills held great promise and value for the military operating in Afghanistan and Iraq. Unlike typical military professionals, social scientists understand how culture shapes beliefs, values, and behavior and are comfortable with multidimensionality, including the lack of perfect prediction and control inherent in understanding human nature. In addition to their content expertise, social science methods and tools (such as making observations and conducting interviews) were germane for eliciting and identifying socio-cultural considerations pertinent to the military's engagement with local populations. A detailed discussion of social science epistemological assumptions and orientations from positivism to constructivism is beyond the scope of this chapter.[12] However, it is important to note that while quantitative approaches were useful at higher theater levels, in general HTS focused on qualitative, naturalistic methods. Although they came from a broad variety of disciplines, the social scientists selected for HTTs were expected to be seasoned field researchers, rather than novices or even journeyman researchers.

Although social scientists were expected to be experts in their craft, they were not expected to be savvy with regard to the profession of arms. If they were going to be deployed and embedded with a brigade combat team in an active war zone they would need some help. The HTT "Team Leader" position was designed to provide this linkage between the HTT and the brigade. The team leaders were expected to understand the military. Active component uniformed personnel were not available for HTS and thus the team leaders were selected from military retirees or available members of the Reserves. Whereas retirees were recruited and hired under the BAE contract, reservists or members of the National Guard were recruited through an individual process of negotiating with each volunteer's unit. Other positions such as human terrain and/or cultural analysts and research managers rounded out the HTT and were designed to aid the conduct and communication of the social science research.

The HTT was not a typical team and especially not a typical cohesive military team. Not only were HTT members deployed individually, but the team had no goal of its own. The team was to conduct research and provide situational awareness to the brigade commander. Neither the social scientist nor the team leader defined the goal. Not only did this model run counter to the typical military idea of a "team," it also ran counter to the typical academic research role where an individual researcher determines the parameters of the study.[13] As for the HTT leader, well, this flew in the face of leadership theories such as "path–goal theory" where leaders generate performance motivation by defining goals, clarifying the path, removing obstacles, and providing support.[14] The HTT leader did not set the goal; that was the purview of the brigade commander. While the HTT leader did get some training regarding social science, he or she was not really able to help the social scientist to overcome research obstacles. Path–goal theory also suggests that a directive leadership style is best for subordinates accepting an authoritarian environment and a task that is is ambiguous and complex. Reserve or retired team leaders were generally accustomed to a directive style, whereas the typical academic social scientist was often less comfortable with this management style.

Although this civilian and military melding of five to nine members per HTT developed expertise in their respective areas, training was still required to fuse the capabilities for operational purposes. The training should have created team cohesion, but unfortunately it did not. The balance between teamwork and "taskwork" was, out of necessity, tipped in favor of the latter. Once hired as contractors (or under orders for reservists), prospective HTT members reported for four and a half months of training at Fort Leavenworth, Kansas. The curriculum evolved in response to operational needs but included an overview of HTS, military culture, military decision-making process, counterinsurgency theory, research methods, basic language, area background, and team building. After the schoolhouse training, HTT members attended a combat simulation exercise with an active duty unit at a combat training center (CTC). And then they deployed for at least nine months.

After the initial fielding of an HTT with a brigade, HTT members rotated onto existing teams as individuals and not as intact units. While this is not optimal for team development and orientation, it was a necessary "evil." To mitigate the loss of knowledge and relationships with local nationals as brigades came and went, the HTT was designed to stay put and accept the burden of individual replacements for the good of the military unit and mission. Therefore, in deference to operational needs, HTT members did not train or deploy as a team. Neither could they do their capstone CTC exercise with the brigade to which they would eventually be attached. As with individual replacements, this unfamiliarity between the HTT and the BCT inevitably delayed team orientation and the development of shared mental models.

OBSTACLES

As an experimental program, HTS needed a flexible, adaptable management structure that could accommodate the iterative nature of the program and enable control over personnel and human resources to produce HTTs. Unfortunately, HTS had neither. What HTS had were plenty of obstacles.

Contractor Crisis

For the sake of expediency, HTS was housed in the Army's Training and Doctrine Command (TRADOC) and more specifically within the TRADOC Intelligence Support Activity (TRISA). The TRADOC Deputy Chief of Staff for Intelligence (DCSINT or G-2) had learned of the burgeoning concept during a stint with the Joint Improvised Explosive Device Defeat Organization (JIEDDO), an organization that was an early champion and funder of HTS.[15] TRISA had some sociocultural capabilities, including the Foreign Military Studies Office (FMSO) at Fort Leavenworth, Kansas. However, while TRADOC ran schools, conducted war games, and developed training and doctrine for the Army, it was not geared toward team fielding and management. TRADOC had never deployed anything in its organizational existence before HTS. Deployment is the purview of the US Army Forces Command (FORSCOM). This organizational mismatch became problematic as HTS grew and was institutionalized.

In 2006, HTS was approved for implementation as a proof-of-concept *project*. It was not a government program, agency, or activity; HTS was not a government anything. Because of HTS's status as a project that did not officially exist, the project had access to neither active duty military members nor DOD civilians. But what the TRADOC G-2 had was a so-called omnibus contract with BAE. From its office in Hampton, VA, BAE had been providing information technology and personnel support services (e.g., data entry and database management) to TRADOC G-2 on site in such places as Fort Monroe, VA and Fort Leavenworth, KS. And so, without a competitive bidding process, BAE was tasked under its existing contract to hire all the HTS human resources, including the HTT members, trainers, and support staff. Even key HTS leadership was brought on board under Intergovernmental Personnel Act (IPA) assignments. Qualified subcontractors under the BAE contract also hired personnel, and after ninety days in contractor status these people would become quasi-government personnel. This was a cash cow for BAE and put them in the enviable catbird seat.

While the controversy and criticism levied by the academic anthropology community made HTS's recruiting of anthropologists more difficult, an additional problem was that recruiting efforts were conducted via BAE Systems under contract to TRADOC. Although the contract was meant to expedite the typically onerous and untimely government hiring process, the critical ongoing problems with contractor performance, support, and responsiveness negated this ostensible benefit. Furthermore, BAE did not know how to locate, recruit, or select social scientists with the requisite skills. The contractor was perusing internet job sites, waiting for replies to newspaper ads, or holding job fairs. BAE did not have dedicated, informed staff members who were knowledgeable about the program and the qualifications of applicants. Social science professionals with the requisite expertise tended not to be looking for a job but looking for a professional challenge. The potential candidates had options, were savvy, and demanded information regarding the program, working conditions, remuneration, and so forth. HTS needed not just any field-experienced social scientists, but those who were willing and physically and mentally fit to work for the military in a war zone; those who were security clearance eligible; and those with the temperament for teamwork. BAE would not or could not provide accurate, realistic information to HTT candidates about the nature, context, or details of the HTS project and their assignments in particular. Questions from candidates (who were expected to deploy to a war zone) were often met with disdain, hostility, or silence. As noted above, the BAE contract included a few subcontractors, but their candidates were often wait-listed in favor of direct BAE hires. BAE also ignited perceptions of inequity with regard to compensation. Rather than tying salary to duties and experience, BAE would try to get the best deal for itself and would low-ball subcontractor candidates. HTS did warn BAE that affronts to equity could be expected to hurt team cohesion and functioning; this fell on deaf ears.

In addition to recruiting, the selection and management of personnel was inadequate, deficient, arbitrary, and capricious. While bona fide occupational qualifications, position descriptions, performance objectives, and performance management required a comprehensive job analysis, which was outside BAE's purview, one would nevertheless have expected some technical expertise on the part of the contractor. Given federal contracting regulations, HTS was not allowed to screen résumés and curricula vitae nor otherwise vet prospective HTT members. But other interim measures that BAE could have taken, based on sound professional judgment and experience and continuing project feedback, were eschewed or ignored. BAE could not or would not develop and implement sound, professionally recognized personnel practices for the HTS effort. HTS staff members were precluded from interviewing or interacting with potential HTT candidates. Job descriptions provided by HTS were not used in job advertisements. Candidates were given a cursory interview over the phone, or none at all. Requests that applicants be screened on the basis of personnel security, physical and psychological fitness, relevant team and technical experience were resisted and ignored. Among the consequences were wasted time and resources spent on candidates who were too frail (e.g. an 81-year-old man with obvious physical limitations), morbidly obese (posing a serious health risk in a war zone), unable to meet security requirements, and in other ways unable to adapt to the unique technical and deployment demands of HTS. Although highly unlikely, it is plausible that BAE thought the 300-pound man would get thinner by the end of training; there is no way the octogenarian would get any younger. It appeared to HTS management that BAE was simply delivering bodies to Fort Leavenworth for training. They made money on every hire, for every day that a candidate was in training, regardless of quality and regardless of whether that person was fit for deployment. Misfit training dropouts may have been lucrative for the contractor but they wreaked havoc on HTS, affecting deployment plans and team processes.

In addition to poor interaction with candidates, many of whom withdrew from the recruitment process, HTT members reported feeling cast adrift. This is no small wonder, since BAE continued to be responsible for HTS human resources through deployment and redeployment. Pay issues forced deployed civilians to argue with BAE via email about errors in their pay stubs. BAE's response to requests from employees regarding logistics, deployment schedules, and insurance was inconsistent, owing to deficient personnel tracking and coordination systems (a supposed core competency of the contractor). There was no support lifeline for dealing with personal affairs (e.g. family emergencies, finances, etc.) once downrange. As for performance management, there was anarchy, with undefined reporting and accountability chains. Deployed military team members and civilian personnel in theater were confused and suffered from a lack of clarity regarding who supervised and appraised whom. As contractor employees, civilian HTT (and CONUS HTS staff) members were not obligated to comply with performance requirements set by HTS leadership/management or HTT leadership. TRADOC undermined HTS's authority and abdicated its own responsibility.

Frustration with BAE was palpable and pervasive within HTS. The morale of team members and the cohesion of teams in theater were negatively affected. HTT members were distracted from performing their duties for the brigade because of the lack of trust and confidence in their ostensible employer. HTT members even quipped that BAE stood for Bad At Everything! The potential consequences of these failings in recruiting, selection, training, movement, and support were more than a nuisance and had repercussions for individual safety, team performance, brigade integration, and mission success.

Family Feud!

The omnibus support nature of the BAE contract with TRADOC, while expected to be flexible, adaptive, and responsive to the needs of the developing and evolving HTS, did not serve HTS's mission requirements. The task statement was vague at best and there were no standards of performance.[16] The contractor could not be held accountable for failing to meet requirements because there were no requirements. Although there is the expectation that the government oversees a contract, the perception of HTS leadership and HTT members was that functionally the contractor was in charge. BAE, tasked with providing support to HTS, refused to take direction from HTS leaders. BAE representatives asserted that they would only respond to contractually relevant requests from the TRADOC Contract Officer Technical Representative (COTR). Sadly the COTR apparently was not knowledgeable about or interested in HTS. HTS had all of the responsibility but none of the authority—not even to terminate the BAE contract.

HTS was toggling between strategic and tactical issues as they worked to build the program and overcome the obstacles posed by BAE. They were developing and modifying program specifications, updating job descriptions, managing the evolution of training, conducting site visits to evaluate performance, and briefing Army and Pentagon officials. When the numerous efforts of HTS leadership to fix the situation with BAE failed, HTS lobbied TRADOC for a new contract designed and written to mission requirements. HTS was unique, transformational, and human resource intensive. HTS needed a contract that would at least allow them to tell contractors the general requirements for personnel and would put HTS in control of compliance. Calls for a new contract seemed to be blocked by TRADOC. Furthermore, TRADOC would not relinquish control of the HTS task order to HTS. HTS was denied control over human resources, control over budget, control over facilities—control over everything. TRADOC even resisted moving the program to another command more experienced with deploying forces. Neither TRADOC nor BAE was evil or unethical per se. But the non-operational part of the DOD bureaucracy often tends not to be focused on the mission or soldiers downrange but on amassing power through fiefdoms and allocating budgets to pet projects.

HTS battled not only BAE but its parent organization, TRADOC, to guard its budget, adjust the program, and meet the mission.[17] A significant battle was fought over whether TRADOC would allow HTS to bid for a contract for job analysis, which would provide the technical and legal basis for HTT personnel decisions. Job analysis entails systematically collecting, analyzing, and interpreting job-related information so as to define a job in terms of tasks performed and the competencies, knowledge, and characteristics needed to perform those tasks. It also provides the basis for defensible performance standards, allowing for the counseling and, if need be, the termination of poor performers. In 2007 HTS recommended that a job analysis be conducted, but TRADOC declined to authorize it.[18] This was an unfortunate decision, as the basic building block of any reliable, valid, effective, and legally/ professionally defensible human resource system is a job analysis.

After a great deal of argument, in 2008 TRADOC reluctantly authorized the conduct of a professional job analysis. After the completion of the job analysis in 2009, HTS now had a credible footing on which to base HTS recruitment, selection, training, and performance management decisions.[19] During the course of conducting the job analysis, the processes, procedures, and policies regarding HTS personnel were documented. This documentation clarified responsibilities and work to promote a consistent process on the part of the HTS contractor and its subcontractors. Furthermore, it promoted process equity for HTS candidates by articulating a validated salary and benefit policy. In addition to laying the groundwork for interview protocols and tools for scoring résumés, the job analysis was also a key part of reconfiguring the training program based on input from sound samples of returning team members and data from Program Development Team reports.

Another windfall for HTS human resources and personnel accountability was transferring HTT positions from contractor to civil service status. In December 2008, the pending rules of the new Security Agreement between the US and Iraq forced TRADOC to change its manning approach. This agreement placed contractors within the primary jurisdiction of Iraqi civil and criminal law rather than US law, which left the long-term impacts on the contractor workforce unclear. HTS management believed that the situation placed the safety, security, support, and mission effectiveness of deployed HTT members at risk, and that the best way to mitigate potential problems was to convert all deployable HTS positions to government term-hire civil service positions. This transition was complex and did not eliminate BAE from the picture. Although all deployed team members became civil servants, for reasons of expediency, HTS candidates entered training as temporary contract employees and were converted to government status at the end of the training cycle. Although this conversion was associated with a spike in attrition because of the reduction in pay for personnel, it (along with the personnel decisions based on the job analysis) did have long-term positive effects on personnel quality and accountability.

The growing animosity between TRADOC and HTS, and especially the program manager, led to an internal review with regard to the contracting situation. The topline result of the Office of Internal Review and Audit Compliance (IRAC) stated that "The contract management and oversight framework for the HTS contract needs significant improvement. We recommend re-competing the current contract as soon as possible."[20] The IRAC report validated all of the problems that HTS had raised over the years concerning the BAE contract. Essentially the report concluded that BAE had too much power and control and that HTS should not be working for the contractor. It needed dedicated government personnel who were accountable to the HTS mission rather than to the contractor. IRAC observed that the conversion of HTT members was a step in the right direction and reinforced HTS's call for earlier and improved screening of recruits and trainees in accordance with the job analysis results. There were costs paid for this showdown with TRADOC and BAE. The IPA-status program manager, who was acting as a good steward of HTS resources and had welcomed the internal review, was dismissed shortly thereafter. Of course the TRADOC DCSINT was also sent packing a short time later.

HTT ACCOMPLISHMENTS

Despite the urgency and the parade of obstacles that HTS faced, it did enhance the operational effectiveness of military units in Afghanistan and Iraq. HTTs conducted operationally relevant research and analysis and enabled more culturally astute decision-making by the units that they supported. HTTs represented the voice of the local community, and helped them communicate their needs more effectively to US and Coalition forces. HTTs contributed to decisions regarding the security of the area, infrastructure restoration, and economic development. Social scientists served as advisors to the brigade and as interlocutors between the local people and the commander. They provided situational awareness about how the local people made a living and how they governed themselves.

Teams interacted, chatted, interviewed, observed, and took notes. Social scientists didn't just "look," but they "observed" and they knew what they were observing. Social scientists, well versed in theory and practice, had cross-cultural competence and were adept at perspective taking. They did not apply their own cultural lens to understand the society within the unit's AOR, but picked up on the local customs and beliefs. They had a tolerance for ambiguity and had a framework that enabled them to pick up on body language and non-verbal behaviors like gestures, facial expressions, and personal space. They interpreted others' behavior and interaction and suggested to the unit how to act accordingly. Because they could read the poker "tell" within the social context, they were able to judge whether or not a person was a true leader.

Teams went beyond "Islam for dummies" and mere "dos and don'ts." Instead, they explored local clans and their loyalties and disputes. They came to understand the social structure, allegiances, and physical, economic, and security needs. They mapped the political power grid. They did damage-control following cultural incidents, such as a soldier shooting a Qur'an[21] or after a patrol inappropriately flex-cuffed and detained a local sheikh's elderly uncle. They understood that rituals such as celebratory gunfire at an Arab wedding were not aggressive acts. They explained the pique of Kabul residents endangered by combat patrols speeding on narrow roads in their 5-ton trucks to avoid IEDs. They drank tea and talked about tribal disputes and grievances. They focused on relationships rather than weapons, on harm mitigation and conflict resolution. And according to account after account of former HTT members, every reasonable effort was made to conduct their research ethically.[22]

The HTTs listened to the brigade as well as the population. They advised the brigade on how to interact with local residents and the complexity of the social system. They coached the commander before meetings with elders and political actors. They explained their perceptions and provided insight as to why the people supported the Taliban. Because HTS was alien to military culture, team leaders were instrumental in fitting the social science square peg into the brigade's round hole. Team leaders informed the brigade commander how to use an HTT. While social scientists were experienced professionals in their disciplines, the team leader helped them to interpret vague orders, kept them centered on the unit's needs and limited timelines, and helped them conduct their research in the fog of war. Team leaders along with research analysts and managers were the lynchpin in dealing with the puzzle of getting social science to fit into the military decision-making process.[23]

Teams did not do ideal or even typical social science research. It was practical, on the fly, "action research."[24] They collected their data not just on Forward Operating Bases (FOBs), but in physically rigorous conditions while on patrol with soldiers. They provided quick and dirty data about tribes in remote territories. In Chapter 3 of this volume, Callahan described what he did as an HTT social scientist as "combat ethnography"—random cursory interviews rather than in-depth participant observation.[25] The research was more like a series of pilot tests than well-designed theses.[26]

HTT contributions were often small but critical. Before HTS, no one knew what commanders wanted or needed to know about the socio-cultural environment. The commanders themselves often did not know. HTTs provided a non-engineering framework for observing the AOR in real time, further opening the Johari window of each AOR for the brigade by collecting data on what they didn't know and what they didn't know they needed to know.[27] For example, the brigade might not have *wanted* to know about pine nuts in a remote Afghan village, but they *needed* to know. By knowing that pine nuts were an economic key for the Zadran tribe, the brigade came to understand that the people were harvesters not insurgents and so they should not be shot. Such seemingly simple information had second- and third-order effects. As Dorough-Lewis's chapter notes, social scientists knew the art of asking questions (rather than conducting interrogations) and could make sense of the unique characteristics of the area of operations and the people who lived there.

HTS EVALUATIONS

Certainly not all HTTs were as useful as those whose stories comprise the preceding chapters. But there is compelling evidence that HTS provided valuable socio-cultural knowledge that improved situation awareness and resulting courses of action. This evidence comes from multiple sources. Subsequent to the fielding of the first HTT in Afghanistan in 2007, the demand for teams from senior leaders of both combat theaters steadily increased. Army brigade and Marine corps regiment commanders are tough and discerning customers who take their missions and the lives of their troops seriously. Given the incredible demands that vie for their precious time and attention, asking for HTTs to be embedded with them downrange is not only the highest of compliments but a strong indicator of mission success. The demand for HTTs (or HTATs) at brigade/regiment and higher levels, as well as support for expansion to other combatant commands, is proof positive that HTTs successfully narrowed the socio-cultural gap for which the project was created.

Underlying the orders for rapid fielding of over forty teams were endorsements from the field regarding HTS success. Beginning with Colonel Schweitzer, the commander of the first brigade to receive an HTT (4th Brigade from the 82nd Airborne Division), HTTs were praised for enabling the brigade to reduce kinetic operations, develop more effective courses of action, improve situational awareness, improve consequence management, increase support for the host nation government, improve humanitarian assistance efforts, improve village assessments, and decrease attacks by enemy forces, among other things. Similar testimonials came from both war theaters and were extended by their subordinate battalion and company commanders in addition to their direct staff members. Moreover, where HTTs worked with FAOs, or those from CA or MISO and embedded Provincial Reconstruction Teams (e-PRTs) or even chaplains, the feedback generally was positive.

In a January 2009 email to scores of military personnel regarding HTS, Lieutenant General John Kimmons, *the* Army Deputy Chief of Staff for Intelligence, expressed his tremendous support of HTS to the community. He noted:

> Embedded HTS teams provide tactical units a neighborhood/village-level understanding of the local population & culture; that feeds better operational decisions.... They present "Human Terrain" considerations for analysis & planning. One commander recently stated that a patrol augmented by an HTS element was more effective than six patrols without one.[28]

Internal Assessments

Such examples of kudos were collected not for the purpose of basking in glory but as part of detailed, multidimensional, internal assessments of HTS that were planned and conducted to develop and improve the program further. In addition to routinely soliciting and receiving informal feedback from HTS staff, trainees, and participants, HTS conducted formal evaluations in the field, beginning with the first HTT location in Afghanistan (AF1) in July/August 2007. The first five proof-of-concept teams in Iraq (IZ1–5) were evaluated in February 2008. These evaluations were mostly formative, but there were summative components as well. That is, the primary focus was on further developing and refining the program rather than zeroing in on outcomes and providing a simple "thumbs up/thumbs down" verdict on HTS.

Multidisciplinary assessment teams collected data from brigade commanders, brigade staff, as well as HTT members, using semi-structured interviews and observations as well as questionnaires, surveys, and checklists.[29] An additional PDT assessment took place in 2009, visiting HTAT and eight (or 42 percent) of the HTTs. Assessments or evaluations did not simply solicit positive comments from the brigade. In addition to such appreciative inquiry, all feedback was welcomed; problems were documented, and follow-up actions were recommended. Among the subjects covered by the PDT were HTT roles and relationships, research conducted, HTT integration with the host unit, and the value of training. Based on assessment findings, training evolved to be more tailored to the HTT role, to include practical exercises, and to facilitate unit integration. Training could not and did not turn on a dime, but reliable and valid changes to improve training fidelity, efficiency, and effectiveness were put into the pipeline expeditiously. And not only were HTS trainees the beneficiaries, so too were unit leaders by HTS's efforts to improve their knowledge and management of HTS assets.

External Assessments

Beyond the multiple internal assessments, HTS welcomed and provided access to external evaluators. In addition to being of interest to the popular press and the subject of academic theses, HTS was formally evaluated by faculty members from the US Military Academy (USMA) at West Point, by two Federally Funded Research and Development Centers (FFRDCs)—the Center for Naval Analysis (CNA) and the Institutes for Defense Analyses (IDA)—and most recently by the National Defense University (NDU). While these external assessments paled in comparison to the depth and detail provided by internal assessments documented in HTS Yearly Reports, the outside perspectives are important nonetheless.

At the behest of TRADOC, West Point faculty members (who were Army officers themselves) were tasked to assess the value of the HTT construct for providing cultural information and analysis for the commander.[30] In 2008, they visited HTS locations in Fort Leavenworth, KS and Oyster Point, VA as well as eight FOBs in Iraq. All in all, West Point conducted over 100 interviews with brigade commanders and staff, HTT members and HTS and TRADOC representatives. They noted the challenge of integration and differential placement within the brigade and the variation in operating environments. The bottom-line finding was that HTTs did add value. Despite unfamiliarity or initial misperceptions regarding HTTs, "[a]ll commanders stated that they highly valued the HTT's work."[31] It is also notable that these Army officers from West Point relied on, valued, and urged the Army to embrace process and not just outcomes. That is, HTTs contributed to the BCT's understanding of and relationships with the local populations, for which quantitative metrics are deficient. They urged recruiting and training improvements and some future directions, including the continuation of HTS and extension to other command levels and to earlier phases of warfare.

Next the CNA evaluation was directed by Congress in 2010. This independent assessment focused on the organization, management, and human resource related aspects of HTS. As CNA was constrained by a ninety-day time period to conduct the assessment, they relied primarily on the review of existing records and interviews with HTS and TRADOC personnel in the US. A serendipitous, convenience sample of eighteen commanders in Afghanistan were interviewed by two CNA analysts who were supporting the Marine Corps but agreed to lend a hand for this requirement.

Following a cogent description of HTS, CNA independently documented the criticisms and problems that HTS faced. Their biggest concern was the friction between TRADOC and HTS and the concomitant human resource repercussions. Recommendations included proper resourcing of HTS, putting HTS in control of recruiting, and continuation of training improvements. In contrast to the West Point assessment, CNA lamented the lack of independent outcomes measures to document the success of the program in meeting objectives. The report captured the quandary regarding the appropriateness of quantitative metrics, such as the number of products produced, the number of meetings with local people, or the frequency of off-FOB excursions for such a subjective mission. There is an adage in organizational behavior that what gets measured gets done. The reification of "counts" can misrepresent effectiveness and inadvertently lead to rewarding a "check the box" mentality, even for tasks like drinking tea with villagers or attending *shuras*. Despite the deficient personnel, equipment, and training metrics, military readiness remains an elusive and subjective construct.[32] Regardless of the obstacles and subjective nature of success, the CNA final report concluded that HTS was unique, dynamic, innovative and "in many ways, a success."[33]

Yet another observation of HTS was sponsored by the Joint Chiefs of Staff and conducted by IDA in 2012.[34] The Joint Staff were looking at innovations developed during the wars in Iraq and Afghanistan that were worth sustaining. So the purpose of the IDA study was to distinguish effective from less effective HTTs. IDA identified pairs of former HTT members and the military commanders whom they served, and administered a structured interview to elicit effectiveness ratings on a scale of 0 (failure) to 3 (success) and relevant HTT/BCT/AOR factors.

From among thirty-eight paired observations, teams were coded as effective if both the HTT member *and* supported commander indicated that the team was at least partially successful (score of 2 or 3). Less successful teams were so designated if the HTT member *or* the commander said that the HTT had no impact or was a complete failure (score of 0 or 1).

Among the factors that statistical analysis suggested detracted from HTT performance were poor integration/relationship with the supported unit; lack of frequent communication with the brigade; conflicts within the HTT; and limitations to getting access to the local population. HTT composition, in terms of size or academic discipline, was not a significant factor. Commanders reported that it was the non-military perspective—the on-site assessment of the current situation—that was important to team success. Although the point of the IDA report was not to determine the success rate of HTTs as a whole, outside reporting of their data shows that the overwhelming rating provided by commanders was a 3 (successful). Approximately 72 percent of commanders said that the BCT could not have been successful without the HTT. Another 25 percent indicated that the HTT was a partial success, that it did more good than harm. Only one reported that the HTT was not effective. None reported it as a failure.[35]

The latest evaluation was conducted by NDU in 2011 and published in 2013. In addition to providing a critical review of the HTS program and previous assessments, NDU conducted approximately 100 interviews with prior HTT members and HTS staff. The evaluators also interviewed thirteen commanders and again found that most rated HTT contributions as effective. Only one commander provided a "not effective" rating.[36] The NDU study noted commanders' appreciation of HTS and recognized its importance as well as its challenges. This study, along with the others, also provides some useful recommendations regarding HTS organization and development. For example, housing HTS within the US Special Operations Command rather than TRADOC seems worthy of consideration. There is certainly no argument that program improvements should include human capital investments in recruiting, selection, training, and team development.

Overall, however, NDU's conclusions sometimes seem contradictory, contra-indicated, internally inconsistent, and incompatible with the military's evolving irregular warfare missions. Perhaps the most unsettling feature was the myopic focus on a model of cross-functional team performance as informed by academic literature on organizations. The NDU report faulted HTS because it "did not adopt a theory of small cross-functional group performance from management and organizational literature."[37] Certainly this literature is relevant to HTS, but it seemed as if the researchers had a pet theory in search of a problem; an answer in search of a question. The literature on teams is just now burgeoning, with valid studies pertinent to the complexities and *in extremis* situations found in the military still evolving.[38] Much of the literature that shows promise for the military's highly stressful and complex operations has been published only recently, that is within the last five years.[39] The military could not push the pause button and wait for this nascent literature to advance its understanding of team competencies, team performance, team characteristics, team emergent states and team leadership.[40]

Just as CNA had done, NDU criticized the lack of objective measures that the evaluators believed would explain the HTT performance variation. They highlighted measures such as the number of times a patrol was invited for tea, the number of conversations patrols initiated, and the like. As pointed out above, these measures are deficient and only give the illusion of actual accomplishment. The critical acknowledgment that one should not rely exclusively on quantitative measures was relegated to a footnote. The affinity for quantitative data is curious, given that NDU relied upon qualitative assessments primarily from HTT members whom they interviewed by telephone or by email. Furthermore, NDU was disappointed that HTTs were not evaluated based on their impact on local population attitudes, yet they hesitated to accept commanders' attitudes regarding HTTs.

Related to this apparent discomfort with inductive methods, NDU found the lack of HTT standardization troubling. They denigrated HTS for its ambiguous mission and not having a "single, coherent, well-understood team purpose." They frowned upon HTTs not having a standard, well-recognized staff role, and for brigade integration difficulties owing to commander unfamiliarity and/or skepticism. They claimed that HTTs should have been larger to cover the entire battlespace; they should have had longer deployments; they should have deployed as a whole team with considerable time overlap with the HTTs they replaced; they should have had more specific training and with the brigade to which they would be attached; they should have used soldiers as the primary ethnographers for collecting human terrain data in the field; and so on. Also, NDU seemed to be scapegoating HTS for failures in Afghanistan as they concluded: "Ultimately, the HTTs failed to ameliorate growing cross-cultural tensions between U.S. forces and Afghans and were unable to make a major contribution to the counter-insurgency effort."[41]

All in all, NDU seemed to be saying that HTS should have existed before it existed and it should have been ideal—with no challenges or obstacles. It should have had more resources; it should have defined the mission clearly; and it should have been standardized across the board. However, counterinsurgency was the military's mission and they were in charge; the situation varied by location and across time; socio-cultural understanding was lacking; civilian social scientists were hard to come by and unfamiliar with team research or the military; soldiers are not social scientists; nothing like this had been done before and learning how to do it took time, energy, and attention. Furthermore, HTS faced obstacles galore.

In many ways, the NDU report mirrored the same mechanistic, deductive, engineering perspective that commanders downrange were transcending with the help of social science. The overly negative tone and haphazard suggestions detract from the gold nuggets scattered in the wide but shallow pan of the evaluation. While calling attention to weaknesses can lead to corrective action, it must be balanced with appreciative inquiry and the perspectives of key stakeholders. If you only ask "what's wrong" and only ask those who may not fully comprehend the irregular warfare mission, you may fail to maintain or strengthen what's right.

THE FUTURE OF HTS

Although US forces have withdrawn from Iraq and the footprint in Afghanistan is getting smaller, the demand for understanding the human terrain remains. With seemingly intractable conflict in the Middle East and potential and actual hot spots elsewhere around the globe, US participation in irregular warfare is likely to continue. Social science has operational relevance for military missions[42] involving not only sustained combat (so-called phases 1 to 4), but especially for the purposes of conflict deterrence and stability operations (phase 0), or as the pre-conflict period has ethnocentrically[43] been called, "left of boom."[44]

Outside Partners

The capability should not be allowed to languish,[45] but what concatenation of HTS should emerge for the future? Arguments for a wholly organic program devoid of civilian social scientists are shortsighted. Even relegating them to non-deployable training and education roles is troubling.[46] Beefing up special operations, military intelligence, civil affairs as well as other support operations may be in order. And so too may be cultural training programs for the entire force. But consider the possibility that warfighters and social scientists may have orthogonal personality characteristics and dispositions. That is, if you select and train for perspective-taking and tolerance for ambiguity, you might select out or stifle engineering-like precision and the warrior ethos. Soldiers may not like doing social science and they may not be good at being social scientists. Those in military intelligence or civil affairs or even a new HTS occupational specialty may have more in common with academics, but they do not bring the unique non-military perspective that proved so valuable to commanders. It would be unwise to let the chasm grow between academic social scientists and the military. Civilian partners are in keeping with the Pentagon's endorsement of developing a total defense workforce to include not just the Active and Reserve components but civilians as well.[47] Such civilian partners will be needed if the deep cuts to the Army come to fruition. Even if "tooth and tail" are cut proportionately, it seems unlikely that the Army would compromise its lethal enterprise.

Inclusion of civilian social scientists does not preclude smoothing the uneasy relationship between academics and soldiers. The DOD should consider providing graduate education in military-relevant applied social science to military officers *and* civilians *together*. For example, the Uniformed Services University of the Health Sciences (USUHS) might wish to expand and add another H to its acronym to become the Uniformed Services University of the Health and *Human* Sciences (USUHHS). USUHS already houses a Center for Deployment Psychology, a Center for the Study of Traumatic Stress, and a Center for Disaster and Humanitarian Assistance Medicine.[48] Adding a program geared towards social science for military operations would help to build a further bridge across the academic/military divide. Civilians would come to understand military missions, military people, and might be required to serve as a condition of their graduate education.

This would foster team development and effectiveness. Civilians would be better prepared for the pace, nature, and requirements for practical, operationally relevant research. The military would better understand social science offerings. Together this would work towards the synergy of a proactive team and an open-minded unit.

A new USUHHS or other such military–civilian educational entity should not preclude HTS preparation by means of other military education establishments. Nor should it preclude the entry of civilians from non-military related institutions. Multiple pathways would not only enhance recruiting but engender discourse about alternative approaches and from different disciplinary and theoretical vantage points. Of course, proper indoctrination and preparation of civilians for military missions is critical. And, on the military's side, building awareness and appreciation of social science and cultural competence is invaluable as well.

Tackling Other Challenges

HTS was ahead of its time, but it was assembled to meet an urgent timeline. Lest dire conditions strike again, now is the time to begin tackling the challenges and to build HTS better, stronger, but more slowly. Besides the HTS pipeline and academic preparation, there are additional issues surrounding HTS integration and organization. Where HTS should be housed is among the critical questions that still remain to be answered. Evaluators have noted its poor fit with TRADOC and suggested that an operational command such as Army Special Operations would be a good home. In addition to the inclusion of civilian academics, points about the military side of HTS should be raised as well. How should Reservists come to be part of HTS? Should active duty members be available for HTS assignment? And, beyond organization and resourcing matters, there are issues surrounding training, teams, and leadership to be discussed.

Discussion and debate are in order. It is time to bring HTS evaluators, originators, proponents, practitioners, and other forward thinkers and stakeholders to the HTS table. Military psychologists are one contingent that should participate in the dialogue. Representing several specialties and subfields but united by the military context, military psychologists have grappled with the exigencies of the military environment.[49] They bring expertise in clinical practice, military training, *in extremis* leadership, and military team situations, to name a few. One relatively new sub-discipline, operational psychology, has even navigated complex and challenging ethical considerations in the course of their research and practice in support of national security.[50]

Mission variation can be expected to continue or increase, and so flexibility and adaptability must be key considerations. The operational military is at center stage, so the ecological validity of recommendations for the military is crucial. There must be honest discussion that is centered on operational concerns and not on egos, fiefdoms, or turf wars. The HTS experiment in Iraq and Afghanistan has shown the value of bringing social science to war. Warfighters cannot afford a cold start or even a phoenix rising from the ashes. Let the next chapter of HTS or its successor begin.

APPENDIX

INTERVIEW QUESTIONS FOR HTS PERSONNEL

(interviews took place between 2/24/12 and 12/20/2012)

1. Do you wish to be acknowledged for or any quotes potentially used in publications or remain anonymous?
2. What is your discipline and training?
3. What are/were the specifics of your HTS training, work, dates and place(s) of your deployment?
4. Did you consult your professional code of ethics before working with HTS? If yes, was this a satisfactory exercise, your considerations, concerns?
5. What were/are your motives for joining/volunteering for HTS? Doing some good, preventing/ameliorating harm? Concerns for causing harm? Career advancement, level of compensation?
6. When were you made aware of the controversies surrounding the HTS program, it at all?
7. Describe the nature of and value of the prior cultural preparation you received once in theater.
8. How is/was your HTS work assessed?

NOTES

FOREWORD

1. I have noted in the past that we did not get the inputs even close to right in Afghanistan until late 2010, some nine years into that operation. And we didn't get the inputs right in Iraq until the spring of 2007, when a new civil-military counterinsurgency campaign was implemented and enabled by the addition forces deployed.

1. INTRODUCTION: UNVEILING THE HUMAN TERRAIN SYSTEM

1. Sun Tzu, *Illustrated Art of War*, trans. Thomas Cleary (Boston, MA: Shambhala, 1998), 109.
2. Gal Luft, *Beer, Bacon and Bullets: Culture in Coalition Warfare from Gallipoli to Iraq* (Lexington, KY: BookSurge, 2009), x.
3. Peter Chiarelli, Commanding General, MNC-I. Available at: humanterrainsystem.army.mil/testimonial.html.
4. Declan Walsh, "US Had 'Frighteningly Simplistic' View of Afghanistan, says McChrystal," *Guardian*, October 7, 2011. Available at: http://www.guardian.co.uk/world/2011/oct/07/us-frighteningly-simplistic-afghanistan-mcchrystal.
5. Williamson Murray, *Military Innovation in the Interwar Period* (Cambridge: Cambridge University Press, 1998).
6. Barry Posen, *The Sources of Military Doctrine: France, Britain, and Germany Between the World Wars* (Ithaca, NY: Cornell University Press, 1984), 56; Graham Allison, *Essence of Decision: Explaining the Cuban Missile Crisis* (Boston: Little, Brown, 1971), 85. Note, however, Rosen's argument to the contrary, that failure is neither a necessary nor a sufficient condition for military innovation. Steven P. Rosen, *Winning the Next War* (Ithaca, NY: Cornell University Press, 1991), 8–9. While military adaptation refers to a change in tactics, techniques, or technologies to improve operational performance, military innovation refers to a major change institutionalized in new doctrine, organizational structures or technologies. Theo Farrell, "Improving in War: Military

319

Adaptation and the British in Helmand, 2006–2009," in *Contemporary Military Innovation: Between Anticipation and Adaption*, ed. Dima Adamsky, Kjell Inge Bjerga (New York: Routledge, 2012), 131. Another definition proposes that military innovation, broadly defined, means the development of new warfighting concepts and/or new means of integrating technology, such as revised doctrine, tactics, training, or support. Jeffrey A. Isaacson, Christopher Layne, John Arquilla, *Predicting Military Innovation* (Santa Monica: RAND, 1999), 8.

7. Farrell, "Improving in War," 132.
8. Rajiv Chandrasekaran, *Imperial Life in the Emerald City* (New York: Alfred A. Knopf, 2006), 73–5.
9. Quoted in Michael R. Gordon and Bernard E. Trainor, *Cobra II: The Inside Story of the Invasion and Occupation of Iraq* (Vintage, 2007), 463.
10. President George H. Bush, "Remarks" (speech at the US Naval Academy Commencement, Annapolis, MD, May 25, 2001). Available at: http://georgewbush-whitehouse.archives.gov/news/releases/2001/05/20010525-1.html.
11. William D. Wunderle, *Through the Lens of Cultural Awareness: A Primer for US Armed Forces Deploying to Arab and Middle Eastern Countries* (Fort Leavenworth, KS: Combat Studies Institute Press, 2006), 65–78.
12. Anthony H. Cordesman, *Iraq's Evolving Insurgency: The Nature of Attacks and Patterns and Cycles in the Conflict* (Washington, DC: Center for Strategic and International Studies, February 3, 2006), 1.
13. Cordesman, *Iraq's Evolving Insurgency*, 2.
14. Quoted in George Packer, *Assassin's Gate: America in Iraq* (New York: Farrar, Straus and Giroux, 2005), 302.
15. William A. Knowlton Jr., *The Surge: General Petraeus and the Turnaround in Iraq: Industrial College of the Armed Forces Case Study* (Washington, DC: National Defense University Press, December 2010), 1.
16. David H. Petraeus, "Learning Counterinsurgency: Observations From Soldiering in Iraq," *Military Review* 86, no. 4 (January–February 2006): 2.
17. House of Representatives Committee on Un-American Activities, "Guerilla Warfare Advocates in the United States: Report by the Committee on Un-American Activities," 19th Cong., 2nd sess. (1968), 63.
18. Ralph Peters, "The Human Terrain of Urban Operations," *Parameters* XXX, no. 1 (Spring 2000).
19. William G. Boykin, "From the Commandant," *Special Warfare* 14, no. 2 (March 22, 2002): 1. The term "human terrain" was then broadened out to apply specifically to counterinsurgency: as Lieutenant Colonel Adrian Bogart III has written, "In a counterinsurgency... the center of gravity is the population—what the enemy fights for and what we defend. Counterinsurgency is a war fought over human terrain. Influencing, convincing, managing perceptions, and protecting the populace are keys to a successful COIN campaign." Adrian Bogart III, "The Nine Principles of Combined Arms Action in a Counterinsurgency Environment," *Military Review* (March–April 2006): 112–13.

20. Joseph D. Celeski, *Operationalizing COIN*, Report 05–2 (Hurlburt Field, FL: Joint Special Operations University, September 2005), 40.

21. Navy captain, email to first author, April 13, 2006. All emails were sent in confidentiality, and the names of interviewees are withheld by mutual agreement.

22. Department of the Army, Field Manual 7–15, *Army Universal Task List* (Washington, DC: Department of the Army, February 2009). Available at: http://armypubs.army.mil/doctrine/25_Series_Collection_1.html.

23. Field Manual 7–15, ix.

24. Department of the Army, Army Doctrine Publication 7–0, *Training Units and Developing Leaders for Full Spectrum Operations* (Washington, DC: Department of the Army, February 23, 2011), para. 2–2. Available at: http://armypubs.army.mil/doctrine/25_Series_Collection_1.html.

25. Army Doctrine Publication 7–0, para. 3–27.

26. Army Doctrine Publication 7–0, para. 3–19.

27. Department of the Army, Regulation 71–9, *Warfighting Capabilities Determination* (Washington, DC: Department of the Army, December 28, 2009), para. 6–1(a). Available at: http://armypubs.army.mil/epubs/pdf/R71_9.PDF.

28. Human Terrain System, "Mission Statement" (2008). This mission statement was developed through a series of workshops and approved by the Program Manager in 2008. It follows guidance from Department of the Army, Field Manual 5–0, *Army Planning and Orders Production* (Washington, DC: Department of the Army, January 2005) and utilized a variety of materials to include the HTS CONOPS, the HTS Concept Plan, the JUONS, and the HTS Annual Report 2007–2008. HTS has since updated their mission statement to read: "The US Army Human Terrain System functions as the primary and enduring social science-based human domain research, analysis, and training capability, focused on enabling leaders to remain adaptive when shaping current and future complex strategic and operational environments which support Unified Action Partners world-wide." Available at: http://humanterrainsystem.army.mil/index.html.

29. John R. Galvin, "Uncomfortable Wars: Toward a New Paradigm," *Parameters* 16, no. 4 (Winter 1986): 6.

30. Not all counterinsurgency theorists agree on this point, however. See Gian P. Gentile, "Freeing the Army from the Counterinsurgency Straightjacket," *Joint Forces Quarterly* 58, 3rd Quarter (July 2010). Available at: http://www.ndu.edu/press/counterinsurgency-straightjacket.html.

31. Brigade S3, interview with first author, 2007.

32. Marine Corps battalion commander, interview with first author, 2007.

33. HTS has occasionally been compared to the Civil Operations and Revolutionary Development Support (CORDS) program, established during the Vietnam War to assist in pacification of South Vietnam. See Jacob Kipp, Lester Grau, Karl Prinslow, and Don Smith, "The Human Terrain System: A CORDS for the 21st Century," *Military Review* (September–October 2006). Available

at: http://usacac.leavenworth.army.mil/CAC/milreview/English/sepoct06/kipp. pdf. While CORDS did include some civilians from other US government agencies, its mission was not social science research in support of the US military but rather military advising and rural development in support of the Army of South Vietnam. See, for example, John A. Nagl, *Learning to Eat Soup with a Knife: Counterinsurgency Lessons from Malaya and Vietnam* (Chicago: University of Chicago Press, 2005).

34. In addition, there were two part-time staff members. This figure does not include the contracting company that executed the early training program. Just to put this in perspective, the academic department of which the first author is currently a member has a director and three full-time staff people to manage six faculty members. This is an established enterprise and is not attempting to deploy teams into a war zone.

35. For a discussion of the reading habits of US soldiers, see for example Colby Buzzell, *Killing Time in Iraq* (New York: Berkley Trade, 2006), 175.

36. See, for example, Nathan Hodge, *Armed Humanitarians: The Rise of the Nation Builders* (New York: Bloomsbury, 2011), ch. 11.

37. The PDT also did debriefs with returning team members which was challenging since we could not require many of them to return through Leavenworth until we got authority from the Army to issue equipment at Leavenworth. Before that teams were getting equipment at Fort Bragg or Fort Benning when they deployed.

38. As recommendations from the PDT, team members, and external observers flowed in, HTS made a variety of adjustments to training, organization, and recruiting processes. As a result, after a couple of years, the program grew organically rather than according to a strategic plan.

39. See, for example, Nathan K. Finney, "Human Terrain Support For Current Operations," *Infantry* (March–June 2009): 4–6; Katherine Blue Carroll, "Tribal Law and Reconciliation in the New Iraq," *Middle East Journal* 65, no. 1 (Winter 2011): 11–29; Norman Nigh, *An Operator's Guide to Human Terrain Teams* (Newport, RI: Center on Irregular Warfare and Armed Groups, US Naval War College, 2012); Lieutenant Colonel Jonathan D. Thompson, "Human Terrain Operations in East Baghdad," *Military Review* (July–August 2010): 76–84; Rheanna R. Rutledge, "HTT Coverage of Afghan Women's Perceptions and Perspectives: The Commonly Forgotten Community," *Military Intelligence Professional Bulletin* 37, no. 4 (October–December 2011); Gregory Cabrera, "A Case Study of the Rural Human Terrain and Deep Engagements in Kandahar," *Military Intelligence Professional Bulletin* 37, no. 4 (October–December 2011); Brian Gunn, "Building Credibility: Engaging Local Religious Leaders in the Central Helmand River Valley," *Military Intelligence Professional Bulletin* 37, no. 4 (October–December 2011).

40. Marcus Griffin, "An Anthropologist among the Soldiers: Notes from the Field," in *Anthropology and Global Counterinsurgency*, ed. John D. Kelly, Beatrice Jauregui, Sean T. Mitchell, and Jeremy Walton (Chicago: University of Chicago Press, 2010), 215–29.

41. However, the conceptual development and much of the heavy data collection and analysis was actually performed by three incredibly talented young men: 1Lt Robert Holliday, Sgt Britt Damon, and Sgt Dan Lawrence.
42. The revised training program was implemented in 2011.
43. Montgomery McFate, Britt Damon, and Robert Holliday, "What Do Commanders Really Want to Know? US Army Human Terrain System Lessons Learned from Iraq and Afghanistan," in *The Oxford Handbook of Military Psychology*, ed. Janice H. Laurence and Michael D. Matthews (New York: Oxford University Press, 2012), 92–113, 111.
44. "Key leader engagements" seemed important and common enough to be included as a method, but were difficult to define, since they might include direct observation, interviewing or observing someone else conduct an interview, networking and socializing, "being quiet in the room," facilitation, etc.
45. See Montgomery McFate and Steve Fondacaro, "Reflections on the Human Terrain System during the First Four Years," *PRISM* 2, no. 4 (2011).
46. Brian Michael Jenkins, "Safer, But Not Safe," *San Diego Union-Tribune*, September 10, 2006, http://www.rand.org/commentary/2006/09/10/SDUT.html.
47. Brigade S3, interview with first author, 2009.
48. Ibid.
49. Department of the Army, Army Posture Statement, Addendum F, "Army Force Generation (ARFORGEN)," 2011. Available at: https://secureweb2.hqda.pentagon.mil/vdas_armyposturestatement/2011/addenda/Addendum_F-Army%20Force%20Generation%20(ARFORGEN).asp.
50. Nigel Aylwin Foster, "Changing the Army for Counterinsurgency Operations," *Military Review* (November–December 2005). Available at: http://www.army.mil/professionalWriting/volumes/volume4/february_2006/2_06 1 pf.html.
51. Email from Isaiah (Ike) Wilson III to the author. See also Isaiah (Ike) Wilson, "Saving Westpahalia: Countering Insurgency through 'Tribal' Democratization," in *Countering Insurgency and Promoting Democracy*, ed. Manolis Priniotakis (Washington, DC: CENSA, 2007), 245–62; Isaiah (Ike) Wilson, *Thinking beyond War: Civil–Military Relations and Why America Fails to Win the Peace* (New York: Palgrave Macmillan, 2007).
52. James Dobbins, James, Seth Jones, Keith Crane, and Beth Cole Degrasse, *The Beginner's Guide to Nation-Building* (Santa Monica, CA: RAND, 2007), xxiii; James Dobbins, John G. McGinn, Keith Crane, Seth G. Jones, Rollie Lal, Andrew Rathmell, Rachel M. Swanger, Anga R. Timilsina, *America's Role in Nation-building: From Germany to Iraq* (Santa Monica, CA: RAND, 2003); James Dobbins, Seth G. Jones, Keith Crane, Andrew Rathmell, Brett D. Steele, Richard Teltschik, and Anga Timilsina, *The UN's Role in Nation-building: From the Congo to Iraq* (Santa Monica, CA: RAND, 2005).
53. "Notably absent from the list was any mention of cultural study or awareness." R. Bryan Christensen, *Weight of Culture in Nation Building* (Thesis, US Army Command and Staff College, Fort Leavenworth, Kansas, 2007), 37.
54. Lt Col. Andrew Kennedy, interview with first author, 2006.

55. Clyde Kluckhohn, *Mirror for Man: The Relation of the Anthropology to Modern Life* (New York: Whittlesey House, 1949), 172.
56. Human Terrain System, "Mission Statement" (2008).
57. Brigade deputy commanding officer, interview with first author, 2009.
58. Battalion commander, interview with first author, 2008.
59. See, for example, Katherine Carroll, "Not Your Parents' Political Party: Young Sunnis and the New Iraqi Democracy," *Middle East Policy* XVIII, no. 3 (Fall 2011): 101–21.
60. Brigade commander, interview with first author, 2008.
61. Brigade executive officer, interview with first author, 2008.
62. Brigade commander, interview with first author, 2008.
63. HTT social scientist, email to author, 2010.
64. Brigade S9, interview with first author, 2009.
65. David Price and Hugh Gusterson, "Spies in our Midst," *Anthropology News* 46 (2005): 39–40.
66. Seymour M. Hersh, "The Gray Zone," *New Yorker*, May 2004.
67. Scott Jaschik, "Torture and Social Scientists," *Inside Higher Education*, November 22, 2006. Available at: www.insidehighered.com/layout/set/print/news/2006/11/22/anthro.
68. Alan Goodman, "From the President: Engaging with National Security," *Anthropology News* 47 no. 2 (February 2006): 63.
69. Catherine Myser, "Ethics under Fire at Abu Ghraib: Unresolved Questions," *Anthropology News* 45, no. 6 (September 2004), 16.
70. American Anthropological Association Executive Board, *Statement on the Human Terrain System Project* (October 31, 2007). Available at: http://www.aaanet.org/about/policies/statements/human-terrain-system-statement.cfm.
71. Susan Andreatta, "President's Letter," *Society for Applied Anthropology Newsletter* 19, no. 2 (May 2008): 4.
72. Network of Concerned Anthropologists, *Pledge of Non-participation in Counter-insurgency*. Available at: http://concerned.anthropologists.googlepages.com.
73. American Anthropological Association, Ad Hoc Commission on the Engagement of Anthropology with the US Security and Intelligence Communities (CEAUSSIC), *Final Report on US Army's Human Terrain System Proof of Concept Program* (October 14, 2009): 55–6. Available at: http://www.aaanet.org/cmtes/commissions/CEAUSSIC/Proposal-for-Examination-of-the-Human-Terrain-System-A-CEAUSSIC-Project.cfm.
74. Carolyn Fluehr-Lobban, email communication to authors, 2011.
75. American Anthropological Association, "Final Report," 4.
76. HTS social scientist, email communication to authors, 2009.
77. American Anthropological Association, "Final Report," 24.
78. American Anthropological Association, "Final Report," 54.
79. HTS social scientist, email to authors, 2009.
80. Army infantry officer, interview with author, 2007.
81. Army infantry officer, email to author, 11 November 2005.

82. John A. Nagl, "Constructing the Legacy of Field Manual 3–24," *Joint Forces Quarterly* 58, 3rd Quarter (July 2010). Available at: http://www.ndu.edu/press/constructing-3–24.html.

83. John A. Nagl, "Learning and Adapting to Win," *Joint Forces Quarterly* 58, 3rd Quarter (July 2010). Available at: http://www.ndu.edu/press/adapting-to-win.html.

84. Gian P. Gentile, "Freeing the Army from the Counterinsurgency Straightjacket," *Joint Forces Quarterly* 58, 3rd Quarter (July 2010). Available at: http://www.ndu.edu/press/counterinsurgency-straightjacket.html.

85. Charles J. Dunlap Jr., "We Still Need the Big Guns," *New York Times*, January 9, 2008. Available at: http://www.nytimes.com/2008/01/09/opinion/09dunlap.html?_r=0.

86. II Marine Expeditionary Force (Forward) G2, interview with author, 2008.

87. Second Infantry/8 Battalion commander, interview with author, 2008.

88. US Army, *QDR 09—Former Brigade Commanders Seminar #3*, June 1, 2009.

89. Ben Connable, "All our Eggs in a Broken Basket: How the Human Terrain System is Undermining Sustainable Military Cultural Competence," *Military Review* (March–April 2009): 58.

90. Ben Connable, "All our Eggs," 64.

91. In 2013, for example, the DOD Inspector General discovered $900 million dollars' worth of mostly outdated Stryker parts that appeared nowhere on the books. Adam Ashton, "DOD Inspector General finds $900M stockpile of Stryker parts," *The (Tacoma, Wash.) News Tribune*, April 2, 2013. Available at:http://www.stripes.com/news/army/dod-inspector-general-finds-900m-stockpile-of-stryker-parts-1.214680.

92. Robert A. Rubinstein, Kerry Fosher, and Clementine Fujimara, "Preface" to *Practicing Military Anthropology: Beyond Expectations and Traditional Boundaries*, ed. Robert A. Rubinstein, Kerry Fosher, and Clementine Fujimara (Sterling, VA: Kumarian Press, 2013), x.

93. Roberto J. Gonzalez, *American Counterinsurgency: Human Science and the Human Terrain* (Chicago: Prickly Paradigm Press, 2009), iii, 3. Other anthropologists have argued that the information gathered by the teams could be used for kinetic targeting and is therefore an unethical activity for anthropologists. R. Brian Ferguson, "Plowing the Human Terrain: Toward Global Ethnographic Surveillance," in *Dangerous Liaisons: Anthropologists and the National Security State*, ed. Laura McNamara and Robert Rubinstein (Santa Fe: School for Advanced Research, 2011).

94. John D. Kelly, Beatrice Jauregui, Sean T. Mitchell, and Jeremy Walton, "Introduction: Culture, Counterinsurgency, Conscience," in *Anthropology and Global Counterinsurgency*, ed. John D. Kelly, Beatrice Jauregui, Sean T. Mitchell, and Jeremy Walton (Chicago: University of Chicago Press, 2010), 7.

95. David H. Price, *Weaponizing Anthropology: Social Science in Service of the Militarized State* (Oakland, CA: Counterpunch/AK Press, 2011), 28–31.

96. Mark Dawson, "Intelligence Work: the Mundane World of High-Consequence

Analysis," in *Anthropologists in the Security Scape: Ethics, Practice and Professional Identity*, ed. Robert Albro, George Marcus, Laura A. McNamara, and Monica Schoch-Spana (Walnut Creek, CA: Left Coast Press, 2012). See also Nathan Hodge, *Armed Humanitarians* (New York: Bloomsbury, 2011); Montgomery McFate, Britt Damon, and Robert Holliday, "What Do Commanders Really Want to Know? US Army Human Terrain System Lessons Learned from Iraq and Afghanistan," in *The Oxford Handbook of Military Psychology*, ed. Janice H. Laurence and Michael D. Matthews (New York, Oxford University Press, 2012), 92–113; Marcus B. Griffin, "An Anthropologist Among the Soldiers: Notes From the Field," in *Anthropologists in the Security Scape: Ethics, Practice and Professional Identity*, ed. Robert Albro, George Marcus, Laura A. McNamara, and Monica Schoch-Spana (Walnut Creek, CA: Left Coast Press, 2012).

97. Roberto Gonzalez notes that "little official information about HTS exists" and relied instead on newspaper accounts, radio transcripts, military journal articles (many outdated), job descriptions, and three HTS personnel who were fired from the program as sources. Roberto J. Gonzalez, *American Counterinsurgency: Human Science and the Human Terrain* (Chicago: Prickly Paradigm Press, 2009), 22. Similarly, David Price relies on a number of outdated manuals, blogs, and one disgruntled employee who resigned from training and never deployed to make his case against HTS. David H. Price, *Weaponizing Anthropology: Social Science in Service of the Militarized State* (Oakland, CA: Counterpunch/AK Press, 2011).

98. George Lucas, *Anthropologists in Arms: The Ethics of Military Anthropology* (Walnut Creek, CA: Altamira Press, 2009), 145.

99. John D. Kelly, "Seeing Red: Mao Fetishism, Pax Americana, and the Moral Economy of War," in *Anthropology and Global Counterinsurgency*, ed. John D. Kelly, Beatrice Jauregui, Sean T. Mitchell, Jeremy Walton (University of Chicago Press, 2010), 68.

100. Katherine Blue Carroll, "Tribal Law and Reconciliation in the New Iraq," *Middle East Journal* 65, no. 1 (Winter 2011); Katherine Blue Carroll, "Not Your Parents' Political Party: Young Sunnis and the New Iraqi Democracy," *Middle East Policy* XVIII, no. 3 (Fall 2011); Adam Silverman, "Preliminary Results from Voices of the Mada'in: A Tribal History and Study of One of Baghdad's Six Rural Districts," *Cambridge Review of International Affairs* 23 no. 2 (June 2010): 223–6; Bradley Trainor, "Mitigating Kuchi Settlement Issues in Kandahar [or] Reflections on Ethnic Group Identities and the Confound of Emotion," *Practicing Anthropology*, 35, no. 2 (Spring 2013): 4–7; Kay Kautz, "Practicality of Ethnic Group Self-Identification in a Military Zone," *Practicing Anthropology* 35, no. 2 (February 2013).

101. Christoph Markson, *The US Army in Iraq: A Discussion of "Militarized Humanitarianism"* (PhD diss., School of Oriental and African Studies, 2010); Nick Krohley, *Insurgency and Civil Society in Occupied Baghdad: A Case Study of the Mehdi Army in Tisa Nissan Political District* (PhD diss., King's College London, 2012); Melvin Hall, *Words, Substance, War: The Rhetorical*

Constitution of Iraqi's Combined Security Mechanism (PhD diss., University of Wisconsin, Madison, 2013).

102. Ted Callahan, "Ein Ethnologe im Krieg," *Geo* 3 (May 2010): 50–70.

103. AnnaMaria Cardinalli, *Crossing the Wire: One Woman's Journey into the Hidden Dangers of the Afghan War* (Havertown, PA: Casemate, 2013).

104. Melvin Hall, "Integrating Social Science Research into Military (Division) Staff Planning," *Military Intelligence Professional Bulletin* (October–December 2011); Matthew Arnold and Anthony Vinci, "The Need for Local, People-Centric Information Does Not End in Afghanistan," *Small Wars Journal* (2010), available at: http://smallwarsjournal.com/blog/journal/docs-temp/469-arnold.pdf; Nathan K. Finney, "Human Terrain Support for Current Operations," *Infantry Magazine* (March–June 2009); M. Shands Pickett, "Co-Opting the Afghan Taleban," *Small Wars Journal* (February 23, 2012); Donald Rector, "Afghan Local Police: An Afghan Solution to an Afghan Problem," *Small Wars Journal* (January 10, 2012); Timothy Gusinov, "Green on Red: the Soviet Experience," *COIN Common Sense: COMISAF Advisory and Assistance Team Publication* (December 2012); Karl A. Slaikeu, "Winning the War in Afghanistan: An Oil Spot Plus Strategy for Coalition Forces," *Small Wars Journal*, April 20, 2009, available at: http://smallwars-journal.com/jrnl/art/winning-the-war-in-afghanistan; Karl Slaikeu and Faieq Zarif, "Five Questions for America to Answer about Afghanistan, the Arab Spring, and Nation Building at Home," *Small Wars Journal*, April 23, 2012, available at: http://smallwarsjournal.com/jrnl/art/five-questions-for-america-to-answer-about-afghanistan-the-arab-spring-and-nation-building; David W. Pendall and Alec Metz, "Non-traditional Intelligence Functions and the Use of Human Terrain Elements in Combat," *Military Intelligence Professional Bulletin*, April 1, 2012; Jonathan D. Thompson, "Human Terrain Team Operations in East Baghdad," *Military Review* (July–August 2010); Marcus B. Griffin, "Talking Trash with the Locals: Garbage and Situational Awareness," *Small Wars Journal*, February 14, 2013; M. Shands Pickett, "The Village Engagement Center: Stabilizing One Village at a Time," *Small Wars Journal*, September 30, 2010; *Military Intelligence Professional Bulletin* 37, no. 4 (October–September 2011) is entirely dedicated to HTS.

105. Janice H. Laurence and Michael D. Matthews, "The Handbook of Military Psychology: An Introduction," in *The Oxford Handbook of Military Psychology*, ed. Janice H. Laurence and Michael D. Matthews (New York: Oxford University Press, 2012), 2.

106. Henry Tomes, "Giving Psychology Away," *APA Monitor* 32, no. 6 (June 2000). Available at: http://www.apa.org/monitor/jun00/itpi.aspx.

2. MIND THE GAP: BRIDGING THE MILITARY/ACADEMIC DIVIDE

1. Brigade commander interview, 2009. All interviews unless otherwise noted were conducted in confidentiality, and the names of interviewees are withheld by mutual agreement.

2. David H. Petraeus, "Learning Counterinsurgency: Observations from Soldiering in Iraq," *Military Review* 86, no. 4 (January–February 2006): 8.

3. Robert H. Scales, "Clausewitz and World War IV," *Armed Forces Journal* (July2006).Availableat:http://www.armedforcesjournal.com/clausewitz-and-world-war-iv.

4. Anthropologist employed by the State Department interview, 2006.

5. A variety of authors have noted the gap between the policy and academic communities. Alexander George, *Bridging the Gap: Theory and Practice in Foreign Policy* (Washington: United States Institute of Peace, 1993); Joseph Lepgold and Miroslav Nincic, *Beyond the Ivory Tower: International Relations and the Issue of Policy Relevance* (New York: Columbia University Press, 2001); Bruce W. Jentleson, "In Pursuit of Praxis: Applying International Relations Theory to Foreign Policy-Making," in *Beyond the Ivory Tower: International Relations and the Issue of Policy Relevance*, ed. Joseph Lepgold and Miroslav Nincic (New York: Columbia University Press, 2001); Bruce W. Jentleson, "The Need for Praxis: Bringing Policy Relevance Back In," *International Security* 4 (2002): 169–83; Joseph Nye Jr., "International Relations: The Relevance of Theory to Practice," in *The Oxford Handbook of International Relations*, ed. Christian Reus-Smit and Duncan Snidal (New York: Oxford University Press, 2008); Joseph Nye Jr., "Scholars on the Sidelines," *Washington Post*, April 13, 2009, A15.

6. Pew Research Center, *War and Sacrifice in the Post-9/11 Era* (Washington, DC: Pew Research Center, October 5, 2011). Available at: http://www.pewsocialtrends.org/files/2011/10/veterans-report.pdf.

7. Shanea Watkins and James Sherk, *Who Serves in the US Military? The Demographics of Enlisted Troops and Officers* (Washington, DC: Heritage Foundation, August 21, 2008). Available at: http://www.heritage.org/research/reports/2008/08/who-serves-in-the-us-military-the-demographics-of-enlisted-troops-and-officers.

8. According to Gallup, 77 percent of Americans identify as Christian. Frank Newport, "In US, 77% Identify as Christian," *Gallup Politics* (December 24, 2012). Available at: http://www.gallup.com/poll/159548/identify-christian.aspx. According to the Pew Research Center, 60 percent of military veterans describe themselves as Christian (the figure includes "Protestant," "Catholic," and those describing themselves generally as "Christian"). Pew Research Center, *War and Sacrifice in the Post-9/11 Era* (Washington, DC: Pew Research Center, October 5, 2011), 133. Available at: http://www.pewsocialtrends.org/files/2011/10/veterans-report.pdf.

9. Jeff Sharlet, "Jesus Killed Mohammed: the Crusade for a Christian Military," *Harper's* (May 2009), available at: http://harpers.org/archive/2009/05/jesus-killed-mohammed/; Christopher Hitchens, "In Defense of Foxhole Atheists," *Vanity Fair*, December 15, 2009, available at: http://www.vanityfair.com/politics/features/2009/12/hitchens-theocracy-200912.

10. Christopher F. Cardiff and Daniel B. Klein, "Faculty Partisan Affiliations in All Disciplines: A Voter-Registration Study," *Critical Review* 17 (2005). Available at: http://www.criticalreview.com/2004/pdfs/cardiff_klein.pdf.

11. Neil Gross and Solon Simmons, "The Social and Political Views of American Professors" (Working Paper, Department of Sociology, Harvard University, 2007): 27, 28. Available at: www.studentsforacademicfreedom.org/file_download/38. This is similar to the results of other studies, which show that the Democratic to Republican vote ratio is 30.2:1 in anthropology. Daniel Klein and Charlotta Stern, "Political Diversity in Six Disciplines," *Academic Questions* 18, no. 1 (Winter 2005): 40–52; Daniel B. Klein and Charlotta Stern, "Democrats and Republicans in Anthropology and Sociology: How Do They Differ on Public Policy Issues?" *American Sociologist* 35, no. 4 (2005): 79–86.

12. Alexander L. George, *Bridging the Gap: Theory and Practice in Foreign Policy* (Washington DC: USIP Press, 1993), 15–16.

13. Ben Zweibelson, "How PowerPoint Stifles Understanding, Creativity, and Innovation Within Your Organization," *Small Wars Journal*, September 4, 2012, available at: http://smallwarsjournal.com/jrnl/art/how-powerpoint-stifles-understanding-creativity-and-innovation-within-your-organization; Edward Tufte, "PowerPoint Is Evil," *Wired* (September 2003), available at: http://www.wired.com/wired/archive/11.09/ppt2.html.

14. McMaster banned PowerPoint presentations under his command in Tal Afar, Iraq in 2005. Elisabeth Bumiller, "We Have Met the Enemy and He Is PowerPoint," *New York Times*, April 26, 2010. Available at: http://www.nytimes.com/2010/04/27/world/27powerpoint.html?hp&_r=0.

15. Probably political science and economics have a different core reading list and would be an exception to this broad generalization.

16. I base my statements here on my own graduate school experience, and an informal straw poll taken of sixteen of my colleagues who have served in the military and who have taught in professional military education institutions. The other top nominees were the works of Morris Janowitz and Samuel Huntington. Specific books mentioned were: Harold G. Moore and Joseph Galloway, *We Were Soldiers Once...and Young* (New York: Random House, 1992); Anton Myrer, *Once an Eagle* (New York: HarperCollins, 2000); H. R. McMaster, *Dereliction of Duty: Johnson, McNamara, the Joint Chiefs of Staff, and the Lies That Led to Vietnam* (New York: Harper Perennial, 1998); Mark Bowden, *Black Hawk Down* (Grove/Atlantic, 1999); Michael Walzer, *Just and Unjust Wars: A Moral Argument With Historical Illustrations* (New York: Basic Books, 2006); Robert Heinlein, *Starship Troopers* (New York: Ace,1987).

17. Michael W. Mosser, "Puzzles versus Problems," *Perspectives on Politics* 8, no. 4 (December 2010): 1077–86, 1078–9.

18. Lisa Anderson, *Pursuing Truth, Exercising Power: Social Science and Public Policy in the 21ˢᵗ Century* (New York: Columbia University Press, 2003).

19. Philip E. Tetlock, "Thinking the Unthinkable: Sacred Values and Taboo Cognitions," *Trends in Cognitive Sciences* 7, no. 7 (July 2003): 320.

20. US Army, "Army Values." Available at: www.army.mil/values/index.html.

21. Leonard Wong, "Leave No Man Behind: Recovering America's Fallen Warriors," *Armed Forces & Society* 31, no. 4 (Summer 2005): 599–622.

22. John Tierney, "Social Scientist Sees Bias Within," *New York Times*, February 7, 2011. Available at: http://www.nytimes.com/2011/02/08/science/08tier. html?_r=0.

23. Jonathan Haidt, "The Bright Future of Post-Partisan Social Psychology," *Edge*, February 11, 2011. Available at: http://www.edge.org/3rd_culture/haidt11/ haidt11_index.html.

24. On the distinction between the "cultural gap" and the "connectivity gap" between the military and civil society, see Lindsay Cohn, "The Evolution of the Civil–Military 'Gap' Debate" (paper presented at the Triangle Institute for Security Studies, 1999). Available at: http://lpcohn.squarespace.com/storage/ Cohn_Evolution%20of%20Gap%20Debate%201999.pdf.

25. Katherine Yester, "Inside the Ivory Tower," *Foreign Policy*, March 1, 2009. Available at:http//www.foreignpolity.com/article/2009/02/16/inside_the_ivory _over.

26. For example, as of 2004 of the 73,000 officers in the Air Force, about 1.4 percent hold doctoral degrees and 7.7 percent have professional degrees. Chuck Roberts, "Is There a Doctor in the Dorm?" *Air Force News Service*, May 25, 2004. Available at: http://usmilitary.about.com/od/airforcetrng/a/phd.htm.

27. Richard D. Lambert, "DoD, Social Science, and International Studies," *Annals of the American Academy of Political and Social Science* 502 (March 1989): 94–107, 95; Peter Buck, "Adjusting to Military Life: Social Scientists Go to War, 1941–1950," in *Military Enterprise and Technological Change*, ed. Merritt Roe Smith (Cambridge: MIT Press, 1985), 203–52.

28. Richard D. Lambert, "DoD, Social Science, and International Studies," *Annals of the American Academy of Political and Social Science* 502 (March 1989): 94–107, 96.

29. Ibid., 94–107, 98.

30. Ibid., 94–107, 100.

31. Noam Chomsky, *American Power and the New Mandarins* (New York: Pantheon Books, 1969), 41.

32. DOD Research, Development, Test, and Evaluation funds expended by non-academic institutions, including their own laboratories, increased from $3.9 billion in 1955 to $32.6 billion in 1986. Richard D. Lambert, "DoD, Social Science, and International Studies," *Annals of the American Academy of Political and Social Science* 502 (March 1989): 94–107, 99. See also James G. McGann and R. Kent Weaver, eds., *Think Tanks and Civil Societies: Catalysts for Ideas and Action* (New Brunswick, NJ: Transaction Publishers, 2002).

33. Richard D. Lambert, "DoD, Social Science, and International Studies," *Annals of the American Academy of Political and Social Science* 502 (March 1989): 94–107, 99.

34. The number of ROTC programs appears to be on the rise again. Larry Gordon, "Once a Campus Outcast, ROTC is Booming at Universities," *Los Angeles Times*, June 1, 2011. Available at: http://articles.latimes.com/2011/jun/01/ local/la-me-rotc-20110601

35. Joseph Nye Jr., "Scholars on the Sidelines," *Washington Post*, April 13, 2009, p. A15. Available at: http://www.washingtonpost.com/wp-dyn/content/article/2009/04/12/AR2009041202260.html.

36. Stephen M. Walt, "The Cult of Irrelevance," *Foreign Policy*, April 15, 2009. Available at: http://walt.foreignpolicy.com/posts/2009/04/15/the_cult_of_irrelevance.

37. Bruce W. Jentleson and Ely Ratner, "Bridging the Beltway–Ivory Tower Gap," *International Studies Review* 13, no. 2 (March 2011): 6–11, 7.

38. Juan Campanario, "Rejecting and Resisting Nobel Class Discoveries: Accounts by Nobel Laureates," *Scientometrics* 81, no. 2 (November 2009): 549–65.

39. Sophie Petit-Zeman, "Trial by Peers Comes Up Short," *Guardian*, January 16, 2003.

40. Michael J. Mahoney, "Publication Prejudices: An Experimental Study of Confirmatory Bias in the Peer Review System," *Cognitive Therapy and Research* 1, no. 2 (1977): 161–75.

41. Stephen M. Walt, "International Affairs and the Public Sphere," Social Science Research Council (undated). Available at: http://publicsphere.ssrc.org/walt-international-affairs-and-the-public-sphere/. "Should it really be the case that a book with a major university press and an article or two in the *American Political Science Review*, *International Organization*, *World Politics*, or other such journals can almost seal the deal on tenure, but books with even major commercial houses count so much less and articles in journals such as *Foreign Affairs* often count little if at all?" Bruce W. Jentleson, "The Need for Praxis: Bringing Policy Relevance Back In," *International Security* 26, no. 4 (Spring 2002): 169–83, 179.

42. No studies have been done to my knowledge on readership of academic journals. Here is discussion on the topic: http://academia.stackexchange.com/questions/1206/how-many-people-read-an-individual-journal-article.

43. Stephen M. Walt, "International Affairs and the Public Sphere," Social Science Research Council (undated). Available at: http://publicsphere.ssrc.org/walt-international-affairs-and-the-public-sphere/.

44. Ibid.

45. Ibid.

46. Ibid.

47. Cris Shore, "Anthropology's Identity Crisis: The Politics of Public Image," *Anthropology Today* 12, no. 2 (April 1996): 5.

48. Max Boot, *Savage Wars of Peace: Small Wars and the Rise of American Power* (New York: Basic Books, 2002).

49. Robert M. Gates, "A Balanced Strategy: Reprogramming the Pentagon for A New Age," *Foreign Affairs* (January 2009): 7.

50. See, for example, Russell Weigley, *The American Way of War: A History of US Military Strategy and Policy* (Bloomington, IN: Indiana University Press, 1973); Robert Tomes, *US Defense Strategy from Vietnam to Operation Iraqi Freedom: Military Innovation and the New American Way of War, 1973–2003* (New York: Routledge, 2007). For a critique, see Antulio J. Echevarria

II, *Toward an American Way of War* (Carlisle, PA: Strategic Studies Institute, US Army War College, March 2004); Robert M. Cassidy, *Counterinsurgency and the Global War on Terror: Military Culture and Irregular War* (New York: Praeger, 2006).

51. David W. Barno, "Military Adaptation in Complex Operations," *PRISM* 1, no. 1 (December 2009).

52. Analysts writing at the time all agreed that some sort of revolution was occurring, but disagreed on whether it was technological or informational, and whether it was major or minor. Alvin and Heidi Toffler, *War and Anti-War: Survival at the Dawn of the 21st Century* (Boston: Little, Brown, 1993), 32; Andrew F. Krepinevich, "Cavalry to Computer: The Pattern of Military Revolutions," *National Interest*, no. 37 (Fall 1994): 30.

53. Steven Metz and James Kievit, *Strategy and the Revolution in Military Affairs: From Theory to Policy* (Carlisle, PA: Strategic Studies Institute, US Army War College, June 27, 1995).

54. Metz and Kievit, *Strategy and the Revolution in Military Affairs*, vii, 2.

55. Quoted in Kathleen T. Rhem, "Rumsfeld Tells Pentagon Workers Transformation Critical to Success," *American Forces Press Service*, August 6, 2002. Available at: http://www.defense.gov/news/newsarticle.aspx?id=43578.

56. Linda D. Kozaryn, "Military Works to Meet Transformation Goals," *American Forces Press Service*, April 10, 2002. Available at: http://www.defense.gov/News/NewsArticle.aspx?ID=44179.

57. William M. Darley, "Strategic Imperative: The Necessity for Values Operations as Opposed to Information Operations in Iraq and Afghanistan," *Air & Space Power Journal* (Spring 2007). Available at: http://www.army.mil/professional-Writing/volumes/volume5/april_2007/4_07_2.html.

58. Department of Defense, Joint Publication 1–02, *DOD Dictionary of Military and Associated Terms* (April 12, 2001, as amended through April 14, 2006). Available at: www.dtic.mil/doctrine/new_pubs/jp1_02.pdf.

59. National Science Foundation Division of Science Resources Statistics, *Federal Funds for Research and Development: Fiscal Years 2002, 2003, and 2004* (Arlington, VA: National Science Foundation, 2005). Available at: http://www.nsf.gov/statistics/nsf05307/.

60. For FY04, appropriators provided $12.1 billion for Department of Defense S&T. The 2004 budget for behavioral, cognitive, neural, and social science was $376.7 million. American Psychological Association, "Behavioral and Social Science in the Administration's FY 2005 Budget," *Science Policy Insider News* (March 2004). Available at: http://www.apa.org/about/gr/science/spin/2004/03/budget.aspx.

61. The science and technology budget is subdivided into basic research, including the production of new knowledge in a scientific area of interest to the military (6.1); applied research, which supports the development of new technologies for specific military applications (6.2); and advanced technology development, which supports the development of hardware and the conduct of experiments that can demonstrate operational capability (6.3). Once a technology goes into

prototype (6.4), it is no longer funded through the science and technology budget but falls under Research, Development, Technology and Engineering (RDT&E). For a review of S&T budgets by year, see Association of American Universities, https://www.aau.edu/budget/article.aspx?id=4660.

62. A compounding problem is that, unlike the United Kingdom which has only a single defense S&T agency, in the US each of the branches of the military have their own S&T divisions and laboratories that make policy, distribute funds, and conduct research. The scientific needs of the US Navy, for example, are met through the Office of Naval Research (ONR) and the Naval Research Laboratory (NRL). Similarly, the Air Force has both an Air Force Office of Scientific Research (AFOSR) and the Air Force Research Laboratory (AFRL). In addition to the service S&T divisions and laboratories, the US also supports S&T research through agencies such as DARPA and DTRA whose research, in theory, benefits the entire defense community.

63. Army Research Lab, "Organizations," undated. Available at: http://www.arl. army.mil/www/default.cfm?page=231.

64. Army Research Institute for the Behavioral and Social Sciences (ARI) generally supports social science research on training, leadership development, recruiting, job performance, and morale and welfare of soldiers. ARI's research areas were not directed towards understanding foreign societies. See, for example, US Army Research Institute for the Behavioral and Social Sciences, "List of US Army Research Institute Research and Technical Publications," (Alexandria, VA: US Army Research Institute for the Behavioral and Social Sciences), January 2003. Available at: www.dtic.mil/dtic/tr/fulltext/u2/a437361.pdf.

65. Deputy Under Secretary of Defense for Science and Technology, *Behavioral, Cognitive and Social Science Research in the Military, Report to Senate Appropriations Committee* (Washington, DC: Department of Defense, August 2000), 3–4. Available at: handle.dtic.mil/100.2/ADA529662. While some of the research funded by NSF might prove useful, much of this research never reaches the end-user due to the weak institutional links between the operational, planning, and policy functions of the DOD and program managers at the NSF. Furthermore, since the NSF provides funding to institutions and individual academic researchers who themselves often have weak ties to the DOD, much of this research is never disseminated to defense agencies and individuals who might find it useful.

66. NSC staff member interview, 2005.

67. In theory, commanders' action groups (CAGs) ought to conduct this type of outreach. CAGs, however, are only as knowledgeable in the realm of social science as their collective membership, which more often than not includes engineers and others trained in the "hard" sciences.

68. With a defense S&T organized in such a distributed manner, coordination of research should be a priority. Yet, the federal government lacks any mechanisms to coordinate the social science research it funds and conducts, which has consequences both for policy-makers and warfighters. In theory, the Office of Science and Technology Policy (OSTP) could take the lead in coordinating

social science research across the US government. Congress established OSTP in 1976 with a broad mandate to advise the President and others within the Executive Office of the President on the effects of science and technology on domestic and international affairs. When Mark Weiss was appointed as assistant director for social and behavioral sciences at OSTP, he noted that his top challenge would be "to get a handle on the range of SBE science being pursued across the government." Paul J. Nuti, "Washington Wire," *Anthropology News* 46, no. 8 (November 2005): 31. Alas, Mark Weiss left his post after a year and whether he ever identified the range of social science being conducted by the various US government agencies remains a mystery. Unfortunately, OSTP has not been actively involved in coordinating social science research across the government. Like OSTP, the National Science and Technology Council (NSTC) is a federal government entity that could be used for the coordination of research, but which currently does not serve this function. Established by an Executive Order on November 23, 1993, the NSTC is a cabinet-level council, and is composed of various cabinet secretaries and agency heads with significant science and technology responsibilities, and other White House officials. The NSTC sets investment goals for federal science and technology and prepares research and development strategies. Like OSTP, the NSTC does not coordinate research. Rather, it coordinates science and technology *policies* across the federal government.

69. Michael A. Vane and Daniel Fagundes, "Redefining the Foreign Area Officer's Role," *Military Review* 84, no. 3 (May–June 2004): 15–19, 18.

70. Vane and Daniel Fagundes, "Redefining," 17. Until recently, being selected as a FAO was a "career killer." Because FAOs were assigned to State Department posts as attachés rather than completing assignments at battalion and brigade levels, Army FAO promotion rates were consistently below the Army average. In addition, FAOs had to compete against other officers from different branches such as Military Intelligence or Air Defense for promotion. Jon E. Shearer, "The FAO Experience," *Marine Corps Gazette* (February 2000): 66. An expansion of the FAO program to meet the military's socio-cultural requirements would be a costly investment for the military: the Army invests two and a half to four years to train each FAO-qualified officer. Peter Schirmer, Dina G. Levy, Harry J. Thie, Joy S. Moini, Margaret C. Harrell, Kimberly Curry, Kevin Brancato, Megan Abbott, *New Paths to Success: Determining Career Alternatives for Field-Grade Officers* (Arlington, VA: RAND, 2004), 35.

71. Department of Defense, Joint Publication 2-0, *Joint Intelligence* (June 22, 2007): I-1. This language has been removed from the 2013 revision, reflecting some consensus perhaps that the scope of military intelligence has broadened. Available at: www.dtic.mil/doctrine/new_pubs/jp2_0.pdf.

72. Former US Army military intelligence officer interview, 2006.

73. David H. Petraeus, "Learning Counterinsurgency: Observations From Soldiering in Iraq," *Military Review* 86, no. 4 (January–February 2006): 2.

74. US Army, Field Manual 3-24, *Counterinsurgency* (December 15, 2006): para. 1–3. Available at: https://rdl.train.army.mil/catalog/view/100.ATSC/41449AB4-

E8E0–46C4–8443-E4276B6F0481–1274576841878/3–24/chap1.html. The 2014 version does not contain this language. Available at: http://armypubs. army.mil/doctrine/Active_FM.html.

75. David Galula, *Counterinsurgency Warfare: Theory and Practice* (New York: Praeger, 1968), 89, 88.

76. One could certainly make the case that the preferences and perspectives of civilians matter greatly during major combat operations in regards to the popular will required to sustain a war.

77. Civil affairs core tasks are those "normally the responsibility of civil government." Department of the Army, Field Manual 3–57, *Civil Affairs Operations* (Washington, DC: Department of the Army, April 18, 2014): 3–1.

78. Christopher Holshek, "Integrated Civil–Military and Information Operations: Finding Success in Synergy," in *Cornwallis Group IX: Analysis for Stabilization and Counter-Terrorist Operations*, ed. Alexander Woodcock and George Rose (Ottawa: Canadian Peacekeeping Press, 2005).

79. Mark Benjamin and Barbara Slavin, "How Rumsfeld Abandoned the Peacemakers," *Newsweek*, February 6, 2011.

80. David H. Petraeus, "Learning Counterinsurgency: Observations from Soldiering in Iraq," *Military Review* 86, no. 4 (January–February 2006): 12.

81. USMC officer in email to author, April 14, 2007. Italics are added.

82. Anthony Zinni, "Remarks" (speech at the US Naval Institute and Marine Corps Association, September 4, 2003). Available at http://www.usni.org/ Seminars/Forum/03/forum03zinni.html.

83. Different types of military operations generate different types of knowledge requirements. In a major combat operation, for example, understanding the enemy order of battle and the physical terrain are critical pieces of information. During a humanitarian aid mission, on the other hand, understanding local food preferences and basic infrastructure for delivery of equipment and supplies are equally critical. Stability operations, which often entail reestablishing government, rebuilding infrastructure, and kick-starting the economy, demand a comprehensive understanding of the local environment.

84. McChrystal quoted in Declan Walsh, "US Had 'Frighteningly Simplistic' View of Afghanistan, says McChrystal," *The Guardian*, October 7, 2011. Available at: http://www.guardian.co.uk/world/2011/oct/07/us-frighteningly-simplistic-afghanistan-mcchrystal.

85. The author served on the DSB, but did not contribute to this particular report.

86. Only Southern Command, whose geographic area of responsibility includes Central and South America, seemed to feel that they were in possession of all the facts. Defense Science Board, *Summer Study on Transition to and from Hostilities* (Washington, DC: Office of the Under Secretary of Defense for Acquisition, Technology, and Logistics, December 2004), 113.

87. Platoon leader in the 101st Airborne Division, email to author, 2006.

88. Of course, whether policy-makers and military leaders would have utilized the information to inform policy and strategy is another question, beyond the scope of this chapter.

89. Joint Chiefs of Staff, Joint Publication 3–06, *Doctrine for Joint Urban Operations* (Washington, DC: Joint Chiefs of Staff, November 20, 2013): IV-12.

90. Jeffrey B. White, "Some Thoughts on Irregular Warfare," *Studies in Intelligence* 39, no. 5 (1996). Available at: https://www.cia.gov/csi/studies/96unclass/iregular.htm.

91. John P. Coles, "Cultural Intelligence and Joint Intelligence Doctrine," *Joint Operations Review* 1, no. 3 (2005). Available at: www.au.af.mil/au/awc/awcgate/ndu/jfsc_cultural_intelligence.pdf.

92. Robert H. Scales Jr., "Culture-Centric Warfare," *Proceedings of the US Naval Institute* 130, no. 10 (October 2004). Available at: http://www.usni.org/magazines/proceedings/2004–10/culture-centric-warfare.

93. David S. Cloud, Eric Schmitt and Thom Shanker, "Rumsfeld Faces Growing Revolt by Retired Generals," *New York Times*, April 13, 2006. Available at: http://www.nytimes.com/2006/04/13/washington/13cnd-military.html?_r=0.

94. Quoted in Mark Perry, "US Military Breaks Ranks, Part 2: Troops felled by a 'trust gap,'" *Asia Times*, January 23, 2008. Available at: http://www.atimes.com/atimes/Middle_East/JA23Ak02.html.

95. Quoted in Eric Schmitt, "Pentagon Contradicts General on Iraq Occupation Force's Size," *New York Times*, February 28, 2003. Available at: http://www.nytimes.com/2003/02/28/us/threats-responses-military-spending-pentagon-contradicts-general-iraq-occupation.html.

96. Paul D. Eaton, "A Top-Down Review for the Pentagon," *New York Times*, March 19, 2006. Available at: http://www.nytimes.com/2006/03/19/opinion/19eaton.html?pagewanted=print.

97. According to Lieutenant General Greg Newbold, the former operations director for the Joint Chiefs of Staff, "I now regret that I did not more openly challenge those who were determined to invade a country whose actions were peripheral to the real threat—al-Qaeda. ... [T]he Pentagon's military leaders ... with few exceptions, acted timidly when their voices urgently needed to be heard. When they knew the plan was flawed, saw intelligence distorted to justify a rationale for war, or witnessed arrogant micromanagement that at times crippled the military's effectiveness, many leaders who wore the uniform chose inaction. ... It is time for senior military leaders to discard caution in expressing their views and ensure that the President hears them clearly. And that we won't be fooled again." Gregory Newbold, "Why Iraq was a Mistake," *Time*, April 9, 2006, 42–3. Available at: http://content.time.com/time/magazine/article/0,9171,1181629,00.html.

98. Thomas E. Ricks, *The Generals: American Military Command from World War II to Today* (Penguin Press, 2012).

99. Robert H. Scales Jr., "Statement" (Statement Before the House Armed Services Committee, United States House of Representatives, October 21, 2003). Available at: http://www.au.af.mil/au/awcgate/congress/03–10–21scales.htm.

100. Sandra I. Erwin, "US Military Training Fails to Grasp Foreign Cultures, Says Rep. Skelton," *National Defense Magazine*, June 2004. Available at: http://

www.nationaldefensemagazine.org/archive/2004/June/Pages/US_Military35 51.aspx.

101. For example, James Baker, "Winning Hearts with Cultural Awareness," *Soldiers* 58, no. 7 (July 2003); Barak Salmoni, "Beyond Hearts and Minds, Culture Matters," *Proceedings of the Naval Institute Press* (November 2004); George W. Smith, "Avoiding a Napoleonic Ulcer: Bridging the Gap of Cultural Intelligence (Or, Have We Focused on the Wrong Transformation?)," in *Essays 2004: Chairman of the Joint Chiefs of Staff Strategy Essay Competition* (Washington, DC: National Defense University Press, 2004): 21–38, available at: http://www.mcu.usmc.mil/mcwar/IRP/Documents/ CJCS%20Essay%20-%20Smith.pdf; Montgomery McFate, "The Military Utility of Understanding Adversary Culture," *Joint Forces Quarterly* 38 (2005): 42–52; Richard L. Taylor, *Tribal Alliances: Ways, Means, and Ends to Successful Strategy* (Carlisle, PA: Strategic Studies Institute, 2005).

102. Benjamin C. Freakley, "Cultural Awareness and Combat Power," *Infantry* 94, no. 2 (March/April 2005): 1–2.

103. David H. Petraeus, "Learning Counterinsurgency: Observations From Soldiering in Iraq," *Military Review* 86, no. 4 (January–February 2006): 8.

104. The US Army's Limited-War Mission and Social Science Research Conference took place in March 1962.

105. In a 2005 report, for example, the National Science and Technology Council (which advises the White House Office of Science and Technology Policy) noted, "The necessity of substantive research in the social sciences for the creation of effective counterterrorism strategies cannot be overstated." National Science and Technology Council, *Combating Terrorism: Research Priorities in the Social, Behavioral and Economic Sciences* (Washington, DC: National Science and Technology Council, 2005), 20.

106. Donald Rumsfeld quoted in William D. Wunderle, *Through the Lens of Cultural Awareness: A Primer for US Armed Forces Deploying to Arab and Middle Eastern Countries* (Fort Leavenworth, KS: Combat Studies Institute Press, 2006), 4.

107. Department of Defense, Directive 3000.05, *Military Support for Stability, Security, Transition, and Reconstruction (SSTR) Operations* (Washington, DC: Department of Defense, November 2005, superseded 2009).

108. US government agencies focused on "cultural intelligence" during the post-Somalia period were the Marine Corps Intelligence Activity (MCIA) in Quantico, VA and the Strategic Studies Detachment of the 4th Psychological Operations Group in Fort Bragg, NC.

109. *Stanford Encyclopedia of Philosophy*, s.v. "Knowledge How," http://plato. stanford.edu/entries/knowledge-how/

110. The classic example is Polanyi's explanation that one does not need to understand mechanical physics to ride a bicycle. Michael Polanyi, *Personal Knowledge: Towards a Post-Critical Philosophy* (Chicago: University of Chicago Press, 1958), 50–52.

111. Ben Connable, "Cultural Intelligence in Iraq" (PowerPoint briefing, November 2004).

112. Allison Abbe, Lisa M. V. Gulick, and Jeffrey L. Herman, *Cross-Cultural Competence in Army Leaders: A Conceptual and Empirical Foundation* (Fort Belvoir, VA: US Army Research Institute for the Behavioral and Social Sciences, October 2007), 2.

113. W. Arthur and W. Bennett, "The International Assignee: The Relative Importance of Factors Perceived to Contribute to Success," *Personnel Psychology* 48 (1995): 99–114; W. Arthur, W. Bennett, P. S. Edens, and S. T. Bell, "Effectiveness of Training in Organizations: a Meta-analysis of Design and Evaluation Features," *Journal of Applied Psychology* 88 (2003): 234–45.

114. R. A. Detweiler, "Intercultural Interaction and the Categorization Process: A Conceptual Analysis and Behavioral Outcome," *International Journal of Intercultural Relations* 4 (1980): 275–93.

115. Montgomery McFate, Britt Damon, and Robert Holliday, "What Do Commanders Really Want to Know? US Army Human Terrain System Lessons Learned from Iraq and Afghanistan," in *The Oxford Handbook of Military Psychology*, ed. Janice H. Laurence and Michael D. Matthews (New York, Oxford University Press, 2012), 92–113.

116. Brigadier General Benjamin C. Freakley, "Cultural Awareness and Combat Power," *Infantry* 94, no. 2 (March/April 2005): 1–2.

117. In the words of Franz Boas (arguing against the common museum practice of nineteenth-century naturalists of taxonomic organization of material objects in 1887): "We have to study each ethnological specimen individually in its history and in its medium.... By regarding a single implement outside of its surroundings, outside of other inventions of the people to whom it belongs, and outside of other phenomena affecting that people and its productions, we cannot understand its meanings.... Our objection ... is that classification is not explanation." Franz Boas, "The Principles of Ethnological Classification," in *Franz Boas Reader*, ed. George W. Stocking Jr. (Chicago: University of Chicago Press, 1974), 62.

118. Anthony C. Zinni, "Non-Traditional Military Missions: Their Nature, and the Need for Cultural Awareness and Flexible Thinking," in *Capital "W" War: A Case for Strategic Principles of War*, ed. Joe Strange (Quantico, VA: Marine Corps University, 1998), 267.

119. Human Terrain System, "Mission Statement" (2008). HTS has since updated their mission statement to read: "The U Army Human Terrain System functions as the primary and enduring social science-based human domain research, analysis, and training capability, focused on enabling leaders to remain adaptive when shaping current and future complex strategic and operational environments which support Unified Action Partners world-wide." Available at: http://humanterrainsystem.army.mil/index.html.

120. For an additional list of cultural barriers between the military and anthropology in particular, see David Edwards, "Counterinsurgency as a Cultural System," *Small Wars Journal*, December 27, 2010: 12. Available at: http://smallwarsjournal.com/jrnl/art/counterinsurgency-as-a-cultural-system.

121. US Army major, interview with first author, 2008.

122. Social scientist, interview with first author, 2008.

123. Ibid.

124. Ibid.

125. David Edwards, "Counterinsurgency as a Cultural System," *Small Wars Journal*, December 27, 2010: 12. Available at: http://smallwarsjournal.com/jrnl/art/counterinsurgency-as-a-cultural-system.

126. Department of the Army, Army Doctrine Publication 5–0, *Operations Process* (Washington, DC: Department of the Army, May 2012).

127. Social scientist, interview with first author, 2008.

128. IZ13 team leader, interview with first author, 2008.

129. "Operationally relevant" does not mean that the information is used to identify and prosecute targets; military operations in counterinsurgency and stability operations transcend the lethal operations that are usually associated with major combat operations. In wars such as those in Iraq and Afghanistan, the military has multiple, overlapping lines of operations focused on strengthening local governance, developing local economies, and providing security to the population. It is in these non-lethal domains of military operations that HTTs were designed to be employed, and where their research supports the warfighter.

130. Montgomery McFate, Britt Damon, and Robert Holliday, "What Do Commanders Really Want to Know? US Army Human Terrain System Lessons Learned from Iraq and Afghanistan," in *The Oxford Handbook of Military Psychology*, ed. Janice H. Laurence and Michael D. Matthews (New York, Oxford University Press, 2012), 92–113.

131. For a nice discussion, see David Edwards, "Counterinsurgency as a Cultural System," *Small Wars Journal*, December 27, 2010. Available at: http://smallwarsjournal.com/jrnl/art/counterinsurgency-as-a-cultural-system.

132. IZ1 team leader, interview with first author, 2008.

133. Pauline Kusiak, "Sociocultural Expertise and the Military: Beyond the Controversy," *Military Review* 88, no. 6 (Nov./Dec. 2008): 72.

134. Social scientist, interview with first author, 2008.

135. Ibid.

136. Montgomery McFate and Steve Fondacaro, "Reflections on the Human Terrain System during the First Four Years," *PRISM* 2, no. 4 (2011): 74–5.

137. USMC lieutenant colonel, interview, 2009.

138. Assistant G3, II Marine Expeditionary Force (Forward), interview with first author, 2009.

139. Although human intelligence collectors (HUMINT) have excellent interview skills, their role is to concentrate on identification of threats not the general situation of the local civilian population.

140. Platoon leader from the 1st Battalion of the 112th Infantry Regiment, interview with first author, 2009.

141. Stephen Downes-Martin, "Operations Assessment in Afghanistan is Broken," *Naval War College Review* 64, no. 4 (Autumn 2011).

142. Some examples are offered in Montgomery McFate and Steve Fondacaro, "Reflections on the Human Terrain System During the First Four Years," *PRISM* 2, no. 4 (2011): 64, 75; Martin P. Schweitzer, "Statement" (testimony before the House Armed Services Committee, 110th Cong., 2nd sess., hearings on the role of the social and behavioral sciences in national security, April 24, 2008), available at: http://gop.science.house.gov/Media/hearings/research08/april24/schweitzer.pdf; David Edwards, "Counterinsurgency as a Cultural System," *Small Wars Journal*, December 27, 2010, available at: http://smallwarsjournal.com/jrnl/art/counterinsurgency-as-a-cultural-system, 44; Montgomery McFate, "The Military Utility of Understanding Adversary Culture," *Joint Forces Quarterly* 38 (3rd Quarter 2005); Dan G. Cox, "Human Terrain Systems and the Moral Prosecution of Warfare," *Parameters* (Autumn 2011); Paul Joseph, "Changing the Battle Space? How Human Terrain Teams Define 'Success' in Iraq and Afghanistan" (paper prepared for the Seventh Interdisciplinary Conference on War and Peace, Prague, Czech Republic, April 30–May 2, 2010).

143. Mobile training team commander, interview with first author, 2008.

144. Brigade effects coordinator, interview with first author, 2009.

145. Ben Connable, "All our Eggs in a Broken Basket: How the Human Terrain System is Undermining Sustainable Military Cultural Competence," *Military Review* (March–April 2009).

146. By 2006, the wars had been going on for a number of years with a full accompaniment of FAOs, Civil Affairs, PRTs, and Military Intelligence personnel. The existence of the JUONS, signed by both US Army and USMC, tends to indicate that despite all these enablers on the staff, the downrange cultural knowledge gap was not being filled.

147. Brigade deputy commanding officer, interview with first author, 2009. One analytical control element chief serving in Iraq in a brigade S2 shop put it this way: "Typically the brigade relies on intel to provide what HTT provides to us. We [the S2] don't have the knowledge, haven't been there for a long time. We have no time and no manpower resources to focus on population and environment. It really helps us out because I don't have the time to dedicate to it. We're so focused on the bad guy. Now, with the reconciliation process and pull-out from the cities, there is a bigger emphasis on the non-lethal piece." Interview with first author, 2009.

148. American Anthropological Association Executive Board, *Statement on the Human Terrain System Project* (October 31, 2007). Available at: http://www.aaanet.org/about/policies/statements/human-terrain-system-statement.cfm.

149. Network of Concerned Anthropologists, *Pledge of Non-participation in Counter-insurgency*. Available at: http://concerned.anthropologists.googlepages.com.

150. See, for example, American Anthropological Association Commission on the Engagement of Anthropology with the US Security and Intelligence Communities, *Final Report* (November 4, 2007), available at: http://www.aaanet.org/cmtes/Commission-on-the-Engagement-of-Anthropology-with-the-

US-Security-and-Intelligence-Communities.cfm; American Anthropological Association, Ad Hoc Commission on the Engagement of Anthropology with the US Security and Intelligence Communities (CEAUSSIC), *Final Report on US Army's Human Terrain System Proof of Concept Program* (October 14, 2009), 55–6, available at: http://www.aaanet.org/cmtes/commissions/CEAUSSIC/Proposal-for-Examination-of-the-Human-Terrain-System-A-CEAUSSIC-Project.cfm.

151. Philip E. Tetlock, "Thinking the Unthinkable: Sacred Values and Taboo Cognitions," *Trends in Cognitive Sciences* 7, no. 7 (July 2003): 320.

152. American Anthropological Association, "Code of Ethics" (November 1, 2012). Available at: http://ethics.aaanet.org/ethics-statement-1-do-no-harm.

153. Hugh Gusterson quoted in Scott Jaschik, "If CIA Calls, Should Anthropology Answer?" *Inside Higher Education*, September 1, 2006). Available at: http://insidehighered.com/news/2006/09/01/anthro.

154. Ibid.

155. See, for example, American Sociological Association, "Code of Ethics" (undated), available at: http://www.asanet.org/about/ethics.cfm; American Political Science Association, "Guide to Professional Ethics in Political Science" (2012), available at: http://www.apsanet.org/media/PDFs/ethics-guideweb.pdf. The ethical principles of the American Psychological Association do note that "Psychologists strive to benefit those with whom they work and take care to do no harm." American Psychological Association, "Ethical Principles of Psychologists and Code of Conduct" (2010). Available at: http://www.apa.org/ethics/code/index.aspx?item=3#

156. American Anthropological Association, "Code of Ethics" (November 1, 2012). Available at: http://ethics.aaanet.org/ethics-statement-1-do-no-harm.

157. American Anthropological Association, "Statement of Purpose" (undated). Available at: http://www.aaanet.org/about/Governance/Satement-of-Purpose.cfm. The long-range plan of the AAA removes the word "science" from the mission statement. See Dan Berrett, "Anthropology Without Science," *Inside Higher Education*, November 30, 2010. Available at: http://www.insidehighered.com/news/2010/11/30/anthroscience. The meaning of "science" to anthropologists has changed over time, as the discipline has changed. See Susan R. Trencher, "The American Anthropological Association and the Values of Science, 1935–70," *American Anthropologist* 104, no. 2 (June 2002): 450–62.

158. Roy D'Andrade, "Moral Models in Anthropology," *Current Anthropology* 36, no. 3 (June 1995): 399.

159. Talal Asad, ed., *Anthropology and the Colonial Encounter* (London: Ithaca Press, 1973); George W. Stocking Jr., ed., *Colonial Situations: Essays on the Contextualization of Ethnographic Knowledge* (Madison: University of Wisconsin, 1991); Marc Pinkoski, "Julian Steward, American Anthropology, and Colonialism," *Histories of Anthropology Annual* 4 (2008).

160. Evie Plaice, "Comment on Adam Kuper, 'The Return of the Native,'" *Current Anthropology* 44, no. 3 (2003): 397.

161. See, for example, Roger Bastide, *Applied Anthropology* (London: Croom Helm, 1971); Sol Tax, *Horizons of Anthropology* (Chicago: Aldine Publishing Company, 1964).

162. Sol Tax, "Action Anthropology," *Current Anthropology* 16 (1975): 171–7.

163. Marshall Sahlins, "The Established Order: Do not Fold, Spindle or Mutilate," in *The Rise and Fall of Project Camelot*, ed. Irving Louis Horowitz (Cambridge, MA: MIT Press, 1967), 72.

164. Philip E. Tetlock, "Thinking the Unthinkable: Sacred Values and Taboo Cognitions," *Trends in Cognitive Sciences* 7, no. 7 (July 2003): 321. For example, among Christian fundamentalists the will of God manifest in the life of Jesus Christ is a powerful sacred value. In one experiment Christian fundamentalists were "outraged by heretical counterfactuals that implied that the life of Jesus was as subject to the vagaries of chance as the lives of ordinary mortals."

165. Philip E. Tetlock, "Thinking the Unthinkable: Sacred Values and Taboo Cognitions," *Trends in Cognitive Sciences* 7, no. 7 (July 2003): 322.

166. Franz Boas, "Scientists as Spies," *The Nation* 109 (December 20, 1919): 797.

167. Gerald C. Hickey, *Window on a War: An Anthropologist in the Vietnam Conflict* (Lubbock: Texas Tech University Press, 2002), 298.

168. Seymour J. Deitchman, *Best-Laid Schemes: A Tale of Social Research and the Bureaucracy* (Cambridge, Massachusetts and London: MIT Press, 1976), 204.

169. Thomas A. Gregor and Daniel R. Gross, "Guilt by Association: The Culture of Accusation and the American Anthropological Association's Investigation of 'Darkness in El Dorado,'" *American Anthropologist* 106, no. 4 (December 2004): 687–98. See also Roy D'Andrade, "Moral Models in Anthropology," *Current Anthropology* 36, no. 3 (June 1995).

170. See Robert Rubinstein, "Master Narratives, Retrospective Attribution, and Ritual Pollution in Anthropology's Engagement with the Military," in *Practicing Military Anthropology*, ed. Robert Rubinstein, Kerry Fosher, and Clementine Fujimura (Sterling, VA: Kumarian Press, 2012), 119–33; Peter Stone, "Introduction: the Ethical Challenges for Cultural Heritage Experts Working with the Military," in *Cultural Heritage, Ethics and the Military*, ed. Peter G. Stone (Rochester, NY: Boydell Press, 2011). Over the years, I have heard from a number of graduate students who feel they cannot express their opinions to their faculty nor make free career choices. One graduate student wrote: "I want to explore this subject further, that is, Military Anthropology, but I must do so cautiously. The faculty members of the anthro department who would best serve as mentors for such a focus are vehemently opposed to your program." Another budding anthropologist wrote, "It seems that if I did work with the HTT, that would be academic career suicide. There is a witch-hunt for everyone involved in this project." Anthropology graduate student at George Mason University, email to the first author, 2007.

171. Philip E. Tetlock, "Thinking the Unthinkable: Sacred Values and Taboo Cognitions," *Trends in Cognitive Sciences* 7, no. 7 (July 2003): 321.

172. Thanks to Chris V. for this observation.
173. United Nations, "Mandates and the Legal Basis for Peacekeeping" (undated). Available at: http://www.un.org/en/peacekeeping/operations/pkmandates. shtml.
174. Simon Chesterman, *Use of Force in UN Peace Operations*, Department of Peacekeeping Operations of the United Nations (August 2004): 7; Trevor Findlay, *Use of Force in UN Peace Operations* (Oxford: SIPRI and Oxford University Press, 2002).
175. American Anthropological Association, "Code of Ethics" (February 2009). Available at: http://www.aaanet.org/issues/policy-advocacy/Code-of-Ethics. cfm.
176. Jeremy Keenan, "Conspiracy Theories and Terrorists: How the War on Terror is Placing New Responsibilities on Anthropology," *Anthropology Today* 22, no. 6 (2006): 9.
177. Laura A. McNamara, "Culture, Decision Making, and Computational Modeling: Where are the Anthropologists?" Available at: http://est.sandia. gov/consequence/docs/05_7679C.pdf; Roberto J. Gonzalez, "Why We Must Fight the Militarization of Anthropology," *Chronicle of Higher Education*, February 2, 2007. Available at: http://chronicle.com/article/We-Must-Fight-the/9640.
178. The Office of Personnel Management shows 144 anthropologists and 1,150 archaeologists working for the federal government. This statistic probably underestimates the actual number. Shirley J. Fiske, "Working for the Federal Government: Anthropology Careers," *NAPA Bulletin* 29, no. 1 (2008): 111. Fiske notes that the federal government is probably the largest employer of anthropologists outside of universities. However, her study does not compare the number of anthropologists to members of other disciplines working within the federal government, such as political scientists.
179. Anne Francis Okongwu and Joan P. Mencher, "The Anthropology of Public Policy: Shifting Terrains," *Review of Anthropology* 29 (2000): 109. Dorothy Willner, "Anthropology and Public Policy," *RAIN*, no. 24 (February 1978):1, 3–4. A title search in May 2014 of public policy journals in JSTOR, for example, turned up three articles on anthropology and public policy—all of them published before 1966. A title search of the entire JSTOR database for anthropology and public policy turned up a total of 24 articles. A 2005 editorial in *Anthropology Today* noted that "anthropology as a discipline has not given policy—a social, cultural and political construct—the explicit attention that it deserves." But instead of calling on anthropologists to aspire to policy-making as a professional goal, or even policy analysis as a job, the authors called for anthropologists to *study* policy. Janine R. Wedel and Gregory Feldman, "Why an Anthropology of Public Policy?" *Anthropology Today* 21, no. 1 (February 2005): 1.
180. James Peacock, "The Future of Anthropology," *American Anthropologist* 99, no. 1 (1997): 9–17.
181. Roberto Gonzalez, "Anthropologists in the Public Sphere: Speaking Out on

War, Peace, and American Power," in *Anthropologists in the Public Sphere*, ed. Roberto Gonzalez (Austin, TX: University of Texas Press, 2004).

182. Catherine Besteman and Hugh Gusterson, "Introduction" to *Why America's Pundits are Wrong*, ed. Catherine Besteman and Hugh Gusterson (Berkeley, CA: University of California Press, 2005), 6.

183. Dr Margaret Mead, "The Study of Cultures," publication no. L61–63 (Washington, DC: Industrial College of The Armed Forces, November 1, 1960), 24.

184. President Bush quoted in George Packer, *The Assassins' Gate* (New York: Farrar, Straus and Giroux, 2005), 111.

185. David Edwards, "Counterinsurgency as a Cultural System," *Small Wars Journal*, December 27, 2010: 3. Available at: http://smallwarsjournal.com/jrnl/art/counterinsurgency-as-a-cultural-system.

186. Brigade commander, interview, 2008.

187. Navy Seal, interview, 2008.

188. US Department of Defense, "First Minerva Research Initiative Awards Announced," US Department of Defense news release (December 22, 2008). Available at: *www.defense.gov/releases/release.aspx?releaseid=12407*.

189. Department of Defense, "Introduction to the Human Social Culture Behavior Modeling Program," *Human Social Culture Behavior Modeling Newsletter* 1 (Spring 2009): 1. Available at: http://www.dtic.mil/biosys/files/HSCB-news-spring-2009.pdf.

3. AN ANTHROPOLOGIST AT WAR IN AFGHANISTAN

1. Both fire a 7.62 mm round, but the PKM is a belt-fed machine gun, capable of shooting farther and faster.

2. As it turned out, the unit rotated out before they had a chance to return to Harawara.

3. Unable to find many qualified individuals and under intense pressure from the Army and CENTCOM to field additional teams, the architects of the program chose to emphasize the power of social science as a generic discipline, as well as the "different way of thinking" that academics would bring to the military. It wouldn't matter if a person had never been to Afghanistan, didn't speak Pashto, and hadn't ever studied anthropology, since his or her social science *bona fides*—psychology, economics, and religious studies—were really what allowed HTS to make a difference. In many instances, this actually seemed to work. In other cases, it backfired spectacularly. The overarching need for personnel meant that recruitment and training received scant attention, but unless someone had a medical condition making them unsuitable for deployment, such as having greater than 40 percent body fat or a *diagnosed* psychiatric disorder, they usually headed downrange. As one HTS administrator put it, "Many of the people in this program are too old, too fat, or too unstable for a war zone—but they go anyway."

4. George Packer, "Knowing the Enemy: Can Social Scientists Redefine the 'War on Terror'?" *New Yorker*, December 18, 2006.

5. "American Anthropological Association Executive Board Statement on the Human Terrain System Project," American Anthropological Association, October 31, 2007. Available at: http://www.aaanet.org/about/policies/statements/human-terrain-system-statement.cfm.

6. David Rohde, "Army Enlists Anthropology in War Zones," *New York Times*, October 5, 2007. See also Vanessa M. Gezari, "Rough Terrain: The Human Terrain Program Embeds Anthropologists with the US Military in Afghanistan," *Washington Post*, August 30, 2009.

7. Roberto J. Gonzalez, "Towards Mercenary Anthropology? The New US Army Counterinsurgency Manual FM 3–24 and the Military–Anthropology Complex," *Anthropology Today* 23 (2007): 14–19.

8. George Lucas, *Anthropologists in Arms: The Ethics of Military Anthropology* (Walnut Creek, CA: Altamira Press, 2009).

9. "Final Report on US Army's Human Terrain System Proof of Concept Program," American Anthropological Association, Ad Hoc Commission on the Engagement of Anthropology with the US Security and Intelligence Communities (CEAUSSIC), October 14, 2009. Available at: http://www.aaanet.org/cmtes/commissions/CEAUSSIC/Proposal-for-Examination-of-the-Human-Terrain-System-A-CEAUSSIC-Project.cfm.

10. Adam Geller, "From Campus to Combat: 'Professor' Pays Heavy Price," *Associated Press*, March 10, 2009.

11. Bhatia wasn't the only HTS casualty. In June 2008, Nicole Suveges, a social scientist, was killed in Iraq when a bomb planted under the floor of a District Council building exploded during a meeting. A more bizarre incident involved Paula Loyd, a social scientist who was working on AF4 in Kandahar. In the bazaar just outside her base, Abdul Salam, a man she was interviewing, doused her in gasoline and set her alight. Loyd suffered horrific burns and died two months later; see Vanessa Gezari, *The Tender Soldier: A True Story of War and Sacrifice* (New York: Simon & Schuster, 2013). Don Ayala, a former Army Ranger on Loyd's team, had subdued Abdul Salam and, when told of the extent of Loyd's injuries, executed Salam with a gunshot to the head. Ayala was tried in the US, pleaded guilty to voluntary manslaughter, and was sentenced to five years' probation and given a $12,500 fine; see Matthew Barakat, "Ex-Contractor Given Probation in Slaying of Afghan," *Associated Press*, March 8, 2009.

12. The airfield at FOB Salerno is named after 1LT Laura Walker, who was killed by an IED.

13. Richard Tapper, "Who are the Kuchi? Nomad self-identities in Afghanistan," *Journal of the Royal Anthropological Institute*, n.s., 14 (2008): 97–116.

14. General McChrystal, the former commander of International Security Assistance Force (ISAF), captured the paradox in his koan-like example of 'COIN mathematics': "Let us say that there are ten [insurgents] in a certain area. Following a military operation, two are killed. How many insurgents are left? Traditional mathematics would say that eight would be left, but there may only be two, because six of the living eight may have said, "This business of insurgency is

becoming dangerous, so I am going to do something else." There are more likely to be as many as twenty, because each one you killed has a brother, father, son and friends, who do not necessarily think that they were killed because they were doing something wrong. It does not matter—you killed them." Stanley McChrystal, "Special Address on Afghanistan" (speech at the International Institute of Strategic Studies, October 1, 2009). Available at: http://www.iiss.org/recent-key-addresses/general-stanley-mcchrystal-address.
15. McChrystal, "Special Address."

4. WHAT DO YOU BRING TO THE FIGHT?: A YEAR IN IRAQ AS AN EMBEDDED SOCIAL SCIENTIST

1. Jeff Emanuel, "On Patrol with the Quarter Cav: A Modern Day Band of Brothers on the Streets of Baghdad," *Weekly Standard*, May 16, 2007, available at: http://www.weeklystandard.com/Content/Public/Articles/000/000/013/648ard.asp?page=1; Thomas J. Sills, "Counterinsurgeny Operations in Baghdad: The Actions of 1–4 Cavalry in the East Rashid Security District," *Military Review* 89, no. 3 (May–June 2009): 98.
2. "US Soldier Uses Quran for Target Practice; Military Apologizes," CNN.com, May 18, 2008. Available at: http://edition.cnn.com/2008/WORLD/meast/05/17/iraq.quran/.
3. Kim Gamel, "US soldier removed from Iraq for shooting Quran," *USA Today*, May 19, 2008. Available at: http://www.usatoday.com/news/topstories/2008–05–19–4110462503_x.htm.
4. David Olson, "The Importance of Cultural Awareness Training," *Dave's Field Notes* (Blog), October 6, 2009. Available at: http://davesfieldnotes.blogspot.com/2009/10/importance-of-cultural-awareness-training.
5. Robert Spencer, "US Official Kisses Quran," *Jihadwatch Blog*, May 18, 2008. Available at: http://www.jihadwatch.org/2008/05/us-soldier-uses-quran-for-target-practice-us-military-apologizes-us-official-kisses-quran.html.
6. Rofasix, "Shooting Up the Qur'an," *Rofasix Blog*, May 21, 2008. Available at: http://rofasix.blogspot.com/2008/05/shooting-up-quran.html.
7. Qasem Abdul-Zahra, "Bush Apologizes to Iraqi Prime Minister over Qur'an 'Target Practice,'" *Huff Post Politics*, May 21, 2008. Available at: http://www.huffingtonpost.com/2008/05/20/bush-apologizes-to-iraqi_n_102643.html.
8. Mike Nizza, "Reactions: Defusing a Koran Shooting in Iraq," *The Lede blog of The New York Times*, May 20, 2008. Available at: http://thelede.blogs.nytimes.com/2008/05/20/reactions-defusing-a-koran-shooting-in-iraq/?_php=true&_type=blogs&_r=0.
9. Joe Sterling, "Sunni Arabs Embracing Local Iraq Elections," CNN.com, January 27, 2008. Available at: http://edition.cnn.com/2009/WORLD/meast/01/27/iraq.elections/index.html.
10. Roberto González, "Going 'Tribal': Notes on Pacification in the 21ˢᵗ Century," *Anthropology Today* 25 (April 2009): 15.
11. Falah A. Jabar, "Sheikhs and Ideologues: Deconstruction and Reconstruction

of Tribes under Patrimonial Totalitarianism in Iraq, 1968–1998," in *Tribes and Power: Nationalism and Ethnicity in the Middle East*, ed. Falah A. Jabar and Hosham Dawod (London: Saqi Books, 2003), 72.

12. Ben Connable, "All Our Eggs in a Broken Basket: How the Human Terrain System is Undermining Sustainable Military Cultural Competence," *Military Review* (March–April 2009): 57–64.

13. John K. Naland, *Lessons from Embedded Provincial Reconstruction Teams in Iraq* (Washington, DC: United States Institute of Peace (October 2011). Available at: http://www.usip.org/files/resources/SR290.pdf.

5. PLAYING SPADES IN AL ANBAR: A FEMALE SOCIAL SCIENTIST AMONG MARINES AND SPECIAL FORCES

1. Mehmet Yaser Iscan and Richard P. Helmer, *Forensic Analysis of the Skull: Craniofacial Analysis, Reconstruction, and Identification* (Wilmington, DE: Wiley-Liss, 1993); Caroline Wilkinson, *Forensic Facial Reconstruction* (Cambridge: Cambridge University Press, 2008).

2. "Attorney General Gonzales Travels to Baghdad to Visit DOJ Personnel, Military Troops, and Iraqi Officials," Department of Justice. Available at: http://www.justice.gov/opa/pr/2005/July/05_ag_360.htm.

3. Heather Pringle, "Witness to Genocide," *Archaeology* 62, no. 1 (2009). Available at: http://archive.archaeology.org/0901/etc/iraq.html.

4. Human Rights Watch, *Genocide in Iraq: The Anfal Campaign against the Kurds* (1993). Available at: http://www.hrw.org/reports/1993/iraqanfal.

5. For books on USMC Culture, see Nathaniel C. Fick, *One Bullet Away: The Making of a Marine Officer* (Wilmington, MA: Mariner Books, 2006); Thomas E. Ricks, *Making the Corps* (New York: Scribner Press, 2007).

6. Evan Wright, *Generation Kill: Devil Dogs, Iceman, Captain America, and the New Face of American War* (New York: Berkley Trade, 2008).

7. An example might include: "We are a socio-cultural research and advising capability that assists commanders in culturally sound COA development. We also have the capability to bridge the gap between the various staff offices and provide information without stove-piping in order to provide the fastest and most accurate cultural information to the appropriate people for integration into the MDMP (military decision-making process)."

8. R. Lee Ermey was a staff sergeant in the Marine Corps, turned actor. He is best known for his roles as a drill instructor in *Full Metal Jacket*.

9. Jacqueline S. Ismael and Shereen T. Ismael, "Gender and State in Iraq," in *Gender and Citizenship in the Middle East*, ed. Suad Joseph (Syracuse, NY: Syracuse University Press, 2000); Nadje Al-Ali, "Reconstructing Gender: Iraqi Women Between Dictatorship, War, Sanctions, and Occupation," *Third World Quarterly* 26 (2005): 739–58.

10. Joyceen S. Boyle, "Professional Nursing in Iraq," *Image: The Journal of Nursing Scholarship* 21, no. 3 (1989): 168–71.

11. "Iraq and the Kurds: Trouble along the Trigger Line," International Crisis Group, *Middle East Report* no. 88 (2009): 1–37.

12. Michael J. Kelly, "The Kurdish Regional Constitution within the Framework of the Iraqi Federal Constitution: A Struggle for Sovereignty, Oil, Ethnic Identity, and the Prospects for a Reverse Supremacy Clause," *Penn State Law Review* 114, no. 3 (2010): 707–808.

13. "Iraq and the Kurds."

14. Stefan Wolff, "Governing in Kirkuk: Resolving the Status of a Disputed Territory in Post-American Iraq," *International Affairs* 86, no. 6 (2010): 1361–79; Kelly, "The Kurdish Regional Constitution."

15. Ezster Spat, *Yezidi* (London: Saqi Books, 2005); Birgül Acikyildiz, *Yezidis: The History of a Community, Culture and Religion* (London: I. B. Tauris, 2010).

16. Linda Robinson, *Masters of Chaos: The Secret History of the Special Forces* (New York: Public Affairs, 2005); Dick Couch, *Chosen Soldier: the Making of a Special Forces Warrior* (New York: Three Rivers Press, 2008).

17. Mike Tucker, *Now We Are Free: Voices of the Kurds After Saddam* (Parker, CO: Outskirts Press, 2014).

6. THE FOUR PILLARS OF INTEGRATION: HOW TO MAKE SOCIAL SCIENCE WORK IN A WAR ZONE

1. Ali Abad, Shewak District Governor, interview, October 2010.

2. Tribalism in Afghanistan, particularly in the Pashtun areas, has long been considered a complex topic. See Thomas Barfield, *Afghanistan: A Cultural and Political History* (Princeton: Princeton University Press, 2010); Frederick Barth, *Political Leadership Among the Swat Pathans* (New York: Berg, 1959); Christine Noelle-Karimi, *State and Tribe in Nineteenth Century Afghanistan* (London: Curzon, 1997); Bernt Glatzer, "War and Boundaries in Afghanistan: Significance and Relativity of Local and Social Boundaries," *Die Welt des Islams* 41, no. 3 (2001): 379–99; Richard Tapper, ed., *Conflict of Tribe and State in Iran and Afghanistan* (New York: St Martin's Press, 1983).

3. Joint Chiefs of Staff, Joint Publication 3–24: *Counterinsurgency Operations* (October 2009), II–8. Available at: http://www.dtic.mil/doctrine/new_pubs/jp3_24.pdf.

4. Though the military emphasizes it, the definition and relevance of the concept of good governance is not so clear. See M. Doornbos, "'Good Governance': The Rise and Decline of a Policy Metaphor?" *Journal of Development Studies* 37, no. 6 (2001): 93–108; Merilee Grindle, *Going Local: Decentralization, Democratization, and the Promise of Good Governance* (Princeton: Princeton University Press, 2007); Adrian Leftwich, "Governance, the State and the Politics of Development," *Development and Change* 25, no. 2 (2008): 363–86.

5. Center for Army Lessons Learned, *Handbook 10–41: Assessment and Measures of Effectiveness in Stability Ops: Tactics, Techniques, and Procedures* (Fort Leavenworth, KS: Center for Army Lessons Learned, May 2010). Available at: http://usacac.army.mil/cac2/call/docs/10–41/10–41.pdf.

6. Department of Defense, *Report on Progress Toward Security and Stability in Afghanistan* (Washington, DC: Department of Defense, April 2011), available

at: http://www.defense.gov/news/1230_1231report.pdf; Ian Livingston and Michael O'Hanlon, *Afghanistan Index* (Washington, DC: Brookings Institute, July 31, 2012), Available at: http://www.brookings.edu/~/media/Programs/foreign%20policy/afghanistan%20index/index20120731.pdf; Thomas Joscelyn and Bill Roggio, "Analysis: The Taliban's 'Momentum' Has Not Been Broken," *Long War Journal* (September 2012), available at: http://www.longwarjournal.org/archives/2012/09/analysis_the_taliban.php.

7. The use of indirect speech acts to "save face" is common in many Asian cultures. Min-Sun Kim, "Cross-Cultural Comparisons of the Perceived Importance of Conversational Constraints," *Human Communication Research* 21, no. 1 (2006): 128–51; Thomas Holtgraves, "Language Structure in Social Interaction: Perceptions of Direct and Indirect Speech Acts and Interactants Who Use Them," *Journal of Personality and Social Psychology* 51, no. 2 (1986): 305–14.

8. See Commission on the Engagement of Anthropology with the US Security and Intelligence Communities, "Final Report on US Army's Human Terrain System Proof of Concept Program," October 14, 2009, available at: http://www.aaanet.org/cmtes/commissions/CEAUSSIC/Proposal-for-Examination-of-the-Human-Terrain-System-A-CEAUSSIC-Project.cfm; Roberto Gonzalez, *American Counterinsurgency: Human Science and the Human Terrain* (Chicago: Prickly Paradigm Press, 2009); Hugh Gusterson, "Do Professional Ethics Matter in War?" *Bulletin of the Atomic Scientists* (March 4, 2010), available at: http://www.thebulletin.org/web-edition/columnists/hugh-gusterson/do-professional-ethics-matter-war; Network of Concerned Anthropologists, *The Counter-Counterinsurgency Manual* (Chicago: Prickly Paradigm Press, 2009).

9. In the event of a death or serious injury in a deployed environment, all unclassified systems, both work and personal, are shut off until the families can be notified directly. These actions prevent families learning about the loss of a loved one via Facebook or a similar site, but this also means that during heavy fighting seasons the unclassified network can go down for weeks at a time; so if you wanted to disseminate information, the classified network was more reliable.

10. At least not of the local population. However, living and working with the US Army for 15 months was certainly a form of participant observation when it came to understanding the society and culture of deployed American soldiers. I would contend, however, that while ethnographic research is the cornerstone of anthropology, it is by no means the only method that anthropologists utilize, especially in restrictive settings like refugee camps or development initiatives. See Akhil Gupta and James Ferguson, eds., *Anthropological Locations: Boundaries and Grounds of a Field Science* (Berkeley: University of California Press, 1997).

11. For example, Jean Comaroff and John Comaroff, *Modernity and Its Malcontents: Ritual and Power in Postcolonial Africa* (Chicago: University of Chicago Press, 1993); Sidney Mintz, *Sweetness and Power: The Place of Sugar in Modern History* (New York: Penguin, 1986); Nancy Scheper-Hughes, "The

Global Traffic in Human Organs," *Current Anthropology* 41, no. 2 (2000): 191–224.

7. INVESTING IN UNCERTAINTY: APPLYING SOCIAL SCIENCE TO MILITARY OPERATIONS

1. Kevin Avruch, *Culture and Conflict Resolution* (Washington, DC: United States Institute of Peace Press, 1998).
2. While several writers have explored this topic, for a fairly complete representation from the perspective of two founding leaders of HTS see Montgomery McFate and Steve Fondacaro, "Reflections on the Human Terrain System During the First 4 Years," *Prism* 2, no. 4 (2011): 63–82.
3. During my HTS experience, I recalled more than once a statement I ran into during one of my doctoral classes on anthropology: "Sociologists stand guard in the garrison and report to its masters on the movements of the occupied populace. The more adventurous sociologists don the disguise of the people and go out to mix with the peasants in the 'field', returning with books and articles that break the protective secrecy in which a subjugated population wraps itself, and make it more accessible to manipulation and control." M. Nicolaus, "Remarks at ASA Convention," *American Sociologists* 4, no. 2 (1969): 154–5.
4. Robert M. Clark, *Intelligence Analysis: A Target-Centric Approach*, 2nd edn (Washington, DC: CQ Press, 2007).
5. Mark Lowenthal, *Intelligence: From Secrets to Policy*, 5th edn (Thousand Oaks, CA: Sage Press, 2012), 110.
6. Sharon MacDonald, "British Social Anthropology," in *Handbook of Ethnography*, ed. Paul Atkinson, Amanda Coffey, Sara Delamont, John Lofland, and Lyn Lofland (Los Angeles: Sage Press, 2001): 60–79.
7. Christopher Wellin and Gary Alan Fine, "Ethnography as Work: Career, Socialization, Settings and Problems," in *Handbook of Ethnography*, ed. Paul Atkinson, Amanda Coffey, Sara Delamont, John Lofland, and Lyn Lofland (Los Angeles: Sage Press, 2001), 323–38.
8. Exec. Order No. 12,333, 46 Fed. Reg. 59941 (December 4, 1981); Army Regulation 381–10, *US Army Intelligence Activities* (May 3, 2007). This includes natural-born or naturalized citizens, permanent resident aliens, US corporations, and even informal associations with a substantial number of United States citizens or permanent residents.
9. As a matter of fact, Section 2.10 of Executive Order 12333 specifically states, "No agency within the Intelligence Community shall sponsor, contract for or conduct research on human subjects except in accordance with guidelines issued by the Department of Health and Human Services. The subject's informed consent shall be documented as required by those guidelines."
10. John H. Miller and Scott E. Page, *Complex Adaptive Systems: An Introduction to Computations Models of Social Life* (Princeton, NJ: Princeton University, 2007).

11. Edward A. Smith, *Complexity, Networking, and Effects-Based Approaches to Operations* (Washington, DC: Department of Defense Command and Control Research Program, 2006).

12. Melanie Mitchell, *Complexity: A Guided Tour* (New York: Oxford University Press, 2009).

13. Clark, *Intelligence Analysis: A Target-Centric Approach*, 11.

14. Colonel Harry Summers quoted in "New Civilian Tasks for the Military," *American Defense Monitor*, television show, 1993.

15. Elizabeth Kelleher, "US Military Humanitarian Efforts Planned for 99 Nations," *Washington File*, July 13, 2006. Available at: http://www.america. gov/st/washfile-english/2006/July/20060712172520berehellek0.4737207.html.

16. George Ritzer, *Sociological Theory*, 7th edn (Boston: McGraw-Hill, 2008).

17. James N. Mattis, "USJFCOM Commander's Guidance for Effects-based Operations," *Parameters* 38 (Autumn 2008): 18, 20.

18. For a more detailed description of these events, see Michael Silverman, *Awakening Victory: How Iraqi Tribes and American Troops Reclaimed al Anbar and Defeated al Qaeda in Iraq* (Havertown, PA: Casemate Publishing, 2011).

19. Tim Arango, "Iraq's Tribal Chiefs Step into the Breach with Swift Justice," *New York Times*, March 13, 2012.

20. See, for example, R. Alan King, *Twice Armed: An American Soldier's Battle for Hearts and Minds in Iraq* (St Paul, MN: Zenith Press, 2006); Michael Eisenstadt, "Tribal Engagement Lessons Learned," *Military Review* (September–October 2007): 16–31.

21. Daniel Druckman, *Doing Research: Methods of Inquiry for Conflict Analysis* (Thousand Oaks, CA: Sage Press, 2005).

22. C. P. Kottak, *Window on Humanity: A Concise Introduction to Anthropology*, 3rd edn (New York: McGraw Hill, 2008).

23. John Winslade and Gerald Monk, *Narrative Mediation: A New Approach to Conflict Resolution* (San Francisco, CA: Jossey-Bass Publishers, 2001).

24. Center for Army Lessons Learned, *CALL Handbook 10–41: Assessments and Measures of Effectiveness in Stability Operations* (Fort Leavenworth, KS: Department of the Army, 2010).

25. Todd S. Bascatow and D. Bellafiore, "Redefining Geospatial Intelligence," *American Intelligence Journal* (Fall 2009): 38–40.

8. ALLIED CIVILIAN ENABLERS AND THE HELMAND SURGE

1. Frank Ledwidge, *Losing Small Wars: British Military Failure in Iraq and Afghanistan* (London: Yale University Press, 2011), 38.

2. Ibid., 28.

3. Ibid., 47.

4. Ibid., 54–5.

5. Tom Westmacott, Nick Dowling, and Tom Praster, *Helmand Provincial Handbook: A Guide to the People and the Province* (Arlington: IDS International Government Services, 2010).

6. Ledwidge, *Losing Small Wars*, 46.

7. Michael Clarke and Valentina Soria, "Charging up the Valley: British Decisions in Afghanistan," *RUSI Journal* 156, no. 4 (2011): 80–88.

8. Ledwidge, *Losing Small Wars*, 128.

9. See, for example, Theo Farrell, "Improving in War: Military Adaptation and the British in Helmand Province, Afghanistan, 2006–2009," *Journal of Strategic Studies* 33, no. 4 (2010): 567–94; Clarke and Soria, "Charging up the Valley"; Anthony King, "Understanding the Helmand Campaign: British Military Operations in Afghanistan," *Journal of International Affairs* 86 (2010): 311–32.

10. King, "Understanding."

11. Ibid.

12. Ibid., 314, 315.

13. Clarke and Soria, "Charging up the Valley."

14. Ledwidge, *Losing Small Wars*, 79–80.

15. King, "Understanding," 9.

16. Farrell, "Improving in War," 580, 590, 591.

17. Ledwidge, *Losing Small Wars*, 61.

18. Farrell, "Improving in War," 574.

19. Congressional Research Service, "Afghanistan: US Foreign Assistance" (2010): 6. Available at: https://opencrs.com/document/R40699/

20. The United States Government Accountability Office, "Afghanistan: Improvements Needed to Strengthen Management of US civilian presence," GAO-12-2985 (2012): 4–5, 9, 10. Available at: www.gao.gov/assets/590/588869.pdf.

21. US GAO, "Afghanistan," 2.

22. Ibid., 16, 21.

23. King, "Understanding."

9. ASSESSING THE HUMAN TERRAIN TEAMS: NO WHITE HATS OR BLACK HATS, PLEASE

1. Carolyn Fluehr-Lobban, "Ethics and Anthropology: 1890–2000," in *Ethics and the Profession of Anthropology*, 2nd edn, ed. Carolyn Fluehr-Lobban (Walnut Creek, CA: AltaMira Press, 2003), 1–28; Carolyn Fluehr-Lobban, "Informed Consent in Anthropological Research: We are Not Exempt," *Ethics and the Profession of Anthropology*, 2nd edn, ed. Carolyn Fluehr-Lobban (Walnut Creek, CA: AltaMira Press, 2003), 159–77; "Code of Ethics of the American Anthropological Association," American Anthropological Association, approved June 1998, available at: http://www.aaanet.org/issues/policy-advocacy/Code-of-Ethics.cfm.

2. David Price, *Anthropological Intelligence: The Development and Neglect of American Anthropology in the Second World War* (Durham, NC: Duke University Press, 2008).

3. David Price, "Gregory Bateson and the OSS: World War II and Bateson's

the Profession of Anthropology, 2nd edn, ed. Carolyn Fluehr-Lobban (Walnu Creek, CA: AltaMira Press, 2003), 51–83.

11. Montgomery McFate and Steve Fondacaro, "Reflections on the Human Terrain System: the First Four Years," *Prism* 2, no. 4 (2011): 63–82. Available at: http://www.ndu.edu/press/lib/images/prism2–4/Prism_63–82_McFate-Fondacaro.pdf.

12. "Failure in the Field: The US Military's Human Terrain Programme Needs to be Brought to a Swift Close," *Nature* 456 (December 11, 2008): 676.

13. Benjamin Connable, "All Our Eggs in a Broken Basket," *Military Review* (March–April 2009): 57–64; J. P. Sullivan, "Partnering with Social Scientists," *Marine Corps Gazette* 93, no. 1 (2009): 53–7; Dan Vergano and Elizabeth Weise, "Should Anthropologists Work Alongside Soldiers?" *USA Today*, December 9, 2008, 5D.

14. "Principles of Professional Responsibility," American Anthropological Association, November 1, 2002. Available at: http://www.aaanet.org/issues/policy-advocacy/Code-of-Ethics.cfm.

15. "American Anthropological Association Executive Board Statement on the Human Terrain System Project," American Anthropological Association, October 31, 2007, available at: http://www.aaanet.org/about/policies/statements/human-terrain-system-statement.cfm; Carolyn Fluehr-Lobban, "New Ethical Challenges for Anthropologists: The terms 'secret research' and 'do no harm' need to be clarified," *Chronicle of Higher Education Review* 55, no. 12 (November 2008): B11.

16. Hugh Gusterson, "Anthropology and Militarism," *Annual Review of Anthropology* 36 (2007): 155–75; see also Roberto J. Gonzalez, "We Must Fight the Militarization of Anthropology," *Chronicle of Higher Education Review* 53, no. 22 (February 2, 2007): B20.

17. David Price, "Anthropology *Sub Rosa*: The CIA, the AAA, and the Ethical Problems Inherent in Secret Research," in *Ethics and the Profession of Anthropology*, 2nd edn, ed. Carolyn Fluehr-Lobban (Walnut Creek, CA: AltaMira Press, 2003), 29–49.

18. John Stanton, "US Army Human Terrain System in Disarray: Millions of Dollars Wasted, Two Lives Sacrificed," *Pravda*, July 23, 2008, available at: http://english.pravda.ru/topic/Human_Terrain_System-607; John Stanton, "Expanding Human Terrain Systems?" *Counterpunch*, August 7–9, 2009, available at: http://www.counterpunch.org/2009/08/07/expanding-human-terrain-systems/.

19. "American Anthropological Association Executive Board Statement on the Human Terrain System Project," American Anthropological Association, October 31, 2007. Available at: http://www.aaanet.org/about/policies/statements/human-terrain-system-statement.cfm.

20. David Rohde, "Army Enlists Anthropology in War Zones," *New York Times*, October 5, 2007. Available online at: http://www.nytimes.com/2007/10/05/world/asia/05afghan.html?pagewanted=1&_r=1&sq=David%20Rohde&st=cse&scp=2.

Assessment of Applied Anthropology," *Human Organization* 75, no. 4 (1998): 379–84; David Price, "Cold War Anthropology: Collaborators and Victims of the National Security State," *Identities* 4, nos. 3–4 (1998): 389–430; David Price, "Anthropologists as Spies," in *Ethics of Spying: A Reader for the Intelligence Professional*, ed. Jan Goldman (Lanham, MD: Scarecrow Press, 2000), 336–42; David Price, "Anthropology *Sub Rosa*: The CIA, the AAA, and the Ethical Problems Inherent in Secret Research," in *Ethics and the Profession of Anthropology*, 2nd edn, ed. Carolyn Fluehr-Lobban (Walnut Creek, CA: AltaMira Press, 2003), 29–49; David Price, *Threatening Anthropology: McCarthyism and the FBI's Surveillance of Activist Anthropologists* (Durham, NC: Duke University Press, 2004); David Price, *Anthropological Intelligence: The Development and Neglect of American Anthropology in the Second World War* (Durham, NC: Duke University Press, 2008); David Price and Roberto J. Gonzalez, "When Anthropologists Become Counterinsurgents," *Counterpunch*, September 27, 2007, available at: http://www.counterpunch.org/gonzalez09272007.html.

4. George R. Lucas Jr., *Anthropologists in Arms: the Ethics of Military Anthropology* (Lanham, MD: Altamira Press, 2009).

5. Peter Pels and Oscar Salemink, eds., *Colonial Subjects: Essays on the Practical History of Anthropology* (Ann Arbor: University of Michigan Press, 2000).

6. Albert R. Jonson, *Short History of Medical Ethics* (Oxford: Oxford University Press, 2000).

7. Alexander Lesser, "Franz Boas," in *Totems and Teachers: Key Figures in the History of Anthropology*, 2nd edn, ed. Sydel Silberman (Walnut Creek, CA: AltaMira Press, 2004), 1–25; Price, "Anthropologists as Spies."

8. Margaret Mead, *And Keep your Powder Dry: An Anthropologist Looks at America* (New York: Berghahn Books, 2000); Sidney W. Mintz, "Rutʃ Benedict," in *Totems and Teachers: Key Figures in the History of Anthrʌ pology*, 2nd edn, ed. Sydel Silberman (Walnut Creek, CA: AltaMira Preʃ 2004), 103–24; David Price, "Gregory Bateson and the OSS: World War II aʃ Bateson's Assessment of Applied Anthropology," *Human Organization* ' no. 4 (1998): 379–84; David Price, "Cold War Anthropology: Collaboraʲ and Victims of the National Security State," *Identities* 4, nos. 3–4 (19 389–430.

9. Irving Louis Horowitz, *The Rise and Fall of Project Camelot: Studies ʲ Relationship between Social Science and Practical Politics* (Cambridge MIT Press, 1967); Marshall Sahlins, "The Established Order: Do Noʲ Spindle, or Mutilate," in *The Rise and Fall of Project Camelot: Studieʃ Relationship between Social Science and Practical Politics*, ed. Irvin Horowitz (Cambridge, MA: MIT Press, 1965), 71–9.

10. Eric R. Wolf and Joseph G. Jorgensen, "Anthropology on the Wa Thailand," *New York Review of Books* 15 (November 19, 1970): 26 Wakin, *Anthropology Goes to War: Professional Ethics and Counteri in Thailand* (Madison, WI: University of Wisconsin Press, 200ʲ D. Berreman, "Ethics Versus Realism in Anthropology: Redux," in

21. In this regard the controversy over anthropologists in war zones was comparable to the last major controversy over the allegation that anthropological conduct in the field harmed the Indigenous people: the Yanomami in Darkness in Eldorado revelations. In the end the concern was more about the reputation of the anthropologist than the well-being of the Yanomami.

22. "Final Report of the AAA Ad Hoc Commission on the Engagement of Anthropology with US Security and Intelligence Communities," November 4, 2007. Available at: http://www.aaanet.org/pdf/Final_Report.pdf.

23. George R. Lucas Jr., *Anthropologists in Arms: the Ethics of Military Anthropology* (Lanham, MD: Altamira Press, 2009).

24. Perhaps because Montgomery McFate was then a USIP fellow, as was Fluehr-Lobban.

25. Noah Shachtman, "Army Social Scientist Set Afire in Afghanistan," *Wired Magazine/Danger Room*, November 6, 2008, available at: http://blog.wired.com/defense/2008/11/army-social-sci.html; Farah Stockman, "Anthropologist's War Death Reverberates," *Boston Globe*, February 12, 2009, available at: http://www.boston.com/news/world/middleeast/articles/2009/02/12/anthropologists_war_death_reverberates/?page=1.

26. Pamela Constable, "A Terrain's Tragic Shift: Researcher's Death Intensifies Scrutiny of US Cultural Program in Afghanistan," *Washington Post*, February 18, 2009, C1, C8.

27. Kerry Fosher, Review of "Anthropologists in Arms," *Journal of Military Ethics* 9, no. 2 (2010):177–81. Available at: http://philpapers.org/rec/KERAIA.

28. Laurie Rush, "Archaeological Ethics and Working for the Military," in Robert Rubinstein, Kerry Fosher, and Clementine Fujimura, *Practicing Military Anthropology* (Sterling, VA: Kumarian Press, 2012), 9–28.

29. George R. Lucas Jr., *Anthropologists in Arms: the Ethics of Military Anthropology* (Lanham, MD: Altamira Press, 2009).

30. Robert Rubinstein, Kerry Fosher, and Clementine Fujimura, eds., *Practicing Military Anthropology* (Sterling, VA: Kumarian Press, 2012).

31. Robert Rubinstein, "Master Narratives, Retrospective Attribution, and Ritual Pollution in Anthropology's Engagement with the Military," in Robert Rubinstein, Kerry Fosher, and Clementine Fujimura, *Practicing Military Anthropology* (Sterling, VA: Kumarian Press, 2012), 119–33, 127.

32. George R. Lucas Jr., *Anthropologists in Arms: the Ethics of Military Anthropology* (Lanham, MD: Altamira Press, 2009).

33. Rohde, "Army Enlists Anthropology"; Giles Clarke, "A Marine Goes the Distance in Iraq," *Washington Post*, November 27, 2008, A29; Vanessa M. Gezari, "Rough Terrain," *Washington Post*, August 30, 2009, available at: http://www.washingtonpost.com/wp-dyn/content/article/2009/08/21/AR2009082101926.html; Patricia Cohen, "Panel Criticizes Military's Use of Embedded Anthropologists," *New York Times*, December 3, 2008, available at: http://www.nytimes.com/2009/12/04/arts/04anthro.html; Alexander Star, "Afghanistan: What the Anthropologists Say," *New York Times Book Review*, November 18, 2011, available at: http://www.nytimes.com/2011/11/20/books/

review/afghanistan-and-other-books-about-rebuilding-book-review.html?page-wanted=all; Dahr Jamail, "When Scholars Join the Slaughter," *Truthout*, February 3, 2010, available at: http://truth-out.org/archive/component/k2/item/87789:when-scholars-join-the-slaughter.

34. "Pledge of Non-Participation in Counterinsurgency," Network of Concerned Anthropologists. Available at: https://sites.google.com/site/concernedanthro-pologists/.

35. Carolyn Fluehr-Lobban, "No Black Hats or White Hats, Please: the Complexities of Anthropological Engagement" (paper presented at the International Society for Military Ethics, San Diego, January 26–29, 2010).

36. DS2, interview with first author, 2012.

37. Lachlyn Soper, interview with first author, 2012.

38. Others cited motives of patriotism, opportunity for experience on the ground, a chance to conduct focus groups with locals, being part of a local reconstruction team, informing public policy, the interesting nature of the program, career enhancement, and the well-known pay for working with the program.

39. Eli Corin, interview with first author, 2012.

40. Phil Carlson, interview with first author, 2012.

41. David Southworth, interview with first author, 2012.

42. Lachlyn Soper, interview with first author, 2012.

43. Larry Katzenstein, interview with first author, 2012.

44. Eli Corin, interview with first author, 2012.

45. Michael Albin, interview with first author, 2012.

46. *HTT Sangin Population Final Analysis Report*, 2010.

47. *HTT Sangin Population Final Analysis Report*, 2010, 3–4.

48. Michael Albin, interview with first author, 2012.

49. Larry Katzenstein, interview with first author, 2012.

50. Eli Corin, interview with first author, 2012.

51. Phil Carlson, interview with first author, 2012.

52. Lachlyn Soper, interview with first author, 2012.

53. Montgomery McFate, personal communication to first author, January 9, 2013.

54. 32 CFR 219.101 (b)(2) exempts human subjects research from an IRB process "when it involves survey, interviews and observation" unless (1) individuals can be identified; and (2) disclosure might place subjects at risk of harm.

55. Montgomery McFate, personal communication to first author, January 2013.

56. Phil Carlson, interview with first author, 2012.

57. Michael Albin, interview with first author, 2012.

58. Larry Katzenstein, interview with first author, 2012.

59. Fred Chapman, interview with first author, 2012.

60. Michael Albin, interview with first author, 2012.

61. DS2, interview with first author, 2012.

62. David Southworth, interview with first author, 2012.

63. Michael Albin, interview with first author, 2012.

64. Lachlyn Soper, interview with first author, 2012.

65. Lachlyn Soper, interview with first author, 2012.

66. Michael Albin, interview with first author, 2012.

67. Michael Albin, interview with first author, 2012.

68. William Post, the first author's son-in-law, shared this based on his 18 months' experience in Afghanistan.

69. Fred Chapman, interview with first author, 2012.

70. Fred Chapman, interview with first author, 2012.

71. DS2, interview with first author, 2012.

72. DS2, interview with first author, 2012.

73. Fred Chapman, interview with first author, 2012.

74. Nathan Hodge, "Help Wanted: 'Human Terrain' Teams for Africa," *Wired Magazine: Danger Room*, January 12, 2009. Available at: http://www.wired.com/2009/01/help-wanted-hum/.

75. David Southworth, interview with first author, 2012.

76. Michael Albin, interview with first author, 2012.

77. Michael Albin, interview with first author, 2012.

78. The first and second authors are both faculty members in professional military education institutions.

10. TANGI VALLEY: THE LIMITATIONS OF APPLIED ANTHROPOLOGY IN AFGHANISTAN

1. Roberto J. González and David H. Price, "When Anthropologists Become Counter-Insurgents," *CounterPunch*, September 28, 2007. Available at: http://www.counterpunch.org/2007/09/28/when-anthropologists-become-counter-insurgents/.

2. Ray Rivera, Alissa J. Rubin, and Thom Shanker, "Copter Downed by Taliban Fire; Elite U.S. Unit among Dead," *New York Times*, August 7, 2011. Available at: http://www.nytimes.com/2011/08/07/world/asia/07afghanistan.html?pagewanted=all&_r=0.

3. US Army, Field Manual 3–24, *Counterinsurgency* (Washington, DC: Department of the Army, 2006), 3–2.

4. Sarah Rainsford, "Row over Afghan Wife-Staving Law," *BBC News*, August, 16, 2009. Available at: http://news.bbc.co.uk/2/hi/south_asia/8204207.stm.

5. Montgomery McFate, "The Military Utility of Understanding of Adversary Culture," *Joint Forces Quarterly* 38 (2005): 43.

6. Montgomery McFate and Andrea Jackson, "An Organizational Solution for DOD's Cultural Knowledge Needs," *Military Review* (July–August 2005): 19–20.

7. Jack Marr, John Cushing, Brandon Garner, and Richard Thompson, "Human Terrain Mapping: A Critical First Step to Winning the COIN Fight," *Military Review* (March–April 2008): 19.

8. Ibid., 22.

9. Ibid., 21–2.

10. David Glenn, "Anthropologists in a War Zone: Scholars Debate Their Role,"

Chronicle of Higher Education, November 30, 2007. Available at: http:// chronicle.com/article/Anthropologists-in-a-War-Zone-/34710.

11. Fred Renzi, "Networks: Terra Incognita and the Case for Ethnographic Intelligence," *Military Review* (September–October 2006): 17.

12. Jacob Kipp, Lester Grau, Karl Prinslow, and Don Smith, "The Human Terrain System: A CORDS for the 21st Century," *Military Review* (September–October 2006): 11.

13. David Rohde, "Army Enlists Anthropology in War Zones," *New York Times*, October 5, 2007. Available at: http://www.nytimes.com/2007/10/05/world/ asia/05afghan.html? pagewanted=all&_r=0.

14. Ibid.

15. Dell Hymes, *The Use of Anthropology: Critical, Political, Personal* (Ann Arbor: University of Michigan Press, 1969), xxxiii.

16. Kipp et al., "The Human Terrain System," 12.

17. "American Anthropological Association Executive Board Statement on the Human Terrain System Project," American Anthropological Association, October 31, 2007. Available at: http://www.aaanet.org/about/Policies/statements/Human-Terrain-System-Statement.cfm.

18. Glenn, "Anthropologists in a War Zone."

19. "Literacy Rate in Rural Afghanistan," Ministry of Rural Rehabilitation and Development, 2010. Available at: www.mrrd.gov.af/.../Literacy%20rate%20 and%20primary%20 education%20.pdf.

20. González and Price, "When Anthropologists Become Counter-Insurgents."

21. Roberto J. González, "Human Terrain: Past, Present, and Future Applications," *Anthropology Today* 24, no. 1 (2008): 25.

22. Maureen Dowd, "Seven Days in June," *New York Times*, June 22, 2010. Available at: http://www.nytimes.com/2010/06/23/opinion/23dowd.html.

23. Glenn, "Anthropologists in a War Zone."

24. "Human Terrain System," US Army Training and Doctrine Command, 2010. This language has been removed from the 2012 website. Available at: http:// humanterrainsystem.army.mil/.

25. Barry G. Silverman, "Human Terrain Data—What Should We Do With It?" (paper presented at the Winter Simulation Conference in Washington, DC, December 9–12, 2007).

26. Matthew Arnold and Anthony Vinci, "The Need for Local, People-Centric Information Does Not End in Afghanistan," *Small Wars Journal* (July 2010): 4.

27. Nevin S. Scrimshaw and Gary R. Gleason, eds., *Rapid Assessment Procedures— Qualitative Methodologies for Planning and Evaluation of Health Related Programs* (Boston: Nutrition Foundation for Developing Countries, 1992); James Beebe, *Rapid Assessment Process: An Introduction* (Walnut Creek, CA: AltaMira Press, 2010).

28. McFate, "The Military Utility," 44.

29. Kevin Baron, "Petraeus Issues Afghanistan COIN Guidance," *Stars and Stripes*, August 2, 2010. Available at: http://www.stripes.com/blogs/stripes-cen-

tral/stripes-central-1.8040/petraeus-issues-afghanistan-coin-guidance-1.113
193.

30. Marr et al., "Human Terrain Mapping," 20.

31. Montgomery McFate and Steve Fondacaro, "Reflections on the Human Terrain System During the First 4 Years," *Prism* 2, no. 4 (2011): 68.

32. Arnold and Vinci, "The Need for Local, People-Centric Information," 2–3.

33. Marr et al., "Human Terrain Mapping," 18.

34. Greg Jaffe, "US Retreat from Afghan Valley Marks Recognition of Blunder," *The Washington Post*, April 4, 2010. Available at: http://www.washington-post.com/wp-dyn/content/article/2010/04/14/AR2010041401012.html. Alissa J. Rubin, "US Forces Close Post in Afghan 'Valley of Death'," *New York Times*, April 15, 2010. Available at: http://www.nytimes.com/2010/04/15/world/asia/15 outpost.html?_r=1&hpw.

35. Glenn, "Anthropologists in a War Zone."

36. Marr et al., "Human Terrain Mapping," 21.

37. Fred Renzi, "Networks: Terra Incognita."

38. Ibid., 16–17.

39. Laurel Richardson, "Evaluating Ethnography," *Qualitative Inquiry* 6, no. 2 (2000): 254.

40. González, "Human Terrain," 23.

41. McFate, "The Military Utility," 46.

42. "Office of the Coordinator of the Foreign Policy Advisor Program," US Department of State, http://www.state.gov/t/pm/polad/.

43. Cooper T. Cash, "TF Warrior Transitions COP Tangi to ANSF," Afghanistan: International Security Assistance Force, April 11, 2011. Available at: http://www.isaf.nato.int/article/isaf-releases/tf-warrior-transitions-cop-tangi-to-ansf.html.

44. González and Price, "When Anthropologists Become Counter-Insurgents."

45. González, "Human Terrain," 26.

46. González and Price, "When Anthropologists Become Counter-Insurgents."

47. Hymes, *The Use of Anthropology*, 47.

48. Chris Hedges, *American Fascists: The Christian Right and the War on America* (New York: Free Press 2006), 34.

11. THE HUMAN TERRAIN SYSTEM: SOME LESSONS LEARNED AND THE WAY FORWARD

1. Janice H. Laurence, "Military Leadership and the Complexity of Combat and Culture," *Military Psychology* 23, no. 5 (2011): 489–501.

2. P. Christopher Early and Soon Ang, *Cultural Intelligence: Individual Interactions Across Cultures* (Stanford, CA: Stanford Business Books, 2003).

3. Human Terrain System Program Development Team, *Human Terrain System Yearly Report 2007–2008* (Fort Monroe, VA: US Army Training and Doctrine Command, August 2008).

4. Department of Defense, "Population Representation in the Military Services,

2011" (Washington, DC: Office of the Under Secretary of Defense (Personnel and Readiness), no date). Available at: http://prhome.defense.gov/portals/52/Documents/POPREP/poprep2011/download/download.html.

5. Janice H. Laurence, "Behavioral Science in the Military," in *Handbook on Communicating and Disseminating Behavioral Science*, ed. Melissa K. Welch-Ross and Lauren G. Fasig (Thousand Oaks, CA: Sage, 2007), 391–405.

6. Samuel A. Stouffer, Arthur A. Lumsdaine, Marion Harper Lumsdaine, Robin M. Williams Jr., M. Brewster Smith, Irving L. Janis, Shirley A. Star, and Leonard S. Cottrell Jr., *The American Soldier: Combat and its Aftermath, Volume II: Studies in Social Psychology in World War II* (Princeton, NJ: Princeton University Press, 1949).

7. Daniel D. Mouton, "The Army's Foreign Area Office Program: To Wither or to Improve?" *Army* (March 2011): 21–4.

8. Mark Benjamin and Barbara Slavin, "Ghost Soldiers: The Pentagon's Decade-Long Struggle to Win Hearts and Minds Through Civil Affairs," *Center for Public Integrity* (February 6, 2011), available at: www.publicintegrity.org, http://militarylegitimacyreview.com/?page_id=163; Bruce B. Bingham, Daniel L. Rubini, and Michael J. Cleary, "US Army Civil Affairs: The Army's Bridge to Stability," *Civil Affairs*, updated December 2010, available at: http://militarylegitimacyreview.com/?page_id=163.

9. Ben Connable, "All our Eggs in a Broken Basket: How the Human Terrain System is Undermining Sustainable Military Cultural Competence," *Military Review* (March–April 2009): 57–64.

10. Department of Defense, *Quadrennial Defense Review Report* (Washington, DC: Office of the Secretary of Defense, February 2006); Department of Defense, *Quadrennial Defense Review Report* (Washington, DC: Office of the Secretary of Defense, February 2010). Available at: http://www.defense.gov/qdr/qdr%20as%20of%2029jan10%201600.pdf.

11. The Johari window is a model used to improve self-awareness and improve interpersonal relationships. It has four panes: the first known by self and others; the second known by others but not the self; the third is known by the self but hidden to others; and the fourth is unknown by self and others.

12. For a relevant discussion, see Egon S. Guba and Yvonna S. Lincoln, "Competing Paradigms in Qualitative Research," in *Handbook of Qualitative Research*, 2nd edn, ed. Norman K. Denzin and Yvonna S. Lincoln (Thousand Oaks, CA: Sage, 1994), 163–94.

13. See Montgomery McFate, "Mind the Gap: Bridging the Military/Academic Divide," in *Social Science Goes to War: The Human Terrain System in Iraq and Afghanistan*, ed. Montgomery McFate and Janice H. Laurence (New York: Oxford University Press/London: Hurst, 2014), Chapter 2 of this volume.

14. See for example Peter G. Northhouse, *Leadership: Theory and Practice*, 6th edn (Thousand Oaks, CA: Sage, 2013), 137–59.

15. Montgomery McFate and Steve Fondacaro, "Reflections on the Human Terrain System During the First 4 Years," *PRISM* 2, no. 4 (2011).

16. See Janice H. Laurence, "The Human Terrain System's Human Resource

Challenges: Preliminary Assessment and Recommendations," report submitted to HTS PM and TRADOC (October 2007).

17. It should be noted that HTS also had to guard its budget against critics who wanted the funds for their own "rice bowl" programs. See Ben Connable, "All our Eggs," 57–64.

18. Janice H. Laurence, *The Human Terrain System's Human Resource Challenges*.

19. For details of the HTS job analysis see Erin C. Swartout and Nicholas L. Vasilopoulos, *US Department of Defense—Human Terrain System (HTS): Job Analysis for Human Terrain Team Members in the Team Leader, Social Scientist, Research Manager, and Human Terrain Analyst Jobs, Technical Report No. 630* (Arlington, VA: PDRI: A PreVisor Company, February 2009).

20. US Army Training and Doctrine Command, Office of Internal Review and Audit Compliance (IRAC), *Review of Human Terrain System, Results Briefing* (Fort Eustis, VA: US Army Training and Doctrine Command, May 12, 2010), 4.

21. See Leslie Adrienne Payne, "Allied Civilian Enablers and the Helmand 'Surge'," in *Social Science Goes to War: The Human Terrain System in Iraq and Afghanistan*, ed. Montgomery McFate and Janice H. Laurence (New York: Oxford University Press/London: Hurst, 2014), Chapter 8 of this volume.

22. See Brian G. Brereton, "Tangi Valley: The Limitations of Applied Anthropology in Afghanistan," in *Social Science Goes to War: The Human Terrain System in Iraq and Afghanistan*, ed. Montgomery McFate and Janice H. Laurence (New York: Oxford University Press/London: Hurst, 2014), Chapter 10 of this volume; Carolyn Fluehr-Lobban and George R. Lucas Jr., "Assessing the Human Terrain Teams: No White Hats or Black Hats, Please," in *Social Science Goes to War: The Human Terrain System in Iraq and Afghanistan*, ed. Montgomery McFate and Janice H. Laurence (New York: Oxford University Press/London: Hurst, 2014), Chapter 9 of this volume; and James Dorough-Lewis Jr, "Investing in Uncertainty: Applying Social Science to Military Operations," in *Social Science Goes to War: The Human Terrain System in Iraq and Afghanistan*, ed. Montgomery McFate and Janice H. Laurence (New York: Oxford University Press/London: Hurst, 2014), Chapter 7 of this volume.

23. See Kathleen Reedy, "The Four Pillars of Integration: How to Make Social Science Work in a War Zone," in *Social Science Goes to War: The Human Terrain System in Iraq and Afghanistan*, ed. Montgomery McFate and Janice H. Laurence (New York: Oxford University Press/London: Hurst, 2014), Chapter 6 of this volume.

24. Action research is an applied, participative, and iterative approach to problem solving and intervention assessment. That is, it involves active participation in an organization change situation while conducting research.

25. See Ted Callahan, "An Anthropologist at War in Afghanistan," in *Social Science Goes to War: The Human Terrain System in Iraq and Afghanistan*, ed. Montgomery McFate and Janice H. Laurence (New York: Oxford University Press/London: Hurst, 2014), Chapter 3 of this volume.

26. Brian G. Brereton, "Tangi Valley."

27. Montgomery McFate, Britt Damon, and Robert Holliday, "What Do Commanders Really Want to Know? US Army Human Terrain System Lessons Learned from Iraq and Afghanistan," in *The Oxford Handbook of Military Psychology*, ed. Janice H. Laurence and Michael D. Matthews (New York, Oxford University Press, 2012), 92–113.

28. John F Kimmons, email to staff, January 26, 2009.

29. It should be noted that in some cases data were collected at the battalion level and from non-military support staff such as the PRT. In at least one case, an interview with a local sheikh was conducted to triangulate accounts provided by a company commander and the HTT. Also during these assessments, the collection of preliminary job analysis data was attempted with survey instruments of duty functions and job tasks as well as by eliciting critical incidents of job demands.

30. Cindy R. Jebb, Laurel J. Hummel, and Tania M. Chacho, *Human Terrain Team Trip Report: A "Team of Teams"* (West Point, NY: Interdisciplinary Team in Iraq, United States Military Academy, 2008).

31. Ibid., 3. Underlined in original.

32. See Chairman, Joint Chiefs of Staff, *CJCS Guide to the Chairman's Readiness System* (Washington, DC: Joint Chiefs of Staff, November 15, 2010). Available at: http://www.dtic.mil/cjcs_directives/cdata/unlimit/g3401.pdf.

33. Yvette Clinton, Virginia Foran-Cain, Julia Voelker McQuaid, Catherine E. Norman, and William H. Sims, *Congressional Directed Assessment of the Human Terrain System*, CRM D0024031 A1 (Alexandria, VA, CNA Analysis & Solutions, November 2010), 2.

34. The official report has not yet been released, but the following PowerPoint and paper were provided by IDA: S. K. Numrich, P. M. Picucci, and D. Wright, "Effective Employment of the US Army's Human Terrain Teams: Views of Team Members and Unit Commanders" (Alexandria, VA: Institute for Defense Analyses), PowerPoint, no date; "Effective Employment of the US Army's Human Terrain Teams: Views of Team Members and Unit Commanders" (Alexandria, VA: Institute for Defense Analyses), draft paper, no date.

35. See Christopher J. Lamb, James Douglas Orton, Michael C. Davies, and Theodore T. Pikulsky, "The Way Ahead for Human Terrain Teams," *Joint Forces Quarterly* 73, no. 3 (2013): 21–9.

36. In the NDU report, the prose says that 9 commanders were interviewed while the table provided shows a total of 13 cases. See Lamb et al., "The Way Ahead for Human Terrain Teams"; and Christopher J. Lamb, James Douglas Orton, Michael C. Davies, and Theodore T. Pikulsky, *Human Terrain Teams: An Organizational Innovation for Sociocultural Knowledge in Irregular Warfare* (Washington, DC: Institute of World Politics, 2013).

37. Lamb et al., *Human Terrain Teams*, 49.

38. See Marissa L. Shuffler, Davin Pavlas, and Eduardo Salas, "Teams in the Military: A Review and Emerging Challenges," in *The Oxford Handbook of Military Psychology*, ed. Janice H. Laurence and Michael D. Matthews (New York, Oxford University Press, 2012), 282–310.

39. Shuffler et al., "Teams in the Military: A Review and Emerging Challenges," 304.

40. See Donald J. Campbell, Sean T. Hannah, and Michael D. Matthews, "Leadership in Military and Other Dangerous Contexts: Introduction to the Special Topic Issue," *Military Psychology* 22, suppl. 1 (2010): S1–S14.

41. Lamb et al., "The Way Ahead," 22.

42. Robert H. Scales Jr., "Clausewitz and World War IV," *Military Psychology* 21, suppl. 1 (2009): S23–S35.

43. If one comes from a Middle Eastern culture, it would be "right of boom."

44. Hriar Cabayan, David Adesnik, Chandler Armstrong, Allison Astorino-Courtois, Alexander Barelka, Thomas Bozada, David Brown, Charles Ehlschlaeger, Dana Eyre, Michael Flynn, John Ferrell, LeAnne Howard, Robert Jones, David Krooks, Anne McGee, Timothy Perkins, Dan Plafcan, and Lucy Whalley, *Operational Relevance of Behavioral & Social Science to DoD Missions*, March 2013. Available at: http://www.fabbs.org/files/7613/6396/3846/U_Social%20Science%20White%20Paper%20Approved%20for%20Public%20Release%2014Mar13%20Final.pdf.

45. Defense Science Board, *Report of the Defense Science Board Task Force on Understanding Human Dynamics* (Washington, DC: Office of the Under Secretary of Defense for Acquisition, Technology, and Logistics, 2009).

46. Connable, "All our Eggs," 57–64.

47. Department of Defense, *Quadrennial Defense Review*.

48. More information on USUHS can be found on their website: http://www.usuhs.edu/centers.html.

49. Janice H. Laurence and Michael D. Matthews, "The Handbook of Military Psychology: An Introduction," in *The Oxford Handbook of Military Psychology*, ed. Janice H. Laurence and Michael D. Matthews (New York, Oxford University Press, 2012), 1–3.

50. See for example Thomas J. Williams, James J. Picano, Robert R. Roland, and Paul Bartone, "Operational Psychology: Foundation, Application, and Issues," in *The Oxford Handbook of Military Psychology*, ed. Janice H. Laurence and Michael D. Matthews (New York, Oxford University Press, 2012), 37–49; Stephen H. Behnke and Olivia Moorehead-Slaughter, "Ethics, Human Rights, and Interrogations: The Position of the American Psychological Association," in *The Oxford Handbook of Military Psychology*, ed. Janice H. Laurence and Michael D. Matthews (New York, Oxford University Press, 2012), 50–62.

INDEX

INDEX